Uncommon Dominion

THE MIDDLE AGES SERIES

Ruth Mazo Karras, General Editor
Edward Peters, Founding Editor

A complete list of books in the series
is available from the publisher.

Uncommon Dominion

Venetian Crete and the Myth of Ethnic Purity

Sally McKee

PENN

University of Pennsylvania Press

Philadelphia

10 9 8 7 6 5 4 3 2 1

Published by
University of Pennsylvania Press
Philadelphia, Pennsylvania 19104-4011

Library of Congress Cataloging-in-Publication Data
McKee, Sally.
  Uncommon dominion : Venetian Crete and the myth of ethnic purity / Sally McKee.
    p.   cm. — (Middle ages series)
  Includes bibliographical references and index.
  ISBN 0-8122-3562-2 (alk. paper)
    1. Ethnicity — Greece — Crete — History.   2. Crete (Greece) — Ethnic relations —
History.   3. Crete (Greece) — History — Venetian rule, 1204–1669.   I. Title: Venetian
Crete and the myth of ethnic purity.   II. Title.   III. Series.
DF901.C83 M35   2000
305.8'009495'90902 — dc21   00-028658

Contents

A Note on the Sources

Since almost all the material presented in this book comes from archival sources, I ought to explain what those sources are and the parameters within which I interpreted them. In the course of my research, it occurred to me that some scholars of Venetian Crete have a greater familiarity with Candiote society than they do with the sources they studied to gain that familiarity. Basic methodological problems plague the field of Venetian Cretan studies and Venetian studies, and the problem transcends a number of the sources' layers. First, scholars of an earlier generation typically based their conclusions about Crete on governmental sources, without taking into sufficient account what those sources represent and without undertaking a systematic survey of all the surviving notarial records, which reflect the commercial, patrimonial, and proprietorial activities of the residents of Candia. In general, I believe that by an evolving tacit consensus among scholars in various disciplines, smaller and smaller samples are being used to support broadly conceived generalizations, a procedure that has led to certain kinds of sources supporting historical observations for which they are not well suited. For example, the extent to which testamentary dispositions can reveal social practices *inter vivos* needs more discussion and greater precision.

Given that the body of surviving documents from fourteenth-century Venetian Crete is relatively small, at least in comparison to the seemingly infinite fund of documents in the State Archives of Venice, I set myself the task of making the various components of that archival body work together in tandem, rather than confining myself to a selection of kinds of sources. I ranged those components broadly between governmental and literary sources, on the one hand, and notarial sources, on the other. Historians of Venetian Crete have traditionally relied more on the former component than the latter. As a result, a skewed vision of the social relations prevalent in the colony currently prevails. Therefore, my concern is just as much in the interplay between the components as it is in what they tell us prima facie.

The first century of Venice's rule, the thirteenth, is not as amply documented as the second, although the historian Silvano Borsari has made the most of what has survived from that earlier period.[1] The loss of the vast majority of the sources for thirteenth-century Crete is lamentable, but the following century, for which a substantial body of documents has survived, is in retrospect a far more interesting time in Crete, from the perspective of social relations. Moreover, the overwhelming majority of the material surviving from the Venetian colony of Crete comes from and concerns the principal city and capital, Candia (modern-day Irakleion), a name by which the island was also known in the medieval and pre-modern periods. The Cretan archives do not reflect the colony as a whole, but the sources have the virtue of emanating from its political, economic, and administrative center. This is not, for our purposes, as great a handicap as it might appear, since we are interested in the interaction between Greeks and Latins, the latter of whom were found mostly in Candia. Consequently, I am not investigating the entire island, so much as I am focusing on the extremely important role of urban life in the colony's history and the evidence for a fundamental and ongoing tension between countryside and town in the second century of Venetian rule. The sources do not extend far beyond the walls of Candia, but it is far enough to understand what was important about the colony.

After the Ottomans captured Crete in 1669, Venice negotiated the removal of all the records in the Cretan chancery, which were brought to Venice and eventually incorporated into the State Archives.[2] The contents of the Cretan chancery were then divided into two parts. One consists of the governmental and judicial records, now known collectively as the Archive of the Duke of Candia (hereafter, the ADC). Although the ADC is large, there are significant gaps in the government's records for the early part of Venetian rule. Only one register of the deliberations of the three advisory councils of Candia, which begins only in 1344 and ends in 1363, and only one register of government proclamations covering a slightly greater span of years in the same century, have survived. Court records, one land register, and some state correspondence constitute some of the other contents of the archive. These are the sources on which the overwhelming majority of scholars have very largely relied.

The other category of documents to come from Crete are the notarial records, which were separated from the Archive of the Duke of Candia and incorporated into the Notarial Archives of the State Archives of Venice, in a section called the *Notai di Candia* (hereafter, NDC). The notarial archive has not been completely ignored, but it has received far less attention and certainly no systematic treatment, in spite of its manageable size in comparison to the more forbidding notarial archive of Venice. Moreover, the unfortunate scholarly tendency to use the data from the protocols of one notary to generalize about economic and social trends not surprisingly has led in many cases to unwarranted conclusions that a survey of the entire corpus of notarial records would not support.

Although it constitutes the largest portion of the surviving Cretan sources, the notarial archive is nevertheless incomplete. First, only the protocols of notaries who worked inside the city walls of Candia have survived, even though we know there were also notaries who lived and worked in the burg and villages. Therefore, although villagers from the greater district of Candia often had cause to come to a notary in the city, most of the names in the protocols are residents of the city and its suburb. The Cretan notarial sources consist of over thirty-three files, or *buste*, for the entire 450-year period of Venetian rule.[3] For the fourteenth century alone, with which we are here exclusively concerned, there are the protocols and fragments of protocols of 57 notaries who worked in Candia. I have culled 56 additional names of fourteenth-century notaries, none of whose protocols have survived, but who are mentioned in court records, government deliberations, proclamations, and other notarial transactions as working in Candia. This amounts to a total of 113 known Cretan notaries working in Candia in the fourteenth century. When distributed across the century according to the years in which they worked, I estimate that there were sometimes as many as twenty Latin, Greek, and Hebrew notaries, more or less, working at one time, serving a population of perhaps five to eight thousand.[4]

The Cretan chancery had come into being by the fourteenth century, but we do not know how far back in the thirteenth century its existence went. Furthermore, there is little we can learn about how notaries acquired their skill and license to work in Candia. No mention of a notarial school has surfaced in the Archive of the Duke of Candia nor in the notarial records, just as in Venice notarial schools have a very shadowy existence in the sources and can be traced only to the end of the thirteenth century.[5] Still, most notaries in Candia appear to have been locally trained. Only a few of the notaries in Crete call themselves a Venetian notary, meaning that they came from Venice, where they received some kind of training and recognition of their profession by the Venetian government.

In Candia, there were two types of notaries. Members of one group were official employees, attached to the colony's chancery, known variously as notaries or scribes of the palace, who copied down the government's business. Others were public notaries, whose services included the redaction of private charters, such as contracts, bills of sale, procurations, acquittances, wills, and other instruments pertaining to civil law.[6] Occasionally, the two types of notary overlapped. For instance, Domenico Grimani not only drew up transactions of a private nature for individuals, but also served as the colony's chancellor for much of his career, which spanned the middle part of the fourteenth century.[7]

Customarily, the population of Candia took their affairs to notaries trained in their own language. Thus Greeks tended to patronize Greek notaries, Latins went to Latin notaries, and Jews sought out notaries trained in Hebrew,[8] but Latin notaries always greatly outnumbered the notaries working in other languages. Since practically no Greek or Hebrew documents from the fourteenth century remain, we might expect there to be few Greeks and Jews in the transactions, or at least only so many as had business dealings with Latins, which automatically would have required the services of a Latin notary. This is indeed a problem that prevents us from generalizing about the activities of Greeks and Jews as aggregates. Luckily, the protocols do contain transactions between Greek and Greek and between Jew and Jew in more than sufficient numbers to prove their historical worth. The convenience of conducting one's business in the official language of the colony's court ensured that Latin notaries would attract clients from all the colony's communities. A document first redacted in Latin did not need to be translated before being brought to court, as would have been the case of a document first drawn up in Greek or Hebrew.

Notaries whose primary language of record was Greek were occasionally called in the sources *tabelliones*, but not always.[9] Although there were Greek notaries who worked in the city, most of them could be found in the villages.[10] In 1365 a Greek priest, Georgios Spilioti, resident of a smaller town at the western end of the island, Chanea (and therefore not included in the above estimation), was created "in scriptura greca notarium publicum" after being judged to be a person of good reputation, legal standing and trained "ad tabellionatus officium exercendum."[11] These Greek notaries undoubtedly knew Latin as well, but had the ability to take the first rough notes from a Greek-speaking client orally, before making a fair copy in Latin, if that is indeed what Greek notaries did. We cannot be sure. For the fourteenth century, the notaries whose registers have survived, among which figures a protocol of at least one Greek notary (Emanuel Focha), all recorded their business in Latin.

Whereas in Venice the notariate was composed exclusively of priest-

notaries for most of the thirteenth century,[12] the Cretan notaries throughout the fourteenth century appear to have been mostly laymen, since only
11 of the 113 notaries' names can be identified confidently as belonging to
priest-notaries.[13] Yet because priest-notaries did not consistently identify
their clerical status in the transactions they redacted, more of the notaries
might have been clerical than the documents lead us to believe.

As a final note, when I distributed the 113 notaries' names over the
years of the fourteenth century, I noted the longevity of the careers of
numerous notaries. Nine of the notaries' careers lasted more than twenty
years, four of those for over thirty.[14] Fifteen notaries have left traces of ten
to twenty years of their careers.[15] Thus the Candiote notariate was not a
large group in the fourteenth century, but it was a relatively stable one.

On the basis of the information I have just provided, I estimate that
notarial protocols from approximately half the notaries active in Candia
during the fourteenth century have survived. This is not at all to say, however, that half the Cretan chancery has survived. For each of the 57 notaries
only some of whose transactions still exist, there must have been at least
several protocols for each notary that have not survived. In other words, a
small fraction (a quarter to a third?) of the protocols of perhaps half of
all the fourteenth-century notaries is still in existence. But the problem
in working with these sources goes deeper than simply the fraction that
have survived.

As I mentioned earlier, the surviving notarial archive's small size has
not discouraged some historians from manipulating the data contained
there in an overly ambitious way. A thorough acquaintance with the protocols will make it clear that notaries tended to group particular types of
documents in separate protocols, as evidenced by *busta* 295, a large, cum-
bersome bundle containing protocols dedicated entirely to wills. Occasionally, a notary recorded a will in a protocol containing other kinds of documents, such as contracts or documents of obligation, perhaps for reasons of
time or its lack or perhaps merely because that particular protocol was
closest to hand. It must be assumed that it was also true that other kinds of
transactions, like those of obligation, were recorded out of order. Therefore, although the absence or the infrequent appearance of a kind of transaction may in the end reflect a genuine trend, it is just as likely to reflect the
loss of the protocol in which a notary normally recorded those types of
transactions. For this reason, not only is it questionable to use the data in
one notary's protocol to derive percentages and generalizations pertaining
to trade and other economic trends, because we cannot divine the contents

of the protocols that have not survived, but percentages based on the multiple protocols of one notary's labors are only slightly more meaningful than those based on only one protocol of one notary.

Those are the sources and the limits any scholar must face when studying Venetian Crete. Given the small percentage that the surviving records represent, tracking economic and social changes over the course of the century through the notarial transactions is an imaginative exercise that I have mostly foregone. The documents have their limits and I have mine. But lest the methodological outlook of my approach seem too gloomy, I maintain nonetheless that even if change over time is hard to detect, there is still much to learn about any given moment in the colony's history.

My approach was to arrange the sources into two conventional groups. On the one hand, there are the official and literary sources, in which category I include government deliberations, proclamations, and court records, along with chronicles written by Venetian officials who were also members of the metropolis's burgeoning intellectual circles in the fourteenth and fifteenth centuries. On the other hand, there are the notarial sources: specifically, notarial registers into which were recorded formulaic transactions mostly of an economic nature, ranging from bills of sale, acquittances, contracts for employment, and apprenticeships to marriage contracts.

The notarial document that is an exception to this arrangement is the will, which embodies both the impersonal formula of a transaction guided by law and the personal inclinations of its maker and, thus, spans both groups of sources. Scattered among the protocols are the wills of 793 inhabitants of the colony and over one hundred marriage contracts. The clearest stamp of the population's individuality appears in the wills. For instance, the economic and social status of individuals in Candiote society is apparent in the wills. Because the wills give the values of the property they allot as legacies or as dowries assigned to daughters, members of Candia's elite are on the whole easy to identify. Titles and occupations are also indicative of the social level of the testators. Although, in the spirit of humility appropriate to making a will, testators rarely identify themselves by their noble titles, noble testators reveal their status nonetheless by referring to their parents or other close relatives as "dominus" or "nobilis." At the lower end of the social scale, artisans and other skilled workers or professionals listed their occupation after their name. Many women identified themselves as the wives of artisans, workers, and professionals. Although testators rarely set out to list all their children, the information contained in wills provides the best data for the reconstruction of families in the colony, at least on the upper levels of society.

Marriage contracts also contain valuable information. The text of these documents tends to be brief, unless complicated arrangements for the payment of the dowry are involved. Each marriage contract has two parties, one representing the bride, the other the groom. Typically, fathers represented their children, but in the absence of the father, mothers and siblings were equally likely to step in as the principal parties to a contract. The only other variable information found in marriage contracts was the date by which the groom promised to carry the bride to his household and the value of the dowry and nuptial gifts. Unfortunately, it was not a standard practice to do more than outline the kinds of property of which the dowry consisted without specific details. Coin, gold and silver objects, clothing, linen, household effects, and occasionally rights to real estate were the most common elements of a Candiote woman's dowry.[16]

Notarial documents are seldom appealed to in discussions of ethnicity in the history of medieval and Renaissance Europe. When relations between Latins and Greeks have been the subject of discussion, presumably it is the intentionality of the governmental sources that has lent them greater credibility in characterizing those relations. Governments say in their records what they intend to happen and occasionally why. Chronicles and other literary works are expressions of their authors' conscious and unconscious intentions. In contrast, notarial documents display a less obvious intentionality, in that they are witnesses to people's actions — what they do, not what they say. They reflect the practice of people's lives, as opposed to the theory that human beings are so fond of attributing to themselves and their actions. Notarial sources, however, have the underappreciated advantage that they can, through cautious study, display the material basis of the social and political changes appearing after the fact in official and literary texts. In our case they present a picture of Cretan colonial society at variance with the one which emerges from the diplomatic and literary sources. As I came to see it, the governmental records provided a partial theory for living in the colony, while the notarial sources partially depict the actual practice of living there. It is the gap between theory and practice that makes Candia so interesting.

Introduction

Crete is Greek, despite the variety of imprints on its landscape and population made by Romans, Byzantines, Muslims, and the people of western Europe, the Latins. No one would deny that Cretans speak demotic Greek, or a dialect of it, and have done so for centuries. The legendary ferocity of the Cretan people came to stand for the Greek nation as a whole during the Second World War, when the army of the Third Reich invaded the island and met furious, bloody resistance. The image of Zorba the Greek, jubilantly dancing on the Cretan shoreline, drawn vividly by the Cretan author Nikos Katzanzakis and brought cinematically to life by Cacoyannis, furnished another side of the stereotype of the quintessential Greek man. Even Eleutheros Venizelos, who became in the early part of the twentieth century the first prime minister of a united Greece that included the island, was a Cretan. In the West, and to a certain extent in modern Greece itself, the island of Crete became a metonym of the modern Greek nation.

A little less than four centuries before the *enosis*, the proclamation of the Union of Crete with the mainland issued by the Assembly of Crete in 1908, and well before the founding of the Greek state in 1821, the Ottoman Turks had wrenched possession of the island from Venice after a protracted war that ended in 1669. In 1211, 458 years before that, Venice sponsored its first settlement of Crete. The Byzantine emperor's grip on the island had already been lost by that date.[1] The so-called Second Byzantine period had lasted for only one hundred and fifty years, from the time that the military general and subsequent emperor Nicephorus II Phocas managed to expel the Muslims, who themselves had previously captured Crete in the mid-tenth century. Prior to the Muslim period, the first Byzantines, the heirs of the Roman world, ruled the island.

Measuring the impact of conquerors on a conquered people simply by comparing the number of years each power's occupation lasted would be to simplify grossly the process whereby people become acculturated to one another. Nevertheless, it gives a twentieth-century student of history pause when the over four and a half centuries of Venetian rule are placed alongside the three hundred and ninety years of Ottoman rule, the one and a half centuries of later Byzantine rule, and the century of Muslim rule. The pause lengthens with the realization that the Venetian Comune kept possession of the largest Mediterranean island after Sicily for nearly five centuries, longer than the English held India, Spain held Mexico, or France held Québec. Consequently, it is not unreasonable, even if rather ahistorical, to wonder why Crete's culture and people do not resemble more than they do italianized Sicily, hispanized Mexico, or anglicized India, whose most evident link to the power that once colonized them is language. Obviously, at least in the case of Crete, the length of occupation does not play an essential role in the process of colonization and acculturation. Otherwise would not the Cretans resemble more closely in their cultural aspect the Venetians?

A few years ago, on a warm day in early May, I stood talking with two Greek colleagues, both of whom I much admire, in the courtyard of one of Athens's libraries, well beyond the reach of the traffic noise and shaded from that spring's unusually strong heat. We three were participants in a conference, one of those whose principal aims were to bring together a relatively small group of scholars from around the world to talk about the subject to which most of those attending had devoted their careers, in this case, Latin Greece. As often happens at such gatherings, what was said in conversation outside the conference hall was as instructive as what was formally presented within.

One of the men with whom I was speaking took collegial exception to a comment I had made during the afternoon's discussion period. The point I had sought to make earlier was in response to the frequent and — so it seemed to me — very vague use of the word, "identity," a concept ill-defined and ill-understood by historians, including myself, if there ever was one. To prompt further thought about the use of "identity," I proposed half provocatively and half seriously that for the next few years we observe a moratorium on the use of the word itself, in order to force ourselves to explain more precisely what we mean at those moments when it is the easiest word at hand.

Afterward, in the courtyard, my interlocutor was having none of it. "You in the United States and western Europe have an identity crisis. We Cretans do not. A Cretan knows who he is. His identity is Cretan and Greek." Being both, he stressed, does not preclude other identities, such as a masculine identity or perhaps even a Mediterranean one. Even if what it means to be either Greek or Cretan has changed over the centuries, the question, "who or what are you?" would not be as complicated for a Cretan to answer as it apparently would be for American and European academics casting about for fresh, relatively untrammeled fields of investigation at the beginning of the twenty-first century. In other words, he was implying, why make something more complicated than it really is?

The question brought me up short, if only because it is a question that I have often asked myself while reading in my broadly defined field of medieval studies, in which the concepts of "politics of identity," "alterity," "ethnic identity," and "national identity" have appeared more and more often in recent years. My colleague's comments forced me to reassess whether an individual's statement of his or her own "identity" ought to be taken at face value and dealt with from there. More to the point of this study, why does it matter whether or not there was a material basis for the ethnic distinctions between Greeks and Latins in the Venetian colony of Crete during the fourteenth century, if that population and the powers that governed them believed those distinctions to be real and acted on that belief accordingly? To what extent is my subject being driven by the scholarly fashions of the day?

My response to that question will not satisfy many, because I admit to a moral stance towards my subject. The aim of this book is not principally to answer the question I posed earlier, why are the Cretans not more like the Venetians? I am instead more interested in contributing to the school of thought that recognizes collective sentiments and ethnic identity to be and always to have been shifting beds of sand. I do not treat the history of the intellectual concept of "ethnic identity" so much as I argue, using the example of one society, that ethnic categories, which presuppose a cognitive ordering of human beings according to some implicit or explicit criteria, exist independently of and are shaped and fueled by forces other than people's daily, material lives. By now, in this post-Kosovo world, it might seem obvious to most participants in ethnic strife (and there are very few humans on the planet who are not in some way participant, regardless of how aware they are of it) that ethnic identity is to a large extent a politically generated, or at least manipulable, phenomenon, which exists in either a benign or a malignant state. Americans and western Europeans, however, cannot afford to look down their noses at the seemingly inexplicable ethnic conflicts of the former Yugoslavia or the genocide in Rwanda, since ethnicity lies at the core of so many social ills in their own countries. Whether of African, native, or European descent, all Americans, to take one people, are imbued with the idea of objective ethnicity and so cast their world unconsciously in its terms, thereby ignoring the reality of a world with no set, tangible ethnic boundaries. Ethnicity is everywhere, yet nowhere.

To my way of thinking, ethnic presuppositions so infuse scholarly investigations today that it is a little like the left hand forgetting to take into account what the right hand is doing. We decry the malignant expressions of ethnicity, on the one hand, and advocate the preservation and perpetuation of the benign forms, on the other, without exploring dispassionately the idea that, to mix similes, the malignant and the benign are two sides of the same coin. I believe that the more conscious we are of the unnatural character, literally, of ethnicity, the more we can protect ourselves from its virulent forms. I am very sympathetic to the sentiment recently expressed by Edward Said, although he might not subscribe wholesale to my position.

Identity as such is about as boring a subject as one can imagine. Nothing seems less interesting than the narcissistic self-study that today passes in many places for identity politics, or ethnic studies, or affirmations of roots, cultural pride, drum-beating nationalism and so on. We have to defend peoples and identities threatened with extinction or subordinated because they are considered inferior, but that is very different from aggrandizing a past invented for present reasons. Those of us who are American intellectuals owe it to our country to fight the coarse anti-intellectualism, bullying, injustice and provincialism that disfigure its career as the last superpower.[2]

For my part, I do not believe that Americans are alone in "aggrandizing a past for present reasons." Europeans also contribute their share of inflated pasts and presents.

Nowadays, interest in ethnicity has grown, albeit unevenly, across the various geographic fields of medieval history. There is no question that the study of ethnic definition and self-definition in the medieval period is a field that promises many things, many of which are still to be delivered. If the literature on ethnic identity and relations between people of different ethnic backgrounds reveals anything thus far, it is that ethnic identity is a very slippery concept that depends on a pool of factors, including class, law, culture, politics, and religion. Not even anthropologists, from whose discipline historians today have adopted many tools with which to delve into the past, relish the task of pinning down the fairly recent coinage, "ethnicity."[3] It comes as no surprise, then, that historians fear to tread where anthropologists are reluctant to go, with the result that they, too, are unable to reach a consensus on the meaning of such terms as "race" or "nation" and their derivatives, much less on how they were understood by the people in the past that used them.[4] This state of ambiguity may be unavoidable, since the multiplicity of uses to which ethnic terms have been put in any age defies easy generalizations.

In the meantime, the difficulties inherent in the subject have not prevented scholars from proceeding with investigating forms of definition and self-definition in the past, if only because ethnic classification and self-classification in history have had a palpable impact on human beings in a multitude of contexts. A key area to which such questions are particularly suited is colonial history and frontier societies, where encounters between two or more ethnic groups have typically occurred. There we find a growing recognition of the interaction between governing systems and the ethnic divisions within a population.[5]

In the social relations prevailing in Venetian Crete, I realized that state-sponsored colonization of territory inhabited by people who were culturally, linguistically, and religiously distinct from the people who carried out the task of conquest presented remarkably similar conditions to those that would come to characterize the European colonial experiences of the sixteenth and seventeenth centuries. The colonial experiment on Crete had no direct influence or impact on later ventures. Rather, that particular colonial society in the southern Aegean during the fourteenth century constitutes one piece of a complex puzzle, not a point on a linear spectrum. The puzzle, in other words, the symbiotic relationship between ethnicity and colonization, has yet to be explored in depth.

The Venetian colony of Crete, which began in 1211 and lasted until 1669, is the premier example of pre-modern colonization and deserves its place in medieval and early modern colonial history as such.[6] The second century of its existence is a fitting period in which to explore these ideas. If the colony were a stew, then, by the fourteenth century, the ingredients would have had time to blend and intensify. The fourteenth century was a time when Turkish raiders had begun to harass the coastline, the plague reached the island, revolts led by Greek noble families put continual pressure on the colonial regime, and the Latin colonists themselves declared their independence from Venice for one remarkable year.

What distinguished the colony from nearly every other one in the medieval period is the unprecedented intervention of the state in its direct governance. Instead of delegating the task of ruling and administering the colony to individual subjects or commercial companies, the Venetian state established an administration directly accountable to the Senate, the highest ruling body of the city on the lagoon. To this day, the anomalous manner of the Venetian state's rule of Crete remains largely unappreciated by nearly all historians of colonization and state-building outside the field of Latin Greece and still by many within it.[7]

The importance of Crete, however, only begins with and extends from its structure and governance. Two recognizably distinct ethnic communities, the Greeks and the Latins, lived side by side in the colony of Crete, although the Greeks as a whole were subordinated to the Latins economically, politically, and juridically. With the passing of the first century of Venetian rule, Latin and Greek people adopted some of each other's cultural customs. As I will show, the two groups intermarried, many of them learned each other's language, and some even chose to worship according to the rites of the other's church. Visible signs of ethnic membership, therefore, became blurred over the course of the first two centuries of Venetian rule, without either the Greeks and or the Latins ceasing from referring to themselves and the other as such. On a practical level in daily life, with the shifting of the cultural boundaries separating them from the indigenous population, members of the Latin community had less and less incentive, to varying degrees depending on their rank, to call themselves Latins. This cultural convergence proved politically crucial at certain times during the fourteenth century, because, despite this acculturation, the Venetian regime continued to treat Latins and Greeks differently before the law.

Here I must say a word about what I will not discuss in this work, because anyone familiar with Venetian Candia will note the absence of an important component of the population: the Jews.[8] The Jewish community of Candia is an old one, predating the arrival of the Venetians. Individually, Jews appear throughout the sources, although, like the Greeks of Candia, they went to their own notaries, whose protocols have not survived. They are readily identified by the epithet *iudeus* or *iudea* required by law to be appended to their names in any legal document or record. That obligatory usage marked them off from the rest of the population. A rich source of prosopographical information, the Cretan archives contain much material that deserves more attention than it has received in the years since Joshua Starr published his still standard study of the community.

Nevertheless, I do not include them in my discussion for two reasons, the more practical of which is for the sake of brevity. The more important reason has to do with the way I have defined my subject. I focus almost exclusively on the Greek-Latin paradigm, since the language of the sources forces on us a Latin-Greek dichotomy, with its stress on ethnically motivated strife. The paradigm reflects how the sometimes volatile atmosphere in the city of Candia and the island as a whole was perceived by the Venetian state, the colonial regime, and the people themselves. Other groups, such as the Armenians, who arrived as refugees and stayed to found their own communities and leave their own cultural imprint on Candia, inhabited the city, but the relations that were vital in the colonial context were those between Latins as a group and Greeks as a group.[9] For this reason, the Jews of Candia, as well as the Armenians, the Turkish slaves, and others, are largely absent.

Venetian Crete stands on its own as a rich field in which to work. But by placing its history into a broader context, I hope to show that the history of Venetian Crete offers many valuable lessons about how being ruled by agents of a distant colonial power had a profound impact on concepts of ethnicity and race in the pre-modern era. The context needs explaining, however, in order to make that argument, because colonies were by no means all alike in how they were governed or in how their populations were affected by colonial rule. Therefore, I offer a brief framework within which to compare the colonial social relations active in Crete with those of other forms of colonization in approximately the same period.

Colonization and Colonies in the Medieval World

To observe, as R. R. Davies has done in the Scottish context, that colonization does not necessarily lead to colonies is to open a pathway toward discriminating among the various kinds of expansion and migration that historians of Mediterranean colonization in the Middle Ages in particular have tended in the past to ignore.[10] It has perhaps by now gone out of fashion to place merchant quarters in eastern Mediterranean cities, semi-autonomous lordships and principalities in the Aegean, and territorial possessions under the direct control of distant powers all within the category of "colony." The late Freddy Thiriet, the French historian who did most to lay the foundation for all subsequent work on Venetian activities in the eastern Mediterranean, found it useful to treat all forms of Venetian presence as colonial ones, on the reasonable grounds that they were all closely administered back in Venice by the same governing body, the Senate. Still, whether it was a question of a merchant compound in Constantinople or of a direct possession like the island of Crete, the differences in status, in his mind, were negligible.[11] More recently, the historian of the crusader states, Joshua Prawer, likewise spent little time distinguishing among the various forms of Italian merchant and colonial activities. In his view, even those Italians who lived in overseas commercial compounds qualified as colonists.[12]

Although economic and social historians since Thiriet's and Prawer's syntheses reached publication have teased apart to a limited extent the differences in the ways Venice made its presence felt in the Byzantine Empire and the crusading states, the question of which were colonies and which were simply settlements remains largely unaddressed. The difference among the various endeavors lies in the maturity of the state. State-sponsored colonization was not to be the form of colonization that proved most efficient to the colonizers of the western hemisphere, but the Spanish state set those later enterprises in motion, and set the stage for the crucial linkage of colonization and racially defined slavery.

Unfortunately, the state as an institution in medieval or early modern times has come under fire in recent decades. Ever since historians have grown shy of attributing too much reality to the existence of the state in the Middle Ages, the political and bureaucratic processes of domination over land and people have suffered neglect, falling into a desuetude similar to other traditionally defined areas of study, like constitutional and parliamentary history.[13] I would argue, however, that the subject's retirement is premature. There is insufficient attention given to the impact of governing systems on how people see themselves and see others. Even in such a valuable and magisterial synthesis as Robert Bartlett's *The Making of Europe* the need to generalize eclipsed important exceptions that could have led us to more fruitful insights into the ways ethnicity worked in western European societies of the past. Davies's dictum that colonies are not always the outcome of colonization is sometimes lost, for not everywhere where Europeans migrated or conquered did administrative and judicial control and domination buttress settlement and thus create ethnic conditions that were peculiarly colonial.

My examples of colonization, Genoa, the Spanish crown, and Ireland, are neither exhaustive nor arbitrary. Capturing, occupying, and governing distant territory by the use of salaried agents was, however, beyond the abilities of most states in the Middle Ages. For example, the establishment of the crusader states in the Levant at the beginning of the twelfth century and the dismemberment of the Byzantine Empire after 1204 brought into being sovereign states, despite a nod to the papacy as nominal lord. The conquerors themselves stayed to rule, but in order to do so they were obliged to accommodate their newly acquired subjects, or at least the nobles among them. Moreover, those that came from the Italian maritime states made themselves beholden to their cities of origin in a loosely defined form of vassalage, in which they exercised a considerable amount of freedom in their jurisdiction.

Of all the examples of expansion and conquest in the Middle Ages, Genoa, Aragon, Castile, and England work best as a foil to my primary subject of study, Venetian Crete. I will unabashedly suggest that the primary difference among those twelfth-, thirteenth-, and fourteenth-century choices is the existence of a stable bureaucratic state in two of them. Which powers in the pre-modern Christian world, other than Venice and, to a lesser extent, England, successfully kept possession of and ruled directly a distant, noncontiguous territory through the agency of its own salaried representatives for nearly five hundred years? The methods of the Venetians and the English differed from one another in significant ways, but their accomplishment after a great deal of effort indicates a remarkable degree of stability and centrality. That only two powers were capable of such bureaucratic colonial control of distant territory is key to understanding Crete's importance to the history of European colonization. It took a high and stable level of political organization to govern directly for more than fifty years, much less for more than four-and-a-half centuries, a large tract of territory, geographically distant from its base of power and populated by people with a culture different from its own. A brief exploration of the differences among Genoa, the Iberian crowns, and England should make the point.

Since the revival of interregional Mediterranean trade in the eleventh century, most of the region's Christian states had sponsored the establishment of communities of their own merchants in the emporia of the Mediterranean and the Aegean Seas.[14] Competition in trade was fiercest between the two most powerful economic states, Venice and Genoa, which jockeyed for position as the dominant commercial presence in the Byzantine Empire and in the crusader states.[15] Prior to 1204 and the conquest of Constantinople, the fortunes of both cities depended in large measure on the privileges granted to them by the Byzantine emperor. When Genoa's fortunes ran hot in the empire, reaping great financial advantage from the monopolistic trade concessions it enjoyed in the Black Sea, Venice's prospects tended to run considerably colder. Then, when Venice underwrote the expedition that resulted in the expulsion of the emperor and his court from the capital city, carrying with them in their wake the Genoese, Venetian fortunes ascended once more.[16] With the reestablishment in 1261 of the Byzantine Emperor in his traditional capital, Genoa once again rose to prominence, buttressed by its relationship with the emperor and fortified within its merchant quarter, Pera, which was granted to the Genoese on the northern shore of the Golden Horn.

Pera is a good example of what many historians of Mediterranean trade and colonization would call a merchant colony.[17] Essentially a suburb of Constantinople, this quarter of the city was home to Genoese merchants and transplanted Genoese families who settled in the empire. Although Genoese law obtained in the quarter, the colony was embedded in a larger sovereign polity to which it was in fundamental ways subject. Nevertheless, it grew increasingly independent of the Byzantine emperor over time to the point where he lost all practical jurisdiction over the Genoese who resided there permanently. Despite these developments, the autonomy and political hegemony of the quarter were limited by the sovereign status of the polity in which it thrived.

There were many other merchant quarters similar in nature to Pera around the Mediterranean. Any power whose merchants were involved in the lucrative long-distance trade between the Levant and western Europe sought to acquire a base of operations in the ports out of which they operated. Pisa, Amalfi, and other Italian cities enjoyed varying degrees of privilege in those ports. Genoa had a colony in Kaffa on the Crimean peninsula, and prior to 1346 on the island of Chios, in some of which locations Venetian merchant colonies were also to be found. The port cities of the crusader states held important merchant colonies of western European, mainly Italian, maritime powers.[18]

Genoa made several attempts to create territorial colonies, over which the Comune tried to exercise full control, but ultimately failed to sustain the effort. Individual subjects of Genoa were more successful.[19] The Genoese Comune's attempt to colonize Corsica and Sardinia occurred around the same time that Venice consolidated its control over Crete in the early thirteenth century. Lured by the silver and salt of Sardinia and by the agricultural products of Corsica across the straits that separated the islands from the Ligurian coast, the Genoese state sponsored the settlement of some of its subjects in Corsica's principal town, Bonifacio. The establishment of a colony capable of supporting itself off the land faltered and, unable to govern the colony because of its own internal political instability at home, Genoa allowed the settlement in Bonifacio to become yet one more merchant colony enjoying a good deal of autonomy.[20]

Even Genoa's acquisition of Chios in the fourteenth century was mediated by a company of private shipowners. At the start of that century, members of the Zaccaria family, originally from Genoa but long established in the Byzantine Empire, took possession of Chios and the city of Phocaea on the Anatolian coast opposite the island, but their recognition of Byzantine sovereignty placed them and the island outside Genoese dominion. The mastic of Chios and the alum mines of Phocaea drew the Zaccarias, who exploited these profitably. But in 1329 they were expelled by the indigenous noble families of Chios. Political instability in Genoa had the unintended effect for a while of bolstering Byzantine efforts to keep the Genoese from reasserting any claim to the island. Nevertheless, after several false starts, a fleet of Genoese galleys captured Chios in 1346. The Comune, trying to recover from the devastating effects of Guelph-Ghibelline civil war, agreed to allow the Mahona, the company that furnished and funded the victorious fleet, to rule in the Comune's name and interest.[21] One signal feature of the agreement between the Genoese Comune and the Mahona was the confirmation of the Chiote nobles in their place of privilege. No noble family was dispossessed; no attempt was made to subvert the Greek church in favor of the Roman, or as it is more commonly called, the Latin one.[22] The Mahona's rule of the island lasted, however, until 1566.[23]

Another opportunity to create a territorial colony presented itself in the early fourteenth century when Genoese vessels reached the Canary Islands, off the coast of northwestern Africa in the Atlantic.[24] In the end, the Genoese were not the ones who turned the islands into a territorial colony. It took nearly one hundred years before anyone tried to settle the islands, and those efforts came about only with the initiative of people from the Iberian peninsula.[25] Colonization, however, was not on the minds of the first Iberian conquerors, who were after slaves and plunder. In the early fifteenth century, first Franco-Norman forces under the patronage of the Castilian crown, and then an invasion of Castilian and Andalusian adventurers, began the slow process of making the Canary Islands the first Atlantic colony. They began by establishing bridgeheads, in the form of merchant compounds, on the largest islands, and slowly extended their political control over the islands once their Portuguese rivals gave up their claim to the same territory.[26] Later in the century, the Genoese were still on the scene, for they helped introduce sugar production into the colony.[27] The resistance of the native islanders made the process of colonization lengthy and costly. Tensions were further exacerbated by the constant threat of enslavement, notwithstanding the crown's decree in 1500 that the native islanders were not subject to servitude.[28] That vulnerability to enslavement eventually became a symptom of the crown's weakened authority.

Although the Castilians began to raid the island for slaves in the 1340s, when they subsequently got around to settling the islands, Stevens-Arroyo argues, their harsher measures reflected the increasingly brutal modes of colonization applied during the conquest of Grenada in the fifteenth century under a united Castilian-Aragonese crown. Well before that, the Reconquista proved to be the laboratory in which the future Spanish crown derived its experience in conquest and settlement.[29] At the same time that the Genoese established their commercial, if not strictly speaking colonial, presence in the port cities of the Mediterranean, the crown of Aragon was acquiring considerable experience of its own in the conquest and colonization of territory. The influence on Aragonese activities attributed to Genoa was hardly necessary, given that the king of Aragon went about colonizing Valencia in a way that Genoa could only dream of doing in its own bridgehead on Chios. Much of Genoa's influence on Iberian expansion stemmed less from the methods of Genoese colonial rule than from features of its commercial activities that propelled the Genoese to attempt colonization. The experience in long-distance trade and involvement in local industries where Genoa's merchants set up business furnished Aragonese merchants with an example of efficient commercial organization.[30] But the Aragonese, it must be said, had not been slow in acquiring their own kind of colonial experience. The kind of colonization adopted at first by the crown of Aragon was a mixture of state direction and feudal delegation.

Jaume I (1213–76) was known as the Conqueror for very good reasons. In 1233 he began the conquest of Muslim Valencia, and later on he conquered the largest of the Balearic Islands, Majorca. In Valencia his intention seems to have been to maintain it as a kingdom separate from Aragon.[31] He established an administration composed of his son as procurator general, a lieutenant, two sub-lieutenants, and two bailliffs, the general scope of whose duties was the collection of revenue and protection of the king's rights.[32] Most of the land and the cities of greatest importance he kept for himself, distributing the rest among his supporters, the church and military orders.

The colonization of Majorca proceeded along much the same lines. In the first half of the thirteenth century, Jaume I conquered Majorca with the intention of establishing a regime supported by a nobility to whom the crown granted estates, while keeping a considerable portion of the island under direct crown control.[33] Jaume dispatched magistrates to the island to dispense royal justice, a signal feature of centralized state dominion. During his lifetime, trade flourished and the merchants in the port towns grew in number and strength. At the same time, the system of land tenure instituted by Jaume and perpetuated by his heirs led to a decrease in the number of feudal lords and an increase in the complexity of royal administration and in the system of justice.[34] With the death of Jaume in 1276, however, the kingdom of Valencia and the colony of Majorca underwent a fundamental change. Jaume I divided his kingdom into two parts as a solution to the rivalry for succession between his two eldest sons, Pere and Jaume.[35] He gave his eldest son, who became Pere II, most of the peninsular territory, including Aragon and Valencia. The second son, Jaume II, became king of Majorca, which included the other Balearic Islands, the provinces of Rosellón and Cerdaña, and the seigneurie of Montpellier.[36] Although Pere forced his brother to become his vassal, Majorca ceased being a colony and instead became a sovereign kingdom.

Aragonese colonial ambition did not stop there. Jaume the Conqueror's descendants in the fourteenth century succeeded in unifying around the Aragonese crown a far-flung kingdom. Pere IV (III in Catalonia, 1336–87) reconquered Majorca and struggled to remove Sardinia from Genoese influence. Although firm possession of Sardinia eluded the Aragonese kings, the kingdom eventually came to consist of the Balearic Islands, Naples, and Sicily. The degree of control over the Italian territory exercised by the crown is not well understood. Nevertheless, this kingdom that was slowly pieced together over the fourteenth and fifteenth centuries bears close resemblance to the Venetian colony of Crete. Aragonese history, however, was troubled by the political and dynastic instability of the crown, which was unable to maintain a sure, consistent hold on its territories.[37]

The example of Ireland offers the most useful contrast to bear in mind during the extended treatment of Crete that follows. Its history is not an exact analogue to Crete's, but aspects of its colonization and subsequent rule mirror many of the same social developments that occurred in the Mediterranean island colony. There are similarities in the method of rule, the imposition of juridically defined ethnic boundaries on the populations, the assertion of the English church at the expense of the Irish one, and the creation of an elite that was in many respects neither Irish nor English in the eyes of the colonial power and of the colony. Finally, its relevance for later adventures in colonization in the western hemisphere has more direct application to history than perhaps does the history of Venetian Crete, for, as Robert Bartlett has succinctly put it, the planters of Virginia had already been the planters of Ireland.[38]

At the same time that they were wealthier and more powerful in their kingdom than French kings were in theirs, the English kings still had to rely to a great extent on the feudal aristocracy to fulfill any expansionist ambitions they might have had.[39] Dominion over conquered territory took sev-

eral forms, ranging from exaction of tribute to direct rule. Although the
various forms could and did co-exist in the same territory, most often, as
Davies has put it, "The assumptions were those of hegemony and clientship
rather than those of direct or territorial lordship."[40]

The English conquest of Ireland lacked all the resolve of purpose evident in Venice's acquisition of the rights to and conquest of Crete. Nevertheless, once embarked on the project, the two powers' policies proceeded
along similar lines. In response to appeals for aid from the Irish king of
Leinster, Dermot MacMurrough, Anglo-Norman adventurers initially
made their way to Ireland from Wales beginning in 1169, without, however, the initial encouragement of the English king, Henry II.[41] Prominent
among Dermot's new supporters was Richard fitz Gilbert de Clare, earl of
Pembroke, otherwise known to history as Strongbow. When Dermot died
in 1171, Strongbow, now married to Dermot's daughter, stepped to the
fore and laid claim to Leinster, thereby attracting the active enmity of the
late Irish king's foes and the wrath of Henry, who landed at Waterford with
an armed force in tow.[42] Once Henry required the submission of all parties,
the English crown's lordship over Ireland was established. It is important to
note that Henry became lord, not king, of Ireland. Retaining Dublin, Waterford, and Wexford directly in the hands of the crown, he confirmed the
position of some of the Irish kings and Strongbow's lordship of Leinster
minus Dublin, as well as handing the lordship of Meath and the office of
justiciar to Hugh de Lacy for balance.[43] The English presence in Ireland
depended on the Irish chieftains' acceptance of Henry's lordship, no easy
matter to maintain. The situation was made even more precarious by the
risky ventures of other ambitious Anglo-Normans in search of lordships for
themselves. The lordship of Ulster became a sort of principality on the
strength of John de Courcy's reckless raids on the province in 1177, but he
was eventually brought down by Anglo-Normans rivals in 1205.[44] Before
his defeat, he had established in his lordship a seigneurial administration,
including chamberlain, seneschal, constable, and a cohort of vassals. In
short, Anglo-Norman domination of Ireland had many of the attributes of
feudal relations.

It is just that derogation of the crown's prerogatives to the lords of the
Irish provinces, who held them in fief, that distinguishes the rule of Ireland
from the rule of Crete. The Norman conquerors brought with them to Ireland knights' fees of the kind that they had instituted in England after that
earlier conquest.[45] Tenants of fiefs had all the obligations that marked a
feudal system of territorial rule: military service, attendance and counsel

given at one's lord's court, and money grants.[46] Notably, the private construction of fortifications, especially the mote castle, was also a hallmark
of military tenancy in Ireland, a feature entirely missing from Venetian
Crete. While establishing that fiefs could be held directly or indirectly of the
crown, Henry II and his son John as his representative granted in charter
numerous legal and economic privileges to Dublin, among whose population recent emigrants from England and Wales predominated.[47] The chief
justiciar, who operated as the king's main representative at the head of the
colonial administration and judiciary, and his council oversaw the feudal
arrangement set up by the crown. One of the chief justiciar's main tasks was
to make war, since resistance to English domination was continuous. Additionally, judicial administration constituted a very important component of
the justiciar's function. Feudal lords from England and also from among the
Anglo-Norman lords of Ireland were chosen to be governors and council
members, where they acted with a limited degree of autonomy. Throughout
the twelfth, thirteenth, and most of the fourteenth centuries, royal direction
was close.[48] Thus, it is possible to agree with Davies with respect to the
relationship between the lordship of Ireland and the English crown that
Ireland, under the close tutelage of the king of England's governance, constituted a colony, albeit one whose governance was interwoven with feudal
relations.[49]

Although King John brought English common law to Ireland in 1210,
it was not uniformly applied to the population. In this age when the personality of law predominated, those of Gaelic Irish descent stood away
from the bar of English law, unless they received a special grant from the
crown that brought them under its protection. In their rule of Ireland,
however, the English formulated a distinction between the English and
Irish peoples on all social levels that is indeed reminiscent of the distinctions
that Venice made among her subjects in Crete. Although the English crown
endeavored to apply English common law in Ireland in such a way that
England and Ireland would be seen to be governed by the same law, it
nevertheless did not make that law available to everyone in Ireland. From at
least the middle of the thirteenth and throughout the fourteenth centuries,
the courts did not recognize suits made by Irishmen precisely because they
were just that, Irish. Moreover, there was a clear implication of unfree status
in that legal incapacity, much resented by the Irish commoners, who now
had to compete under English rule with newcomers to the island.[50] In
addition to sanctioning the conquest of Ireland by English nobles, the
government also promoted immigration of English peasants to Ireland in

an attempt to bring the land under cultivation to a degree that the island
had not experienced before. They held the privilege of access to English law,
while Irish peasants did not. In some respects, ethnic law was no innovation
of either the English or the Venetians, since the concept of the personality
of law was and would remain for centuries to come a characteristic feature
of *ius commune* on the Continent. People carried the law of their place of
birth with them always.[51] To the same extent as language and religion, law
ethnically defined an individual. What will emerge from Venetian Crete, as
I suspect would be true as well of Ireland, is that ethnic law, in practical
application, gradually edges aside religion as a primary criterion for free
status, while in other respects law in general becomes responsive more to
custom and less to nature. Historians see in the crown's restricting access to
English law a racialization of legal categories of persons in the midst of the
judicial pluralism typical of medieval polities where more than one ethnic
group permanently resided. The Gaelic Irish were governed according to
their own traditions, customs, and laws that had grown out of native conditions, but this policy had the effect of locking them into a socially and
economically inferior status. By the end of the fourteenth century, birth, or
rather biological descent, was a principal criterion for gaining access to
English law.[52] In contrast, the Anglo-Norman conquerors, who eventually
evolved into the Anglo-Irish nobility, enjoyed the benefits of English law, as
was considered their right by birth. Although, like Venice, the English
crown borrowed from Irish law certain institutions, such as some pertaining to criminal law and judicial procedure, English law remained open only
to a colonial elite until the sixteenth century, when Henry VIII promoted
himself from Ireland's lord to the island's king, and therewith extended
English law to all.[53]

   Unlike the course of action chosen by Venice in Crete, the English
conquerors of the twelfth century did not dispossess the Irish lords, since
the feudal bond was able to provide a basis for a realignment of fealties. Recognizing the English king's overlordship, the Irish lords made little complaint. Whatever resentment they felt grew out of the fiscal burdens placed
on them by the king and not out of political subjection.[54] Partly as a consequence of the judicial pluralism of the colony, the Anglo-Normans who
settled in Ireland became a group distinct not merely from their Gaelic-Irish
cohabitants but, equally significantly, from their Anglo-Norman peers in
England. The development of this colonial elite provides another striking
parallel with the feudatories in Crete in the same period. By the fourteenth
century, the English of Ireland came to think of themselves as separate, as a

"middle nation," although we ought not to rush to an anachronistic under-standing of that latter word.[55] Just as significantly, the English of England came to perceive the Anglo-Irish as separate from themselves, existing in a state of being somewhere closer to the Irish than to the middle. Tensions between the Anglo-Irish colonial elite and the nobility of England appeared early in the fourteenth century. There are clear instances of the Anglo-Irish nobility throwing in their lot with the Irish against English authority. Nev-ertheless, well before that, the government's thirteenth-century insistence on wearing one's Englishness on one's sleeve, almost literally, forms the basis of what at bottom was a fear of diluted allegiance among the colo-nists.[56] Strictures against "going native" in terms of dress, style of hair, and language show up in the records of the Irish Parliament in 1297, but even as early as 1170 Gerald of Wales testifies to the complaints of the Anglo-Normans that they were despised by both the Gaelic Irish and the English in England.[57] One possible consequence of such tension was a potential alliance of the Anglo-Normans with their Gaelic Irish peers against the English crown. Therefore, it behooved the government to make sure that the colonial elite's aspirations were firmly tied to the fortunes of court politics and life.

England differed from Venice in its relationship to the church hier-archy of its acquired colony. In contrast to the ecclesiastical situation in Venetian Crete, the process of anglicization of the Irish church was a grad-ual process, stretched out over three centuries, in which natives of England slowly monopolized the episcopates of the Irish dioceses. There is even a divergence of sentiment, or at least emphasis, among historians of medieval Ireland. While one believes that the process of anglicization formed part of a larger process of bringing the Irish into line with the uniform practices of the English church, another sees the imposition of uniformity with English ecclesiastical practice as an extension of widespread perjorative views of the Irish.[58] To substantiate the latter viewpoint, Watt cites the opening of the papal bull that validated Henry II's lordship over the island: the Irish were "a barbarous people, undisciplined, uncivilized and ignorant of the divine law."[59] It is interesting, moreover, that Otway-Ruthven pinpoints the early thirteenth century as the time when Ireland's ecclesiastical organization finally matched that of the rest of Europe, which is precisely the same period in which Watt situates the demise of the Irish church's constitutional unity.[60] Obviously there is more at work here than the attitude of "glass half empty" competing with "glass half filled," for the differences in emphasis have clear political overtones today. Regardless of this difference, there can

be no doubt that, in spite of the Irish and Anglo-Normans belonging nomi-
nally to one church, there was a perception of two churches well into the
fourteenth century, a reflection no doubt of the colonial nature of Irish society.[61] By the end of that century, however, English royal authority in Ireland
was declining, only to be resuscitated towards the end of the fifteenth.

What the crowns of Aragon and England attempted to accomplish,
Venice had already accomplished long before. The neglect of Venetian colonial history can only be explained by the unimaginative view that failures in
the long term holds few lessons of value. Even among scholars of Venetian
history there is a tendency to ignore the social and political implications of
colonization for Venice, as opposed to its economic benefits, which have in
contrast received a great deal of attention. The Venetian state was sufficiently stable and complex in its organization to adapt to and mold the
circumstances prevailing in an island hundreds of miles away from its bases,
with the result that the colony of Crete lasted longer than any other territorial colony in the European Mediterranean.

The chapters that follow ought not only to provoke interest in the
colony of Crete, about which very little is known outside a small group of
specialists, but also to carry forward a few steps our understanding, first, of
how governing Crete changed Venice, and, secondarily but more broadly,
how Venetian Crete offers the first signs of the conditions in which colonization adopts ethnicity as one of its principal tools of domination. Here on
this island is one society where the periphery ought not to be as peripheral
to the central field as it currently is.

The insularity of Venetian Cretan studies is more than geographic.
What the many aspects of the colony's history have to teach us should by
rights extend beyond its shorelines, out beyond its current location within
the confines of Greek history, to take up a position closer to the center of
Venetian studies and, more generally, of colonial history.

I

The Colony of Crete

"Our City's Eye and Right Hand"

In 1368, Pope Urban V wrote to the Latin archbishop of Crete to express his concern that the Greek church in the Venetian colonies was gaining ascendancy over the indigenous populations that Venice ruled. After studying the reports he had received of Greek priests ministering to those faithful to the rites of the Greek church, he instructed the archbishop to invoke the assistance of the Venetian colonial regime in Crete, in order to prevent learned Greeks there from being ordained in any other rites but the Latin ones. For, he wrote, "as we have been pleased to learn, our beloved sons, the doge and the comune of Venice, wield in the island of Crete uncommon dominion over Latins and Greeks."[1] The pope arrived at the heart of the matter concerning the colony's unusual character more easily than most historians have done in hindsight. Venice had established in its Mediterranean possession a regime that fit no ordinary model.

It would be anachronistic to ascribe to Urban an insight that only in the present day begins to make sense, now that modern states, their huge apparatus, and their capacity to rule distant territory have long been a reality. Yet contained in his single observation is a hitherto unnoticed clue to the roots of modern colonization and modern ethnicity. At the heart of the colony's novel character is the role of the Venetian state and its impact on the people it ruled. It shaped the colonial government and, as a consequence, the lives of the island's inhabitants, both Latin and Greek. The pope correctly perceived that Venice exercised a greater dominion over Crete than over any other of the colonies that made up the Venetian overseas empire and than any other state power had achieved thus far.

Two principal features that set the colony apart from every Venetian-ruled territory, including the city of Venice itself, were its size and the distance between the city and the colony. Until it acquired the island in 1211, the Venetian state had governed no land mass greater than the collection of one-hundred-odd tiny islands that formed its city and a thin strip of ports on the mainland lying along a short arc around the lagoon. Crete was the largest territory the Venetian state would rule until the fifteenth century, when the Comune made its first foray onto terra firma.[2] No previous experience, except for that acquired in ruling itself, had provided a template for the government of Venice, when they set about securing and settling Crete. Furthermore, the distance of the island from the metropolis and consequently the time it took to communicate with the island meant that ruling Crete was no mean achievement for a fledgling colonial power. Crete lay approximately a month away by galley from Venice, and so direct rule required a more sophisticated bureaucracy and methods of communication than mere expansion into contiguous territory would have demanded.

Prior to the conquest of Crete, communicating with Venice's merchant community in Constantinople furnished the most comparable experience in long-distance direction of policy.[3] Like Genoa, Aragon, and other commercial powers of its time, Venice during the eleventh century sponsored merchant quarters in foreign cities around the Mediterranean, the most prestigious and powerful of which was located in Constantinople.[4] Although the *podestà* of the most important Venetian overseas base had to answer to the Senate back in the metropolis, the great distance between the cities, in combination with the importance of Venetian trade in the Byzantine empire, afforded that Venetian magistrate considerable power and autonomy in negotiations with the Byzantine emperor.[5] It has become virtually an axiom in Venetian historiography that the community in the Byzantine capital rivaled the metropolis in importance to Venice's economic health. Its importance did not come without its dangers. The civil servants at work in the Palazzo Ducale overlooking the lagoon must have realized that there were problems inherent in such a community, which was large in comparison to the Venetian communities in other port cities, and distant enough to threaten to slip out of the Senate's control, as indeed the Venetian community in the Byzantine capital had once threatened to do.[6] Implicit and occasionally explicit in all its communications with the community in Constantinople was a reminder that there but for the grace of the Senate went the Venetians of Byzantium, and therefore obedience to the mandates issuing from the lagoon was of the highest necessity. Consequently, the administrators and magistrates of Crete would never experience anything other than close supervision, thanks to the political stability that Venice, unlike Genoa, enjoyed.

Urban's inclusion of Latins as first among those whom Venice ruled in Crete underscores another important feature of the colony that set it apart from almost every other in that period. When the island came under its

nominal dominion in 1211, the Venetian state chose not to delegate rule of
the island to noble colonists who would govern in its name, as it did elsewhere in Latin Greece. Why it made such a choice in the case of Crete will
remain essentially conjecture, but the island's size and strategic importance
undoubtedly had something to do with the reasoning. Regardless why
Venice chose that path, its choice had social and political consequences. For
the first time in the medieval Mediterranean, a group of Latin colonists and
their descendants were not synonymous with those who ruled the colony.
By imposing an administrative structure staffed by salaried employees sent
from the metropolis for two-year terms of office, Venice made subjects of
both the Latin colonizers and the colonized Greek people of the island,
even if one group held considerably more privileges than the other. Conquerors and colonized peoples occupied similar shared space in other colonies of the Middle Ages, such as the crusader states, but not as subjects of a
third, geographically-distant state exercising direct rule. As subjects of Venice, the Latins and Greeks of Crete stood on common ground, on which
common interests might be found, a potential complication the danger of
which was not lost on the Venetian state.

For all that the colonizers and the colonized were both subjects of Venice, each portion of Candia's population embodied in its own way what was
new about that colonial society. At the top of the Candiote social hierarchy
stood the feudatories, the group of military settlers, mostly (at least in the
beginning) from Venice's oldest families, who received grants of land and
other kinds of property that enabled them to perform their martial obligations to the Venetian Senate and its representative regime based in the city.
Since their military service was for a long time the linchpin of Venice's continued possession of the island, the feudatories' allegiance mattered in a way
that the allegiance of those further down the social scale did not. Below the
feudatories came the commoners, both Greek and Latin, many of whom
were artisans and professionals, but also servants and unskilled laborers of
free status. Slaves and villeins, on whose backs the economy of Crete in part
rested, formed the mass of the entire island's population, living mostly in
the villages. We will see that at both ends of the social spectrum, rather than
in the middle, the unique features of the colony emerged.

The Establishment of the Colony in Candia

As broker for the armies that used its city as their departure point, Venice
profited substantially from the dubious enterprise known to history as the

Fourth Crusade. After the unprecedented fall of Constantinople to the Latin forces and the expulsion of the Byzantine imperial authorities in 1204, the conquerors set about looting the city and dividing up the territorial spoils. In a secret pact during the same year, one of the leaders, Boniface of Montferrat, and the Venetian doge Enrico Dandolo swapped their shares of the prizes. Boniface took four-fifths of northern mainland Greece, including the city of Salonika, and gave to Venice the island of Crete and two cities, Coron and Modon, on the tip of a Peloponnesian peninsula.[7] At least as far as the island of Crete was concerned, the acquisition of the island was more potential than real. Venice had to face the task of making good its newly negotiated claim.

It might have been, as Freddy Thiriet supposed, that by exchanging the territory of northern Romania for rights over the island of Crete Venice had in mind only a minimal occupation of the island.[8] The Comune's lack of previous experience in territorial conquest is as good an argument as any for that view. The ports of Crete, and the possibility of a permanent base for Venetian merchants in Venetian territory, were what the doge had his eye on. The island's interior with its peasantry and the fields of grain and viticulture they worked, betokening an agricultural economy, had less appeal to the maritime commercial power. But like it or not, secure possession of the ports turned out to depend on securing as much of the island as possible and as soon as possible. Venice was not the only power at that time seeking to conquer Crete. Genoese pirates, primarily Enrico Pescatore, who acted with the evident approval of the Genoese government, also had their eyes on the island. They even managed to take possession of the city of Candia for a short time before Venetian forces arrived to begin their own conquest and installation. The contest between Venice and Genoa over Crete went on for some years, concluding with the defeat of the Genoese in 1211. Thereafter, they made no further attempts to establish a base anywhere on the island from which to extend their possession.[9] With the elimination of the Genoese from the scene the Venetians, left to face only indigenous resistance to their presence, first gained a foothold in the island's principal city of Candia.

The towns of Crete, Candia, Chanea, Rethimno, and Sithia, all ports on the northern shore, face mainland Greece many miles to the north. Although endowed with a variety of landscapes, prominently including plains cultivated in grain, Crete had few large settlements in the interior of the island. The many villages filled with the Greek-speaking peasantry remained largely immune to the introduction of Latin culture in the coastal towns.

Very little of Candia from the Venetian period and still less from the Byzantine period have survived to this day. The few existing Venetian public buildings and churches, such as the loggia and the church of St. Mark, have been restored to their sixteenth- or seventeenth-century condition, but virtually nothing remains of the public and private buildings of the medieval period.[10] Much of what we know about the medieval city comes to us from the writings of visitors to the island and from archaeology, although there have been relatively few excavations within the modern city. One visitor, an Irish monk by the name of Symon Semeonis, passed through Crete in the course of his pilgrimage to the Holy Land in the early fourteenth century. He visited Candia for a short time after a brief stop in Chanea, the port at the western end of the island. His impressions of the city, appearing in the account of his travels that he subsequently wrote, are the earliest ones we have from the period of Venetian rule.

This city, like those of Istria, Albania and Romania through which we passed, abounds in most excellent wine, in cheese, and in fruit. It exports the famous Cretan wine to every country of the world. Here also ships and galleys are loaded with cheese; also pomegranates, lemons, figs, grapes, melons, water-melons, gourds and other most excellent kinds of fruit can be bought here for a very small price. To those at sea it presents a beautiful appearance, but it has nasty, dirty, narrow, torturous and unpaved streets.[11]

Founded by the Muslims who conquered the island in the ninth century, Candia lay clustered around its harbor. It was an old city even in the fourteenth century, though not so old as the famed one hundred Cretan cities of antiquity or those ancient city-states on the mainland. Since the geographic position of its harbor was never advantageous, the port's importance as an entrepôt developed in spite of rather than because of its natural features.[12] Storms blowing into the harbor from the north and the constant influx of silt made necessary the construction of a breakwater (*mole*) and the periodic removal of the accumulated sand in the harbor, for which project taxes were levied on the city's population.[13]

It was not until Venice took possession of the island that Candia's strategic importance in the trading networks reached its height. Candia was a port town, possessing all the attributes normally associated with any maritime city host to merchandise-laden vessels constantly arriving and departing. Much of Candia's economic value to Venice came from its role as a harbor, where galleys traversing the Mediterranean put in on their way east or west, or used it as a terminus, leaving their goods to be picked up and carried on by another galley heading in the opposite direction.[14] Thus there were always strangers from all around the sea, except from those Muslim territories proscribed by the papacy. Though small, Candia was nonetheless cosmopolitan in the variety of its visitors.[15] From the early thirteenth century through the sixteenth, Candia welcomed a steady stream of merchants and pilgrims. The traffic of galleys moving in and out of the harbor resounds through the proclamations issued by the colonial government. In those records we hear galley crews being recalled to their ships and tavern-keepers being ordered to close their shops until the crews were safely, if not soberly, back on board their vessels.[16] Uprooted immigrants, like Armenians and those from the island of Tenedos fleeing lands that yielded to the incursions of the advancing Turkic peoples, were arriving in the second half of the fourteenth century. Christian and Jewish pilgrims en route to the Holy Land disembarked at Candia; some remained, some continued on their travels.

From the water's edge in the port, looking south with the sea at one's back, the city spread east to west in a semi-circle delineated by ramparts. At some point after the island came into imperial possession for the second time, the representatives of the Byzantine emperor erected fortifications around the city, which remained the city boundary until the Venetians in 1462 built another series of ramparts to encompass the additional area into which the population of Candia had spilled during the first two centuries of Venetian rule.[17] In the early thirteenth century, there were two main gates leading inside the city walls: one by the port, called the Sea Gate, that opened immediately onto the city's main street (*ruga maistra*) and one, known as the Land Gate, or *Voltone*, at the end of that street, which led south into the suburb.[18] Over the next two centuries the authorities would open more gates in the city walls. Along the main street stood private houses and warehouses containing merchandise from all over the Mediterranean.[19] On either side of it lay a rabbit-warren of narrow, crooked streets, lined with one- and two-storied buildings and dotted with churches in the Byzantine architectural style of small basilicas.

The city covered 192 acres, of which fifty were built up in the Venetian period.[20] At the heart of the city was the central piazza, commonly referred to in the sources as the Platea, which was located toward the southern end of the *ruga maistra*. Here were the principal public buildings, the ducal palace, the merchants' and exchangers' loggia, the church of St. Mark, and, farther toward the east outside the Platea, the cathedral dedicated to Crete's patron saint, St. Tito. Prior to the construction of the second set of walls in

1462, Candia was divided into two parts, one within the walls and one outside them. In contemporary documents, the part inside the walls is referred to as the *civitas*. A suburb called the *burgus* in the sources extended south of the city's walls. Unusual for a Christian Mediterranean city, Candia's walls enclosed the Jewish quarter, the existence of which has been attested prior to the arrival of the Venetians.[21] Also directly up against the interior of the walls were gardens tended by city residents, from which they harvested much of Candia's fresh foodstuffs. Moreover, judging from the bequests of *terrae vacuae* in wills made by residents of that period, there were green fields and pasture throughout the city's outer fringes, also within the walls.

But despite the sense of space created by pasture and fields under cultivation on the outer perimeter, contemporaries thought the city center crowded, crammed with people at certain periods of the century and characterized by two-storied flat-roofed buildings lining the narrow streets. The appearance of the city, host to profitable Mediterranean merchants with their wares, was not too small a detail for the Great Council of Venice. It decreed that, in order to ensure the attractiveness of the outer aspect of Candia's main street, buildings were to be faced in stone and plaster.[22] With such a pleasing blend of Byzantine and Italian features, Candia's buildings must have recalled those of Venice, whose own vernacular architecture in the late Middle Ages was much influenced by the Byzantine style.[23] An opportunity to improve the city's appearance arose when a severe earthquake shook the island in 1303 and reportedly destroyed a considerable portion of the city's private dwellings. Carpenters and masons came to Crete from Venice to supplement and assist their Candiote confreres in rebuilding the city, and their work is thought to have lent the city characteristics common to Venice's appearance. But the artisans of Venetian origin already settled on the island may have just as likely have already put a Venetian stamp on Candia well before.[24] Slightly later accounts attest to the Levantine look of the city, conveyed primarily by the flat roofs of the buildings. A visitor to Candia at the end of the fifteenth century extolled the beauty of the city, with its many churches, flat-roofed houses, and warehouses filled with barrels of cheese in brine ready for export, but, like the Irish monk, he found the city filthy from lack of proper sanitation.[25] Garbage deposited by the city's sea walls and washed into the sea remained a continual problem.[26]

Candia's suburb began to spread from its beginnings in the southeast corner outside the city walls and extended around its entire perimeter, taking in the overflow of artisans and the newer religious establishments.

Eventually the suburb became the place for anyone unable either to afford or find a suitable dwelling inside the walls. The smaller port of Dermata, abutting the walls on the southwestern corner where a narrow river once emptied northward into the sea, witnessed the rise of mills, tanneries, and a cloth industry. Gardens could be found here too, dotting the landscape and providing additional produce for the residents of both suburb and city.

This busy port city, hundreds of miles from the northern Adriatic sea, whose small size and population were out of all proportion to its strategic and economic importance to Mediterranean trade, prospered under the close supervision of the Venetian Senate. Most of the credit for achieving this unprecedented level of direction at a distance belongs to one man. Of all the dukes of Candia, the first, Giacomo Tiepolo, a Venetian from one of the oldest and most prestigious families, made the greatest impact on the colony. His career after he left the position of duke of Candia shows him to have been one of the most important Venetian politicians of the thirteenth century, if not in all Venetian history. After leaving Candia, he twice served as *podestà* of Constantinople (1219–21, 1224–27), where he effectively put an end to all questions of the Constantinopolitan colony's independence from Venice. Two years after his last term as *podestà*, he was elected doge of Venice (1229–49). During this tenure he made another important contribution to his city, through his sponsorship of the compilation of Venetian law, thereafter known as the Statutes of Venice. This set of ducal legislation became in the succeeding century the principal source of law for Venetian judges.[27]

Back in Candia during the first years of the colony's existence, Tiepolo took charge of the campaign to secure Venice's possession of the island. Apart from expelling the various other claimants to Crete, including the Greek noble families, this Venetian functionary also had the task of setting up a system of administration. He established the city of Candia as the military headquarters of the island's occupation and as its administrative center, although how much of the hinterland Venice actually controlled is open to doubt. The duke of Candia, with two councillors to assist him and three advisory councils, corresponded roughly to the doge, the College or Signoria, and the other legislative councils of Venice.[28] The burden of keeping their duty always before the eyes of the military settlers fell principally on the duke of Candia, whom the Signoria chose from among its own politicians, and whose appointment the Great Council of Venice confirmed. In this office, the term of which lasted two years before a replacement arrived, he not only was charged with the island's administration, but also was responsible for serving as chief magistrate, assisted by other judges and officers of the peace.[29] The duke's two councillors also came from Venice's *case nobili* and served terms of two years. These three civil servants constituted the high court of the colony, but there is little in the sources to make clear the practical differences in their duties from one another. In an effort to minimize the potential for corruption, all three were prohibited from engaging in trade.[30] The Signoria kept close watch on the activities of its functionaries in Candia through the teams of inspectors (*provisores* and *sindaci*) who regularly visited the colony, although these visits do not seem to have been regular before the second half of the fourteenth century.[31] Their role was not merely to investigate the operation of the ducal regime, but also to function as circuit judges.[32]

From what we can infer from the sources, the duties of the duke and the councillors do not appear to have changed much over the course of the thirteenth and fourteenth centuries. The extent of their jurisdiction, however, underwent transformation as ruling the colony became an increasingly complex affair and the need to foster new settlements of Latins in other parts of the island became apparent. The western towns of the island, Chanea and Rethimno, eventually had rectors, appointed by the Venetian Senate, who by the end of the thirteenth century carried on day-to-day rule. In the mid-fourteenth century the business of governing the eastern half of the island became even more demanding, with the increase in Turkish raids along the coast. When the duke and the councillors began to spend more and more time traveling outside the city to inspect the situation in Sithia and other towns in the eastern districts, changes had to be made to the rules about their replacements in Candiote court and council sessions during their absence. So great did the job of ruling and defending Crete become that by the last quarter of the fourteenth century the responsibility of organizing the military defense and maintaining the peace of the colony had shifted entirely away from the duke and his councillors to a Venice-appointed Captain of Crete. Nevertheless, in spite of the increase in the number of functionaries, the duke of Candia remained the senior representative of the Venetian Signoria.

More than fifty and probably closer to one hundred men, most of them appointed in Venice, filled the ranks of the colony's bureaucracy. In Crete, its first territorial possession, the Venetian state launched a miniaturized version of its own political structure, down to and including the administration and dispensation of justice. As in Venice, three judges *di proprio* handled the litigation involving inheritance and three judges *di petizion* dealt with debts and commercial matters. Together, these six judges heard cases between Latins and between Latins and either Greeks or Jews. Another kind of judge (*iudex di prosopo*) handled cases involving Greeks and Jews alone. When the Great Council of Venice dispatched judges on two-year tours of duty in the Venetian colony of Crete during the fourteenth century, the oath of office (*capitularium*) administered to the appointees laid out very clearly the sources of law to which they were to turn in their adjudications. Those sources are interesting for what they do and do not include. The source of first recourse was the Statutes of Venice. Case law, or precedent (*de simili ad simile*), was a judge's second resort in the event that a fitting solution could not be found in the Statutes. Failing the first two, judges were to turn to approved custom; the text does not specify Venetian or Byzantine. Finally, lacking all three sources, judges must fall back on their good consciences to guide them to what was right in the particular circumstances of the cases before them.[33]

With such a hierarchy of sources of law at work, most historians have assumed that the Statutes of Venice trumped all other sources of law. The Cretan notarial records make clear that Venetian statutory law prevailed most clearly in civil law matters, unlike the situation in the territory Venice conquered in the fifteenth century, where the law of the conquered city in fact supplanted the Statutes of Venice.[34] But in practice judges exercised far more flexibility than even the judges' *capitularium* allowed. As was mentioned, a separate court with the specially designated judges *di prosopo*, some of whom in the later stages of the colony's history were of Greek ancestry, oversaw cases involving the disputes of Greeks and Jews. Very little is known about the workings of this court, since none of its records have survived, except for the judges' oath of office. In the *capitularium* of the judges *di prosopo*, the same hierarchy of sources of law appears, in which Venetian statutory law takes precedence over approved custom, when appropriate to the circumstances, with one exception.[35] An explicit exception to Venetian law was made for dowries: "Except in the accounting (*ratio*) of dowries, where I must proceed and adjudicate according to Greek custom."[36] The existence of the two courts strongly suggests that free Greeks and Jews had limited access to their own customs and laws under Venetian rule, as long as their affairs did not involve persons of Latin descent. Venetian law often had one answer and Byzantine law allowed for another, but Venetian judges in practice made allowances for local customs, even when they contradicted Venetian and canon law. There were situations in which Venetian judges applied Byzantine law also in cases involving only Latins, for the very good reason that Venetian law could not provide solutions to the unprecedented problems that the colonial officials encountered in administering the island. Thus they had to rely on the customs and laws of the previous rulers. Chryssa Maltezou has found several instances of Venetian judges resorting to Byzantine law in cases involving Venetian noblemen and the inheritance of land.[37] Land tenure was one principal area in which the Venetian state had had little experience prior to occupying the island of Crete.

Forming the backdrop to all sources of law explicitly recognized was *ius commune*, the traces of which are so faint that hardly any thought has been given to the way its presence might have been felt in this colony. Common law crops up in mysterious ways in the sources. In a document from 1328, an archdeacon, Antonio Rizardi, agent and administrator (*iconomo procurator*) of the see of Chiron, presented to a notary his credentials contained in a public instrument drawn up by Bartolomeo de Hengelardis, "imperiale auctoritate notarius."[38] There is nothing in the transaction itself to suggest that the imperial notary resided in Crete, which his non-Venetian name would seem to support. However, Bartolomeo's will, made in 1342, fourteen years after the date of the transaction, shows that he was indeed a resident of Candia. Imperial notaries are not unknown in Venetian territory; indeed they performed a function not unlike the three additional sources of law to be found in Crete, by rendering in the form of *consilia* their opinions based on their training in *ius commune* in civil law matters to which Venetian positive law failed to respond. Not only did *ius commune* serve that function, but it also was closely related to the law upon which ecclesiastical institutions relied. Thus the notarial transaction in which Bartolomeo, or other any imperial notary, played a role often involved the property of an ecclesiastical institution.

At issue in Crete was more than the Venetian state's willingness to let each community be governed by its own customs, as in the matter of Greek dowries, or as the Jewish community did, rather than impose Venetian law on all its subjects in the colony.[39] Rather, the concurrent spheres of law provoke thought. Just as Patrick Geary has suggested that ethnicity was a situational construct, one might say that law was situational as well, at least in the minds of Venetian colonial administrators.[40] Venetian judges used law that was previously conceived of and applied in local or imperial terms as was best suited for the circumstances. Whatever works, the judges might have said. Law and notarial practice in Crete have also very much to do with the same areas of study in the metropolis itself. When we remember that

Venice ruled Crete for almost two hundred years before it set foot on the Italian peninsula, the earlier methods of rule it devised for an island a great distance from it take on added significance. Before Venice acquired its great territorial empire on the mainland, it had been experimenting with ruling non-Venetians for quite some time. Ruling the colony of Crete instilled in the Venetian colonial system of justice a flexibility that other territorial powers of Italy scarcely achieved.

The system of governance installed by Tiepolo at the behest of the Signoria was designed to regulate and modulate the participation of the military settlers, who came to be known as the feudatories. When the Venetian state elected to rule Crete through an administration headed by the duke of Candia and two councillors, the men who conquered the island and their successors amounted to little more than a militia, albeit one that enjoyed a privileged position in the colony.[41] The Venetian state charged those colonists with the defense of the island, but did not trust them to rule themselves. Therefore the colonists dispatched to Crete did not devise a system of rule for themselves, nor did they rule the land they had conquered, as did their Frankish counterparts in the nearby Morea. The feudatories of Crete themselves, along with everyone else in the colony, had to conform to the laws and regulations that Venice imposed on them.

The feudatory group was small in proportion to the total population, but their importance considerably outweighed their small number. During the thirteenth and part of the fourteenth centuries, Venice's possession of the island depended largely on them and their heirs, thus posing a special problem for the Signoria. Whereas in the first century of occupation, the princes and nobles of the Morea had to be loyal only to themselves, the problem for Venice in Crete was the preservation of the loyalties of second-, third-, and fourth-generation Venetian colonists. As long as the political, economic, and cultural interests of the Venetian Cretan colonists coincided with those of Venice more than they converged with the interests of their cohabitors, especially the Greek Cretan nobility, the colonists' allegiance to Venice was for the most part assured. Venice's hold on the island became threatened at the times when its interests diverged from those of the feudatories.

Ensuring that Venice's interests continued to converge with those of the feudatories explains in large part the functions of the councils in which the feudatories participated. Three councils assisted the duke and his councillors in administering the colony: the Great Council of Candia, the Council of Feudatories, and the *Consilium rogatorum*, or the Council of the Rogati, otherwise known as the Candiote Senate. Only one register containing a record of all three councils' deliberations, beginning in 1344 and ending in 1363, has survived in the Archive of the duke of Candia. It is possible that other registers have been lost, but it is more likely that no other record in that century existed, since there does not appear to have been a systematic commitment to write down the decisions reached by governmental bodies in Venice, much less in Crete.[42] The *Quaternus consiliorum*, as the register of deliberations is called, probably contains as complete a record of the deliberations as was likely to exist, in that there are no internal signs that more than one register was used to record the councils' decisions. In addition to the councils' deliberations, a register of the local regime's proclamations has survived. It, too, was very likely the only one produced at the time.

The functions of these councils were not legislative or executive, in the sense that they constituted the agencies through which the feudatories exercised any rights in governance. On the contrary, mandatory attendance at the council and its evil twin absenteeism say as much about the obligatory nature of the feudatories' involvement in the councils as they do about the reluctance of feudatories to fulfill their obligations to the regime. The councils were the regime's way of keeping an eye on the feudatories and of securing their assistance in the management of the colony. Whether the councils existed from the start of the colony is not clear. They are not mentioned in the charter of concession, to which we will turn shortly, according to the terms of which the first settlers were granted land in Crete.[43] They were formed at some unknown point in the thirteenth century. No description of their purposes and jurisdictions has survived, if indeed one ever existed, and a superficial resemblance to Venice's legislative bodies of governance points only vaguely in the direction of their primary roles.

The Great Council

To understand the function and importance of the Great Council in the colony of Crete, several questions must first be addressed. Very little is known and too much has been assumed about the social composition of the council's members. For instance, it has too often been assumed that the members of the Great Council were uniform in interest and status. A glance at the studies of the Venetian patriciate in the Trecento and Quattrocento ought to have hinted at the possibility of that not at all having been the case.

The process of defining and delineating the upper stratum of Venetian society points to analogous processes operating on Crete.[44] But perhaps an equally important possibility is that the evolution of the Venetian Cretan nobility has a bearing, thus far unrecognized, on the process taking place in Venice.

By the time the documentary evidence in the ADC begins in the fourteenth century, there existed the Great Council and there existed the group of feudatories, and the assumption has been that the two had always been one and the same. Here a different tack will be taken. Instead of studying the Great Council and the feudatories in the fourteenth century as if they were synonymous, my purpose is to establish the historical link that supposedly led to them becoming so. Just as the Venetian patriciate in the same period was defining itself, so it will be evident that the feudatories were undergoing a similar development.

The question has never been posed as to whether there is a connection between the members of the Great Council and the feudatory group of the fourteenth century, about whom the most documentary information exists, and the first military settlers sent by Venice to Crete in 1211. The word "feudatory" appears nowhere in the few thirteenth-century documents whose contents are still available. Furthermore, there are changes, only hinted at in the sources, effected by the Venetian Senate over time as it worked out the fine points of a method of rule. Three documents from the first half of the thirteenth century will give a clearer idea of the evolution of the feudatory group.

The first document is the *Concessio insulae Cretensis*, the charter of Venice's concession of the island to a group of mostly its own subjects, drawn up in 1211 just prior to the first settlement.[45] In this charter, after locating the boundaries of the land in the district surrounding the city of Candia that would remain under the direct control of the Comune, the Venetian Signoria divided the island of Crete into six districts, which in the early thirteenth century were called *sestieri*, in imitation of the districts of Venice.[46] Each of the districts was further divided into thirty-three and a third units of land called *cavallerie* or *miliciae*. Of the island's total two hundred *cavallerie*, 132 were granted to *milites*, the mounted men-at-arms. The remaining 68 *cavallerie* were each divided into six parts called *serventarie*, or sergeantries, amounting to 408 in all and earmarked at the beginning for footsoldiers (*pedites*).[47]

The mission of these first settlers in Crete was clear: they were to occupy the island, subdue resistance to the occupation, and organize themselves in such a way as to ensure their continued presence. In return, the military settlers received from the Venetian state property with which they might support and equip themselves for the task of defense. The *cavalleria* and sergeantry referred to in the charter of concession, both of which categories of property constituted a *feudum*, were distinguished primarily by their value, which in turn directly corresponded to the kind of military service the Comune expected the tenant to provide.[48] The more valuable, and therefore the more prestigious, category of property was the *cavalleria*. According to the charter of concession of 1211, the revenue of a *cavalleria* had to be of sufficient worth to support at least the cost of a warhorse, two additional horses, a minimum of armor and weapons, and two squires. The *serventaria*, the category of lesser value, had to support the cost of outfitting a footsoldier. Additionally, both knights and infantry were obliged to maintain residences in the city of Candia, to possess adequate pasture for their horses and livestock, and to swear allegiance to the Venetian state. They could sell or alienate their property as they wished, but only to other Venetians and only with the consent of the island's government. In contrast to the privileges and duties of the duke and the other civil servants, the military settlers were permitted to engage in trade.[49]

The words "feudatory" and "fief" imply that Venice intended to impose some sort of feudal relations on the colony when it sponsored the establishment of the colonial regime. This is not an unreasonable assumption, since strictly speaking a feudatory was the tenant of a fief, which was granted to him in exchange for aid, almost always in the form of military service, and counsel, always in the form of participation in the colony's advisory councils. Moreover, since feudal relations characterized the system of landholding instituted in the Morea by the Frankish knights in the same period, it might be supposed that Venice, lacking experience in this sort of endeavor, would follow their lead.[50] Despite these similarities, there is little that is feudal about the colony of Crete beyond the terminology employed to describe property and status. As David Jacoby has stressed, a key characteristic of feudal relations, the decentralization of state prerogatives, is entirely missing in Venetian Crete.[51] When the Venetian state distributed land among its first settlers, it in no way relinquished any of its rights over that land, as can be seen in the system of land allotment. Justice and taxation also remained firmly the prerogatives of the colonial regime.

From subsequent sources we learn that both kinds of grants, the *cavalleria* and the sergeantry, consisted generally of three kinds of property, the most valuable of which was land.[52] By the fourteenth century, this system of land allotment evolved into one whereby the government auctioned off land to feudatories and others, whose length of tenure was fixed by term, and in return for which they had to provide for its defense.[53] The Comune also auctioned off the rights to individual houses, lands, and villages in twenty-nine-year terms. As was the case under Byzantine rule, the grantees enjoyed sole right of possession, including the right to sublease the property in various ways and titles, but they could not do so without the permission of the Comune.[54] The value of the land derived largely from viticulture, whose importance to the economy grew over the fourteenth century, and grain, the most important crop in the fourteenth century, which landholders were obliged to sell to Venice at fixed prices, sometimes to their advantage and sometimes not.[55] Other agricultural products supplemented their incomes, cheese, oil, and wine being the most prominent ones.

Land was not, however, the only kind of real estate to make up a *feudum*. It was not unusual for a *cavalleria* and a sergeantry to comprise, among other property, buildings in the cities and fortifications of Crete, in addition to the feudatories' residences. Rent from the additional buildings was another important source of revenue. After real estate, rights to villages formed the next important component of the *feudum*. Those holding either *cavallerie* or sergeantries often rented their portions of village lands, consisting of orchards, vineyards, and gardens, for varying lengths of time to others to cultivate.[56] The third component typical of the *cavalleria* and sergeantry were the villeins, the unfree peasantry, whose duty was to provide free labor and a portion of the product of their labor to their lords.[57] A *cavalleria* had to have no less than seven villeins attached to it. A miscellany of other revenue-generating properties, such as rights to a mill, also could be included in a *feudum*.[58]

The settlers who received either *cavallerie* or sergeantries from the Comune came from all levels of society in the Italian peninsula and from other parts of southern Europe, but at the start of the project to gain a foothold on the island, Venice attempted to rely exclusively on its own citizens and subjects. A list at the end of the charter of 1211 gives the names of the *milites* and the *pedites*.[59] No one in the list held both a *cavalleria* and a sergeantry. Ninety-four *milites*, nearly all with recognizable Venetian cognomina, were to receive *cavallerie*, while twenty-six *pedites*, whose cognomina indicate humble and not necessarily Venetian origin, received *serventarie*.[60] The charter states that the difference in number between the 120 recruits listed and the projected total of 540 military settlers would be made up with men provided by the duke of Candia, who probably had available northern Italian mercenaries recently deployed during the struggle with Enrico Pescatore for the island.[61] Thus, despite its preference for Venetian settlers, the Comune resorted right from the start to recruiting non-Venetians, to make up the majority of the *pedites*. Given the immediate resistance of the indigenous people to Venetian rule, not to speak of the recent contest with Genoa over possession of the island, Venice needed military settlers on whose loyalty it could unfailingly rely. The government reserved the more valuable *cavallerie* for Venetians, especially those from the old patrician families, and conceded the sergeantries to humbler Venetians and non-Venetians. A built-in hierarchy based on class difference played a part in the allocation of the colony's resources from the beginning, but we will see that the hierarchy changed shape and composition over time, causing tensions between noble and non-noble feudatories at a later date.

Because Venice showed a decided preference for its own subjects in its distribution of *feuda*, some historians of Venetian Crete have argued that the granting of land in fief to non-Venetians in the first years of the colony's existence demonstrates an initial shortage of Venetians willing to settle in Crete. On closer inspection, the correlation is not clear. By conflating the concession of *feuda* to non-Venetians in 1211 with the later invitations by the Comune to people of all social ranks to come settle in Crete, those scholars have concluded that Venice was unable to attract more than a handful of Venetian colonists to the new colony.[62] Without question, underpopulation in the towns as well as in the countryside was indeed a problem later in the thirteenth and fourteenth centuries.[63] Epidemics, debtors fleeing the island, and other factors led to the reduction of the Latin population to a point where the Comune tried several times in the fourteenth century to entice new immigrants to the island with an exemption from taxation for the first few years of their residency.[64] None of these enticements to settle in the colony, however, necessarily mean that what Venice lacked at the beginning was a pool of potential recipients of *feuda*.

The second document for us to consider suggests that the colony's apparent dearth of Latin military settlers was indicative of the regime's attempts to find solutions to the problem of consolidating their hold over the island. By 1222, eleven years after the first settlement of colonists in Candia, Venice thought it necessary for the sake of security to increase the number of *cavallerie* and sergeantries in the northern-central region of Crete, around the city of Rethimno. In the document testifying to that increase, the Senate created sixty *cavallerie* or *miliciae*, out of which sergeantries were to be calculated at six sergeantries to one *milicia*, as was the case in the document of 1211.[65] In the document, unlike in the earlier charter of concession, some settlers received both a *milicia* and a sergeantry. What is more, the Venetian Senate appears to have found a group of its own subjects to settle, to judge by the names. Thirty-two Venetians were granted one or two *miliciae*. Of those thirty-two, thirteen received additionally three sergeantries. Another six men, one of whom came from Padua and another of whom was a tailor, received only half a *milicia*. Twenty-eight additional Venetians, several of whom have only a first name or a first name followed by a profession (thereby signifying low social status), received one sergeantry each. Finally, one Venetian was granted two sergeantries with the stipulation that he bring with him to Crete a horse and a Latin squire.

The first difference between the two documents is that in the earlier charter each settler was granted either a *cavalleria*, making him a knight, or a *serventaria*, making him a footsoldier, but no one received one of each. In 1222, a *miles* could possess one or more of both, although by the early fourteenth century the Comune imposed a limit of two *cavallerie* and three contiguous sergeantries per person.[66] As spelled out in the 1222 document, possession of both *cavallerie* and sergeantries entailed increased military duties. A possessor of one *cavalleria* and three sergeantries was obliged to furnish, among other things, both a mounted man-at-arms and three footsoldiers, which comes close to being responsible for raising a small troop.[67] Furthermore, a commitment to stay at least two years and an injunction against taking on Greeks as squires are two other features in the charter of 1222 that do not appear in the earlier document.

These differences suggest that Venice had problems not so much in populating the colony with Venetians and Latins, as in keeping the military ones there, a likely scenario given the resistance of the Greek noble families to the endowment of settlers with what had been their land, and given the hardship normally associated with settling in unfamiliar land. The prohibition of Greek squires is a reflection of that resistance, which we will examine soon in greater depth. The Comune, then, was evidently reconsidering its method of recruiting military forces in Crete. By allowing colonists to hold both *cavallerie* and sergeantries, Venice displaced some of the burden of recruitment onto their shoulders. Very likely it realized that the simple equation of one man to one *cavalleria* or one sergeantry was an inefficient way of raising troops. Since Crete was Venice's first major colonial undertaking, a reform such as this might be expected.

Another sign of reform, or rather experimentation, is in the clause of

the 1222 document pertaining to the two-year residency required of each
new colonist.

When, the Lord willing, you reach Crete an.' after the two years of your continuous
residency have passed, you may change for the time that you will be there those
milites servitores whom you have brought there with you either for Venetians or for
foreigners (*forinsecis*), but not for Greeks, that is to say, knight f   night, footsoldier for footsoldier, provided you have the consent of the duk.   e one there
now or who will be on our behalf and that of our council.[68]

Since neither servant-knights nor a *miles* as the head of a troop play any
role in the first charter of concession of 1211, this further shows that the
Comune had reorganized its recruitment of military forces, no doubt under
the pressure of indigenous resistance. Whether it was prompted also by the
lack of Venetians to settle the colony, or whether the increased amount of
property and military obligations per colonist simply made better organiza-
tional sense, are questions that are not mutually exclusive. The Comune
undoubtedly faced a problem in retaining military settlers on the island, but
there was ample cause to continue to adjust and fine-tune the system by
which it maintained its possession of Crete. Reorganizing the feudatories
and their military cohorts along the lines of small troops had the effect of
diminishing the preference for an all-Venetian landholding group, as long
as there were enough of their own subjects to hold the property of greatest
value, in the form of *cavallerie*. Adaptation to circumstances and reforms in
military organization continued, for troops under the command of merce-
nary leaders (*comestabili*) became common in the fourteenth century.

By the time, thirty years later, that Venice did indeed have to replenish
the Latin population of Chanea, the town furthest west on the island,
military recruitment had changed yet again. The first division of the colony
into districts, *cavallerie* and sergeantries, as described in the charter of concession of 1211, had taken in the entire island. Despite that, the third and
last document we will consider, which dates to 1252, informs us that the
district of Chanea was now divided into ninety *miliciae*, of which seventy-
five were granted to fifty-two men: two each to twenty-six men; one each to
twenty men; and half each to six men. In this charter, however, the burden
of defense was no longer on the concessionaires alone. The 1252 charter
describes the boundaries of the territory where the ninety *miliciae* were
located, fifteen of which remained in the Comune's direct possession, and
specified the areas in the territory that took in the seventy-five allotted to the

settlers, "where you will live and will be with our present army."[69] After forty years of rule, Venice now had a military force independent of the island's military settlers, under the command of a Captain of Crete. Instead of concentrating on how the property was to be divided among the new settlers to Chanea, the Comune now showed much more concern with making clear which land remained directly in the hands of the Comune.

In spite of the existence of Venetian military forces independent of the feudatories, the duties of the knights of Chanea were more demanding than those imposed on the knights of Candia in 1211 and 1222. For every *cavalleria* he possessed, each knight was required to keep a footsoldier, a mounted man-at-arms, and three well-armed Latin squires of at least twenty years of age. In addition, each squire was expected to have two well-equipped crossbows (*balestras de cornu bene redatas*). As for himself, the knight was to have a well-armored warhorse for each *cavalleria* he possessed. Those knights in possession of two *cavallerie*, more than which number no one was allowed to hold, were required to keep also a good associate (*socius*). These conditions were not exclusively applied in Chanea. Similar elements appear elsewhere in the colony, if not in 1252, then certainly at the end of the following century, with, however, some evident relaxation of previously important details. In a contract from 1370, Andrea Corner, son of the late lord Giovanni of the Greater House, took on Frangulio Kyprioti, a resident of the burg and a Greek man, as his "*socius feudalis*," in return for an annual salary of thirty hyperpera.[70]

To return to the charter of 1252, the duties of the sergeants, most of whom were granted three sergeantries, or half a *milicia*, were reduced to a brief paragraph, suggesting perhaps that they had lost some of their importance in the military scheme of things. They, too, had to keep two horses as well as two squires, conditions which resemble closely the requirements of knights in the charter of 1211. And that may have been the key to related changes. Rather than viewing the scant attention to the tenants of sergeantries in the 1252 charter as indicative solely of a loss of status or reduction in their military role, a better explanation may be found in those changes in light of the perceptible changes in the feudatory group itself. When all is said and done, the changes that Venice brought about in its management of the colony's defense had consequences for the nature of the feudatory group. Now is the moment to superimpose the portrait of the first knights and footsoldiers over the picture of the Great Council in the next century to see if they are the same group of people in Candiote society.

A century after the third document we examined was made, in April

1356, the doge and the Senate in Venice responded to a series of petitions placed before it by an embassy of the Candiote feudatories. Among the appeals was a matter concerning the current calamitous state of the Great Council. The petitioners complained that the council was heading towards ruin, because of the "indigenous persons" who had been made members.[71] The Senate ruled for once in the feudatories' favor. Henceforth the duke of Crete and his councillors would not grant seats on the council, which they called a *beneficium*, to anyone without first seeking approval from Venice.

Next, the petitioners asked that membership in the Great Council be regularized, by instituting an annual review of its members and a procedure for election. Every year, the colonial administration was to elect a committee of thirty men, no more than one representative per family. Together with the duke and the councillors (there never being fewer than twenty-five of the thirty present), this committee was to conduct a qualifying examination (*proba*) over the fifteen days prior to Christmas. A look at the lists of examiners tells us that the overwhelming majority of them every year came from the colony's most important and noble feudatory families.[72] The doge went on to rule that the candidates for seats on the council must receive the votes of at least ten of the electors. Failure to win a seat, however, did not extend to the heirs of the unelected candidate, if their heirs won the necessary number of votes. This last provision no doubt came in handy, when the electors wished to relieve heads of families who were too old or infirm to serve usefully on the council and to pass the service on to their sons.

When, thanks to the Senate's rulings, the membership lists of the Great Council of Candia began that year to be recorded in the register of the three councils' deliberations, a proclamation announcing a fine for those who enroll under false pretenses in the Great Council appears in the register of public proclamations seven months after the date of the Senate's decree.[73] The first list of Great Council members appears in the *Quaternus consiliorum* shortly after in the same month. Thereafter, chancery scribes copied out the results of the *proba* every year until 1363, the last year during which council deliberations were recorded in that register. But we still have little idea how a person qualified for a seat on the council and virtually no notion of the criteria the electors used in casting their votes.

For the moment, let us put aside the question of whether the Great Council comprised all feudatories or some portion of them, in order to estimate the number of all feudatories, as constituted by the Great Council membership lists for the years 1357 to 1363, and their families, approximately one hundred and fifty years after the founding of the colony. Not quite all the names written on the folios are legible (less than ten percent are illegible), but we are fortunate that the scribes tended to record names of the council members in the register year after year largely in the same order, so that we can restore some of the faded names by taking into account where in the lists their names fell. Illegibility is, however, the least of the problems we must confront before proceeding with a calculation. How do we distinguish between the branches of one family bearing the same cognomen?

When the Venetian Senate compelled the feudatories in 1356 to undergo henceforth a *proba* each year to determine the membership of the council, the scribes recorded the council members' names for the most part in family groupings. Thus the names of fathers most often appear immediately before their sons and, likewise, brothers whose father was dead appear one directly after the other in the list, indicating as well a legal dependence. Consequently, this suggests additionally that the grouping of brothers signals a fraternal *societas*. For the purposes of this estimation, therefore, I consider a father listed with his sons as one family; and, similarly, a group of brothers without a father or sons of their own listed on the council constitutes a family unit, even though households could comprise family units of three or more generations.[74]

During the six-year period for which membership lists exist, the Great Council fluctuated between approximately 305 and 355 members, sharing 114 cognomina among themselves. Eighty of those 114 represent the sole branch of that clan at that social rank resident in the colony. Thirty-four cognomina consist of more than one family group. Within that group, I have identified a minimum of 109 separate family groups sharing those thirty-four cognomina. The Corner, Gradenigo, Muazzo, and Quirini families, Venetian patricians all, account for thirty-five of the family groups, making them the feudatory families with the most branches in the colony.[75] It is not a coincidence that those four feudatory families were also the most influential and prestigious ones in the Great Council, the Candiote Senate, and the colony at large.[76]

Estimating that each of those family groups consisted of 4.5 members, as ethnographers of late medieval Italy have done with the populations they studied, a figure of nearly 360 individuals constitutes the eighty families with only one branch resident in the colony.[77] The same calculation gives 491 individuals with the 109 families sharing thirty-four cognomina. Together, the feudatory group thus far amounts to 851 people. To this total must be added another 135 individuals bearing the thirty cognomens found in the lists of the Senate during those years, but not in the Great Council.[78]

The resulting figure of 986 is considerably less than the number first projected by the government in its allocation of *feuda*, approximately two thousand individuals. Even allowing for the very real possibility that the estimated 4.5 members per family is low, it is unlikely that the projected figure was ever achieved. Then again, such a low figure may be indicative of this six-year period only. The period in question comes only ten years after the first advent of the plague and seven years after the second, and close on the heels of a third bout in 1360, when we know from the deliberations that the population had been much reduced.[79] The impression remains nonetheless that the feudatory group was always small, in proportion to the total population.

There is still more to be said about the membership lists. A comparison of the family names of the Great Council members from the second half of the fourteenth century with the names in the charters of concession from 1221 reveals that significant changes had taken place in the feudatory group over the one hundred intervening years. To begin with, the *Concessio* of 1211 contained seventy-three cognomina among those who received a *cavalleria*.[80] The Great Council membership lists of 1356–1363 contained 114. Starting with the early list, of the names in the *Concessio*, thirty-five out of seventy-three (nearly 48%) still appear in the council nearly one hundred and fifty years later. Looking at the *Concessio* from the perspective of the Great Council, of the 114 cognomina, only thirty-five (30%) were among the original settlers sent to the island. Where did the other seventy-nine families come from? To be sure, many of the other cognomina shared by the remainder of the council are ones that belonged to families known to be members of the Venetian patriciate in the fourteenth century, but not all of them. Moreover, if we compare the lists of 1358–1363 to one of the few other lists of names that are specifically identified as belonging to newly-created feudatories, ones dated to 1349, there are cognomina that appear in neither the *Concessio* nor the membership lists: Granella, Corario, Milano, Vidore, Pendidari, Modino, Zaco, Armaki, Bevardo, Venetiano, Kavalario, Litore, Sardano, Litini, Gritolo, Ragono, Torcello.[81] Were these seventeen men feudatories, but not members of the Great Council? Were they among those purged from the council in 1356?

To sum up the implications of these figures, the military settlers who received a *cavalleria* in 1211 were a small group of men, relative to the size that the Candiote Great Council would grow to be. By the second half of the fourteenth century the Great Council amounted to approximately three hundred and fifty individuals. A small percentage (30%) of the council possessed cognomina of the original concessionaires at the start of the thirteenth century. A very incomplete list of feudatories seven years prior to the first *proba* contains names of humble men as well as Greek men. They were either not members of the Great Council, that body being constituted according to some other criterion than that of possession of a *feudum*, or they were among the members whom the *proba* instituted in 1356 was meant to purge. My impression is that, in the years between the founding of the colony and the recording of the first membership list, men of ambiguous social standing were gaining entrance into the Great Council. This does not mean that there were no distinctions among those who did survive the rigors of the *proba*, for we saw that after 1358 only 30 percent were from among the original families. This point will become a component of the discussion of the fourth chapter.

Elsewhere in the sources, the notarial records make it clear that possession of a sergeantry was not sufficient to merit a seat on the Great Council. The first instance appears in a notarial contract from 1271, in which Giovanni Bon, a butcher, leases a vineyard belonging to his *milicia* to another person.[82] Although we do not have membership lists of the Great Council for that year, it is unequivocally the case that for most of the fourteenth century men of Bon's humble status did not hold seats on the Great Council. Evidently, then, by the end of the thirteenth century possession of one sergeantry was not sufficient to gain a seat on the Great Council.

At the same time, the regime was anxious that the effects of inheritance and the mounting debt incurred by feudatories meant that the transference of *feuda* from person to person was driven less by the suitability of new owners for the military service required by their newly purchased possessions than by the financial needs of the sellers. In the fall of 1348, the Candiote Senate addressed this concern and set up a committee to investigate the problem of contiguous sergeantries falling into the hands of unsuitable tenants who refused to provide the military service required.[83]

If I am correct in stating that possession of a sergeantry was not sufficient to warrant a seat on the Great Council, then what was? The original charter of concession made no distinction between a *feudum* consisting of a *cavalleria* and one consisting of a *serventaria*. There is nothing explicit in any of the charters pertaining to social rank. The only implicit information derives from the social rank of the Venetian cognomina associated with Venice's newly-formed patriciate appearing in the lists. At the start of the thirteenth century, the term *feudum* encompassed both the *cavalleria* and the *serventaria*, while the term feudatory referred to the tenant of either. The only distinction between the two kinds of *feuda* was the kind of military service that the Comune expected them to provide. Otherwise, both *milites* and *pedites* were under the common expectation to swear allegiance to the Comune and to maintain residences in the city of Candia. By 1222 the situation had changed. Some knights were now in possession of both *cavallerie* and sergeantries and were responsible for providing a troop equivalent to what they possessed. What we see, then, is that by the beginning of the fourteenth century a *feudum* could consist of several sergeantries, but never as many as to equal more than two *cavalleria*; while possessing one sergeantry, as some of the first settlers in Crete had done, was not enough to gain entrance into the colony's councils. The basic criterion for a council seat, and hence feudatory status, must have become possession of either one or more (but not more than two) *cavallerie* or its equivalent worth. In other words, a two-tiered system of *feudum*-allotment had come into play, in which only the tenants on the higher tier gained seats on the Great Council. The conditions that had to be met to gain a seat on that council do not appear to have stopped there.

Since the Great Council of Candia consisted of more members than the number of *cavallerie* allotted to the first settlers, families and not individual feudatories were the constituent units of that council, which is much the same lines as those along which the Great Council of Venice was organized. Heads of family and their sons of age, or groups of brothers after the death of their fathers, enrolled in the council, appearing on the register's folios very often in family groupings. In the one extraordinary grant of membership recorded in the council's deliberations in 1344, testimony that the applicant's father had been a council member is the only condition for membership cited as having been fulfilled.[84] Membership in the Great Council apparently did not depend solely on the amount of property that a head of family possessed. At some point after 1211 and before 1344, heredity became the chief qualification of feudatory rank.

That the process by which the feudatory group was formed resembled the process whereby the Venetian patriciate came to define itself beginning in the late thirteenth century seems clear. Most scholars familiar with Venetian history know of the famous Closing, or *Serrata*, of Venice's aristocracy that took place in the years on either side of 1300.[85] Over a period of twenty years or so the Venetian state enacted legislation that sought to establish once and for all the membership of the city's patriciate. In the colony of Crete, Venetian authorities had been grappling with similar questions of noble status since the colony's inception in 1211. The feudatory group eventually excluded humble tenants of one, perhaps two sergeantries, whom at the start of the thirteenth century the feudatories might have included in their group, but whom the changes in the colony's military organization and the increased rigidity of the Venetian patriciate after 1300 made superfluous. To this extent, the two defining processes seem to run along parallel lines.

Although the issues involving status in Venice and Crete differed from each another, there were points in both processes where the granting of noble status in one place impinged on the process in the other. The impact of Venetian Cretan nobility on Venetian society will be discussed in a later chapter; Venice's internal struggles over power within its own Great Council had a ripple effect that reached as far as Candia. The problem begins with the question of whether all members of the Candiote Great Council were considered noble.

Most scholars of Venice assume that the title "ser" is indicative of nobility, but the use of the title in Crete is more complex. To begin with, not everyone who is called "ser" in the sources is also a "nobilis vir" or a "dominus," but all three titles certainly indicate membership in the Great Council of Candia. The deliberations of the Candiote Great Council themselves reveal that the three titles reflect social stratification within the group. In 1359 the council reiterated that the secretaries, or *camerarii*, of the feudatories, who were chosen from among their own number and who handled the finances and administrative duties of the councils, must be from among the "more noble and worthy of them."[86] After studying the wills and other notarial documents, in addition to the governmental sources, I have discerned the traces of a pattern pertaining to the usage of titles on Crete. The first noticeable feature of the way titles were used is that the titles "nobleman" or "lord" are attached only to offshoots of the patrician families of Venice. In the 790 surviving wills, fifty men, either testator or mentioned in the text of the will, bear the title "dominus" and five the title "nobilis vir." Of those fifty-five, eleven are dukes and councillors, in other words, Venetian patricians sent to the colony for a two-year stint of office.[87] Two others are prominent in the island's ecclesiastical hierarchy,[88] and four are recent immigrant visitors from Venice.[89] The remaining names belong to Latin feudatories (Emo, Barozzi, Contarini, Coppo, Corner, Dandolo, Donato, Falier, Gradenigo, Grimani, Grispo, Giordano, Giustiniano, Liberi, Muazzo, Nani, Pantaleo, Pascaligo, Quirini, Rizardi, Ruzino, Terre, Venier, Vituri, Zeno) and two Greek noble families (Calergis and Ialina). Three points are clear. First, these names correspond with Venetian patrician clans extant in the fourteenth century.[90] Second, it is significant that eleven of these twenty-five noble names that have survived by chance in the sources correspond also to some of the original families of 1211. And lastly, the feudatory families who we will see dominated the councils are all but one represented in this group. Whether their status was explicit or not, whether codified in some way or not, certain feudatory families enjoyed considerably greater prestige than others and they tended largely to be Venetian nobles. Therefore, two groups of nobles have emerged: those of long standing in the colony and those who arrived more recently. As will be seen in later chapters, the difference is significant.

Among the Candiote feudatories were also some of the noblemen who ruled the islands of the southern Aegean. When the Byzantine emperor returned to Constantinople in 1262, he came to terms with Venice, with the result that Venice acquired rights to the islands of Ceo, Serifo, Santorini, and Amorgos.[91] There were, however, others. The Venetian Sanudo family became the dukes of the Archipelago, which consisted of numerous islands, with a capital at Naxos.[92] Through a strategic marriage alliance at the end of the thirteenth century, the Venier family acquired the island of Cerigo. The Corner family of the Greater House were the lords of Scarpanthos. Astimpalia belonged for centuries to the Quirini, and Amorgos had the Ghisi family for its lords. What is less well understood is the extent to which the lords of those islands were for part of the year absentee landlords. Many of the men who possessed the islands of the Archipelago, whose lord in theory ought to have been the Sanudo duke, were instead residents of Candia and participants in the Councils.[93] These adventurers and their families show up consistently in Candia, appearing in the duke's court and applying to the councils for aid when they needed it. Marino Ghisi, feudatory of Candia, sought the support of the Candiote regime in his bid to protect Amorgos from rival claims by the Genoese.[94] In this instance, the regime maintained a studied neutrality.

The Archipelago came under the jurisdiction of the regime in Candia. After the last heir to the dukedom had died in 1362, lordship of the Archipelago passed into the hands of Fiorenza, the daughter of the last duke. The widowed Fiorenza herself was a resident of Candia, perhaps in compliance with the wishes of the Venetian Senate, who no doubt wanted to keep an eye on her.[95] When she died in 1371, her son Niccolo dalle Carceri assumed the title of duke.[96] He was apparently murdered in 1383, after which time the title of duke passed to a new Venetian-backed dynasty, founded by Francesco Grispi.

One previously unpublished document of great interest, dating to

October of 1387, shows that enterprising families even in the late four-teenth century had opportunities to acquire islands. At the beginning of October 1387, a resident of Candia, Gradeniga Pisani, the widow of lord Niccoló, entered into a contract with a galley owner, Niccoletto Dondi, a resident of Candia. Clearly a woman ambitious for her family, Gradeniga engaged Niccoletto to convey her son, ser Giovanni Pisani, ser Domenico Suriano, his associate (*socius*), and all their servants and equipment, on his galley, armed and outfitted with a crew of seven, to the islands of Santorini, Naxos, and Serifos. Once they had reached Serifos, the galley was to lie in port for five days. If within five days the inhabitants of the island "did not accept Giovanni as their lord," then Niccoletto was to bring her son and his companions back to Candia. But if the Serfiotes did accept him within those five days, then Niccoletto was obligated to remain there a further ten days and then carry Giovanni and his men back to Candia. Should Giovanni wish to proceed instead to Nigroponte, Mykonos, or Tinos, in that case Niccoletto was to negotiate a fee directly with Gradeniga's son.[97] Since Gradeniga's late husband is identified as Niccoló Pisani of Venice, and there is no information about the Pisani family in Candia prior to this time, the widow Gradeniga and her son had probably settled in Candia not long before Giovanni set out on his quest.

As was the case with the Great Council of Venice, there does not appear to have been a limit to the number of representatives per family on the Great Council of Candia. On the whole, the family groups were small, usually amounting to a father and his two or three sons, or sometimes three or four brothers in the absence of their father. Not all adult males of a family were elected to the Great Council, for unelected adult sons of council members show up elsewhere in notarial documents during the same years that their fathers appear in the membership lists.[98] But numbers counted. The most influential men of the colony belonged to clans with the greatest number of branches, who tended to vote en bloc. The clans with the great-est number of branches are also the ones whose family groups are the largest.

The size of the Great Council did not vary greatly from year to year; the electors confirmed much the same number of members every December (see Table 1).

The changes in the membership that occurred from year to year are to be found less in the number of families than in the number of their repre-sentatives. Ninety-eight cognomina are recorded in the 1357, 1358, and 1359 lists. The following year, 1360, only one new cognomen was added. In

TABLE I.   Number of Great Council Members, 1357–1363[99]

Year	Number of Members
1357	314
1358	322
1359	320
1360	305
1361	355
1362	320
1363	328

1361, however, there is a marked increase in new families among the council members. Eight families, the Baduario, Damini, Duodo, Freganesco, Lauredano, Mauroceno, Nani, Sanudo, six of whom[100] were attested members of the Venetian patriciate in the fourteenth century, joined the council seemingly for the first time, but that cannot be so. The Baduario, Duodo, Mauroceno, Nani, and Sanuto all appear in the *Concessio*, and the Freganesco are explictly described as feudatory in the incomplete list of 1349. Five other Venetian cognomina (Grimani, Manolesso, Miani, Mocenigo, Trivisano) appear for the first time in the 1362 list and two (Delfino and Signolo) in that of 1363. On the whole, then, family representation in the council did not change significantly, if at all, during the period for which we have lists, which one might expect in light of the resolve to toughen the process of election to the council.

While clan representation remained relatively stable during these six years, the individual members changed significantly from year to year (see Table 2).

The reasons for the additions and deletions of individual members of the Great Council are nowhere stated, but we can easily see in the family groups younger sons joining their fathers and elder brothers once they had reached the age of majority, which, as for Venice, was twenty-five. Often names that had been deleted in one year reappear in others, suggesting that a pattern of rotation was at work, which allowed for different family members to take turns serving on the council. The absence of the colony's most important feudatories in one year and then their presence in another also suggests that feudatories were occasionally absent from the island for extended periods of time, or perhaps incapacitated in some manner that prevented them from participating. For instance, few feudatories were as influ-

TABLE 2.   Additions to and Deletions from the Great Council

Year	Individuals Dropped	Individuals Added
1358	10	21
1359	10	10
1360	22	6
1361	12	62
1362	47	49

ential and prominent as Pietro Quirini, son of the late Romeo. His name appears in each of the lists from December 1356 to December 1359. After that, his name is missing until the *proba* in December of 1361, which determined the council's members for 1362. His name is absent also from the membership lists of the Senate during those same years. Was he away on business? More likely, Pietro suffered from an illness, since he was to die by the summer of 1363.

Attending sessions of the Great Council meant that the feudatories had to reside in Candia several times a year. We need not rely on the membership lists to calculate the number of times that the council met, since the deliberations of the council date back to 1345, when the register begins. Thus, we can calculate the minimum number of times the council met over an eighteen-year period (see Table 3).

The number of times the council met over the period ranged from 3 to 24 times a year. It cannot be a coincidence that the years during which the council seldom met were the initial years of the plague's impact, in 1347 and 1348. It met least often in 1351, when the deliberations of the Council of Feudatories report that a great sickness was depleting the population of skilled workers.[101] By the beginning of the following year, however, the council began to meet once a month. But the devastating effects of a later plague did not prevent the council from meeting twenty-four times in 1362. By that time, the pressing matter of defense, which the feudatories could not afford to ignore, was by then before the council.

In combination with the duke and his councillors, the Great Council attended to matters touching upon the military organization of the district of Candia and the eastern districts of the island, as well as choosing the personnel for the colony's obligations towards Venice. The commanders (*supracomites*) of the colony's galleys slated to join the Venetian fleet in their wars against the emirates of Asia Minor emerged from this group. Here

TABLE 3. Number of Sittings of the Great Council

Year	Number of Sittings	Year	Number of Sittings
1345	10	1354	16
1346	10	1355	20
1347	8	1356	9
1348	9	1357	9
1349	5	1358	14
1350	15	1359	13
1351	3	1360	12
1352	12	1361	11
1353	7	1362	24

captains of the colony's districts, captains appointed to keep the peace during the unruly period of Carnival, and others involved in the maintenance of public order were selected. The need for increased vigilance in the defense of the island led to a rise in the number of sittings of the Great Council after 1357. Many of the Great Council's discussions were now taken up by the threat of the Turks, who had begun to raid the shores of neighboring islands and of Crete itself. Finding an adequate supply of horses became a priority for the island's defense during this period. Numerous entries in the register of deliberations pertain to the licencing of individuals to import horses from Asia Minor.[102] During the same period, the council was also busy appointing its own members to positions relating to the maintenance of public order in the eastern end of the island, where the raids were most common.[103]

It did not wield power in the sense that it affected or altered the mandates handed down to the duke and the councils from the Venetian Senate. The council was, however, the venue in which the feudatories at times registered their resistance to policies that Venice sought to impose on them. For instance, after it had received instructions from the Venetian doge, the council would form a committee to study the dogal letter and consider the feasibility of a positive response. After the committee met, it reported first to the Council of Feudatories, whose response would be subsequently endorsed by the Great Council. Increased fiscal demands were almost always what was in contention. If the committee, following the report of the Council of Feudatories, responded negatively to the request for more funds from the colony, a common recourse was for the Great Council to elect an embassy to go to Venice to lodge an appeal with the

doge and the College. In response to requests from Venice for aid in the
fight against the Genoese, the rebellious Slavs in Dalmatia, or the Turks, the
Council balked on more than one occasion.[104] When the Senate levied a
new tax, or lowered the price at which it bought grain from the feudatories,
the Great Council, under the guidance of the Council of Feudatories, attempted to negotiate with the Venetian government for exactions or for a
price less crippling to themselves.[105] Few of the feudatories' appeals were
resolved to their advantage.

The Council of Feudatories

In contrast to the Great Council, which consisted of the adult males of
feudatory families, the Council of Feudatories consisted of no more than
three representatives per family, no matter how many sons the head of the
family had. Unfortunately, there are no membership lists, but the votes on
motions placed before the council give us some idea of its size. Since attendance at the Council of Feudatories was not mandatory as it was at the
Great Council, the number of votes varied considerably from sitting to
sitting. The attendance numbers range from as few as thirty to as many as
176. On an average, sixty-two members attended any one session of the
Council of Feudatories.

A brief response by the Comune to petitions from an embassy of
Candiote feudatories is the closest we have to a description of any council's
composition and function. It suggests incidentally that the Council of Feudatories may have been formed at this date. In 1325, the feudatories put before the doge and his College a series of questions and issues that needed
resolution, among which figured a complaint that the duke of Candia
would not permit them to advance motions of their own on their own
behalf. They asked the doge to confirm them in this right, just as their
forebears had enjoyed it, for they now would not be able to benefit from
their rights if they could not meet in council and make motions.[106] The
Comune's response was very cautious.

So moved: the feudatories may not meet together on their own initiative or bring
about any gathering or congregation. Whenever they wish to meet about their
business, they are to meet in the ducal palace only after receiving the permission of
the duke and his councillors. The duke and his councillors, after receiving such a
request, are bound to convene by bell and crier a council within three days of the
request. Thus, the Council of Feudatories is constituted, when any feudatory who

· has heard the bell or the crier comes to attend. If it please the duke and councillors to be present at the council, they may do so. Furthermore, they have the liberty of accepting or not accepting the provisions and decisions taken by the council, but they may not invalidate those provisions which are the result of an embassy to Venice, nor may they forbid the feudatories from sending a delegation to Venice. If any secretary [*camerarius*] of the feudatories convenes a meeting contrary to this mandate, they will be fined fifty hyperpera; those who attended the meeting will be fined twenty-five hyperpera.[107]

The degree of mistrust that the Venetian Comune exhibited towards the men whom it was pleased to call when it suited it "flesh of our flesh and bone of our bone" is striking.

Because meetings of the council required the initiative of the feudatories to bring them about, the Council of Feudatories met less often than the Great Council (see Table 4).

Unlike the sittings of the Great Council, which met regularly until the later years when there was a marked increase in the number of sittings, a more haphazard pattern emerges from the above table of sittings. During the plague years, the Council of Feudatories met less often than in other years, but the increase in Great Council sittings, as a result of the increased need for defense, does not find a parallel increase in this council.

The purview of the Council of Feudatories seems to have been two-fold. First, it was timed to coincide with the meetings of the Great Council, when the greatest majority of feudatories would be in the city. It functioned almost like a subcommittee of the Great Council, charged with developing plans for the implementation of projects agreed on by the larger body. This smaller council attended to the issues of greatest concern and interest of the feudatories as a group, to details such as the hiring of a smith to care for their horses, the distributing of salaried positions among themselves, arranging the purchase of horses overseas and the raising of funds for military obligations away from the island. When a feudatory was murdered, the task of pressing for the capture of the malefactor fell to this body.

One concern arises again and again over the eighteen years of the register of deliberations: the constant search for physicians. The Council of Feudatories, supported by the Great Council, frequently sent ambassadors to Venice with instructions to find either a *physicus medicus* or a *physicus cirurgicus*. Normally two physicians received salaries for renewable terms of one year from the council. The search for competent medical care looms large in the deliberations, as well we might expect in a colony beset with frequent epidemics.[108] Finding a good physician who was willing to come

TABLE 4.   Number of Sittings of the Council of Feudatories

Year	Number of Sittings	Year	Number of Sittings
1345	19	1354	6
1346	9	1355	7
1347	11	1356	9
1348	9	1357	2
1349	10	1358	6
1350	12	1359	10
1351	8	1360	14
1352	9	1361	9
1353	4	1362	10

to Crete, a colonial backwater if there ever was one in the late medieval period, many times proved difficult. Low wages and life in what were undoubtedly perceived as less than attractive holiday conditions discouraged many from taking up the offers made. Those physicians who came to Crete applied often for permission to return to Italy on leave.[109]

The Consilio Rogatorum, or the Senate

If power, or at the very least influence, could be said to reside in any one of the three councils on which the feudatories sat, it could only be said of the Council of the *Rogati*, otherwise known as the Candiote Senate. We are fortunate that membership lists survive for this council as well as for the Great Council. A comparison of the two lists reveals that, although it is impossible to reconstruct a complete list in its entirety for any of the years that they were recorded, there were members of the Senate who never appear among the members of the Great Council during the same years (see Table 5).

Apart from the very few names that have become victims of damaged folios on which they were recorded, it is evident that families shifted their members from council to council as the need struck them. For instance, two men of the Magno family, Madio and Sclavo, who may have been brothers, continually show up in the list of the *rogati*, while their sons held seats on the Great Council. Some of the *rogati* families are not represented at all on the Great Council (see Table 6).

How did these men with no obvious family connections to the feuda-

TABLE 5. Comparison of Membership Between the Senate and the Great Council

Year	Rogati in Great Council of same year	Rogati not in Great Council of same year
1357	51	23
1358	53	34
1359	64	27
1360	80	30
1361	72	22
1362	72	22

tory group fit into the scheme of the colony? A likely explanation is that they were Venetians from the metropolis with sufficient commercial interests in Crete to merit a voice in its governance. Some of these men served on the Senate for a few years before they or relatives show up on the Great Council, indicting that they or members of their family had immigrated to the colony. The Dolfin family, who appear again in the fourth chapter, provides a good example of such a case. Even though the court records show that senior members of the Dolfin family were visiting Candia during the late 1350s, and even though they appear among the *rogati*, the first time that a Dolfin appears in the Great Council is 1363, an appearance that may have some crucial significance for our story. The example of that family suggests that the Senate may have served as an entree into the Candiote feudatory group for Venetians whose interests in the colony developed to the point that they immigrated there.

The members of the Senate worked in three groups under the direction of one of the colony's three chief administrators.[110] The administrator under whom the feudatories worked rotated regularly from year to year. Although a pattern of rotation is difficult to discern, the first names in each of the lists' columns under the heading of the duke and his councillors were almost always the most senior feudatories with the greatest responsibility and experience. Their prestige is made evident by their consistent appearance on committees established to look into the affairs of the colony over the twenty-five-year period covered by the register of deliberations. These prominent feudatories took their turn working with each of the regime's administrators. The advantage of this rotation was continuity across the passing generations of dukes and councillors, who benefitted from the experience of the feudatories who spent many years on the councils.

TABLE 6.   Rogati and Their Families Who Are Not Members of the
Great Council[111]

Year	Rogati who are not members of the Great Council	Rogati whose families are not represented on the Great Council
1357	23	11
1358	34	17
1359	27	17
1360	30	15
1361	22	6
1362	22	5

Although Candia was the only town on the island to have a Senate, the most obvious limit on authority of the Candiote Council of the *Rogati* came from the Venetian Senate.[112] In Crete, matters raised in the Candiote Senate pertained largely to the original purpose of the feudatories, namely defense. The duke convened meetings of the council in order to facilitate the staffing of garrisons in the east and to organize the contributions of the feudatories to Venetian military endeavors against the Turks. Economic matters, too, fell within its jurisdiction. Negotiations with the Turkic maritime states, a signal privilege granted to the colony by the Venetian State, were orchestrated there, when trade with the emirates of Palatia and Theologo became a principal concern of this council, beginning in 1347.[113] The Candiote Senate oversaw the levying of taxes and the collection of import duties on the merchandise brought to the colony by the galleys using Crete as an entrepôt. When a dispute over land arose among the heirs of a feudatory, the *rogati* often took a hand in its settlement, even though the court of the duke had the final word. Other deliberations of the *rogati* reveal their interest in city sanitation, the practice of trades, and the sale of food.[114]

Matters concerning the Greek population also came up in the Candiote Senate. The council endorsed several plans to prevent slaves from escaping their owners and the island altogether. The priests of the Greek church had more to do with the regime and the Senate than they had to do with the Latin church hierarchy. It was the Senate which discussed ways of preventing Greeks from seeking ordination away from the island, where they would be ordained according to the rites of the Greek church and not those of the Latin.

The seriousness of the matters that came up in the Council of the *Rogati* says less about the power or influence of the men so called than

TABLE 7.   Sittings of the Senate, 1345–1358

Year	Number of Sittings	Year	Number of Sittings
1345	10	1352	11
1346	7	1353	5
1347	18	1354	3
1348	4	1355	4
1349	4	1356	7
1350	20	1357	10
1351	5	1358	18

about the presence of the duke and his councillors in their midst. For the Senate was, if anything, the closest thing that colony had to an executive committee, whose charge was oversight and execution of the mandates coming from Venice. Their function was practical to an extent not reached by the other two councils. Consequently, they met as the situation required, as the need arose, as Table 7 shows.

Meeting irregularly as they did, the *rogati* were there for the duke to call upon when he needed something to be done. Like the other councils, the Senate seldom met during the years the colony suffered epidemics and, again like the other councils, it met most often during the years when the Turkish raiders menaced the coastline.

But no matter how seldom or how often any of the three councils met, attendance was a problem, whether mandatory or not. The reluctance of some feudatories to attend council, to fulfill their military obligations, and to serve on committees is plain in the register of the councils' deliberations. In 1352 the Great Council elected five men to command a fleet of galleys whose purpose was to protect Crete's coast, a matter of obvious concern to all. All five men refused.[115] Therefore it was necessary at times for the regime to insist that feudatories take on the assignments given to them. On days that the councils were to meet, the city heralds publicly summoned all the members to the meeting, requiring them to sign in and forbidding them, under penalty of a fine, to leave the city before the business of the councils was concluded.[116]

Not all feudatories, however, were remiss in their duties. Indeed, the motion making it more difficult for the feudatories to refuse assignments was put forward by the three most prominent feudatories in the Senate during the 1350s and early 1360s, Alessio Corner of the Greater House,

Pietro Quirini *quondam Romei*, and Marco Gradenigo *maior*. Even if some feudatories considered assisting the duke in the administration and defense of the island onerous, these senior feudatories plainly viewed it as being in their interests to participate in the councils as much as possible. In their view, a little influence was better than none, and by banding together and appealing when necessary to the doge in Venice, they occasionally succeeded in reversing a few decisions detrimental to themselves.[117]

The feudatories of Candia are far more diverse in social composition than has been understood thus far. This point will become even more clear later on. For the moment, it is enough to recapitulate several points. The feudatory group evolved over the course of the first century of the island's occupation, and the evolution of its composition coincided in time with the formation of the Venetian patriciate. Just as the ruling group in Venice did not prevent entry to outsiders as securely as the legislation would suggest, so, too, the feudatory group in Candia changed in membership over the course of the colony's first century and continued to change substantially in the next. By the fourteenth century, membership of the Great Council had become largely hereditary, although new members continued to join it. Indeed the reproduction of the feudatory group, which is the subject of the next chapter, is the next stage of the investigation into ethnicity in Venetian Crete.

2

The Candiotes and Their City

MOST OF THIS CHAPTER concerns the feudatory group, partly because the various segments of Candia's population are not equally represented in the sources. Like aristocracies everywhere, they are easier to study than people of little or no property, whose lineage concerns had little impact on Candiote society. But the feudatories of Candia merit being placed at center stage for another reason. Without them, the colony of Crete would not have lasted as long as it did, not, I stress, that its longevity foreshadowed an optimistic future for the subsequent history of European colonies. My point is instead that the reasons for the colony's survival are what made it a harbinger of modern colonization.

Having said that, I do not view the humble, free residents of Candia as irrelevant to its special status as a state-sponsored colony in the late medieval period. They constitute the essential complement to what I will have to say about the feudatories and the lowest levels of the population. In many respects, the division of what follows falls into two sections, the first treating the feudatories and the second the artisans and professionals of Candiote society. This division reflects the differences in the kinds of sources and information pertaining to the two levels of the population, but it also reflects an actual boundary that ran between the two levels. In spite of Candia's small size, and despite the fact that relations between people of different social ranks had not yet reached the levels of compartmentalization they would in later centuries, the feudatories and the humble people of Candia in many ways inhabited different worlds.

"Flesh of Our Flesh, Bone of Our Bone": The Feudatory Families of Candia

In the previous chapter, the definition of "feudatory" was approached from a corporate perspective. This chapter covers the feudatories as families, heads of households, and prominent and influential members of the councils, before turning to the city's commoners. The loyalty of the Latin landholders, whose main responsibility was to defend Venice's possession of the island, was critical to the colony's survival. Maintaining the loyalty of second- and third-generation descendants of Venetians living in Candia and the other Cretan towns required extraordinary measures to keep their ancestry, and hence their allegiance, in the forefront of their lives.

Just as the Venetian patriciate that emerged at the end of the thirteenth century is now understood to have consisted of divisions, if not factions, so, too, the feudatory group in Candia ought to be viewed.[1] Not only was the group being defined over the same course of time as that of the Venetian patriciate's emergence, the Great Council, too, shows signs of divisions. It remains to be determined how closely connected the evolution of the Venetian aristocracy was to the process taking place in Crete. A close look at the feudatory families may suggest points of connection.

It used to be thought that the Latin conquerors of mainland Greece, the Aegean Islands, the crusader states, and the feudatories of Crete were decidedly urban.[2] Although the greatest portion of their revenues came from the countryside, it is true that their primary residences were in the main cities of Crete: Candia, Chanea, Rethimno, and Sitia. The clause in the *Concessio* of 1211 that obliged colonists to maintain a residence in Candia shows that the choice was not entirely their own, but since many of them were from cosmopolitan Venice they were likely in the early years of the colony to have preferred the town to the country.[3] Some even preferred Candia to other Cretan towns. The regime's decree that all those with *cavallerie* in the district of Chanea must take up residence there and not in Candia speaks to the attraction of the colony's busiest city.[4] Nevertheless, the demands of their estates kept the feudatories outside the city for a portion of the year. The regime had repeatedly to insist in public proclamations that feudatories remain in the city until the work of the councils was completed, although whether they were escaping the chores of administration or eager to return to the work that awaited them in the countryside is impossible to say.[5]

For reasons having to do as much with city congestion as with chang-
ing personal preferences, over the thirteenth century and the next some
members of Candiote feudatory families established their principal, as opposed to official, place of residence beyond the city walls. Michaletto Maufredo's will of 1376 refers to ser Andrea Cornario, son of the late ser Micaliço
and resident of the burg. Even nearly one hundred years earlier in 1285,
however, at a time when a outbreak of resistance was disrupting the countryside, Baldovino Lombardo sought permission from the regime to build a
tower on his *milicia*, so that he might live there more securely.[6] His place of
residence does not appear after his name, as it often does after feudatories'
names, and although we must assume that his official residence was in
Candia, he lived at least part of the year on his country estate. Into the
fourteenth century, more Latin families took up residence outside Candia's
walls. Pietro Dono, the son of a nobleman, identified himself in a notarial
document of 1347 as a resident of the village of Scalari.[7] In 1361, Homo-
bono Gritti, resident of the village of Dhamavolus, oversaw the marriage of
his son, Triadano, to the daughter of Giorgio da Milan, resident of Candia
and member of the Great Council. Giorgio's daughter brought a dowry of
eight hundred hyperpera, typical of the value of feudatory dowries.[8] Other
notarial sources and a chronicle also attest to the presence of feudatories and
their kin in the countryside, presumably residing on their families' estates.[9]
Still, despite an increase in the number of feudatories or family members living on their estates as the fourteenth century progressed, the regime continued to insist on the feudatories' keeping their official residence in Candia.
This requirement, as we have seen, had the effect of keeping them under the
eye of the regime and available for the tasks of administering the colony.

Although no example of a late medieval residence has survived, feudatory dwellings were very likely a shadow of their Venetian counterparts in
the fourteenth century: two or more storied buildings in L- or C-shaped
arrangements, surrounding a courtyard, with a central hall (*portego*).[10] As
in Venice, the family resided on the *piano nobile* (the floor above the ground
floor) and often rented out the upper floor or floors to relatives or even
neighbors.[11] Shops took up the ground floor, from which the family might
derive rent. In general, people referred to their dwelling-place as "domus,"
the same word they used to refer to their clan, but the word's flexibility
could extend to the plural, indicating a suite of rooms (or an apartment)
in a larger structure. The archaeological remains of sixteenth- and seventeenth-century feudatory dwellings have revealed that the façade of the

principal residence of a feudatory family displayed symbols of status similar
to the ones the patrician *palazzi* in the metropolis displayed. Undoubtedly
the feudatories of earlier centuries had similar displays of their rank.

According to the terms of the first charters of concession from the
thirteenth century, discussed in the first chapter, the regime insisted that
each feudatory maintain a residence in Candia. Initially, one residence per
feudatory must have sufficed, but this provision became more complicated
with every passing generation, as families grew and developed into numerous branches. If the feudatory families of Candia followed Venetian
custom in their living arrangements as they probably did in architectural
design, the typical noble household in Venice may serve as a guide to the
arrangement in which the Candiote feudatories lived. Partible inheritance
being the law in Venice as it was in Crete, brothers jointly inherited their
father's property, including his place or places of residence. Even if they
chose to divide the entire estate among themselves and legally separate
themselves from one another, each could still live in a share of the family's
residence. Family compounds consisting of large residential structures that
threatened to fragment into smaller and smaller units with every passing
generation were common among Venice's patriciate.[12] Juergen Schulz believes that, rather than functioning as repositories of large extended families spanning generations and extending laterally to include cousins, the
family compounds of Venice quickly passed out of families within a few
generations.[13]

Candia's feudatory dwellings may well have been as large and as frag-
mented as the patrician family compounds of Venice. In 1340 the Venetian
Senate declared that the retainers (*socii*) and servants of the Chanean feudatories were no longer required to reside in the houses of their masters,
which suggests that, if residences in smaller towns were ample enough to
house kin and non-kin, Candia's domiciles were likely to be as large, if not
larger.[14] The feudatory Pietro Taliapetra, as another example, left to his wife
in his will the *domus* (whether a free-standing structure or a suite of rooms
in a building we do not know) where he was then residing, but earlier in the
same will he instructs his executors to rent out another *domus* (plural)
where he was also then living and to give the rent to the Franciscans. A suite
of rooms in a structure of which he possessed a share or its entirety is
probably what is intended.[15] Other documents show that brothers continued to live within the same building complex after their marriages and
after the deaths of their fathers, while smaller households composed primarily of the conjugal couple and offspring were also common. The Corner

of the Greater House may not be a typical feudatory family, since they were among the colony's most prestigious and wealthiest, but one notarial transaction has survived that suggests that the Greater House on which the family's name was based remained in the family at least through the third generation. In 1386, three first cousins, Andrea Corner, son of the late lord Giovanni, Giovanni Corner, son of the late lord Alessio, and Alessio Corner, son of the late lord Pietro, hired two Latin masons living in the burg to construct a loggia, presumably on top of their residence, but the document does not give the location where it was to be built.[16]

Another document from 1361 sheds a little more light on the arrangements in which various generations lived in their paternal dwellings. Giovanni Bono, son of the late Pietro, with the permission of the judges *di proprio*, gave the equivalent worth of half a sergeantry from his three sergeantries to Niccolò Bono, son of the late Antonio, probably his cousin. In return, Niccolò would receive his *domus*, consisting of a hall and two rooms above it, of Giovanni's large city residence (*domum meam magnam*). This does not mean that Giovanni was moving out of the premises. Instead, he carved out of his section of the building a new apartment for Niccolò. In doing so, he promises not to block the sunlight entering those rooms either from the balcony located above the well (presumably in the courtyard) or from the other balcony above the first, which presumably opened into the two rooms. Giovanni also promised not to put up any pipes on the western wall that would cross the second floor above the hall's large door.[17] For his part, Niccolò had to promise to wall up the door of the portico.[18] This does not sound like spacious or communal living and suggests that some feudatory houses became rather crowded.

If it is difficult to determine the arrangements in which feudatory families lived, it is fortunately easier to learn how those families were formed. The reproduction of the feudatory group was always a precarious business. In such a small society as Candia's, the search for marriage partners must have been constricted. And indeed there were in general only three directions in which the feudatory families had to look to find spouses for their children.

The first direction was towards each other. As Table 8 shows, of the 790 testators, 213 can reliably be identified as belonging to feudatory families.[19]

Over half (57) of the male feudatory testators reveal in the bequest portion of their wills that they are related to other Candiote feudatory families. The remaining 38 testators name only their offspring and the given names of their wives, which means that they too might have had kinship

TABLE 8.   Intermarriage Among the Venetian Cretan Feudatory Families
as Seen in the Wills

	With kin in Candia	Without evident kin in Candia	Total
Male testators	57	38	95
Female testators	101	17	118
Total no. of feuda- tory testators	158	55	213

ties to other feudatory families. The 118 wills of the female relatives of
feudatories exhibit even more clearly kinship with other Candiote feudatories. Of the 118 female feudatory testators, 101 (nearly 87 percent) mention
relatives belonging to other feudatory families in Crete. Putting the male
and female groups together, 74 percent of all feudatory wills show kinship
with other feudatory families in the colony. In the 259 marriage contracts,
56 involve Candiote feudatory families, 19 of which were between Venetian
Candiote families, showing a degree of intermarriage within their own
group similar to that in the wills.[20]

Candiote feudatories were a close-knit group. They exhibit the familiarity and the tension arising from any small group forced by circumstances
to coexist in an environment that was once alien to their forebears yet is
now very familiar to them. In a city as small as Candia, no social rank could
be segregated from another to any great degree, but the feudatories' endog-
amous inclinations worked to separate them from the rest of the population. Many notarial transactions testify to the enterprises undertaken jointly
by families related by marriage, but one aspect of the wills brings into relief
the close-knit character of the Candiote feudatory group. Establishing how
persistent after marriage were the bonds between a daughter and the family
into which she was born is one standard by which to measure the tight
kinship ties binding the group together. Aside from the generally acknowledged advantages a marriage alliance between two families could offer, it is
almost a commonplace in the work of late medieval and Renaissance scholars to depict a woman's position both in the family of her birth and in that
of her husband's as transitional, temporary and therefore marginal, minimizing the opportunities for further contact between families.[21] The absence of married daughters in wills, *ricordanze*, and other remnants of individual family histories has been interpreted to mean that the tie between a

woman and her parents and siblings became attenuated when she was enlisted in the lineage concerns of her husband's family. Unless misfortune brought her back to her father's household in the event of her husband's death, a woman left one family to join another. In this view, by equating changes in the legal relationships within families with changes in affective relationships, the presumption often leads to the perception that women, once married, ceased to exist for their families of birth. From a patrimonial point of view, this was no doubt the case in most families. Once she received her dowry, which represented her share of her father's movable goods, a woman could not legally expect to receive more at her father's or brothers' deaths, although she might receive whatever affection prompted testators to bequeath to her.

To conclude, however, that the end of patrimonial claims spells the cessation of relationships between a daughter and the family into which she was born seems an unduly harsh view of human relations in the past. We have only to ask ourselves whether our own sense of kinship is delimited by those members of our families whose goods we expect to have a share in after their deaths. In the same manner, the absence of women in family records of the past cannot be taken to mean the loss of contact with them or the diminution of their emotional importance to the families into which they were born, not least because of the problem of arguing on the basis of negative evidence. Rather than seeing women as marginal, transient members of families, viewing women as bridges between and among a group of families provides a better basis for understanding both the affective and the economic consequences of kinship.[22] The Candiote wills suggest that families of birth continued to play an active role in the lives of their married daughters and sons-in-law, a suggestion that may well apply to women elsewhere (see Table 9).

One explanation for the wives who made their parents or siblings the executors of their wills, as many of the fifty-five did, was that they were young wives with very young children or none. But about half the female feudatory testators (sixty) appointed siblings and grown married daughters and sons-in-law together as their executors, even though there was no legal requirement for them to do so. This suggests that contact with their birth families persisted for years after the women's marriage. Even when husbands or children alone took on the role of executor, siblings, nieces, and nephews often show up as legatees in the bequest portion of the wills. Fewer feudatory widows mention their birth family in their wills, because of the availability of grown children to take charge of their estate.

TABLE 9.   Female Feudatory Testators and Members of Birth Family

Marital status	Total	Birth family members mentioned in will
Wives	55	48
Widows	57	30
Unmarried	6	6
Total	118	84 (71%)

The same point can be made from the perspective of the wills made by feudatory men. Of 94 feudatory male testators, 19 (20 percent) were sufficiently close to their wives' families of birth or to their married daughters and sons-in-law that they appointed them executors of their wills, even when they had close male relatives of their own to turn to.[23] In some cases, when they were not executors, they were nevertheless witnesses to the making of the will, placing them at the very least in a scene of familial intimacy.[24] Other female kin who married out of the family appear as executors or legatees.[25]

Not only did the feudatories prefer marriage partners from within their own group, but also the most prominent families of Candia, that is, the old Venetian noble families among them, tended to restrict their search for spouses to other noble families. The Corner, Quirini, Muazzo, and Gradenigo families, the very ones with the largest number of branches and the most influence in the colony, very often married among themselves, as well as to a few other noble families residing in Candia. Moreover, certain testators from these particular families demonstrate a decided preference for branches of their own clan. Marco Corner specified in his will that his share of the island of Scarpathos and of the family's great house go to a future son-in-law, on the condition that the prospective groom be a member of ca' Corner.[26] Other wills contain suggestions of other marriages between branches of the Corner family.[27] The Corners were not alone in this intraclan strategy, but they were certainly the most prominent.[28]

Alessio Corner was one of the most prestigious and influential of the feudatories of the fourteenth century. The branch of the Corner clan to which he belonged used the epithet "of the Greater House" (*de domo maiori*). His family had been living in Crete since at least the end of the thirteenth century. The Corners were not among the original settlers mentioned in the *Concessio*, but we know that Alessio's father, Andrea, the first member of this family of whom we have mention, lived in the latter half of that century. Andrea had at least two other sons, Giovanni and Marco, both of whom had died well before 1360.[29] All three sons identified themselves as belonging to the Greater House, but only the sons of Giovanni, probably Andrea's eldest son, carried on the tradition of using the epithet. The sons of Alessio identified themselves simply as his sons. The family was linked in kinship with other Candiote feudatory families, particularly the noble ones. Alessio married Giacomina Miegan, who gave him five sons and at least one daughter. The eldest of his sons was Andrea, named after Alessio's father. Andrea, son of Alessio, made his will in 1360; he apparently died three years later in the violence of the St. Tito Revolt of 1363.[30] His wife, Mariçoli, by whom he had four children, was from the noble Caravello family of Candia and died in the early 1350s.[31] Another of Alessio's sons, Giovanni, married first in 1348 Cecilia Contareno, who died, and then in 1369 Marula, daughter of Andrea Barbarigo.[32] A third, emancipated son, Pietro, married Benicia, daughter of Niccolò Fradello.[33] With the exception of the last, the Caravello, Contareno, and Barbarigo (Barbadico) families were all among the original noble settlers of 1211. Nothing about the spouses of the two remaining sons, Niccolò and Francesco, and of Lucia, his daughter, has thus far come to light. Alessio himself appears for the last time in the council deliberations at the end of 1362. He died at some point in time between then and August, 1363, when his son Andrea is identified as "son of the late lord Alessio."[34]

The family connections continue. Alessio Corner was the brother-in-law of another important feudatory in the same period. Marco Dandolo, from another family of the original concessionaires, appears regularly along with Alessio in the Senate membership lists and on the committees charged with the most sensitive tasks, and was married to Elena, the sister of Alessio Corner *de domo maiori*, by whom he had five children.[35] Like Alessio Corner, Marco married his children to the children of other prominent Candiote feudatories. Marco's son, Giovanni, married Margarita Giordano, who died in 1362.[36] His second wife was named Marchesina (the Venetian form of Margarita), whom he appointed executor of his will in 1376, along with two of his brothers.[37] Niccolò, another son of Marco, was married twice, the first time to Nicolota, daughter of Pietro Taliapetra Boalli, the second time to a daughter of one of the island's most prestigious Greek noble families, to whom we will return further on.[38] Marco's daughters were equally well, if ultimately tragically, placed in marriage. One daughter was married to Tito Venier and the other to Leonardo Gradenigo Baiardo, two of the most notorious rebels of the St. Tito revolt.[39] Once again, Giordano (Iordano), Taliapetra, Venier (Venerio), and Gradenigo (Gradonico) are among the names in the *Concessio*. Marco Dandolo himself died between the fall of 1360 and the early summer of 1362.

Feudatories had other places to look for spouses for their progeny. Venice and the other Cretan towns also supplied a pool of potential husbands and wives.[40] Crete may have been a distant territory with little appeal to the urbane Venetian patriciate, but that did not prevent some Candiote feudatory fathers from successfully luring young Venetian patricians to marry their children. Moreover, it was in the interests of the Venetian Senate to promote marriages between Venetians of the metropolis and those in the colonies, for such marriages added fuel to the government's reminders to the feudatories that they were still Venetians, "flesh of our flesh, bone of our bone."[41] Ambitious Venetian men, wishing to try their luck and make their fortune, immigrated to Candia and some found wives there. Venetian Candiotes, for their part, had many reasons, especially commercial ones, to keep alive ties with their kin in the metropolis.

A network of trade routes bound Candia's feudatories to other ports, including that of Venice. It was not unusual to find them in Rhodes, Alexandria, and the emirates of Asia Minor, in addition to the city of Venice.[42] A few representative examples will suffice. In one contract, Manuele Beto, a feudatory of Candia, sent Marco Beto in 1357 off to trade with 107 hyperpera in the Asia Minor emirate of Palatia.[43] As an another example, in 1366 Giacomello and Marco da Molin, Candiote noblemen and kinsmen, exported to Venice 14,277 pounds of soap and in the same month another feudatory, Naticlero da Bocoli, exported a large amount of wine.[44] The feudatories also had ties with their counterparts in the Morea and the Aegean. Two decades later, in the 1380s, Marco Dandolo, son of the late lord Thomas, hired Anastassios Laudopulo of Nigroponte, a captain of a galley, to transport one thousand pounds of incense, two hundred pounds of linen, and a barrel of wine to Nigroponte, carrying with him however many passengers and equipment Marco wished to send along.[45] Much earlier, in 1331, Pietro Vidro of Candia hired Marcos Cumaniti, a resident of Candia's suburb and the operator of a vessel, to take a letter for the Latin duke of the Archipelago Niccolò Sanudo to the islands of Naxos and Paros, and then to carry his response to the letter to Vidro's agent in Thebes. Once there, Marcos should expect to take possession of eight slaves, whom he would receive within ten days after presenting his letters in Thebes and bring back to Candia.[46] The profits feudatories' commercial ventures such as these examples might be expected to reap were often put back into the

source of the original investment: the land and its cultivation.[47] The feudatories were constrained, however, to seek permission to leave the island
from the colonial regime, whose concern was to ensure that the applicants
left their military obligations accounted for.

The commercial ties and trickle of immigration to the colony over the
course of the century meant that the recent immigrants maintained links
with their kin back in the metropolis. Even with the passage of time and
generations, the kinship links to Venice did not diminish in some of the
feudatory families. One Leonardo Gradenigo, who may have been a recent
immigrant in 1304, applied to the regime for permission to spend four years
with his young children living in Venice. Permission was granted, provided
that he left his lands well garrisoned.[48] When feudatories were unable to
leave their affairs in Crete to travel on business to Venice, it was not unusual
for them to entrust their Venetian relatives with the power to act in their
name.[49] Relatives in Venice appear among the legatees of testators who had
immigrated to Candia.[50]

Although married couples immigrated from Venice, the frequent contact between the Venetian feudatories and the metropolis also resulted in
marriages. Evidence of such alliances appears sporadically throughout the
registers. To take one example, we find a dowry acquittance from 1358, in
which Marco Grioni, formerly of Venice, now a resident of Candia, formally acknowledges payment from his father-in-law, Pietro Longo, a Candiote notary, of his wife's ample dowry of one thousand five hundred hyperpera.[51] A Latin feudatory whom we will meet several times more in this
study, Niccolò Dandolo Bellino, married his daughter to a Venetian nobleman who immigrated to Candia.[52] Nine marriage contracts involve recent
immigrants to the colony and the daughters of Candiote feudatories. But an
interesting aspect of the nine marriage contracts points in the direction of
the third source of marriage partners for the feudatories. Of the nine marriage contracts between Venetians and residents of the colony, eight involve
Venetian males marrying female residents of Candia.[53] Four of these Venetians married Venetian Candiote feudatory women; the other four married
Greek Candiote women from noble (archontic) families. The ninth contract, dated 1347, is unusually between a Greek Cretan nobleman and a
Venetian woman.[54]

How can we explain those immigrants' preference for Greek Candiotes? One answer presents itself after a look at the dowries involved. Table 10 contains in chronological order the values of the dowries of both the
Venetian and Greek women.

Notice that the last example of a marriage between a Venetian man and

TABLE 10.   Dowries in Marriage Contracts Involving Venetians

Year	Value of dowry belonging to Venetian woman	Year	Value of dowry belonging to Greek woman
1346	760 hyperpera	1320	700 hyperpera (dowry received from Venetian woman by Greek man)
1352	1,000 hyperpera	1326	1,000 hyperpera
1357	900 hyperpera	1327	unspecified
1366	600 hyperpera	1345	1,000 hyperpera
		1346	1,000 hyperpera

a Greek woman falls in the very year of the first contract between a Venetian man and a Venetian woman, meaning that all the dowries of the Greek women come from the first half of the century. Since dowries rose in value over the course of the fourteenth century, we might expect those dowries from the earlier part of the century to be of lesser value than those of the second half, even in so small a sample as I have presented.[55] But they are not of lesser value. In fact, they suggest that those Greek noble families who sought to marry their children advantageously to Latins lured Venetian immigrants into marriage alliances, using valuable dowries as bait. Conversely, a sound financial footing on which to begin their new life would appeal to immigrants, particularly if they did not have strong kinship ties with feudatory families already established in the colony. In a group as tightly bound by kinship as Candia's feudatories were, a newcomer from Venice would have found it difficult to penetrate the community and easier to strike a financially rewarding alliance with a wealthy noble indigenous family. One of the men in the contracts, Niccolò Dandolo Bellino, who had come to Candia at some point in time prior to 1327 and had married a woman who was very likely Greek, went on to found one of the more important feudatory families later in the century.[56] Immigrants to Candia, however, were not the only ones who considered the Greek archontic families a source of potential marriage partners. Some long-settled feudatories of Candia also displayed a willingness to link their families with the island's Greek nobility, despite the legal impediments that lay in the way of such alliances.

The origins of Crete's archontes are obscured by the legends promoted by those families to assert their noble status after Byzantine imperial authority had withdrawn from the island and before Venice took possession of it. The archontes' resistance to the Venetians arose far more from a sense of threatened hegemony than from a sense of national violation, as evidenced in part by the Greek nobles' inability ever to unite in coalition against the occupiers. Their anger instead arose out of their being dispossessed of their lands and status. In the process of consolidating their hold of the island, the Venetian authorities had confiscated all the land that had belonged to the Byzantine imperial fisc and to the Greek archontes. The nobility chose either to leave the island or to stay and fight. Needless to say, they had no recourse but to arms, since they had been excluded from sharing any degree of power in ruling the island, similar to that which the Genoese family of the Zaccharia would be obliged to share on the island of Chios in the next century. Over the course of the thirteenth and fourteenth centuries, those Cretan nobles who remained on the island one by one fought to regain as much of their lands as they could force Venice to part with. Some of those who were successful willingly became subjects of the Venetian state; others were permanently impoverished or forced from the island. Therefore, only the archontes most ready to resist succeeded. Their strategy was twofold: to force the Venetian regime into granting them land, and to enhance their status and claims among the mass of Greek peasantry, whose support was necessary to their campaign against the regime. As one historian of Byzantine Crete has noted, they stressed their descent from the legendary twelve "*archontopouploi*," the lesser noblemen from Constantinople, sent to Crete to govern the island in the name of the emperor, in order to enhance their prestige among the Greek population.[57]

Just as its military organization evolved over the thirteenth century, Venice's policy of allowing certain Greek noble families to enjoy some of the privileges held by the Latin feudatories evolved slowly. The regime's stance changed in response to pressure, pragmatism, and the practicalities of defense. To begin with, the Venetian Senate issued decrees aimed at circumscribing contact between Venetian and Greek Candiotes. After half a century of wars conducted by the archontes and their supporters, the colonial regime decreed in 1255 that no more than two Latin men accompanied by eight servants may meet any Greek coming into the city, nor associate with any Greek for any action, nor petition the ducal court.[58] At the same time, however, under growing pressure, the Venetian state opened the circle of feudatories to include a few Greek noblemen who had successfully fought the colonial regime to an impasse. Venice resigned itself to granting them land as long as they fulfilled the same obligations as the Venetian feudatories. As for the archontes, there were economic incentives, beyond the obvious one of acquiring land, for cooperating with the authorities. In 1339 the Great Council of Venice reiterated a fundamental aspect of its commercial policy when it decreed that long-distance trade was the principal activity of Venetian citizens and subjects and thus had to be protected and favored.[59] As long as the archontes were loyal to Venice they enjoyed the fiscal privileges of Venetian subjects. The degree to which these families were involved in Cretan trade is difficult to determine, because a substantial part of the notarial records, in which commercial transactions were recorded, is missing. But the archontes were far more experienced than the first Latin feudatories in the area of agriculture and landowning in general, and so may have continued to concentrate their efforts there. The existing catastico from the Cretan *sestieri* of SS. Apostoli, however, shows that some Greeks received *feuda* in the thirteenth century, which indicates that their revenue was undoubtedly derived in part from the agricultural production typical of *feuda*.[60]

The extension of property-owning rights dates to the thirteenth century, brought about as a result of the wars conducted one-by-one by the powerful archontic families. But at the conclusion of peace negotiations between Venetian authorities and the archon who led the revolt, numerous families besides the leading family benefited from the terms of the resulting treaty. In the first years of the fourteenth century, the duke of Candia granted, with the approval of the Venetian Great Council, a *milicia*, ten villeins, and one thousand *hyperpera* to three men, two of whom were Greek Cretans.[61] In a petition brought forward in 1309 by Nicolaos Plachina, a Greek Cretan member of the Candiote Great Council, whose family had never led but had participated in a revolt, the government noted that his family had possessed the right to hold land since 1289.[62]

In the end, the question for Venice was less whether to grant land at all to portions of the Greek nobility as it was which territory to allot them. The government classified *feuda* in a manner that, like much else, remains obscure, but was, not surprisingly, connected to security. Just as there were apparently *feuda* earmarked for female feudatories (*pro uno varnaçione femineo*), so too were there *feuda* deemed secure enough in their locations to be granted to archontes.[63] An undetermined number of *feuda*, however, probably the great majority, remained out of reach. In 1319, the Venetian Senate prohibited Greek Cretans from acquiring the *feuda* of Latin feudatories, but by the end of the century the situation had changed.[64] The Venetian state had had time to reconsider its policy of restricting the land granted to the archontes. It realized that it was losing money by reserving certain territory exclusively for Latin feudatories, of whom there may have been a shortage at that time, and so in 1395 it decreed that land previously designated only for Latin feudatories could now be sold at auction to both Greek and Latin Cretans.[65]

As evidence of how vigilant the regime could be in protecting its monopoly over the distribution of *feuda*, a remarkable series of documents from the 1340s shows how the feudatories themselves tried to bend the rules and how the regime was there to stop them.[66] To begin with, it goes without saying that Jews could not in any circumstances possess *feuda*. Nor could Greeks own certain *feuda*. Yet that is precisely what two feudatories, one Greek, the other Latin, attempted to bring about. Over the course of these documents, dated May, 1331, we find Lingiaco Mavristiri, a wealthy Candiote Jew, purchasing a *cavalleria* from Niccolò Venier, who is in debt to him. Lingiaco, in turn, arranges to sell the *cavalleria de lo Castri* to the Greek archon, Alexios Calergi, son of Georgios, at a profit. The two parties to the transactions state openly that the *cavalleria* would be registered with the regime in another Latin feudatory's name, although rights to the *cavalleria* would remain with Alexios. Not surprisingly, each of these transactions has a notation entered at a later date that nullifies their contents by order of the regime. Of interest here is not only the arrangement whereby Jews become brokers of feudatories' *feuda*, but also that a man like Alexios Calergi nearly came into possession of an extremely valuable *feudum* not meant for Greek archontes. The only other indication we have that this was a recognized if illegal practice is from a ducal letter of 1416 that expressly forbids consigning *feuda* to Jews.[67] The level of debt incurred by the feudatories in this period was sufficiently high to warrant a delegation to the doge, who issued an extended letter dealing with the details of managing their debt in such a way that it did not interfere with either the security needs of the colony or the military and fiscal needs of Venice.[68]

Along with the right to possess *feuda*, some Greek noble families won for themselves the right to marry their children to the children of Latin feudatories. Those that won this concession pursued their advantage vigorously, but they did so in an ambivalent climate. Venice repeatedly took measures to prevent the feudatories' assimilation into the local population by prohibiting sanctioned unions, or marriages, between Latins and Greeks.[69] Judging from the number of marriages showing up in the notarial sources and elsewhere, the measures were not particularly effective.[70] An official concession to marry Latins appears for the first time in a peace treaty between a Greek nobleman and the Comune of Venice in 1272 and then again in a treaty with another archon, Alexios Calergi, in 1299.[71] It remained the rule, however, that marriages between Greeks and Latins were prohibited. As we shall see, the number of exceptions suggests that permission was regularly granted, although intermarriage on all levels of society continued to be discouraged by the authorities and at times to be prohibited outright.[72]

If the Venetian Senate only reluctantly allowed marriages between Greek archontic families and Latin feudatory families, it nevertheless recognized intermarriage as a way to bring the Greek families into line with Venetian interests and as a way to bolster feudatory numbers. Moreover, some intermarriages were preferable to others. From the Venetian regime's point of view, a Greek woman with a dowry brought wealth (including possibly land) into the Latin feudatory group, whereas a dowered Latin woman removed wealth from it when she married into an archontic family. Exceptions to this rule are in fact the easiest to identify. I have detected seven marriages between Venetian feudatory women and Greek noblemen in the wills, but Greek women married to Latin men appear in greater numbers.[73] Several feudatories had wives with Greek names that generally were not used by Latin families for their children. Paolo Quirini, son of the nobleman Manuele, was married to a woman whose first name was Pothiti, a very unusual name for a Latin woman if she had not had Greek kin or been Greek herself.[74] One of the wealthiest feudatories of the first half of the fourteenth century, Giacomo Cordeferro, also had a wife with a distinctly Greek name, Fenga, who we know was born into the Greek Selopulo family.[75] Other wills reveal even clearer ties between Greek and Latin families. The will of Stefano Bono, a feudatory who was also a notary, begins a trail of kinship ties with Greek nobility through other wills and sources.[76] He appointed as his executor his uncle, Ianni Sachlichi, which shows that his own mother was Greek.[77] This Ianni Sachlichi is to be identified with the member of the Candiote Great Council from 1345 to 1347. In his will, Stefano left small sums to the Dominican and Franciscan churches of Candia, but he also left a small sum to the church of St. Michael the Archangel "where I learned Greek letters." His children's names reflects the amalgam of the two cultures. In addition to such Latin names as Domenico, Pietro, and Francesca, Stefano had a daughter named Pothiti. One of the last bequests in his will is to his cousin, Eleni Sachlichi.

Eleni, it turns out, was herself married to a Latin feudatory, as we learn from the will she made in 1348.[78] Among her bequests is one for commemorative masses for her parents, Ianni and Maria Sachlichi. Her mother, we learn as well, was born into the Greek Ialina family. Eleni leaves a sum as well to an aunt, Pothiti, widow of a Venetian man, Marco Foscari, and to her cousin, Nicolota, daughter of her uncle, Marco Dandolo, although how he was her uncle remains obscure. Stefanos Sachlichi, Eleni's brother, has elsewhere been identified with the Cretan poet Stefanos Sachlichi, who appears among the Great Council members from 1356 to 1361.[79]

The Ialina family, too, into which Eleni's mother was born, had extensive ties to Latin feudatory families. The earliest notable member of this family to appear in the sources is Emanuel Ialina, son of the *papas* Nichiforas, who was named as head of the Greek clergy of Candia (*protopapas*) around the year 1296.[80] Emanuel is described in the Venetian sources as a "fidelis."[81] Since his father was *protopapas*, it is not very likely he was a feudatory himself, no matter how loyal he may have been. In any event, he does not appear to have been closely related to the Ialina on the Great Council or the Candiote Senate. Emanuel's evident wealth is nevertheless a strong indication of his proximity to the important branches of that family. Other members of the Ialina family who appear in the sources can, however, be linked to feudatories. There is Mariçoli, the wife of Ianni Ialina and the daughter of Marco Abramo, a Latin feudatory. Another Latin kinsman of the Ialina, Giovanni da Rogerio, made his will well before the first Great Council membership lists begin, but he was probably a feudatory, since his will shows that he possessed more than one sergeantry.[82] All but one of his pious donations were to churches and foundations adhering to the Latin rite. Giovanni left fifteen hyperpera to the *papas* Petros Ialina, his *propinquus*, so that he would celebrate memorial divine liturgies for the soul of his mother, who was no doubt born a Ialina. Her son was mindful of his mother's attachment to the church of her birth.

These random appearances in the wills of kinship ties between Latin feudatories and Greek noble families undoubtedly represent only a small proportion of the ties that existed. More evidence from the fifteenth century may yet emerge. Two points are worth remembering, however. First, the two groups constituted a small percentage of the population and so it is possible that we may not find many more examples in the fourteenth century. Second, the significance of intermarriages at the feudatory level of Candiote society is disproportionate to their actual number. Because the loyalty of the feudatories was key to the stability of the colony, their unambiguous allegiance to Venetian interests, uncomplicated by potentially conflicting kinship ties, mattered more to the Comune than did the allegiance of social levels further down the scale. Venice did not rely on the middling levels of society for possession of the island as much as it relied on the feudatories. Even if few in number, feudatories of mixed Latin and Greek parentage added new, unwelcome elements to the political situation.

To carry this point further, although relatively few Greek archontic families entered into marriage alliances with Latin feudatory families, the size of those Greek families was not small. The best example of the extent to which the Greek nobility infiltrated the Latin feudatories, and, one might add, vice versa, is the Calergi family. A look at their strategy of intermarriage shows how a Greek clan could be coopted by the Latin feudatories and continue to threaten Venetian interests.

The Calergi Family

At some point during the first two decades of the fifteenth century, Cristoforo Buondelmonti, a Franciscan priest from Florence, paid a visit to Crete. He had spent many years in the Aegean and wrote descriptions of his travels there, which were very popular in his time and thereafter. The first of those travelogues, *Descriptio insulae Cretae*, was written in 1417, after at least two extended visits to the island.[83] In that work a Greek monk takes Buondelmonti, who is interested primarily in the classical and early Christian associations of the island, around to see the sights in the region to the west of Candia. The monk describes to the visitor how an earlier Byzantine emperor abandoned the Catholics of the west to their doctrinal errors and confirmed the empire and its subjects in the true faith. He goes on to explain that the emperor sent a Captain Calergi to Crete to protect it from the treachery of the Latins. The Calergi, he asserts, are still held in such reverence by the islanders that whatever the least of the Calergi commanded, the local population would fulfill with body and soul. The head of the family at that time, Matteo Calergi, happened to be the lord of that very monk, and it is to his estate that the monk leads Buondelmonti. There Matteo Calergi welcomes Buondelmonti graciously, because, in Buondelmonti's view, he is partial to his native city, Florence. Buondelmonti makes a point of saying that the two spoke in Latin and Greek. After the Greek lord takes Buondelmonti on a tour of his estate, the Franciscan and the monk continue on their way. The monk takes up his history once again, recounting the arrival of twelve noble Byzantine families from Constantinople sent to the island by the emperor to govern it. With the arrival of the Venetians the families retreated to disparate estates, weary of fighting, but the monk believes that should they combine forces they would easily take possession of the island. In conclusion, he names the other Greek-Cretan noble families and their numbers.[84]

There are a whole host of textual problems here, not least of which is the possibility that Buondelmonti invented a good deal of what he purports to have learned from the locals. The entire text describing Crete is littered with Virgilian Latin tags, specifically and most suspiciously from Book III of the *Aeneid*, when the Trojans land mistakenly on Crete, thanks to Apollo's vague directions.[85] In spite of this and other significant problems, mostly involving what Buondelmonti's editors in the past few centuries have done to his text, more than one historian has argued that Buondelmonti's report is evidence of the survival of Byzantium in the memories of the island's Greek population and constitutes an example of nascent national sentiment among them.[86] The situation, I believe, is not so simple.

Some of what Buondelmonti reports undoubtedly came from his talks with local people. The details concerning the Calergi family in particular must certainly have come from locals and from Matteo Calergi himself. It would have no doubt come as a surprise to Buondelmonti's readers even today to learn, as we shall, that the imposing Greek lord Matteo Calergi was in fact a member of the Great Council of Venice and had spent a great deal of time there, which might explain his ability to speak Latin with a Franciscan.

Without a doubt, the prestige of the Calergi family as depicted in the *Descriptio* had a basis in reality. They were indeed one of the most powerful, if not the most powerful, Greek-Cretan noble family on the island. Based in the district of Rethimno, to the west of Candia, this family's most famous member was Alexios Calergi, a nobleman who led a formidable revolt against the Venetian rulers at the end of the thirteenth century, nearly one hundred years after the conquest. As head of his family and a small coalition of other archontic families, Alexios entered into a treaty with Venice in 1299, on the basis of which he was given back much land and a considerable degree of juridical and ecclesiastic autonomy on those lands.[87] As a result, he became the most powerful Greek nobleman on the island, although he and his family maintained their estates and political base in the district of Rethimno. The distance between Rethimno and Candia did not, however, prevent the Calergi's influence from reaching into the heart of the Great Council of Candia. In the treaty with Venice, the Calergi and the other families party to it won the right to form marriage alliances with Latin feudatory families.[88]

The Calergi family pursued a strategy of marriage alliances with the Venetian feudatory families of Crete consistently in every generation from the second half of the thirteenth century right through and beyond the fourteenth. The result of all that intermarriage, however, was not the uniform Latinizing of those branches of the Calergi family. Buondelmonti's text is valuable in that it shows that as long as they were on the island, that branch of the family perceived themselves and were perceived by others as Greek-Cretans, even though most branches of the family renewed kinship with the Latin feudatory families in every generation.

Unfortunately, a full reconstruction of the Calergi family tree founders in an abundance of contradictory and incomplete evidence. Ernest Gerland's attempt at the start of the twentieth century to chart the history of the various branches of this family provides a basis on which to start a new reconnoiter of the sources, but even he did not see the pattern of extensive marriages among the scattered and piecemeal evidence.[89] The Calergi family archives in the Museo Correr in Venice and the notarial evidence now make it possible to go beyond the information Gerland found, and, if not always to correct his data, at least to offer plausible alternatives to the genealogical tree he devised. The family archives contain genealogical trees and lists of ancestors compiled by sixteenth-century family members settled in Venice as part of their efforts to retain their Venetian noble status. That knowledge in itself means that we must approach those archives with caution, but their contents differ in enough detail from those Gerland used to make investigation worth our while.

Alexios's grandfather, Varda Calergi, lived during the first years of Venetian occupation.[90] All we know about Varda is that he had four sons, one of whom, Georgios, was the father of Alexios. Gerland had difficulty seeing how other branches of the family fit into the genealogical tree, but one look at the names tells us that those branches are the descendants of Alexios's uncles.[91] First names such as Siphi and Costas show up in Calergi branches other than Alexios's and probably are the names of Varda's other sons. Historians who have studied the Calergi family are aware that some of Alexios's descendants emigrated toward the end of the fourteenth century to Venice, where they were incorporated into the patriciate. Less well known are the descendants of Varda's other sons, who had emigrated to Venice much earlier in the same century. As early as 1347, Georgios and Vassilios Calergi, sons of Siphi, residents of the *confinium* San Vidal, appointed as their commissaries their sisters, Maria and Potha, who still lived in Crete in the village of Calandatea.[92] Their father, Siphi, was very likely the grandson of Varda, the progenitor of the family.

The branch of the family that had the greatest impact on Venetian Crete are the descendants of Alexios, son of Georgios, son of Varda (whom I will refer to as Alexios I in order to distinguish him from his descendants bearing his name). The earliest notice we have of Alexios I comes from the year 1264, when he is mentioned among a group of Cretan archontes concluding a treaty with Venice.[93] In the last decade of the thirteenth century, Alexios I moved out ahead of his cohort when he led an insurrection against Venetian rule. The treaty between him and Venice set the stage for his family's entrance into the feudatory group by means of a continual series of marriage alliances. About Alexios I himself we know very little. He married a woman from another archontic family, Maria Scordili Scanzi, by whom he had numerous children.[94] This legendary warrior, who is always described as "dominus" and "nobilis vir" in the Latin official sources, died at some point before 1317.[95]

Until recently only two Venetian feudatory families, the Sagredo and the Zeno, were known to have married Calergi progeny after the 1299 treaty. [96] The Museo Correr archives and numerous transactions in the notarial registers tell a much more extensive and interesting story. The earliest indication of a marriage between a Calergi and a Latin feudatory comes from 1304. In that year Andre Corner, son of the late lord Marco, undertook some business resulting in a number of transactions on behalf of his uncle (*avunculus*), Alexios Calergi.[97] As an agent of his uncle's, Andrea must have been at least in his late teens, which puts his birth back to the late 1280s, but he was possibly older, since his father was deceased. The kinship link must mean that Alexios's sister had married into the Corner family. Unfortunately, it is impossible at the moment to say with which branch of the Corner family the Calergi allied themselves.

The Calergi policy of intermarriage with Latin feudatory families becomes abundantly clear after the turn of the fourteenth century. Nearly all of Alexios I's children, grandchildren, and great-grandchildren married into Latin feudatory families. These marriages differed from other archontic-feudatory alliances. Although it was unusual for a Latin feudatory woman to marry a Greek man, the Calergi men were extraordinarily successful in making alliances with Latin women. Among the marriage alliances that I have discovered, eleven are between male Calergi descendants of Alexios I and Latin feudatory women; ten are between female Calergi and Latin men.[98] Tracing this marital strategy through the family trees of each of Alexios I's children will bring this into greater relief.[99]

Georgios, Son of Alexios I, and His Descendants

Following the tradition of naming the eldest son after the paternal grandfather, Georgios I was most likely Alexios I's eldest son, and from his line of the family came its most distinguished members (at least from Venice's perspective). All we know of Georgios's wife is that her name was Richiolda, the Venetian form of Ricarda, indicating that she came from a Latin feudatory family.[100] Since Georgios refers to a member of the Bono family as his *cognatus*, it is likely that Richiolda came from that family.[101] Georgios and Richiolda had four children, according to the same archival documents. The eldest was Alexios (hereafter known as Alexios II). He married a woman named Maria, of whom it is not known whether she was Latin or Greek. After having at least three sons and one daughter that we know about, he died sometime before 1352, perhaps in 1346, with his branch of the family firmly ensconced in Venice's favor.[102] Alexios II's children, Matteo, Georgios, Ioannes, and Philipa, became the branch of the family with the closest ties to Venice, and yet they apparently remained in their perception of themselves culturally Greek.

The Matteo Calergi whom Buondelmonti encountered in his circuit of the island was the son of Alexios II.[103] We find relatively little about him in the archival and notarial sources, except a marriage contract and the text of his will, drawn up in Crete but written in the Venetian dialect (equally indicative of the language of the notary as of the likelihood that he dictated it in Venetian), a copy of which survives in the Museo Correr archives (whose existence, incidentally, was initiated by the descendants of Matteo in their bid to maintain their noble status in Venice). The contract, drawn up in 1347 by the fathers of the bride and groom, is for the marriage of Matteo to Cecilia Gradenigo, daughter of Marco Gradenigo of Venice.[104] The year of the will's redaction is 1388 and in it we learn not only that his brother Georgios was still alive, but also that Matteo had married a daughter of the Corner family.[105] Evidently, Matteo's first wife had died and he had taken another from an equally prestigious family.

Georgios, son of Alexios II, brother of Matteo, married twice, the first time to a woman from the noble feudatory family of the Quirini. Her name is given only as Querina, but in a transaction recorded in 1366, Georgios, son of the late Alexios, appears with his brother-in-law, Amorato Quirini.[106] We learn from the Great Council membership lists that Amorato was the son of Bampanino, a relationship confirmed by another notarial transaction.[107] Georgios's second wife was named Beatrice, the daughter of Marco Dandolo, one of the most prominent noblemen of Candia. Georgios had six children from these two women, all of whom married into Latin feudatory families. As indicative of how closely kinship could be forged, even to the point of risking consanguinity, Matteo's and Georgios's brother, Ioannes, also married into the Quirini family. In fact, he married his sister-in-law's first cousin, Madalena.[108] An even closer connection occurred when Querina's daughter, Philipa, married Niccolò Dandolo, the brother of her father's second wife, Beatrice.[109] The link to the Dandolo family does not stop there. Querina's son Alexios III also married into a branch of the Dandolo family, although it is impossible at this point to say which one, and another daughter, Agnes, married Rigo Dandolo, son of the late Lorenzo. Another daughter by Querina married into the Caravello family. The second wife Beatrice's daughter married another son of a noble family, Niccolò Venier, son of the late Giacomo, and her son married Agnes Carandino.[110]

Going back up the family tree to the children of Georgios, son of Alexios I, his and Richiolda's other son, Andrea, married a daughter of Giovanni Abbado, a member of the Great Council, by whom he had two daughters, according to the same family tree in the Museo Correr. One daughter, Maria, also known as Mariçoli, married Andrea Gradenigo son of Leonardo, which made Maria the niece by marriage of Marco Gradenigo, one of the most powerful feudatories in Candia.[111] The other daughter, Agnes, married Pietro Marcello. Both were men from noble Latin feudatory families.

According to the same fragment, Georgios son of Alexios I made his will in 1335, which has not survived, but we know that by 1341 he was dead.[112] Georgios's widow, Richiolda, lived for a long time after his death, which would have been possible if she had been considerably younger than her husband. She and her daughter Agnes appear in a transaction made in 1350, and she is possibly the same Richiolda Calergi whom one testator, Elena, widow of Phylippo Marcello, appointed as one of five executors of her will made in 1365.[113]

Given how extensively the descendants of Georgios, son of Alexios I, infiltrated the Latin feudatory families of Candia, it is worth considering where those families stood in the feudatory group: Abbado, Carandino, Caravello, Dandolo, Gradenigo, Marcello, Quirini, Venier. They represent

eight cognomina, the most influential and wealthy feudatory families in
Candia, distributed over thirteen marriages. Five of the eight are among
the original concessionaire families. The descendants of Georgios son of
Alexios I show a decided preference for Latin families at the top of Candiote
feudatory society.

Andrea Son of Alexios I and His Descendants

The other children of Alexios I display an equal interest in allying themselves with Latin feudatory families. Returning to the top of the tree of
Alexios I's children, we look next at the short-lived line of Andrea, who
married Agnes, daughter of lord Marco Corner. One notarial document
from 1331 involving this son of Alexios shows just how complex was the
kinship network between the Calergi and the Corner families.[114] Andreas
has the transaction drawn up to confer power of attorney on his Corner
relatives. He refers to his *cognato* Giacomo Corner Corneraki, who we will
see was the husband of his sister Agnes; his nephews, Giovanni and Alexios
Corner of the Greater House (which supports the possible connection
mentioned earlier); and to Michele, Giacomo, and Niccolò Corner, brothers, his *cognati*, the brothers of his wife. These Corner kinsmen come from
different branches of the Corner family. From another notarial transaction
dated to 1356, we learn that Andrea's wife Agnes's sister Marchesina was
married to Antonio da Molin and that she had a brother named Niccolò.[115]
Since most of the children of Alexios I must have died in the early part of
the century and the notarial entry dates to 1356, the span of years would be
possible only if Agnes had married young and Andrea, son of Alexios I, had
married after the 1299 treaty.

Andrea and Agnes had only one child, as far as we can tell, a daughter
by the name of Beriola, who appears in records of the Great Council of Venice on more than one occasion. She, too, married a Latin feudatory, Raynucio Zeno, a member of the Candiote Senate from 1340 to 1363. Raynucio
was not one of the more influential members of the *rogati*, to judge from the
infrequency of his appearance on committees or in positions of responsibility. Of the two, Beriola was the one who appears to have garnered the
more respect. In 1349, the Venetian Senate confirmed her right to buy
seven warhorses, as granted in the treaty between her grandfather, Alexios I,
and the Comune.[116] Seven years later the Venetian Senate agreed to pay her
one hundred hyperpera to compensate for the purchase of fifteen war-

horses.[117] One of the only other mentions of the last member, apparently, of this line is in a transaction in which Beriola lends money to a member of the Corner family, perhaps the branch her mother belonged to.[118]

Marcos, Son of Alexios I, and His Descendants

This son of Alexios married a woman from the Quirini family, of whom we know only that her father's name was Paolo.[119] By her, Marcos had a son, Alexios, who married Margarita, daughter of Andrea Pantalio, and who very likely died by 1344.[120] The fragment in the Calergi archive informs us that Margarita made her will in 1371. Another of Marcos' sons, Georgios, married Maria, daughter of Albertino Corner, a feudatory of another prominent branch of that family. This Georgios had numerous children. His three sons bore names that linked them to both sides of the family: Albertino, Leo Trulidi, and Niccolò.[121] A daughter, Elena, married Giovanni Corner, son of Pietro, from another branch of the Corner family.[122] In a notarial transaction of 1361, having to do with the legacies of the late Elena, Georgios appears. This entry mentions, too, that Elena's will was originally given in Greek and subsequently translated into Latin.[123]

Leo Trulidi, Son of Alexios I, and His Descendants

This son of the Greek archon, who bore the nickname Trulidi, and his descendants did not ally himself with the Venetian regime as his brothers and sisters did.[124] In spite of his marriage to Marchesina Gradenigo, who was apparently still alive in 1339, thereby making him and his children kinsmen of a prominent feudatory family, three of Leo's sons led revolts against the regime in the first half of the fourteenth century.[125] Leo, however, had died early in the century, prior to 1317.[126] As a further sign of this branch's detachment from the colonial authorities, one of Leo's sons was the only one of Alexios I's grandchildren to marry a daughter of a Greek archon. The Calergi archives show that Alexios, who was undoubtedly Leo's eldest son, married Maria Scordili Capsalivi. This Alexios died in late 1331.[127] Little is known about Leo's daughters except their names, but we do know that one, Marıçoli, married Andrea Pantalios, son of the late Niccolò; they named their daughter Trulida, who had died by 1357, after marrying into a Candiote branch of the Barbarigo family.[128]

Trulida and Agnes, Daughters of Alexios I,
and Their Descendants

To begin with the daughter of Alexios I that we know least about, Trulida married Pietro Fradello, a Latin feudatory.[129] There is nothing more at this time to say about her.

Agnes, on the other hand, has left us better documentation about her life. Her will has survived, but unfortunately it offers precious little information about her birth family.[130] She had married Cornaraki Corner, whose given name was Giacomo, which we learn from his will made almost twenty years later, after he had remarried.[131] Apparently Agnes died young, since she mentions no children in her will. Her parents, however, were already deceased by that time. In her will, we learn that she had two more sisters about whom we know nothing except that one was a Greek nun; that she had cousins belonging to the Lambardo and Matono families; and that she felt an attachment to the Greek church in spite of her marriage to a Latin. For Giacomo Corner's part, in spite of his remarriage, he kept up some kind of contact with his first wife's family, for in his will he bequeathed five hundred hyperpera to the daughter of Andrea Calergi, who must have been the Beriola we have just met.[132]

Was There a Fifth Son?

In Gerland's outline of the Calergi family, put together on the basis of his own research in the ADC and on the strength of a chronicle by Lorenzo di Monaci (to which we will return in a subsequent chapter), Alexios I had only four sons. Those scholars who have attended to the details of the Calergi family genealogy have taken him at his word, despite the appearance of a fifth son in the Calergi family archives in the Museo Correr. According to those sources, Ioannes, son of Alexios I, was mentioned in the will of a cousin and in the will of one of his sons; neither document has survived. Moreover, there is a family tree dedicated exclusively to the descendants of this mysterious son, from which we learn that Ioannes married into yet another branch of the Quirini family and that he had three children, Leo, Alexios, and Marchesina.[133] A notarial document from 1359 corroborates in part the information in the Calergi archive. Relevant to the existence of Alexios, son of Ioannes, the entry from 1359 concerns a dispute over the will of Beata, widow of Alexios Calergi.[134] Beata's sons are identified as Ioannes, Leo, and Marcus, the same names as those of the sons attributed to Alexios, son of the fifth son, Ioannes, in the Calergi archive.[135] The relevance of Ioannes, the putative fifth son of Alexios I, is that his three grandchildren are the only descendants of the family's patriarch whose names are accompanied by the words "rebelo." The three Calergi sons can be identified with those who led the later stages of the 1363 revolt, the subject of a good portion of Chapter Four. We will return to them again.

Alexios I's descendants married into at least twenty different branches of Latin feudatory families, but they were nearly all Latin feudatory families of the highest order, kin of Venice's patrician families and the original families to settle in the colony. Moreover, we have seen that even the branch most closely associated with the colonial regime still considered itself Greek. Yet portions of the Candiote feudatory group were shot through with noble Greek kinship ties, reflections of which we have seen in the notarial documents, where Greek and Latin kin act in concert as families tend to do. What is most striking, and surprising, is that most of the feudatory families descended from the original settlers could count Calergi among their kin at one point or another during the latter half of the thirteenth and all during the fourteenth century. It is not surprising, then, given the kinship ties that existed, that the Calergi eventually gained admittance to the Great Council of Venice.

Nonsanctioned Unions Between Latin Feudatories and Greeks

Kinship ties with Greeks came not just in the form of marriage alliances with Greek archontic families. There is also evidence that shows it to have been quite common for a Latin man, particularly a feudatory, to have illegitimate children with Greek servile women. These children born outside the supporting structures of matrimony had a legal claim on their fathers, but whether they evoked an emotional one as well is, of course, difficult to determine. Contemporaries in Latin Greece even had a term for people born of Latin and Greek parents and their descendants: *gasmuli* (γασμούλοι), but, unlike similar terminology in succeeding centuries like "mulatto," the word *gasmulus* did not imply a juridical status.

From the legal perspective, illegitimate children had rights to a limited amount of sustenance in their lives in the event that their fathers did not provide fully for their care. When fathers were indifferent to the children that Greek women bore them, the court stepped in to assure a minimum amount of care for the children once paternity had been established. The court compelled Giovanni Paradiso to pay two hyperpera a month, equivalent to the monthly salary of a servant, to Aniça Monovassiotissa, resident of the burg, for the food and clothing of a child she bore him, until the child was weaned.[136] Early in the century, one feudatory, Bampanino Quirini, had an illegitimate son who joined the respectable and lucrative ranks of Candiote goldsmiths, surely a sign of his father's assistance.[137] But several years later another of Bampanino's illegitimate sons wound up in court after his father's death to fight for his status as the son of a Latin man.[138]

Other feudatories looked after the interests of their illegitimate sons in their wills. As noted earlier, arguing for a certain mode of behavior in a person's life on the basis of what one finds in his or her will is problematic, to say the least, and such arguments especially lead to confusion when they involve children born out of wedlock. So, once again, caution is necessary. Twenty of the ninety-three male feudatories whose wills we have mention illegitimate relatives in them. Six bequeath to their own illegitimate offspring less than one hundred hyperpera, which was not an especially large sum.[139] Five other feudatory testators leave their illegitimate children up to three hundred hyperpera.[140] Even though there is always the possibility that the more parsimonious fathers had already provided their illegitimate sons with a portion of their patrimony, the bequests to illegitimate sons in the wills were not substantial enough in value to merit being called preferential for one very good reason.

In all the above cases, the illegitimate sons were competing against legitimate brothers, and there is no question that legitimate sons of feudatories could pose difficulties for their father's illegitimate offspring. It was not so much a question of claiming a share in their fathers' patrimonies, since they legally had no claim at all on their fathers' estate, as it was one of compelling their siblings to honor the promises and bequests fathers made to those sons excluded by law. In 1368 the grandson of a feudatory, Paolo di Rugerio, by Paolo's illegitimate son, convinced the court that his grandfather had bequeathed to him a "burgesia," the rights to which had yet to be transferred to him by the executors of the grandfather's will, who happened to be Paolo's legitimate sons.[141] Andrea and Pasquale Matono, sons of the late Giacomo, were ordered by the court to give ten measures of grain every year for four years to Cali, a seamstress, for her child, Giacobina, born out of wedlock by Giacomo, since, as the court pointed out, they were the child's brothers.[142] Thus an illegitimate child's fortune could be very insecure.

But not always. In the records of the *Avogari di Comune* in Venice from 1327 appears a petition by Constantino Corner, who sought recognition as the son of one of the most important feudatories of the colony, one encountered here before, Andrea Corner of the Greater House, father of the energetic Alessio, kinsman of the great Alexios I Calergi. Constantino explained to the court that he was Andrea's son by a villein, who of course would have been a Greek woman. Unusually, Andrea's legitimate son, Marco, whose will we have examined, supported his natural brother's claim. The Great Council of Venice recognized his claim and Constantino joined his brothers.[143]

Marco's support of his illegitimate brother is not completely surprising or exceptional. He is one of five feudatory testators who displayed a great deal more generosity to their illegitimate kin than did the testators discussed above, which shows that it was not unheard of for a feudatory family to embrace its illegitimate members. A year before Marco Corner *de domo maiori* supported his illegitimate brother's petition, he had made a will, in which he revealed that he also had an illegitimate son. To his natural son Francesco he bequeathed the rights to a village, Mugara, along with ten villeins, and three vineyards in the district of Paraschi, with the understanding that Francesco would provide military service for one sergeantry.[144] Whether this bequest made a feudatory out of Francesco depends on whether possession of one sergeantry merited a seat on the Great Council. There is no way of knowing what property was already in Francesco's possession prior to the execution of his father's will. But Francesco might have been one of the "bastards" purged from the Great Council in 1356. In any case, here is an example of an illegitimate son of one of the island's most prestigious families receiving a substantial inheritance from his father.

Among the other feudatory testators, Pietro Dono and Francesco Caravello were also generous to their illegitimate offspring. In 1347 Pietro, with no legitimate son, bequeathed three hundred hyperpera to Frangula, his illegitimate daughter. To his illegitimate son Paoletto, when he turned eighteen years old, he left two half-sergeantries with villeins.[145] This last bequest, however, was not entirely free and clear, for Pietro allows for the possibility that his wife might yet bear him a legitimate son, which would nullify the bequest to Paoletto. Should that event come about, Paoletto would have to content himself, as his sister would, with a bequest of three hundred hyperpera. In contrast, Francesco Caravello placed no such contingency on his illegitimate son, Andrea, in his will of 1371.[146] He left to Andrea the equivalent of one and a half sergeantries, plus a ten-year loan of two thousand hyperpera against his total estate to invest in commercial ventures. Here are two more illegitimate sons who possibly might have gained entrance to the Great Council on the basis of their fathers' legacies to them.

The Latin feudatory group pursued sanctioned unions (in the form of marriages) and unsanctioned unions (through siring illegitimate children by servile women for whom they were legally obligated to take responsibility) with the indigenous people of the island. This factor alone brought about changes in the previously uncomplicated convergence of Latin feudatory interests with Venetian policy, in a way that was very different from intermarriage on social levels below the rank of feudatory.

The Commoners of Candia

It is a pity that we can in no way analyze the kinship networks of Candia's commoners as we were able to do with the feudatory families. Members of the feudatory group are usually easy to identify when we have the combination of cognomen, demonstrable wealth, and other contextual information. These are the very features that are most often missing in the sources pertaining to humble Candiotes. Yet therein lies one of the most interesting features of that portion of the population. That we cannot easily identify either their kin or their ethnicity is significant, but the problem is a multi-layered one. The first layer is the problem of the commoners' cognomina as they were recorded in the sources; the second is the diffusion of Latin, mainly Venetian, cognomina throughout the Candiote Greek community; the third is the fashion of one ethnic community's adoption of another's given names. Each layer of the sources obscures our vision, and so we must first consider how we will see past and through them. The approach, then, to the majority of the city residents, which the Greek and Latin commoners formed, must differ from that taken in the quest for the feudatory families.

The first layer to pass through is a function of the notary's presence in the document. In ordinary practice, notaries who wrote mostly in Latin tended to latinize the spelling of all names, both given name and cognomen, whether Italian or Greek, whenever possible. The result is that it is difficult and often impossible to determine whether on the face of it the "Iohannes Mauro" who appears in a contract is a Latin rendering of the Greek Ioannes Mavro or the Venetian Giovanni Moro without additional information.

The second and third problems we encounter are that by the fourteenth century, the earliest period to which nearly all notarial sources date, neither cognomina nor given names were the exclusive property of one ethnic group or the other. To take a quite typical example, a woman whose name appears as "Cali Gradonico," a Greek given name combined with a latinized Venetian patrician cognomen, in a notarial protocol or court record might be a person possessing one of several combinations of features. Most obviously, her name suggests that she was a daughter of a Latin feudatory family with a fashionable penchant for Greek names. But she might just as easily have been a daughter of a humble Latin father belonging to a non-noble branch of the Gradenigo family and a Greek mother, or simply a hellenized humble woman of Venetian descent. She might even have been the daughter of parents both of whom considered themselves Greek, if there had been enough intermarriage in the generations of her family that preceded her. Again, without additional information about her, the assumption that she was Latin would be risky and potentially misleading.

The most extreme example of the confusion inherent in the names of humble Candiotes is the practice of manumitted male slaves adopting their former masters' cognomina. The slave population during the early fourteenth century consisted primarily of Greeks, although as the century progressed a growing number of slaves came from the Balkans and the Black Sea region.[147] It was a relatively common practice in Crete for masters to free their slaves or allow them to redeem themselves. In the wills, 125 testators from all social levels, 85 of whom were Latin and Greek men, made arrangements for one or more of their slaves to be freed after their deaths. Although the percentage of testators who acted in this way is not large (16 percent), it does suggest that manumission was not an unreasonable hope for a slave to have, for manumitting a slave constituted a pious act that occurs second only in frequency to donations for masses. In addition to the testators who manumit slaves in their wills, an additional thirty testators mention slaves who had already been freed and to whom they left bequests.[148] Freed slaves, then, were not uncommon in Candia.

Fortunately, the wills of five freed slaves have survived.[149] The two female ex-slave testators did not adopt any cognomen when they were freed, and identified themselves only by stating whose slave they had been and the name of their husbands, if married, a practice typical of women in a dependent legal relationship. The three male ex-slaves, in contrast, bear cognomina of the former master. One will, from 1342, is sufficiently representative. The milieu into which the testator, Lio Taliapetra, ex-slave, en-

tered after gaining his freedom was Greek.[150] He states that he and his wife
Herini are the residents of the Greek monastery of St. Pantaleo, but his
economic status in the world must have been slightly higher than that of the
average ex-slave, for his will informs us that Herini had brought to the marriage a respectable dowry of three hundred hyperpera, three times the value
of the customary dowry assigned to humble Greek women. Ex-slaves like
Lio usually signalled their juridical free status in whatever documents they
had cause to draw up, but we cannot be sure that they always did so or were
even obliged to so so.

It is clear, then, that no easy assumptions about the ethnic background
of any name appearing in the notarial records can be made without running
the risk of presenting a distorted picture of Candiote society. In spite of the
difficulties in ethnic attribution, however, one rule of thumb makes distinguishing between humble Latins and Greeks on the basis of their names
somewhat easier. While it is true that Latin and Venetian family names
often mask people who would consider themselves and be considered by
others as Greeks, Greek cognomina on the humble level of Candiote society, in contrast, always signal Greek people. The problem in attribution,
then, is confined largely to bearers of Latin cognomina, in part because of
the regime's greater tolerance of Greek women marrying Latin men than of
Greek men marrying Latin women. Traditional Greek Cretan family names,
such as Selopulo, continued to belong to Greek families, despite the occasional presence in them of women from Latin backgrounds. In short, a
woman with the cognomen Castrofilacha is without question Greek, while
a woman or a man bearing the patrician names Corner or Venier are not
necessarily Latin.

Given names are also very ambiguous in their ability to reflect the
community to which their bearers belonged. As the thirteenth century
progressed, the Latin and Greek communities developed a growing fond-
ness for assigning certain names from the other community to their children. This fashion is less noticeable among male given names, but it is not
unknown.[151] The two communities shared a small pool of names given to
males. The latinized names Iohannes, Marcus, and Andreas, among others,
were popular among both Greeks and Latins. Not even the diminutives for
these ambi-ethnic names are a useful indicator of the ethnic group to which
its bearer belonged, since each language group's diminutives were shared
by the other group. Thus Zanacki, a Cretan diminutive for Iohannes, can be
found even among the sons of feudatories, although the Venetian diminu-

tive Zuan never appears attached to a recognizably Greek man. The rare occurrence of certain given names in the community with which they were not originally associated, however, ought immediately to provoke suspicion about the ethnic background of their bearers. For instance, Leonardo is a given name rarely belonging to a Greek man. When it is attached to a person who context tells us is Greek, we infer that the man is to a degree latinized, perhaps religiously so. Conversely, Dimitris, or its Latin form Dimitrius, is almost never found belonging to a man whose context argues for his coming from a Latin background. In the few cases where we find a Dimitrius bearing a Venetian cognomen, we are undoubtedly in the presence of a Greek Candiote, perhaps of Latin descent but someone who would identify himself as Greek. Among females, names that were Venetian in origin can be found in Greek families (Mariçoli or Francesca, to name two), just as traditionally Greek female names show up in Latin families (the most common being Cali). When traditionally Greek names like Eudochia, Fenga, Potha, and Pothiti occur in the wills and other kinds of documents made by Latins, both feudatory and humble, it is often a sign of kinship with Greek families.[152]

In addition to names, place of residence in the city has also been thought to follow ethnic patterns. According to this view, the growing number of Latin settlers gradually pushed the Greek inhabitants outside the walls of the city into the suburbs, a metaphor for their marginalization within a Venetian-dominated society.[153] This line of thinking has emerged from a consultation of diplomatic records and an off-hand sampling of a small number of notarial sources. A more thorough sampling reveals a different picture from that more contentious one. The sample must be understood, however, in relation to what the notarial sources represent. Since the great majority of protocols that have survived belonged to Latin notaries working within the city, their clientele would have been mostly Latin people, but that is by no means a hard and fast rule. The protocols of Greek and Hebrew notaries, from which we would have much more positive evidence of the population's residential patterns, have not survived. Therefore in general the protocols that survive are more suggestive of the Latin population's behavior than they are of the Greek and Jewish populations. In spite of this bias built into the sources, there were nonetheless a great many Greeks who patronized Latin notaries. Consequently, if these sources with a built-in bias toward Latin clients contain, as in fact they do, a significant number of transactions made by Greek residents of the city (very

TABLE 11.   Residence of Humble Testators of Wills

	City	Burg	Village, castle or elsewhere
Latin females	103	7	0
Greek females	31	26	2
Females of mixed parentage	56	15	10
Latin males	75	23	3
Greek males	31	37	16
Males of mixed parentage	26	13	2

TABLE 12.   Residence of Humble Parties to Marriage Contracts

	City	Burg	Village, castle or elsewhere
Latin parties	94	28	9
Greek parties	38	48	20
Mixed parentage	5	1	0

TABLE 13.   Residence of Parties to Apprenticeship and Service Contracts

	City	Burg	Village, castle or elsewhere
Latin parties	85	37	4
Greek parties	53	66	9
Mixed parentage	4	0	0

often not even involving Latins as the other parties), then it is reasonable to suppose that they represent the tip of the iceberg, regardless of how large or small the rest of the iceberg was.

I have compiled Tables 11, 12, and 13 to show the residential patterns of the humble testators (all feudatory testators would have without exception been residents of the city), when information is given in the transaction, according to document type, using the criteria discussed above to attribute ethnicity to the names in the transactions.[154]

What these tables do *not* show is that more Latin men and women

lived inside the city than did Greeks or than Latins lived in the burg. Nor
does it show that more Greeks lived in the burg than in the city. I stress
again that the small sample size and the inherent bias towards Italian- or
Venetian-speaking clients of Latin notaries preclude drawing that conclusion. A less ambitious inference from these figures is that Greeks did indeed
dwell within the city walls, even if it is impossible to determine definitively
their proportion of the total population. But an additional 144 names of
Greek men and women of all social levels identified as city residents that
figure among the executors of the fourteenth-century wills suggest that had
the registers of all Candiote notaries survived we would probably learn that
Latins were outnumbered even in the city of their greatest concentration.[155]
That most of the dates of Latin Candiotes living in the burg fall closer to the
second half of the century might point to overcrowding within the city,
with the result that Latin and Greek people alike were pushed beyond the
walls by rising rents and cost of living, but it might just as easily reflect the
greater abundance of notarial documents in some decades of the second half
of the fourteenth century. Suffice it to say that throughout the fourteenth
century Greeks lived in the city walls and out in the burg, forming a majority whose culture remained most visible and palpable.

Although a reliable estimate of the Latin-Greek ratio in Candia is not
feasible given the limitations of the sources, we can attempt a cautious
estimate of Candia's total population. In the previous chapter, we saw that
the feudatories and their families very likely never reached, much less sur-
passed, the figure of two thousand individuals. To find some analogous
number of the commoners, I have had to restrict my sample to the decade
for which the greatest number of protocols survive, the 1380s, by first
counting the names of nearly all the wage earners identified by a job title
working during that decade, with all due attention to the problem of hom-
onyms. From those ten years, I have found 369 names of individuals engaged in 53 professions.[156] For purposes of comparison, I counted 119
names with occupations attached in the decades for which there are the
fewest notarial registers, the 1330s. These numbers are for the most part
meaningless, given the random pattern according to which the notarial
registers have survived, but they are nonetheless suggestive in one limited
way. Broadly speaking, they indicate that there were at the very least a couple of hundred wage-earners (not including domestic servants, of whom
there were many) working in Candia in any one year. Because the surviving
names represent an undetermined and unknowable fraction of the total
number of Candiote wage-earners who went to Latin notaries, their num-

bers were undoubtedly greater. Thus, although some of the wage-earners I counted were fathers and sons or brothers, if we use the same estimate of four members per family as we did with the feudatories, we arrive at a figure of nearly three thousand individuals comprising the wage-earners living in Candia and its burg during the 1380s. My calculations do not take into account the Greek names without any indication of occupation, which may amount to many more than the names I have counted, which appear in contracts and other instruments. At a conservative guess, the Candiote working population fluctuated between five and eight thousand persons at certain times, if we allow as well for unskilled labor and domestic servants.

Because it served an important role as Venice's principal entrepôt in the eastern Mediterranean, the port city was home to people involved in activities related to defense, trade, and the maintenance and operations of galleys. Bowmakers, arrowsmiths, and swordsmiths supplied the weapons needed to defend the island. Sailors, helmsmen (*naucleri*), ship carpenters (*marangoni*), and caulkers were essential to the operation of the port and the galleys harbored there. The colonial administration needed men to carry out the duties of recordkeeping, weights and measures, and quality inspection. Masons, ironworkers or smiths, and stonecutters were kept busy in the upkeep of the colony's public buildings and warehouses. But a significant portion of the non-feudatory population was engaged in the kinds of service and artisanal occupations to be found in any city of its time, ranging from highly skilled, such as goldsmithing, to the unskilled, like domestic service. Cobblers, tanners, and tailors were three of the largest groups of skilled workers engaged in local industry. Another group of workers made their living as butchers, fishermongers, and tavernkeepers. With very few exceptions, all these occupations were carried out by men. Women's traditional options for employment in the city were fewer: nurses, tavernkeeps, servants. We find them, however, occasionally in other occupations, such as textile workers and quite often merchants.[157] In other words, many Candiotes lived out their lives without being directly involved in the colony's strategic role in Venice's overseas empire.

My sample of artisans and wage-earners (Table 14) reveals an ethnically mixed working population. Wishing to remain on the conservative side of my estimates, I counted as Greek only those bearing traditional Greek cognomina or clearly traditional Greek first names in combination with a Venetian cognomina.

The usual caveats apply. These names come from notarial protocols of Latin notaries and therefore are most unlikely to be representative of the

TABLE 14. Ethnic Representation in the Occupations of Candia

Occupation	Total	Latin names	Greek names	Percent Greek
Cobbler	175	113	62	35
Goldsmith	113	74	39	34
Tailor	98	55	43	43
Tanner	66	52	14	21
Mason	55	36	19	34
Sailor	32	20	12	37
Bottlemaker	30	0	6	100

real proportion of Greeks in a field of work. Consequently, the smaller the sample the less meaningful the percentage of Greeks in that field. These numbers serve to show nonetheless that even in the protocols of Latin notaries Greeks generally amount to a third of the crafts for which we have the greatest number of names.

The historian Elisabeth Santschi compiled an extensive sample of 732 contracts of employment and apprenticeship, and published her analysis of them in an article published in a journal of limited circulation.[158] Her conclusions are interesting in many regards, and some are worth summarizing here. It must first be said that she does not explain according to which criteria she judged the names in those contracts to be Greek or Latin, but that does not reduce by much the value of what she has to say. Her sample stretches across the length of the fourteenth century, meaning that the number of contracts she examined, while not so minuscule as to be meaningless, is nevertheless small. She found that in the contracts of employment and apprenticeship, 669 of the workers are Greek and 748 are Latin. She further identified 75 *patroni* as Greek and 242 as Latin.[159] Limiting the significance of the numbers she presents, she observes that they come from Latin notaries and thus cannot be truly representative of the actuality. Broadly speaking, these numbers mirror trends that emerge from my smaller sample of documents in the same notarial sources.

Mapping the residences of the artisans whose names we do have tells us a little more. Although place of residence does not accompany all names of skilled workers, the ones that do are suggestive, as Table 15 shows.

The city and burg of Candia, it would then seem, were fairly well integrated with Latins and Greeks, given that, again, sources with an inherent bias toward higher numbers of Latins reveal a respectable number of

TABLE 15.   Residence of Skilled Workers According to Ethnicity

Artisan	Greek/city	Latin/city	Greek/burg	Latin/burg	Elsewhere
Cobbler	26	25	14	32	0
Goldsmith	25	44	8	8	0
Tailor	11	22	19	21	2
Furrier	3	26	8	5	2
Mason	3	17	8	9	2
Ironworker	4	8	3	6	1
Sailor	5	7	5	7	2
Carpenter	6	4	9	3	1
Cooper	2	14	3	4	0

Greek artisans living in the city and a similar number of Latins living in the Greek-dominated burg. To be sure, Latins in the lowest ranks of society, such as Giovanni from Padua, a herdsman in the employ of a Greek resident of the burg, were always to be found living beyond the city walls.[160] It is also interesting to note that there are no detectable signs of one or another group of artisans favoring either the burg or the city, in spite of government regulations as to where they might allowed to conduct their business. Evidently, not all artisans lived where they worked. For example, the tanners all had their shops outside the city walls near the small port of Dermata to the west, but twenty-nine of them lived in the city. The question that remains to be answered is the extent of segregation within the city and out in the burg. Did Latins and Greeks congregate in neighborhoods on a smaller scale than the city and the burg? This is the kind of question that the sources are not much help in answering.

Let us now consider in detail the largest groups of artisans and skilled workers for whom we have names, once again working in units of decades. The largest group of skilled workers to appear in the notarial protocols across the entire fourteenth century is the 175 cobblers, among whom figure 23 Jews (about 13 percent). Naturally the greatest number come from the 1380s, the decade for which the most records survive and therefore for which we have the most names. The cobblers called themselves by three different titles, *caligarius*, *cerdo*, and *sutor*, with no obvious distinction among them. *Caligarius* and *sutor* were interchangeable titles. The job of *cerdo*, however, differed in function.[161] According to Venetian artisanal statutes, *cerdones* repaired shoes, working with old leather, rather than making them, which is what *caligarii* did with new leather.[162] The distinction between a *cerdo* and a *caligarius* may have collapsed somewhat in Candia. A document from 1346 involves a *cerdo*, Niccolò d'Acri, whose shop is called a "*statio calligarie*."[163] A little over forty years later, in 1387, the distinction appears to apply. Marco Vergici, a Greek *cerdo*, undertook to look after the footwear of the children of a feudatory, a job that involved the maintenance and not the provisioning of their shoes.[164]

The 97 tailors (*sartores* and *iuparii*) make up the second largest group of artisanal names. The 113 goldsmiths, 36 of them from the 1380s alone, formed the third largest group of artisans. Cobblers, tailors, and goldsmiths, then, predominate in the notarial registers, although without necessarily having been in actuality the largest groups of skilled workers in the city. Interestingly, none of these three skills played even a peripheral role in the activities that made the colony so important to Venice.

For a relatively small city, the number of goldsmiths in the 1380s is striking, sometimes reaching as many as 33 working in one year. Churches and ecclesiastical institutions kept up the demand for their services, but gold and silver objects could be found in even humble households, as evidenced by references to them in the contents of dowries. Without doubt there were enough goldsmiths working in Candia to supply the colony with its needs in precious objects.[165] Furthermore, these craftsmen ranked solidly in the middling social ranks of the city, as shown by the values of their wives' and daughters' dowries, which equaled those of other Candiote skilled workers.[166]

Goldsmiths were the object of a series of restrictions typical of the Comune's efforts to regulate all aspects of colonial life. In the years 1357, 1361, and 1364, the government required goldsmiths to have their workshops in the Platea. If there were insufficient stalls for goldsmiths to rent from the Comune, special permission could be granted to a goldsmith either to rent a private shop elsewhere within the walls or to work in his home at night, on condition that he keep his doors shut.[167] Permission to set up a goldsmith's shop, however, apparently did not always come with a ready-made place of business. In 1370, a Greek goldsmith, Giorgos Cavoso, hired Andrea Maladrin, a carpenter, to build him a booth with cupboard space.[168]

The government also mandated that each workshop might have only one master goldsmith, assisted by apprentices and other employees, joint ventures between masters was forbidden. In 1360 goldsmiths were forbidden to send their employees or apprentices to buy gold or silver in the city or the burg.[169] As in so many of its other regulations, the government's restrictions on the goldsmiths were aimed at maximizing the tax and rent it could collect from individual enterprises, and, like the monopoly on grain held by the government, the sale of precious metals fell under the same hegemonic control.

The notarial sources reinforce the notion expressed in the proclamation banning the purchase of precious metals in outlying villages that goldsmithing was an activity that impinged on the countryside as well as the city. In 1326 Costas Scordili, son of the late Sguroiani, resident of the burg, agreed to go to work for Manuel Abramo, resident of the city, for one year at the salary of fourteen hyperpera. Among his responsibilities outlined in the contract between them, he agrees to work in Manuel's shop and "to go when you command me to the villages, according to the custom of goldsmiths."[170] Within seven months Costas had achieved the title of *aurifex* and was now working for two goldsmiths, Manuel Abramo of the earlier contract and another, Georgio Cornario, indicating that two masters were operating one workshop in that year well before the first proclamation forbidding such ventures.[171] In another contract, the goldsmith Georgios Scandolario took as his apprentice a boy, whose father promised that he "would serve you in your craft in your shop, as well as in the burg and villages, wherever you should take him for the purposes of your craft."[172]

Since most workshops functioned as residences as well as places of business, it is not surprising that the majority of goldsmiths whose residence is stated in the notarial protocols lived within the city walls (64 of 80). Fourteen others lived in the burg. We know, too, that at least two goldsmiths moved at some point in their careers from the burg into the city, probably when they managed to acquire a workshop of their own.[173]

If Greeks and Latins had relatively equal access to a lucrative occupation like goldsmithing, another group of skilled workers, the *speciarii* (a kind of pharmacist and maker of candles and "confections"), seems to have been dominated by Latins. The 27 names of *speciarii* throughout the century that have survived belonged mostly to Latins, some Jews, and a few Greeks. Nearly all resided within the city walls. In a contract from 1386, a Greek *speciarius* residing in the city, Dimitrios Salonicheo, agrees to come work for ser Pietro Brocardi of Florence, another *speciarius* living in Candia, for a period of two years, during which time Dimitrios would make candles and "confections" and perform other services in Pietro's shop.[174]

Even more noteworthy than the degree of general ethnic integration among occupations in Candia is the number of Greek Candiotes in crafts connected to defense and military action. Blacksmiths and farriers (*fabri*

TABLE 16.   Ethnic Representations in Defense-Related Occupations

Trade	Total	Latins	Greeks
Blacksmith	48	20	28
Knifemaker	20	10	10
Bowmaker	14	5	9
Swordsmith	11	8	3
Harnessmaker	7	5	2
Arrowmaker	6	5	1
Armorer	1	0	1

and *marescalci*), armorers (*clibanarii*), knifemakers (*cultellarii*), sword-smiths (*spatarii*), bowmakers (*arcerii*), and arrowmakers (*sagittarii* and *fusarii*) were all highly sensitive occupations, inasmuch as the government, the hired troops, and the feudatories relied on these artisans to outfit them for the purposes of war. So important did the Comune consider these crafts-men that it prohibited all those who lived in the burg not only from work-ing outside the city, but also from taking their work home with them.[175] Employing the same means as those we used for Table 15, Table 16 provides similar information.

What makes the information in Table 16 so interesting is that we see that the Comune was willing to depend to some extent on Greek Candiotes for its instruments of war and domination. But there is more to the Latin names in this group of skilled workers than meets the eye. Some of the Latin artisans involved with making war materiel were related by blood or marriage to Greeks. Pietro Polo, a blacksmith, was married to Elena, daughter of the late Nicolas Naptopuli, a resident of the village of Caro-nissi, who had provided his daughter with the respectable dowry of two hundred and thirty hyperpera.[176] Incidentally, after Elena's death in May 1339, Pietro wasted no time in taking another wife, the daughter of a Candiote goldsmith, Michael Pantalio, within the same month.[177] We learn from the 1348 will of another man, Manuel, son of Pietro Polo, a farrier, that his grandmother's name was Nicoletta Naptopulena, the feminine form of Naptopuli.[178] Manuel's will also informs us that he was a kinsman of another goldsmith, Marino Longo, and a Greek man, Georgios Musu-rachi. A Latin swordsmith, Pietro Zane, from Mantua, was married to a Greek woman with a Venetian name, Aniça, daughter of Dionissios Grama-ticopulo, another Greek goldsmith.[179] In the will made by Antonios Chan-

dachyti, the unemancipated son of Michael, a bowmaker and resident of
Candia, we learn that the testator had married Elena Quirini, whose dowry
was worth the respectable sum of three hundred hyperpera. Antonios's
family adhered to the Greek church, had Greek kin who were also bowmakers, and were related to at least one other Latin family, the da Molin.[180]

Physicians were one group of professionals working in Candia who
came from outside the colony, from both the eastern and western ends of
the Mediterranean. Of the forty-three physician names to surface in the
notarial and governmental sources, ten were Jews.[181] Only four bore obviously Greek names.[182] The remainder are an interesting mixture of Latins
and men from further east whose ethnicity is difficult to determine.[183] Some
of those physicians, like the Christian Syrian Benet de Tauresio, were just
passing through. In 1355 he was spending some time in Candia (*morans
Candide*) when Pietro, the son of the prominent feudatory Alessio Corner
de domo maiori, attempted to engage his services. Pietro had been suffering
from a hoarseness in his voice, which Benet undertook to cure within two
months for a fee of fifty Venetian gold ducats, a considerable sum in a
currency seldom seen in the notarial sources. A misunderstanding over the
fee between Pietro and Benet evidently ensued, stemming in part from the
difference in language, for the agreement was canceled. A few days later,
they tried again, this time with the details of payment spelled out and the
necessity for a translator made plain.[184]

Medical care was a constant worry of the feudatories, as the governmental records show. Even before the plague reached the island in the
summer of 1348, from the beginning of the record of the councils' deliberations, the feudatories demonstrated a continual concern to find physicians
willing to come work in the colony.[185] Attracting physicians to Candia and
keeping them there proved difficult. By 1348 the high mortality rate on the
island made retaining physicians especially hard.[186] The depopulation of
the district of Candia had become so dire that the Venetian Senate stepped
in to encourage with fiscal exemptions anyone from the empire *da' mar* to
immigrate to Candia to settle on the lands of the regime.[187]

Similar to the feudatory group, the artisanal population of Candia was
its own marriage pool, but fathers did not always choose prospective husbands and wives for their offspring from colleagues in the same craft. Although it was common for fathers to apprentice at least one of their sons to
someone in their own profession, it was also typical to apprentice second
and third sons to masters of other skills or to marry them to daughters of
masters of other skills.[188] Apprenticing with a master of another profession

from that of one's father was often a son's opportunity to bring his family a step up in the world, as in the case of Matteo Quirini, a fisherman, who apprenticed his son advantageously to a carpenter-caulker for six years, with the condition that his son not leave the island.[189]

Although the focus of this chapter has been the feudatories and the humble people of Candia, the nature of the sources and the consequences of differences in social rank led us to approach them in different ways, with the result that different sorts of conclusions about each group were arrived at. In the case of the feudatories, they were not a homogenous group in either ethnic background or social rank. The lack of like data about the commoners of Candia compelled us to address in a much more direct manner their ethnic composition, patterns of residence, and occupational features, but the results were similar. Therefore it was not, nor is it now, possible to speak in terms of biologically distinct Latin and Greek populations. Far too much intermarriage occurred for either community, but especially the Latin one, to claim ethnic homogeneity. Despite the Venetian Senate's appeal to "flesh of our flesh," the feudatory group was not uniformly "Latin" in any way corresponding to what could be called objective. The ambiguity of the commoners' ethnicity in the sources reveals a degree of acculturation in daily life that must have made it impossible to distinguish reliably and consistently between Latins and Greeks by sight and sound. Consequently the next question must be: where, then, were the boundaries that separated the Greek and Latin communities? The reasonable place to look for them is in the cultural sphere of Candiote life.

3

"The Obligation of
Our Blood"

> *Hector*   Why then will I no more.
> Thou art, great lord, my father's sister's son.
> A cousin german to great Priam's seed.
> The obligation of our blood forbids
> A gory emulation 'twixt us twain.
> Were the commixtion Greek and Troyan so
> That thou couldst say, "This hand is Grecian all
> And this is Troyan, the sinews of this leg
> All Greek, and this all Troy; my mother's blood
> Runs on the dexter cheek, and this sinister
> Bounds in my father's," by Jove multipotent,
> Thou shouldst not bear from me a Greekish member
> Wherein my sword had not impressure made
> Of our rank feud. But the just gods gainsay
> That any drop thou borrow'dst from thy mother,
> My sacred aunt, should by my mortal sword
> Be drained. Let me embrace thee, Ajax![1]

IN SHAKEPEARE'S *Troilus and Cressida*, Hector's appeal to Ajax on grounds of kinship ought to strike the modern reader as ironic. The idea of a person's mixed ethnic heritage manifesting itself corporally like a patchwork quilt is meant to be ludicrous, the Trojan's noble sentiments notwithstanding. His sentiment is furthermore ironic because, when one takes the time to think about it, "the obligation of our blood" is never so strong as to forbid fighting. On the contrary, one might argue that the obligation of blood is most real when bloodshed is its object. The seventeenth century witnessed the slow development of the concept of "blood" and race to replace old, outmoded notions of ethnicity that had once relied so heavily on religion, language, and law for definition. Situated still in the fourteenth century, the colonial society of Candia has not yet arrived at that point. Racial notions of "limpieza di sangre" lie quite a way off in the distance, but, standing at harbor's edge, looking beyond the *mole* emblazoned with the lion of San Marco, they can be seen on the horizon.

In the previous two chapters, my purpose was to establish the historical framework of the colony; to expose some of the intrinsic social relations imbedded in the colony's structure; to excavate, mostly from notarial documents, the kinship networks of the feudatory group; and to examine the non-feudatory population's two main ethnic communities and the degree of integration between them. We have seen how the political, colonial exigencies of the period compelled Venice to allow more Greek archontic families into the circle of feudatories. Even before permission was officially given, neither the archontes nor some portions of the Latin feudatories wasted any time in establishing marriage alliances between themselves, with the result that the feudatory group contained not only Greek noble families, but also key Latin families with kinship ties to those former families, some of whom, like the Calergi, were not even members of the feudatories' councils. A similar state of affairs prevailed among the commoners of Candia, where intermarriage led to a degree of blending, if not of the groups themselves, then certainly of their outward aspect.

With these points in mind, it is time to broach the matter of ethnicity from a modern perspective. Religion, language, customs, and a belief in a common descent are the markers that most scholars interested in the history of ethnicity agree define the populations of Europe.[2] Following Robert Bartlett, I would add law to the list, less because it played a role in ethnicity in Crete, which it decidedly did, but because in that very realm an historically significant change came about.[3] All these markers except law are elective in a fundamental sense. A person can choose which church to worship in and under certain conditions learn another ethnic group's language; cultural customs such as dress or hairstyle may be adopted by anyone. Belief in common descent is seemingly "objective," in that an individual person is or is not biologically descended from a people. Manufacturing mythical pasts, however, constituted a veritable cottage industry among most state-sponsored intellectual programs of the pre-modern era, with the result that it is nearly impossible at times to determine by any so-called objective criteria just exactly from what or from whom a group is descended.[4] I will not belabor further the elective qualities of ethnic markers, except to say that for all their mutability, once pressed into service as the generally agreed-upon defining features of a people, they become nonetheless real and cannot be underestimated in their ability to mobilize that group.

Religion, language, customs, law, and a belief in a common descent are markers that the people of the time, too, would have singled out to delineate the Latin and Greek populations of Candia at the beginning of the colony's existence. As time passed and the populations continued to live side by side, the markers did not so much disappear or converge as they changed shape. The differences at first were obvious. Greeks adhered to the Greek church that rejected the chain of command insisted on by the Latin church, to which the majority of people of Latin descent adhered. At the start of the colony, the indigenous people of the island spoke Greek and the conquerors spoke Venetian. Differences in dress and hairstyle, such as Greek men's beards, made it easy in the early thirteenth century to discern by sight who was a Greek and who a Latin. A uniform belief in a common descent is fairly easy to discern among Latins and Greeks. For one thing, the Venetian Senate had on more than one occasion to remind the feudatories, in particular, of their Venetian descent. Latin people displayed a preference for various aspects of Latin culture, such as funeral rites, in the documents they have drawn up. Among the Greeks, a belief in a common descent emerges from sources relating to the Greek nobility of the island, and there is the occasional expression of collective sentiment among humble Greeks. But there is little direct evidence to confirm such a belief among the peasantry, although I am inclined to believe in its existence, with limitations.[5] Significantly, only one Greek testator expresses a wish for his daughter to marry a Greek, while the only preferences Latin testators display are the wishes of noble Venetian fathers for their daughters to marry noblemen.[6]

And at the heart of this latter minor feature to emerge from the wills is a large lesson. Membership in one ethnic group or the other was deeply conditioned by two factors, class and gender. Existentially, the experience of being Latin and being Greek was not uniform throughout Candiote society. Because in practice the boundaries separating the two communities mattered more than what they enclosed, their location depended on the section of the population they surrounded.[7] A look at religion and language, the two markers most accessible to us through the medium of documentary and literary sources, and a consideration of how they manifested themselves on the different levels of Candiote society and between men and women will make this plain.

Religion as Ethnic Marker

In response to a delegation of feudatories who had complained that "bastards" were acquiring *feuda* as well as seats on Candiote's Great Council, the

Venetian Signoria wrote a letter to the duke of Candia in 1302, in which it equated bastards with Greeks and decreed that they could neither possess a *feudum* nor sit on the Great Council.[8] The Great Council of Candia accepted this decree two months later.[9] Fifty-four years later, in 1356, a delegation of feudatories to Venice once again made the same complaint to the Signoria. They claimed that the Great Council was in a ruinous state because of the presence of "indigenous" members (*personae indigenae*), presumably meaning Greeks. This time, as we saw in the first chapter, even firmer reforms in the election process, the *proba*, resulted in an attempt to ensure that Greeks did not gain access to *feuda* or seats on the council.

And yet there they still are, even in the first *proba* conducted in December 1356 for the following year. At least seven Greek Cretan families won seats on the Great Council between the years 1357 and 1363: Caliva, Flabani, Iallina, Plachena, Poltroni, Saclichi, and Stadi.[10] To make matters even more complicated, the presence of Greeks was not even confined to the larger Great Council. They also appear in the smaller and more influential Candiote Senate. Between 1341 and 1363, the same Greek families consistently had members in that body. The Iallina family had two representatives in 1358 and 1359; the Stadi family had two in 1360. Moreover, Greeks were certainly in positions of responsibility before the 1302 decree, and they are evident in the advisory councils for most of the century after that year. The problem did not end there. In fact, in 1362 the Venetian Senate noted that the election to the Candiote Great Council was once again taking place in great disorder and instructed the duke of Candia and his councillors to ensure that neither Greeks nor bastards gained access to the advisory bodies.[11]

Without question part of the problem was the hostility of noblemen toward the promotion of illegitimate sons of their peers and women of servile rank, who happened to be Greek.[12] Aside from the promotion of illegitimate sons into the feudatory group, the Candiote feudatories and the Signoria appear also to have had in mind people they wished to exclude from their midst other than those whom we would expect. If the aim of both parties was to remove Greeks from the feudatories, how can the continued presence of archontic families on the Great Council and the Senate be explained, given the complaints about them from the feudatories themselves and given Venice's repeated ban? The earlier delegation of feudatories to Venice had complained about "bastards" and the Signoria had taken this to mean Greeks; and I assume that something similar lay behind the complaint of 1356, to which the Signoria responded in like manner. The Signoria and the Latin feudatories either made exceptions for these families or they did not consider them Greek.

Whichever the reason, what made those families acceptable and others not? The most plausible explanation is the church in which they worshiped. Latins and Greeks both were Christian peoples and viewed each other as such, but each side considered the other schismatic, possibly heretical, and certainly intellectually inferior. Although the Latin and Greek churches had more in common theologically with each other than they did with the other churches of the eastern Mediterranean (both subscribing to the canons of the Council of Chalcedon), they disagreed profoundly on questions of ecclesiastical authority.[13] The Greek church rejected the primacy of the see of St. Peter, which of course formed the bedrock of the Latin church. A number of other disputes, including the famous *filioque* debate, the use of leavened (Greek) or unleavened (Latin) bread in the Eucharist, fasting, the manner of crossing oneself, and other differences in customs such as the veneration of icons, all mattered less than the question of authority.[14] Just as the Byzantine emperor did not recognize the papacy's claims to superior authority, the pope as bishop of Rome refused to recognize the authority of a lay ruler, as he thought of the emperor, in ecclesiastical affairs.

After the Fourth Crusade of 1204, when the Byzantine Empire disappeared from the political scene for approximately sixty years, the Venetians and the papacy set about in fits and starts, without, it must be said, a great deal of forethought, establishing a Latin church in the former Byzantine territory.[15] In the decades after it had conquered Crete, Venice sponsored there the installation of a new ecclesiastical hierarchy, in the form of one archbishop and ten bishops, and welcomed the arrival of the mendicant orders. But in Crete as in Venice, the church, Roman certainly, but also, to borrow Giorgio Fedalto's term, *venezianizzata*, was firmly subordinated to the exigencies of the Venetian regime.[16]

When Venice put in place the regime that would govern the island, it allowed the Greek clergy to continue ministering to their flocks more or less as they had been doing, without the benefit, however, of their upper hierarchy and with a liturgy revised to meet the standards of the papacy. The island's Greek episcopate was exiled and replaced by either Latin bishops or Greek bishops recognizing the authority of Rome.[17] All Latin clergy and only a portion of the Greek clergy came under the sole jurisdiction of the Latin archbishop of Crete. As a result, the regime's relations with and security measures concerning the Greek church had to contend with the intervening claims of the Latin church. The Concession of Crete from 1211 set the stage for future conflict between the regime and the archbishop in the clause that addressed the status of the Greek church in the island: "You must maintain the freedom of the churches of the island and their ministers, but their possessions will be at the disposition of the duke, who will be there with his council."[18] A clause such as this was bound to put the archbishop of Crete in an ambiguous position, but not one inconsistent with Venice's pragmatic policies toward the church in the metropolis. Apart from one other clause enjoining military settlers to celebrate the feasts of the Nativity, the Resurrection, St. Mark, and the feast of the principal church of Crete, ecclesiastical matters are completely absent from the document.[19] Later on, the feast of St. John the Baptist would be added to that list.[20] That in those first years of colonization the Greek church was uppermost in the Venetian authorities' mind when it considered the conquest of the island suggests that Venice had not yet envisioned the arrival of Latin ecclesiastics to assume leadership of both the Latin and Greek churches.

Once the emissaries of the Latin patriarch of Constantinople and the papacy set about imposing an ecclesiastical structure over the colony, competing jurisdictions flourished. In the years following the conquest, the Latin archbishop of Crete repeatedly locked horns with the monks of Mt. Sinai, who owned a considerable amount of property on the island. In those circumstances, the papacy time and again came to the defense of the monastery against what the pope considered the abuses of his own prelate.[21] For its part, the Venetian Senate and the regime of Crete did not allow much of its authority to slip through its fingers and into the hands of the Latin church, under the leadership of the archbishop of Crete, with whom it, too, engaged in struggles over jurisdictional rights.[22] Nevertheless, it had to respect the competence of ecclesiastical courts, although the original injunction placed on the regime in the *Concessio* did not leave much room for them. Crete's highest prelate insisted on the primacy of his own jurisdiction in matters that the church felt were rightly adjudicated in an ecclesiastical court, such as cases involving Greek or Latin clergy or the validity or dissolution of a marriage.[23]

Although the archbishop had continual problems in his relationship with the regime in Crete, time and again provoking appeals to the papacy, conflict between secular and ecclesiastical authorities had little effect on the indigenous clergy of the island.[24] From the start of Venetian dominion over Crete, Greek priests continued to minister to their congregants according to the rites of the Greek church. Some Cretan priests living in villages were villeins, but the majority of those in the city and burg were not of servile

status, as Thiriet suggested.[25] The wills show that the population faithful to
the Greek church had access to a complete offering of liturgy, ranging from
the Eucharist to funeral rites. They even had at least one confraternity of
their own.[26] The only restriction on their worship was the requirement that
Greek priests be ordained on the island. In 1326, Pope John XXII allowed
for the creation of a Greek bishop, faithful to the Latin church but a fol-
lower of the rites of the Greek church, who would, among other episcopal
duties, ordain candidates for priesthood in the Greek church. The pope's
policy has been summed up succinctly as "one faith and two rites."[27] The
essence of the restriction, urged repeatedly on the regime by the papacy,
amounted to the prohibition of Greek candidates for priesthood to seek
ordination off the island by a Greek bishop elsewhere in the Byzantine
Empire. Beyond that, the Greek clergy were divided between a group of
130 in the district of Candia, who were answerable solely to the archbishop
of Crete, and the remainder, over whom the regime held jurisdiction. At the
head of the clergy under the jurisdiction of the regime was the *protopapas*,
followed in rank by the *protopsaltes*, both elected by the clergy they directed
with the approval of the regime.[28] The number of 130 Greek priests did not
include the priests of the countryside, about whom little is known because
of lack of sources. But whether in the city or the countryside, those who
sought the Greek liturgy had no trouble finding a church in which it was
celebrated. Greek churches throughout the island formed the majority of
churches, reflecting the population's ethnic makeup. It was primarily in the
towns that they had to take a back seat in status, though not in numbers, to
Latin churches. The Latin church appropriated some Byzantine churches
and converted them to the Latin rite, and a good number more were newly
built. Consequently, throughout the first two centuries of Venetian rule,
and very likely for much longer, the Latin church was a creature of the cities,
for few Latin priests ventured out into the countryside to officiate in village
churches.[29] The dominance of the Latin church, however, did not stem the
natural growth of the Greek church, as the population changed and grew.
Over twenty new Greek churches appeared in Candia's suburbs in the first
part of the fourteenth century, according to one art historian.[30]

The prohibition of the ordination of Cretan priests by Greek prelates
elsewhere in the Aegean remained in force during the thirteenth and fourteenth centuries, but by 1360 a growing number of irregularities had occurred, requiring the attention of the Candiote Senate. Over a period of
nearly a week in the month of October of that year, the *rogati* debated
reforming the manner according to which Greek priests might receive or-

dination. The only point that the members of the Candiote Senate seemed to agree on was the status quo: those seeking ordination in the Eastern rites were not permitted to leave the island. Oddly, the impression one receives from reading the *pars* ultimately voted down by the *rogati* is that it was the Roman clergy, not the secular authorities, who were being too lax in granting special permission to leave the island for ordination. A renewal of the prohibition forbidding any Greek monk or other wishing to become a priest to leave the island finally passed by a vote of forty-five in favor, two opposed and four abstaining.[31] By the end of the century, the climate had obviously changed somewhat. In reward for services unspecified, the duke's court in the first six months of 1391 permitted eight Greek men to seek ordination from a Greek bishop away from Crete.[32] For reasons not given, most of the candidates were supported by the petitions of Latin men.

The resentment these restrictions evoked among the Greek population as a whole can be gauged by the fact that, as we will see in the next chapter, revoking this prohibition became the first official act of the rebel government of 1363, and was later immediately nullified by the reinstated Venetian regime. The rebels' revocation of the prohibition is certainly a testament to the pivotal role that religion played in the relations between the regime and the Greek community.[33] The Greek community's hostility toward the importunate Latin church must have been palpable at the time, as witness the depiction of Franciscans and cardinals on the losing side of the Last Judgement scenes in the fourteenth-century church of St. John at Kritsa, but whether this tension remained an active ingredient dividing the Greek from the humble, lay Latin population is less clear.[34]

To return to the puzzle of why certain Greeks were allowed on the Great Council of Candia and others were not, did the Greek archontes among the members of the Candiote councils follow the rites of the Latin church and recognize the primacy of the pope? Was this what rendered their presence there benign? Did this make them no longer Greek in the eyes of the Venetian Senate?

If we rely on the assumption that an attachment to one church or another expressed in a will is indicative of that testator's practice of worship within his or her lifetime, the wills are our best informants in this regard. To put the information contained in the wills into perspective, the testators comprise 653 Latin and Greek Cretan men and women and 36 Jews.[35] Of those 653 Latin and Greek testators, 119 (16 percent) make bequests exclusively to the Greek church and clerics.[36] Of the 60 male testators who made bequests exclusively to the Greek church, three were Greek feudatories.[37]

The remainder were humble Greek men. Only one of the 59 female testators who left a pious legacy solely to the Greek church was the wife of a
Greek feudatory, and she lived in the early fifteenth century.[38] Of the 653
testators, 283 (43 percent) made bequests exclusively to Latin clergy and/
or Latin religious institutions. Among those testators who left sums of
money to the Latin church figure ten testators who were Greek.[39] Two of
those were feudatories: Petrus Çampani, son of the late ser Ioannes Çampani, and Ioannes Ialina, son of the late ser Michael.[40]

The 1348 will of Ioannes, son of Michael Ialina, one of several wills
made by Greek feudatories, supports the proposition that only Greek noblemen who followed the Latin rites could acquire a seat in the feudatories'
councils. The will is replete with pious bequests to the Franciscans, Dominicans, Augustinians, hospitals, and *scuole*, including a flagellant order (not
surprising, in that year of plague). After bequeathing money to the church
of Santa Maria della Misericordia in Venice, he sets aside a sum for the
construction in Candia of a church to be dedicated to San Giuliano, to
whom he was especially devoted. He even reveals that his own brother is a
member of the Franciscan Order. A thoroughly Roman adherent indeed.

The 1353 will of another Ioannes Ialina stands at first glance in contrast, because this testator left legacies to both churches, suggesting that his
allegiance to the Latin liturgy was not a requirement of his feudatory status,
which latter is indicated by his wealth and the signs that show him to have
been a kinsman of Latin feudatory families.[41] Unlike the first Ioannes, this
one displays an ambiguous attachment to the Greek church, even though
his daughter was married to a Latin feudatory. He leaves money to the
infirmary of San Lazaro and the church of Santa Domenica, two Latin
institutions. He follows with bequests to the church of Santi Apostoli in the
village of Pigaidulia and to the family establishment, the church of the
Mother of God "de Chera Ialini." To address the latter bequest first, this
church of which the Ialina were patrons may have been a Latin church,
since the Ialina family is known to have switched allegiance to the Latin
church at some point during the first two centuries of Venetian rule. One
will casts doubt on the Latin liturgy being celebrated, at any rate exclusively,
in the Ialina church. In 1361 Antonios Chandachyti elected to be buried in
the church of the Ialina and asked that the *presbyter* (a Latin term) there
enter him in his memorial roll, a Greek practice.[42]

There is more to Ioannes' first bequest to the Greek church of Pigaidulia than meets the eye. In his will of 1348, Nicolaos Plachina, a Greek feudatory, also displays an impressive devotion to the Latin church.[43] His first
pious bequest is the very generous sum of three hundred hyperpera to the

new hospital of the *scuola* of Santa Maria of the Crusaders. Numerous other bequests go to individual priests, all with Latin names, at the churches belonging to the orders of the Augustinians, the Franciscans, and the Dominicans. Nicolaos even singled out a *converso* member of the Augustinians, Brother Iohannes de Spoliti. Toward the end of his pious bequests to Latin clergy begin his bequests to the Greek church. To the *papas* Ianni, who lives in the village of Mulia (which apparently belonged to Nicolaos), he bequeaths fifteen hyperpera so that the Greek priest might perform memorial liturgies for the benefit of his soul. He leaves money for the enlargement of the church dedicated to San Nicolaos in the same village, presumably a Greek church, since it is in a village.

Ioannes Ialina's and Nicolaos Plachina's bequests are typical of the feudatories' tendency, whether they were Latin or Greek, to remember in their wills the Greek priest or the church in the villages they possessed. They saw nothing to be lost and possibly salvation to be gained by commending their souls to the village priests on their own land. In fact, either because one of their parents was Greek or out of simple concern for the churches in their villages, sixteen Latin feudatories leave small sums to the churches located in the villages to which they held rights; those churches were undoubtedly Greek.[44] The wills of nine Latin women married to feudatories exhibit the same tendency to make bequests to the Greek churches in villages belonging to their husbands.[45]

To begin with two examples, Giuliano Natale, a Candiote Latin feudatory, made his will in 1334. He appears to have been a pious man, to judge from the number of bequests he made to religious institutions and clergy. The majority of them went to institutions of the Latin church. A few, however, suggest that Giuliano had been immersed in a Greek environment enough to absorb at least a minimal appreciation or tolerance of the Greek church and its clergy. After having left small sums to the Franciscans, the Augustinians, the hospital of St. Mary of the Crusaders, and the nuns of St. George and St. Catherine for prayers, Giuliano set aside ten hyperpera, more than he had thus far dispensed to any one Roman institution, for the painting (*pro pictura*) of the church of St. Anne in his village.[46] Later on in the text of his will, he singled out the priest of the church of St. Anne, *papas* Georgios Calopti, a resident of the same village, who was to officiate at the church for the remainder of the Greek priest's life. Another Latin feudatory testator, Michaletto Maufredo, in 1376 left a sum to help with the repair of the church of Sant'Antonio dei Greci, which he explicitly states is contiguous with the Latin church dedicated to the same saint.[47]

One last example of a Latin feudatory will make the point even more clearly. In 1328, a recent immigrant to Candia who became a feudatory, Niccolò Bellino Dandolo, possessed a *feudum* that included rights to the church of St. Mary, near the cathedral of St. Tito. He contracted with a Latin priest (*presbyter*), Marino Valerio, for its operation and maintenance over a three-year period. Moreover, Niccolò furnished the priest with, among other things, a chalice of gold-plated silver, an amice, a shirt, a linen belt, a golden stole, a missal, and an altar cloth. The priest's salary was to be twelve hyperpera a year, in addition to the revenues and gifts to the church.[48] This is a perfectly sound business transaction between a Latin feudatory and a priest of the church whose rites he followed. But in 1355 Giovanni and Vidal, the sons of the by-then late Niccolò Bellino Dandolo, hired Nemfo, a Greek monk, to restore the ruined monastery of St. Mary of Fraschea that their father held in rent from the Comune. Nemfo was to maintain the monastery according to an ecclesiastical rule (without specifying which one), to live there, and to build a kiln (*fornas*) as quickly as possible, in order to complete the construction of the church, which the monastery lacked. Furthermore, Nemfo was to build cells and install monks in them to live there and care for the church and its land. Whatever they managed to earn from the usufruct of their crops they were to keep, for the love of God and the benefit of Niccolò Bellino's soul. If Nemfo should die, the brothers retained full rights to find other monks to replace them and inhabit the monastery. A small group of men including other Latin feudatories witnessed this document, which for reasons unknown but agreed to by all parties was annulled two months later.[49] What is most interesting about this document is that two noble brothers evidently felt that they were doing their father's soul much good by bringing back to life a Greek monastery inhabited by Greek monks, regardless of their legal responsibility to fulfill their father's last wishes.[50] By a stroke of good luck, their father's marriage contract has survived, and in it we learn that his wife may have been a daughter of a Greek archontic family, if her father's name is anything to go by: Francesca, daughter of Angelos Teocari.[51]

Lest it be thought that this sentiment of responsibility for their land and the people who lived on it emerges only in testamentary moments and does not reflect the same concern in life, a contract from 1386 reveals the same sense of responsibility by a Latin feudatory towards the Greek churches in his villages. In it, Ioannes Mussuro, a *papas* and resident of Candia, agrees to move with his household to the village of Gurnes, which belongs to the Latin feudatory, Giorgio della Porta, son of the late ser Stamati. The *papas* agrees to live in the village for three years to officiate in the church there "according to the custom and rite of the Greeks (*iuxta usum et ritum grecorum*)." In return, Giorgio has to provide the priest with two houses (*domus*) in the village, grain, and wine, and to require every man in the village who has a pair of oxen to give him two measures of grain and those who have no oxen one measure of grain.[52] Thus we can explain the bequest to a Greek village church in the will of the first Ioannes Ialina, discussed above, in a similar way. It was a bequest motivated more by a landowner's concern about the welfare of the residents on his property than it was an indication of his own spiritual inclinations or ethnic allegiances. A bequest such as Ioannes's, like similar bequests made by the other feudatories, Latin and Greek, does not belie the apparent rule that adherence to the rites of the Latin church was an important measure of a Greek nobleman's incorporation into the Candiote feudatory group. Still, I cannot help wondering just how formal the Greek feudatories' devotion to the Latin church was, because the wills of Greek women married to Latin feudatories tell a slightly different story.

Greek female testators married to Latin men reveal in their wills an attachment to the Greek church that needs explaining in light of the evidence that shows a coincidence between the Greek archontes' feudatory status and adherence to the Latin church. For instance, Agnes, the wife of a member of the noble Corner family, was the daughter of the nobleman Alexios I Calergi, with whom and with whose family we have spent considerable time in the last chapter. In the will she made in 1331, she favors Greek churches and clergy almost exclusively in her bequests.[53] Another testator, Elena Muazzo, was born a Ialina and married a Latin feudatory.[54] Even though the Ialina men whose wills we examined were adherents of the Latin church, Elena remembered in her 1360 will both the Latin and Greek churches. At the beginning of her bequests, she expresses a desire to be buried in the Franciscan church, as befitted the wife of a Candiote feudatory. After donating money to that order, she goes on to bequeath sums of money to the monastery of Mt. Sinai in Candia and to a Greek priest, Constantinos Adrianopoliti, who was apparently connected with it. These last two legacies do not correspond to the kind of legacies feudatories tended to leave the people living on their land and in their villages, since the monastery of Mt. Sinai was an institution independent of any *feudum*. In another will, dated 1331, Marina, the widow of a Latin feudatory, Niccolò Zancarolo, states that she is the daughter of Fucha Vanichi, a Greek nobleman.[55] After expressing her wish for the entire Greek clergy of Candia to be present at her burial at the monastery of Mt. Sinai, an indication that she, too, was a woman of some importance, she bequeathed small amounts of money to several Greek churches. One of those bequests was to the church of the Holy Savior of Caloydhena, "so that I might be inscribed in their memorial rolls (*ut scribar in suo condachi*)," a practice typical of the Greek church.[56] The Latin church does not figure at all among her legacies. The exception to this group of Greek women married to Latin feudatories is Agnes, daughter of the late ser Ioannes Caliva, a Greek feudatory, and widow of ser Giovanni Vassalo, a Latin feudatory. The bequests in her will of 1341 fit the pattern seen in the wills of Greek and Latin feudatory men, whose first allegiance is to the Latin church and their status as feudatories. Agnes has a long list of pious donations to Latin religious institutions, at the end of which she bequeaths the sum of fifteen hyperpera to the construction of a church dedicated to St. George in the village of Asimi.[57]

To summarize what has been observed thus far, since none of the Greek male feudatory testators revealed an exclusive devotion to the Greek church, adherence to the Latin rite had something to do with, perhaps was the prerequisite of, a Greek man's membership in the feudatory group of Candia.[58] Furthermore, the regime viewed religion as a Greek ethnic marker, a point that will become clear farther on. Is it possible that Greek feudatory women's attachment to the Greek church had less bearing on their status as feudatory wives than did the religious disposition of Greek men? It was evidently easier for a Greek woman married into the Latin feudatory group to maintain her adherence to the church of her cultural heritage than it was for a Greek man of the same rank. If the men who belonged to the feudatory group were not considered Greek on this basis, were the women married into the feudatory group who continued to worship in the church of their cultural heritage considered more so?

Below the social level of the feudatory group, in the governmental, literary, and notarial sources there is no neat division between the Latin secular and ecclesiastical hierarchy ranged with the Latin population, on the one hand, and the Greek hierarchy and population on the other. In part, clerical labels obscure the boundaries. A Greek priest is usually signaled by the title *papas* and a Greek monastic by *calogerus* or *calogera*. A Latin priest bore the title *presbyter* while a Latin monastic, male or female, was referred to as *monacus* or *monaca*. Unfortunately, the application of these titles falls short of perfect consistency. Occasionally, it is difficult to know whether a Greek man with the title *presbyter* in a document was a priest who officiated according to the Greek or the Latin liturgy. As one example, Cherana, the wife of Nicolaos Corfioti, who lived in the village of Bassia, refers to the priests of her village as *presbyteri*, but, being in the countryside, it is highly unlikely that they were Latin priests.[59] Other examples of loose usage of clerical terms exist.[60]

When we find the word *presbyter* in a will such as Georgio Zeno's used to mean a Greek priest, then we know that the entire field of inquiry is laid with mines.[61] This document, made in 1360, is rich with ethnic ambiguity, typical of the Cretan archives. Georgio may have been Latin, as his name suggests, but there is little among his bequests to support that notion. More than likely, he was born of a Latin father and a Greek mother. He, his mother Irini, and his brother Marco were residents of the burg, while another brother, Franco, resided inside the city. When he made his will, Georgio was a widower with one underage son, Zanaki. To judge from the nature and amounts of his bequests, he was not a wealthy man. He instructed his executors to sell all his movable goods, except for a small bed and its linens that were to go to his son. With the money from the sale, his executors were to find a Greek priest (*alicui presbytero greco*) of good standing to officiate for five years in the church dedicated to St. Anne, to which he possessed the rights. When those five years had passed, the executors were to buy as quickly as possible a slave who was a Greek priest from Turkey or elsewhere and, after freeing him, to give him the position of priest of his church, as his late wife desired. And all this would be for the remission of his, his late wife's, and his family's sins.[62] What Giorgio had in mind was clearly a cleric of the Greek church, yet we have little insight into why he chose the word *presbyter* instead of *papas*.

It is possible that the notary and not the client chose the word, since all clients' desires and instructions passed through the filter of the notaries' written craft. And yet, in one will, we find both terms employed in single bequest. Stefano Capelario, who resided in the fortress of Themenos and made his will in 1339, asked that "the *presbyter* Theodoros, *papas* Georgos, and *papas* Andreas be present at my burial and I leave one hyperperon to each of them."[63] Was Theodoros a Latin priest? It is unlikely, since his name was very atypical of Latin priests' names, even in the fourteenth century. Stefano's other bequests unfortunately do not reveal to which church he principally adhered. Therefore, just as a name was no longer a reliable indicator of the community to which a person belonged, the titles attributed to clergy contain the very real possibility of confusion.

Despite this problem, the bequests of humble testators suggest that within the city and the burg humble Latins and Greeks developed attachments to institutions of both churches perhaps more easily than testators from the feudatory group. Among the feudatories there are few bequests to the Greek church that seem unconnected to either the *feudum* or the memory of a close relative, usually a mother, who was Greek and still adhered to the Greek church. On the lower social levels, however, pious bequests conform to no obvious pattern, least of all one reflecting a sense of proprietarial responsibility. Fourteen male and female testators make bequests to both Latin and Greek religious establishments, a small sample indeed, but not entirely meaningless.[64] I would argue that these testators, who show a desire to benefit from the prayers and masses/liturgies of both churches, are a product of an urban environment in which neither Latin nor Greek churches and institutions could be ignored by either community. If peasants of the countryside had made wills (which I doubt that many did), and if many of them had survived, I doubt that we would find the same spirit of ecumenicism in them as we find in the wills of city residents. Familiarity, contrary to the adage, does not always breed contempt.

Familiarity, in fact, led to a convergence of spiritual sentiment among the Greeks, the Latins, and the regime of Candia during the fourteenth century in the form of a shared veneration of St. Tito, the patron saint of the island, recognized as such by all parties. Both communities apparently played a part in popular forms of worship, involving processions and icons. For instance, the famous and much-revered icon of the Virgin *Mesopanditissa*, which was kept in the cathedral, became a focal point for both communities' devotion and as such was accepted by the Venetian authorities.[65]

This is not to say at all that the people of Candia made little distinction between the two churches. On the contrary, a very clear line, running mostly along liturgical lines, divided the population. To turn again to the wills, some testators specify by which rites they wish to be buried, or commemorated, or according to which custom their dowries were valued.[66] No one in Candia became blind to the existence of a Latin and a Greek community, no matter how much interaction, how much laxity there might have been in which church people attended. A higher standard of behavior prevailed within the Greek male feudatory group, insofar as they had to protect their status by adhering to the politically determined markers of the group, but women at the feudatory level and men and women below the feudatory level relaxed their vigilance over the boundaries of the ethnic groups to which they belonged without relinquishing them entirely. There simply was less at stake, from the regime's point of view, in those more humble sections of the population, which explains to some extent why it is so difficult to tell whether a Candiote commoner is Greek or Latin. Religious worship remained an important ethnic marker, delineating and motivating the two populations, but it is not a coincidence that it is least ambiguous as a marker in the group where it had the most direct political implications, the group whose principal charge was occupation of the island in Venice's name.

Language as Ethnic Marker

Language was another principal medium by which the Latin and Greek cultural spheres manifested themselves, but the manner in which they did so was little more straightforward or easily categorized than were the churches to which the two communities adhered. The sheer numerical superiority of the Greek-speaking population gave a large lead to the Greek language and therefore Greek culture in general. But even though the Latin community was very small, its cultural dominance of the city was great, thanks to Latin being the administrative and judicial language of the colony, and to the regular influx of officials, immigrants, and merchants arriving from Venice. Venetian culture in Crete was, moreover, almost entirely an urban culture, like its prototype. Hence the Greek population's attraction to it for the advantages that familiarity with it conferred helped shift the balance somewhat in favor of Latin culture.

"Language as an ethnic marker" is a somewhat misleading heading for this section, because the day-to-day spoken languages of Candia, unlike the cultural expressions of those languages, were not largely confined to one community or the other. In the eyes of neither Candiotes nor the government was language an ethnic marker. Many people of Latin descent spoke Greek as their first language; not quite so many people of Greek descent spoke Italian, in spite of its advantages in trade, but enough to make that tongue useless as the determining ethnic criterion. On this point most scholars agree: many Latins of Candia spoke Greek fluently, if not as their first language.[67] Furthermore, literacy in general seems to have been at a relatively high level among a restricted group of people in Crete, but it is doubtful how broadly it was achieved through that population. Although he characterized education in Crete during our period as being of "a comparatively high standard," the late Cretan scholar Nikolaos Panagiotakes was struck by how many witnesses to sixteenth-century notarial contracts were able to sign their names.[68] A glance at the signatures at the conclusions of the wills from the fourteenth century reveals that, as labored as some signatures might look, some Candiote men in the fourteenth century knew how to write.[69] The names of the testators who reveal that they composed a document in their own hand, or that another person who was not a notary had done so, suggest that the general level of education in Candia had not yet reached a very high level in our period. With very few exceptions, all those who are capable of writing more than their signature come from the feudatory group. Among those feudatories, moreover, many either had moved to the colony from Venice or were still residents of Venice. The only Greek man, Georgios Filaretis, who states that he wrote his will with his own hand was a notary. No women suggest that they possessed such skills.

At the same time, however, nearly all the 790 wills that have survived from the fourteenth century have the signatures of the witnesses attached. In some instances those witnesses are clerics and/or notaries, but no means all. One entry in the court records suggests that writing was a fairly typical skill for people to have. A widow presented to the court a document purported to contain the last wishes of her late husband, written in his own hand. Because he died before he could have a notary draw it up in a public charter, his widow asked the court to validate the document as her husband's will. The court agreed to her demand, only after two witnesses swore under oath that they recognized the handwriting of the document as that of the late husband. Evidently, handwriting was sufficiently characteristic of an individual to be identified as such.[70]

As I said, language, failing as an ethnic marker, nevertheless remained an important medium by which the two communities marked themselves off from each other. As they did in matters concerning religion, the Greeks and Latins of Candia tended to align themselves with one nominal community or the other when it came to choosing which language to learn, which music to play, which religious or philosophical texts to study, and in which style of painting to adorn the walls of their churches, even though an outsider visiting Crete would be unable to pinpoint where Greek culture left off and Latin culture began. From an historical perspective, their cultural choices were never neutral.

For the people of Candia, both Greek and Latin, limited schooling in Latin and Italian was available. What notice there is of Candiote schools in the fourteenth century is slight, but it shows that an education was usually available for those who could pay for it.[71] Only three teachers, working in the early part of the century, have been found. There is notice of a *grammaticus* named Michael, about whom nothing more is known, except that his title usually denotes a teacher on the secondary level.[72] Master Pietro di Narnia of Spoleto left behind numerous traces of himself in the notarial protocols. He also calls himself a *grammaticus*, suggesting that he, too, taught on a level higher than basic tuition.[73] And then there is Bartholomeo de Hengelardis, briefly met in the Introduction as an imperial notary and owner of legal texts.[74]

Pietro di Narnia ran a school behind the cathedral of St. Tito, adjoined to another church, during the 1320s and '30s. In 1327 he hired an assistant, Galacino d'Arimano, a resident of Candia, for twenty hyperpera a year to help him with teaching his students to read, recite, and write, probably in Latin. Galacino was also put in charge of managing Pietro's account books. In return, Pietro's new assistant had to promise not to teach in any other school in Candia or its suburb so long as Pietro ran a school in Crete.[75] Pietro's school must have been a success, because within the same year he had to hire another assistant, this time the son of a cobbler. Two years later he took on the son of a woolworker to perform the same duties as the others.[76] These two assistants, who came from the lower levels of Candiote society, indicate that in as small a world as Candia's an artisan's son could receive an education, if he could pay for it.

As the reference to Pietro's account books suggests, teaching was not his only source of income. He seems also to have been a moneylender of substance. On two occasions, he lent large sums of money to a surgeon and to a feudatory, which shows that he had more cash at his disposal than did most feudatories.[77] Pietro also bought wine in large enough quantities that he may have been involved in its exportation off the island. In one transaction, subsequently canceled, he even agreed to teach the son of a feudatory in exchange for a considerable amount of wine.[78] No one occupation in Candia sufficed for any resident, and so it is not surprising to find a man like Pietro seeking to extend his income. He appeared indeed to be a man of some substance and reputation, lending money here, taking on employees there, even apparently dabbling in wine export.

Bartolomeo de Hengelardis had a varied career, typical of notaries in that period. By the time he made his will in 1342, he apparently no longer taught school, since he still owed money for the rent of the warehouse where it had once been located.[79] Like Pietro di Narnia, he had other ways of making his living. In the only other document in which his name has appeared thus far, dated to 1327, he is described as an imperial notary residing in Candia, a profession that his will confirms only indirectly.[80] In his will, made fifteen years later, he states that the deacon for whom he worked still owed him forty hyperpera in salary. Furthermore, Bartolomeo reveals that he owned the sort of legal texts a jurist or a teacher of law would need.

Fortunately for us but unfortunately for him, Bartolomeo was obliged to auction off his legal texts in order to bail his son-in-law's business out of debt. In his will, Bartolomeo had to make clear which works he redeemed from whom. He was able to recover the *Decretales* with commentary by Bernardus, the *Codex*, and the *Decretum*. He left another copy of the *Decretales* with commentary by Bernardus, along with a text on judicial procedures by Egidio de Fuscarariis, as surety for a loan from a Latin priest.[81] Here was a man who states that he had his own school, who was evidently trained in canon law and *ius comune*, and was in contact with other local notaries at least familiar with those same subjects. Since there were few Venetians, much less Cretans, trained in either Roman or canon law during the fourteenth century, very likely Bartolomeo, a man from somewhere beyond the metropolis, worked also as a jurist in the colony, advising the colonial administration grappling with the issues brought before them. He might very well also have taught aspiring notaries.

Evidently the colony had difficulty in retaining its schoolteachers. In 1345, the colonial regime decided to subsidize for one year the salary of master Francesco di Bancaria, an Italian, in his school "because it would be very beneficial to students (*qui est valde utilis scolaribus*)."[82] The next notice that we have about schools in Candia comes from 1360, when two teachers decided to pool their resources and students. In anticipation of an upcoming six-month voyage to the west, master Thomas di Ferro accepted master Niccolò Pignatellus of Brindisi as his partner in the school he was then operating. Niccolò was to join his students to Thomas's, with the exception of the sons of the lord Marco Muazzo, who were to remain entirely under Niccolò's tutelage. In exchange for not giving up those students, Thomas took three other students of Niccolò's. When Thomas returned from his travels, they would split the proceeds from the tuition.[83] It is difficult to tell whether these men taught on the elementary or the secondary level. In any case, a transaction from the following year, 1361, shows that Thomas and Niccolò were not the only teachers in Candia. Giovanni Grimani calls himself a *doctor scolarum*, suggesting an elementary schoolteacher, in the document he had drawn up.[84]

More information about teachers comes from the 1380s. There was an elementary school operated by another Italian, master Gentile d'Arezzo, *rector scolarum*, in 1384. In one transaction in which he was named, a noble feudatory of Candia, Vittore Taliapetra, placed his illegitimate son Michael in Gentile's care. Michael was to learn to read and write both Latin and Italian over the course of two years at a cost of twelve hyperpera a year.[85] Simi-

larly another feudatory arranged for his son to learn Latin (*literas latinas*).[86]
Both these illegitimate sons would have had Greek mothers, but once recognized by their fathers they would have been pulled more into the Latin
orbit. Gentile the schoolteacher also took on a Greek student in the same
year, one of the few instances we have evidence for of a Greek in a Latin
school.[87]

Learning Latin and Italian took place outside schools as well, where
the cost of a less well-trained teacher's services was cheaper and more open
to negotiation. In 1384 Nicolaos Theopulo, a Greek shopkeeper in Candia,
hired Lodovico Gradenigo, son of a feudatory, to come to his shop and
teach him over six months to read Latin well enough to read an entire
psalter, the text that students traditionally read after their initial introduction to reading via the *tavola*.[88] If school fees were beyond the reach of more
humble Candiotes, private instruction as part of employment was a less ex-
pensive route toward basic literacy. A Greek man, Nichitas Lagniti, placed
his son Michael in the service of a Venetian man, Domenico Zorzi, who
would feed, clothe, and lodge Michael, as was usual among the lowest of
unskilled domestic labor. In fact, Nichitas specifies that Domenico was
entitled to treat Michael just as he would a slave. But Domenico obligated
himself in the contract to teach Michael how to read.[89]

On an island such as Crete, with its long-established monasteries and
entrenched indigenous clergy, Latin and Italian were of course not the only
languages one could learn for a fee. There was also demand for teachers of
Greek. As early as 1317, a Greek priest, Michali Pedhioti, promised to teach
Manuel, son of Vassili Carochopo, how to read any of his church's manuscripts within a year and to write within four.[90] Later in the century, Ianni
de Rodo arranged for his brother Nicolaos to learn to read Greek from a
priest.[91] In 1387, Costas Salonicheo, who lived in Candia's suburb, agreed
to accept a village boy, Ianni, son of Petros Stria, into his school. At the end
of one year Ianni was expected to know how to read the Greek psalter to the
satisfaction of a priest who would examine him.[92] In the same year a Greek
priest, *papas* Dimitri Corner, took a (possibly) Venetian boy, Niccolò, son
of Giorgos Abramo, as his student. Niccolò's goal was to learn how to read
religious works and write well.[93] In another will, which has attracted attention before now, Stefano Bono, a Venetian notary married to a Greek
woman, refers to his education in Greek at the church of St. Michael the
Archangel in Candia, where he wished to be buried.[94] Even a Latin feudatory might want his son to learn Greek. Ser Pietro Geno arranged for a
village man, Ianni Vlacho, to teach his son Nicoletto how to read the Greek

psalter.[95] Unlike the evidence for Latin schools, nearly all the evidence of Greek learning involves exclusively religious texts. An ability to read the psalter was a prerequisite to ordination.

Jews, too, had their own teachers, but we have no indication of a school prior to the 1380s. Master Melchiel Alemanus agreed to teach Moyses Carvuni "letteras iudaicas," meaning Hebrew, for one year. Moyses's mother, Anastassi Carvunena, promised, for her part, that Moyses would come to the master's home daily, according to the custom of Jewish students. In winter the student would arrive two hours before daylight. Moyses's tuition was twenty hyperpera a year.[96] In 1386, Solomon de Iocuda, called *rector scolarum in litteris iudaice*, suggesting that he operated an elementary school, received Iostef, son of Hergina tu Samuele, as his *discipulus* for one year, in exchange for which Solomon was to receive the rights to two dwellings in the Jewish quarter.[97]

Education, then, could be had across the city, even if teachers were not in plentiful supply. Latin teachers were few, in comparison to the number of Greek priests throughout the island to instruct those who wished to learn Greek, but the most educated people in the colony were usually those Venetians and Italians who were there only temporarily, as either colonial officials or commercial travelers.

A question of greater interest is, what was the level of Greek learning in Crete before the Byzantine refugee scholars arrived there in the fifteenth century? That there are a good number of examples of Greek teachers in sources in which Greeks are underrepresented suggests that we would have found more teachers of Greek in the protocols of Greek notaries had they survived. Furthermore, Crete did not lack its own native poets. A Cretan poet from the fourteenth century, Stephanos Sachlichi, whose work has been studied by Arnold Van Gemert, shows that it was possible to become very well educated in that period.[98] M. I. Manoussacas has contributed an extensive study of the other Cretan poet of the fourteenth century, Leonardo della Porta.[99] Therefore, while there may not have been an intellectual garden in bloom when the Byzantine refugees began to arrive in greater numbers during the fifteenth century, there surely was ample fertile ground by that time.

As further evidence of the relatively high standard of literary culture available in Crete, manuscripts of secular and religious texts were available, if not in great supply. The largest collection of texts in Latin hands that we know of in the fourteenth century belonged to the Franciscan order, whose library of scientific works alone amounted to 195 manuscripts, almost exclusively in Latin, as an inventory made in 1417 shows.[100] Other orders may have had their own libraries. The older Greek establishments were also very likely to have had libraries of books, though none of their titles have survived. There is, however, an interesting entry from 1370, in which the prior of the Augustinians renders his corresponding number in the Greek monastery of Mt. Sinai in Candia secure for the receipt of two manuscripts, "uno nominato Vulgaria et una alio libro psaltereo scriptis in lingua grecorum." These manuscripts had not belonged to the monks of Mt. Sinai, but had been placed in their possession to sell them.[101]

The titles of works are occasionally given, but unfortunately not often enough to give us a vivid impression of what learned Candiotes, both Greek and Latin, were reading. A cleric, Lodovico di Costula of Parma, sold in 1358 to a physician working in Candia eight volumes of medicinal and philosophical texts. For sixty-two Venetian ducats, the physician acquired a weighty collection: a work of Galen, a smaller one by Pietro d'Abono, called the Conciliator, and others by Guillielmo da Piacenza, Giovanni da Masseni, Avicenna (*unum naturalium*), Giovanni Serapion (*In simplicibus et aliud diverssarum questionum*).[102]

We have already seen that Bartolomeo de Hengelardis, who taught school as well as working as an imperial notary, had once possessed several legal texts: two copies of the *Decretales* with a commentary by Bernardo, the *Codex*, the *Decretum*, and a compendium of legal procedure by Egidio de Frascariis. In another will from 1349, Marco Cavalcante bequeathed to the chancellor of Candia a work called "On the property of things" and a gloss on the Book of Solomon. Had Marco once taught school himself? Moreover, he enjoins the chancellor to have his slave educated for five years so that he might eventually be ordained a priest. At the end of the five years, the chancellor was to give the slave his freedom and a volume containing the glossed works of Prosper, Aesop, and Cato, a popular Latin reading textbook in the schools of Italy in that period.[103] Other testators bequeathed religious and medicinal texts to heirs and religious institutions, unfortunately without informing us of their titles.

The Greek texts identified by title are almost all religious in nature and appear in the will of a Greek monk from Troy, Macarios, who taught Greek in Candia in the early 1330s. In his will, he left two religious works, a *Euco-logium* and a *tipicum*, to the illegitimate son of a Latin feudatory. To another student he left a *schimatologium*, and to another a work on poetics (*unum librum gramatice vocatum Prosodhie*).[104] Otherwise, all references to works in Greek are to manuscripts that form part of the property of churches.

Where did these manuscripts come from? Did the manuscript production that became famous in the second half of the fifteenth century actually have older roots on the island? In a recent study, Giuseppe De Gregorio has identified six manuscripts containing bilingual works that were copied in Candia, some of them during the first half of the fourteenth century.[105] The works contained in them are mainly religious in nature, for instance, Gregory the Great's *Dialogues*. De Gregorio argues on palaeographical grounds not only that one manuscript was commissioned by a notary, Andrea Cariola, but that Andrea was also the scribe of the manuscript's Latin text. The Greek text, he further argues, was completed by a Greek ecclesiastic, possibly a deacon.[106] Although one can dispute De Gregorio's characterization of the Greco-Latin cultural life of Candia that reached its culmination in the fifteenth and sixteenth centuries as "ben armonizzato," he is surely justified in bringing our attention to a higher level of cooperative cultural production among Latins and Greeks than was once thought, even if the evidence does not necessarily support the idea of a cultural rapprochement between the two communities.[107] Deno Geanakoplos's depiction of Candiote life as "culturally stagnant" may be further off the mark than has been realized.[108] In addition to the documents I presented above, there is other evidence to lend credence to De Gregorio's evaluation of literary culture in Crete.

Two other previously unpublished documents pertain to manuscript production in Candia. The first example comes, interestingly enough, from the Jewish community in 1326. Samuel, son of Moyses Vilara, promises Isaac, son of Mordochai, that his nephew, Moyses son of Iacuda, would produce within five months a Jewish Bible, or *Chumas*, in his own hand. This Bible, which cost Isaac ten and a half hyperpera (close to the yearly salary of a domestic servant or approximately the cost of 1,000 liters of wine), would contain the Pentateuch and the Prophets, with all the sabbaths and festivals of the year. In this Bible the scribe committed himself to noting the verses and the diacritical points for vocalization of the consonantal text (*stixi ke ta atami*).[109] The finished manuscript was to be bound, covered, and finished.[110]

The second document comes from a few years later, in 1329. In a contract that was ultimately canceled, Domenico Acardo, a cleric of Candia, promises Giacomo de Soleis, the agent for several religious institutions in Candia, to write "de bona littera continuativa" a collection of the lives and passions of the saints for the Latin archbishop of Crete. Domenico was to present his work illuminated and collated. Giacomo was to furnish Domenico with the colors, sheets of vellum, and a collator, in addition to paying him and the illuminator five *grossi* for each quinto of the manuscript. The guarantor of the agreement was Domenico's brother, Santoro, a barber, signifying Domenico's low social origins.[111]

With few exceptions Greeks of all social levels demonstrated an interest in Greek studies and Latins of all ranks tended to pursue Italian and Latin studies. Undoubtedly, there were many more exceptions to this general rule of thumb than the Latin-biased sources allow for. The advantages of learning the language of the economically and politically dominant culture are too obvious. The advantages of learning to read and write Greek are perhaps more subtle, but notaries in particular show a propensity toward being open to the cultural influences of their environment. The contracts pertaining to schooling show that, no matter how humble a free Candiote might be, a rudimentary education was available, if one could pay for it. No women appear among the students, much less the teachers, leading us to conclude that in Crete as elsewhere men dominated the world of education.

Religion and literary culture were not the only modes of cultural expression available to the two communities. Music was another mode, although what relatively little we know about its performance in the fourteenth century comes from the notarial sources. Candia was the site of several festivals and processions throughout the year, most of which were instituted by the Venetian authorities to manifest their dominion over the island. Musicians of course played a major part in those processions. The notarial sources tell us that those players, many of whom came from the Italian peninsula, traversed the city and the countryside.[112] There was at least one music school in Candia. Two musicians from Italy, Master Cecolino, *sonator*, and Bertucio Benno, join together in 1333 to operate a music school for five months.[113] In another document, a musician from Venice, Michael Scolari, described as a *çaramelator*, promises to teach the son of a villager. He was to take the boy with him wherever he went whether in Crete or away from it. Along the way, Michael was to teach him how to play a pipe (*çaramele*), a kind of wind instrument (*flabiole*), and bagpipes (*musacornius*). At the end of seven years of service and instruction, typical of many apprenticeship contracts, Michael would provide his pupil with his own instruments.[114] As for the visual arts, painters of the Byzantine style and those who had learned their craft in Italy have left their imprint, sometimes very western in appearance, on Cretan churches during the fourteenth and fifteenth centuries, examples of which still can be seen.[115] Church frescoes were not the only aspect of Cretan life in which western influence is apparent. Chryssa Maltezou has edited and commented on a notarial document in which a daughter of the Calergi family empowers her uncle to buy for her a dress of golden thread worth at least ninety ducats, in addition to other clothing in Venetian style, indicating the prestige in Crete attached to keeping up with the latest styles in the lagoon.[116]

As ethnic markers, religion and language did not remain stable reference points as to what defined Greeks and Latins of all social ranks and of both genders. Greeks and Latins apparently tended to educate themselves in the tradition of their cultural heritages, except when education in the other community's language promised benefits, such as a broader client base for a Latin notary with a command of written and spoken Greek, or economic reward for a Greek who mastered the language of international trade, Italian. Yet there was acculturation, in that persons of Latin descent increasingly used Greek as their first language. The strength of the boundaries between the two groups depended on which portion of the population they were enclosing. As long as there was the impetus to keep those boundaries in place at the extreme ends of Candiote society, they would never entirely disappear in the middle, no matter how homogeneous the people of Candia looked to outside observers. I would argue that the Candiotes of yesterday would have had just as much trouble articulating why they defined themselves in whatever way they did as we have in defining them today. Yet clearly each social level thought of itself as either Greek or Latin by its own criteria. Whence came, then, the resistance to the assimilation of Latin to Greek? The most obvious answer is that, more than anything else in the colony, political forces kept alive the ethnic categories of Greek and Latin, which is not to say that they would not have survived had it not been for the efforts of the regime. They would have instead taken on an aspect different from the one they had and the one that had lasting implications for ethnic categorization in the early modern period. To pursue this point, an innovative juridical concept that underlay Candiote society deserves attention.

Simply put, in the first half of the fourteenth century the Venetian authorities declared that proven Latin paternity led automatically to free status. In other words, men of Latin descent were by definition free in the colony, whereas men and women of Greek descent were vulnerable to enslavement. Until the 1360s, any villein or slave who was able to prove Latin paternity would gain his freedom.[117] In response to the understandable pursuit of juridical Latinity that rule provoked, thereafter the government arbitrarily closed off that avenue. Furthermore, throughout the fourteenth century the government issued warnings against Greeks who attempted to pass themselves off as Latins.[118]

Significantly, not all Greeks were enslaved or of non-free status. As evidenced by the number who were legally capable to create public notarial instruments without the permission of a master, a substantial number of Greeks in Candia were of free status, although it is very difficult to determine what percentage of the indigenous population they constituted. The majority of the peasantry were of servile status, but in Candia, other towns, and their suburbs, free Greeks of varying social status lived and worked. This must be one of the very first occasions in the pre-modern era when legal enslavement was ethnically and not religiously determined. Up until that time, in theory, canon law forbade the enslavement of a Christian by a Christian, which of course did not stop Christians, such as the Genoese and Venetians, from owning or conducting commerce in the sale of baptized slaves in the European Mediterranean.[119] Nevertheless, legal redress in theory was available, if not easily accessible to an uneducated, propertyless slave. As a result, technically Latins could not own Orthodox Greek slaves.

The way around this problem in Crete, where the majority of slaves at the beginning of the century were Greek Christians, was to shift the legal burden away from religion to that of ethnicity, but not to justify slavery on that basis.[120] In this period, the link between ethnicity and slavery was forged in the effort to establish who could *not* be enslaved. Turning to the Candiote court records will make this clear. In the first half of the fourteenth century, a number of cases involving claims to free status came before the court of the duke and his councillors, interestingly enough, rather than before the judges *di prosopo*, who normally dealt with cases involving Greeks.[121] Each case hinged on the question of whether the father of the defendant, who was claimed by someone to be his slave or a villein, was Latin. In 1319 the duke confirmed the free status of Gerardo Desde, who successfully demonstrated that he was the son of an illegitimate son of a Latin noble feudatory.[122] A few weeks later two other suits came before the court, brought by Francesco Ghisi, who sought three men as his villeins.[123] Other such cases appear in the court records up to 1360, but thereafter disappear.[124] The claims to free status all rest on Latin paternity; some were supported by ancillary evidence, as in the case of a man recently immigrated from Calabria who was ignorant of the Greek language.[125] When doubts about the defendant's paternity still troubled the minds of the duke and his councillors, conditions could be placed on the ultimately successful applicant for free status, as two recorded cases make plain. In the first, dated 1324, the *camerarii* of the Comune, who were charged with overseeing the villeins belonging to the comune, unsuccessfully claimed Michael, the illegitimate son of a Latin man, Paolo Dono, as one of theirs. The court rejected their claim, but stipulated that if Michael ever wore a beard in the Greek fashion or attended the Greek church, or otherwise did not live like a Latin, his status would revert to that of a villein of the comune.[126] In the other case, the court imposed exactly the same conditions on the defendant.

In light of the discussion above about ethnic markers, how may the regime's stipulations regarding beards and religion be interpreted? The absence of language among the distinguishing characteristics that the regime counted on is important. Apparently even as early as 1324 the Venetian authorities could no longer rely on language to tell Greek from Latin. Concerning beards, we will discuss in the next chapter the regime's requirement that its militia members report for duty clean-shaven.[127] With regard to religion, it is not illogical that, if Greek archontes were required to adhere to the Latin church in order to become feudatories, the regime would impose the same standard on those at the servile level. However, the regime's desire for its population to be neatly and tidily distinguishable did not make it so, and it is that unrealistic desire, evident in its official records, that has misled historians. In its efforts to impose social order, within the context of which Latins were to hold pride of place, the duke and his councillors were in effect grasping at straws. The regime could not even control its hired troops. In 1371 the Venetian Senate learned that many soldiers were marrying Greeks and that many Greeks were in the employ of the regime, another indication that the city did not have enough Latins to fill all the necessary posts.[128] In other words, just as it could not prevent marriages between Greeks and Latins on any social level, which in the final analysis was what made the entire situation so confusing to them and to us, it could not keep up with the evolution of ethnic markers by which it hoped to keep the subordinated population distinct from the dominant population.

To return to the claims of Latin paternity, in every case the parents involved are free Latin men and unfree Greek women. Several of the cases make this explicit.[129] In one case from 1324, the court confirmed the free status of Kerana Plumaru of Romania, because she redeemed herself, and her son, Antonio, because he was born of a union between Kerana and her former owner.[130] But a few other cases show that social standing, rather than ethnic ancestry strictly speaking, could also play a part in the outcome of a case. Servile Greeks could advance a claim to free status based on their kinship with the group called *archondopouloi*, or the lesser Greek nobility. In one of the few cases recorded in which the claim to free status did not succeed, the court rejected the claim of a man on the grounds that he did not prove that he was the illegitimate son of a Greek *archondopoulos*.[131] Twenty years later in another case the court ruled that Nicolaus Monovassioti would have to pay the exactions expected of villeins unless he was able to show that he had been an *archondopoulos* where he lived prior to coming to Crete.[132]

Ethnicity and class were inextricably bound together in Crete, especially at the extreme ends of the social spectrum. At the feudatory level, class often overrode ethnic solidarity, with religious allegiance being the conveyor between the two ethnic groups. The noble families of Candia's feudatory group show a decided preference to match their daughters with men of their own status. There were, however, only so many possibilities of intermarriage within the Latin feudatory group, thanks to the extent to which the families were already related to one another. The Greek archontic families, particularly the Calergi, obviously looked very attractive to noble fathers in search of partners of equal or like rank. Indeed, one way to interpret the degree to which the Calergi penetrated the feudatory group through marriages of their progeny is to turn the favor on its head. Instead of viewing marriage alliances as beneficial to the Calergi, kinship ties with the lord Alexios's family (not to mention his wealth and power) might very well have carried with them a patina of exceptionally high prestige and fashion in that colonial society, even within one hundred years of its founding.

The question of whether gender had an impact on the way ethnicity was experienced is less obvious, but the connection is there. Gender, too, comes into play in the formal attributes of ethnicity. It cannot be a coincidence that, as far as the records show, no woman sought Latin status in a court of law. Nor can it be a coincidence that all evidence I have found of marriages between illegitimate daughters and men involves Greek husbands.[133] The ethnicity of women was in general less an issue than it was for men. As a reminder before proceeding, in the previous chapter we saw that female slaves who had been manumitted did not adopt cognomina as male manumitted slaves did. In the present chapter, we have seen that religion served as a firmer ethnic marker for men at the feudatory level than for Greek women at that same level. At the risk of reducing the issue to a functionalist generalization, it is hard to avoid the conclusion that cognomina and socio-juridical labels, such as ethnic categories, mattered less among women than they did among men, because cognomina, emancipation, and ethnic labels implied legal capacities ordinarily beyond the reach of a legally dependent daughter or wife.[134] When they did matter, it was often on the upper levels of society, where women's associations with their husbands' lineages played a paramount role in their social existence. On the lower social levels where the majority of the population were to be found, perhaps the safest way to characterize the difference between men's and women's ethnicity is to say that the socio-political and juridical engine that drove forward the ongoing process of ethnic definition in men ran at fewer revolutions per minute in the social dimensions women inhabited. The pressures on them were not the same as those on men, who lived in a world where the right to engage in local or long-distance trade had as much to do with place of origin or ethnic background or religion as it did with who their father and grandfather were and where they were born. This was generally true in late medieval Italy, but in Crete the long process of distinguishing those who had a right to partake of the economic and social advantages reserved automatically to Latins and already free Greeks coincided in time with a similar evolving process in Venice, which has not been noticed before now.

Although the *Serrata* of the Great Council of Venice is considered the defining moment in the patriciate's corporate identity, the process is now understood to have been an ongoing one throughout the fourteenth and into the fifteenth century. Stanley Chojnacki argues that a second, more definitive *Serrata* took place in the first decades of the fifteenth century, when even more rigorous reforms were passed.[135] The second *Serrata* was spurred on by a sentiment within Venetian ruling circles that undesirable men had been gaining entrance into Venice's Great Council. The perception was, as Chojnacki puts it, that "blemishers had recently penetrated the sacred precincts, necessitating new 'remedies.' "[136]

In response to Chojnacki's interpretation of the early fifteenth-century *Serrata*, I wish to make two observations in regard to the process of defining the Venetian patriciate. The first period during which membership in the Great Council of Venice became fixed and hereditary began in 1297 and ended in 1323, when the last legislation pertaining to the patriciate was enacted. Numerous historians see in Venetian history after this point the rapid convergence of the patriciate with the contours of the Venetian State, meaning that nobility became linked to the functional, bureaucratic needs of the state.[137] In other words, obligatory participation in government increasingly went hand-in-hand with exalted status and prosperity. A little less than a century after the *Serrata*, in 1414, new legislation appears in the

Great Council records. The rules for the lottery to take up council seats prior to the legal age of entry became more complicated and restrictive. The reasons given for the tighter controls make clear that the legislators believed it necessary to prevent the entry of men "who might sully [*maculare*] the reputation, status and honour of the state [*tanti dominii*]."[138] To Chojnacki, this invocation of an ideal purity was a recent innovation, which, I agree, it very well may have been, at any rate in the city of Venice. But elsewhere in the Venetian dominion the same issues had come to the forefront of political life earlier and in much more explicit ways that they would in Venice. They exerted in turn an influence on Venetian society to an extent that has been little appreciated thus far.

During the same period in which Chojnacki places the second *Serrata*, between 1361 and 1427, fifty-four Candiote feudatories with Venetian patrician cognomens successfully petitioned the *Avogadori di Comuni* in Venice to have their noble status, and thus their seats on the Great Council of Venice, confirmed.[139] Five other candidates made the same petition, but failed to prove their noble paternity, thus incurring a three-hundred-*lire* fine.[140] At first sight these applications bespeak a desire to enter into the feudatories' cultural heritage. Undoubtedly some feudatories born in Candia sought to move to the big city and chase their dreams of amassing a fortune there, instead of in a cultural and social backwater, as Crete is thought to have been. Earlier in the century, we find a petition placed before the *Avogadori di Comune* by a nobleman from Candia who had immigrated to Venice. The wording is strongly telling. He states that he left the land where he was raised (*patriam sui ortus*) and moved with his wife, children, and household to Venice because he "was moved by love of and a natural desire for his primordial homeland, that is Venice."[141] He seeks permission to sell the last of his possessions in the colony. The wording suggests that he had not been born in the colony, but had spent a good deal of his life there.

Upon closer examination of those applicants and their families, however, it is striking that most of them do not appear to have immigrated to Venice, or at any rate were still residents of Candia when they made their request. They appear to have been primarily interested in the commercial and employment benefits and prestige that noble status conferred on them out in the colonies.[142] But it is possible that confirmation of noble status was a desirable preliminary step to immigration.

Most of the total of fifty-nine applicants came from families we have encountered before now. All bear cognomina that we recognize to have

been among the colony's most noble feudatory families. The Candiotes
who failed in their attempt are relatively unknown to us, which is perhaps as
it would be expected. However, some of the ones who did succeed are candidates who might have been expected to fail in their petition. In chronological order, the very first petition of a Candiote was put forward in 1361
by Parlato Muazzo, one of the subsequent leaders of the 1363 Revolt of St.
Tito, which is the subject of the next chapter. Six years later, after the
suppression of the revolt, Niccolò, son of Marco Dandolo, one of the
leaders of the colony, whose kin also participated in the revolt and who had
kinship ties with the Calergi family, had his noble status confirmed. Twenty-
five years later four sons of prominent rebels also received confirmation of
their noble rank, in spite of their kinship with the rebels.[143] These last four
may have lived in or near Venice, or elsewhere in the empire *da' mar*; their
petitions do not tell us their official place of residence. Moreover, one
wonders how many of the other applicants were related to Greek archontic
families. For it was in these very same years that senior members of the
Calergi family, Matteo and Georgios, sons of Alexios II, underwent a similar process to acquire seats on the Great Council of Venice. Were they, too,
among the undesirables from the patricians' point of view?

The evidence is purely circumstantial at this point and likely to remain
so, since the Venetian authorities were so reluctant to put the details of
sensitive matters in their registers. That the *probe* initiated by the Candiote
feudatories first appear in the registers in the 1360s and continue up to the
second *Serrata* may be coincidental. The question is nevertheless irresist-
ible: were the undesirable men gaining seats on the Great Council of Venice
coming from the colonies, specifically Crete?[144] If so, did the objection to
their presence there rest on the knowledge that many of them were kinsmen
of Greeks? Aristocratic sentiment in the lagoon may have considered the
Cretan nobility as less than the nominal Venetians and Latins the Venetian
Signoria decreed them to be in the colony. After all, to judge by the rhetoric
of such intellectuals as Petrarch, who was living in the city at the time of the
St. Tito revolt and very much took the side of the government, little distinction was made between Cretans of Greek ancestry and Cretans of Venetian
ancestry. "Venetians in name, enemies by design and character," is how
Petrarch put it in 1363.[145]

It is also worth asking whether the Venetian legislation of 1422, in
which noble status was from then on to be determined by both the lineage
of the father and, what was new, that of the mother, found its motivation in
the desire to contain the influence of Venetian Cretan nobles in the Vene-

tian Great Council.[146] After the turn of the fifteenth century, more and more Cretan feudatories of Venetian descent sought confirmation of their noble status in Venice.[147] By that time, most feudatory families would have been rife with Greek Cretan ancestors, especially recent Greek female ancestors, since the regime in Crete always tolerated marriages between Greek Cretan women and Latin men better than the other way around. No prejudice against the newcomers is anywhere stated. Nevertheless, the number of members of old *case*, some of whose main branches were dying out in Venice, coming to Venice and entering the ranks of the patriciate may very well have given cause for concern to the Senate, who feared being sullied by the integration of Venetian-Greek stock into the pool of patrician purity.

My third and more substantive point is that the process of delineating the nobility in Venice finds its analogue not just in the process of determining who had a right to a seat on the Candiote Great Council, but also in the broader process of identifying legally capable persons. What was played out in the language of class (*patriziano/cittadino/popolano*) in Venice was expressed in Candia in terms of ethnicity (Latin/Greek), even though the same issues of class underpinned both distinctions. But the implications of class hidden under the cover of ethnicity are more disturbing and far-reaching nearer the bottom of the social ladder. The direction ethnic categories would go thenceforth is hinted at in a document from the beginning of the century. Marco Venier, an illegitimate son of the late Bartolomeo, a resident of Candia, and a Greek noblewoman of the island of Cerigo, who himself had successfully brought suit to have his Latin paternity legally recognized, had drawn up in 1301 a charter of manumission for his slave, Ianni Cruschulo of Chios, also a resident of Candia. The transaction is unusual, in that the notary's choice of words to describe the charter's effect is unique in the sources, as far as I know. In the text of the charter, Marco declares that henceforth Ianni will be free and treated as such and "in all things you will be made Roman."[148] In a western context, the connotation "Roman" had more substantial religious than ethnic overtones. Nothing is mentioned in the document about which church rites Ianni followed, but it is possible that, having switched his allegiance to the Latin rites, he thereby increased his chances both for manumission, since manumission was a fairly common pious gesture of both Latins and Greeks, and for transforming himself into a Latin man. The use, however, of the term "Roman" to describe the state the slave would be in after manumission is not a long way from the power of the concept of "blood" to lock people into a juridically determined condition of slavery. Defining who has the right to be free on the basis of ethnicity is one step away from defining who does not have the right to be free on the basis of skin color. Conquest and colonization placed state powers in the position of making those distinctions about people on the lowest and highest levels of society in ways they did not have to do in their own domain. There is a moment in the history of the colony that exemplifies what was occurring at the lowest and highest levels of Candiote society. The tensions inherent in the colony of Crete came to a head in the dramatic events of late summer 1363.

4

High Stakes in
Venetian Crete

"Venetians by Name and Custom,
Enemies by Design and Character"

ON 8 AUGUST 1363, the Candiote feudatories had received word that another tax was about to be imposed on them by the Venetian Senate. The new levy, they learned, was to go toward the cleaning and upkeep of Candia's port. The feudatories objected, viewing the tax as more beneficial to the Venetian merchants who passed through the port than to themselves. When he heard of their opposition, the duke of Candia summoned before him twenty of the resentful feudatories to insist on their compliance with the Senate's decree. When the interview was over, the feudatories withdrew.

Later the same day seventy feudatories gathered in the cathedral dedicated to St. Tito, the patron saint of the island to both Greeks and Latins. After conferring among themselves, they sent the three *camerarii* of the Council of Feudatories, Marco Gradenigo Spiritello, Michele Faledro, and Andrea Pantaleo, to the duke and his councillors. The representatives proposed to the duke that the tax be held in abeyance until a delegation of twenty feudatories had appealed in person to the doge and the Senate in Venice; otherwise they were prepared to resist. The duke was not in a mood to bargain. He responded that the feudatories must agree to pay the tax. To drive the point home to all, he had the tax proclaimed by the city's heralds to the other feudatories waiting in the cathedral, threatening those who continued to resist the new tax with death and confiscation of property. The duke ordered the assembly of feudatories in the cathedral to disperse.

The scene shifted next to the city's central piazza. On the edge of the *Platea* stood the ducal palace and the loggia. In the *Platea*, the duke and his councillors were accustomed to hold court in the open air. During one such session, on the same day as the meeting in the cathedral, some of the

feudatories who resented the new tax expelled from the loggia a small group
of those who had sided with the government. Other adherents to the government's cause, who remained by the duke's side, advised him to call to
arms the approximately fifty Venetians and sailors currently in port, who
were not residents of the island. The duke, however, declined to do so,
fearing that such a step would exacerbate the situation and lay him open to
charges of having ignited a revolt.

On the following day, 9 August, angry feudatories, accompanied by
townspeople, servants, and soldiers, stormed the ducal palace, attempting
to force their way through the main door. But they found that entrance to
the palace could be gained only by climbing over the roofs of the adjoining
goldsmiths' workshops and onto the palace roof. While the angry crowd
outside attempted to break in, the duke, who was in the ducal palace,
ordered the main gate to be opened and commanded the invading army of
feudatories and their abettors to withdraw to their residences. Tito Venier, a
feudatory described as more enraged than the others, cried out in fine
operatic fashion to the duke, "Die, traitor!" Others among the hostile feudatories stepped in to assure the duke that his life was not at risk and took
him and his councillors into custody. The three deposed Venetian functionaries were separated from one another and placed under guard in the residences of three rebel feudatories.

The revolt, which began on 8 August, spread to the rest of the island
within a week. The rebels imprisoned the rectors of Chanea and Rethimno
and installed their own men in those positions. Now in control of the
largest towns along the northern shore of the island, they appointed Marco
Gradenigo *senex* governor and rector (*gubernator et rector*) of the whole
island, with four councillors to assist him, Francesco Muazzo, Marco Fradello, Andrea Pantaleo, and Bartolomeo di Grimaldo. The first usurpation
of a Venetian colonial regime by its own colonists was completed and a new
regime under the leadership of some of the island's most venerable feudatories was installed.

The rebellion of 1363 was not the first to challenge Venetian dominion
on the island. Previous rebellions that had been suppressed involved insur-
gent Greek archontes with their families and followers, who fought to regain the property and prestige Venice took from them in the initial conquest
of the island.[1] In the early thirteenth century, the Hagiostefanites family first
waged war against the Comune for the restoration of their lands.[2] Throughout the century, other Greek noble families, singly or in small coalitions,
fought for economic and social advantages. The Greek nobility, however,

never united in common cause against Venice, so their struggle lacked the quality of a national or patriotic fight. The fourteenth century, in contrast, witnessed fewer, but nonetheless serious, revolts, the suppression of which required considerable resources on the part of Venice.[3]

The Revolt of St. Tito differed from previous revolts in one fundamental respect. For the first time, the Latin colonists initiated the uprising and allied themselves with the Greeks of the island. Nowhere in the territories controlled by Venice had such an event occurred up to that time. The desire for political independence by the Latin colonists was possible only because of the nature of the colony of Crete: a state colony, in which a fiscal and judicial administration was imposed on colonists and colonized alike. State colonization created the potential for an alliance between the colonists and the native population, who found themselves on the same side of the divide separating the governing from the governed. Reinforcing this state of affairs was the fact that, by the time the colonists' frustrations with Venice had reached a breaking point, many of the Latin feudatories had been settled on the island for at least two or three generations, and were immersed in a culture that had initially been alien to their grandparents, but was now more familiar to them than was the culture of Venice.

The first printed account of the little-known Revolt of St. Tito appears in a history of Venice by Lorenzo De Monacis, chancellor of Crete from sometime in the 1380s until his death in 1428.[4] Counting among his correspondents the humanist Leonardo Bruni, De Monacis was acquainted with the fourteenth-century group of learned men from among whom many of the early humanists would shortly emerge, although Lorenzo himself cannot be considered one of them.[5] During the last years of his life, De Monacis began his history of Venice, which included a history of the colony of Crete. In addition to consulting Greek sources for the history he was writing, he also drew on earlier chronicles, such as those of Andrea Dandolo and Niccolò Trevisan, one of the officials sent to Crete to put down the revolt, who described the latter stages of its suppression.[6]

De Monacis had the advantage of living for a time where the revolt had taken place and while it was still within living memory. If he did not actually invent the snippets of dialogue he attributes to a few of the major participants, then he must have spoken with people who knew the participants, remembered the events, and enjoyed or decried the legends that developed around them. Furthermore, he made use of documents in the Cretan chancery, some of which still survive, making it possible to verify his version of the events, at least in part. His account is, however, suspect, since as a

Venetian functionary De Monacis was biased in favor of the regime's point of view. To compound the problem of his prejudice in favor of Venice, in his correspondence he made plain his antipathy toward Greek people and things Greek.[7] Nevertheless, his chronicle is fairly reliable and made even more interesting by his prejudices.

With the exception of a few historians over the centuries, De Monacis' account of the revolt went virtually unnoticed until a historian at the turn of the twentieth century brought the revolt to the attention of the modern scholarly world. J. Jegerlehner's article became in the twentieth century what De Monacis' chronicle had been up to then: the only detailed published account of the revolt.[8] Jegerlehner went further than De Monacis, by exploring in some detail the primary cause of the revolt, namely the tax imposed on the feudatories for the maintenance of the port, and by appending to his study the edited texts of, among other things, the deliberations of the Great Council of Venice relating to the revolt and the proclamations made by the rebels. Because of the article's proximity to our time and the relative inaccessibility of De Monacis' chronicle, Jegerlehner's account became the point of reference for the few historians who have had reason to refer to the events of 1363.[9]

Since Jegerlehner's article appeared, scant attention has been paid to the revolt and virtually none to the rebels themselves. As a result, historians have cast the events of 1363 as the actions of a disgruntled, heavily burdened elite, whose resentments toward the Venetian government grew out of fiscal concerns and frustrated demands for relief. A closer reading of De Monacis' account, along with evidence taken from the ADC and the notarial records pertaining to the rebels and their families, sheds new light on the insurrection and the background to it, and offers a more complex picture of Candiote society.

The sole surviving register of the regime's proclamations during the fourteenth century, the *Quaternus bannorum*, includes the first months of the rebels' government, and is the starting point for our comparison between De Monacis' narrative and the actions of both the rebel government and Venice.[10] After De Monacis describes the events of the first few days, during which the rebels established their own regime and extended their actions to most of the western end of the island, he catalogues the rebel government's first official acts. A new page of proclamations, dated 13 August in the register, begins under the heading, "in the administration of the magnificent Marco Gradenigo, governor and rector, and his council."[11]

The rebel government's first measure marked a sharp departure from the policies of the government which it had overthrown. The revocation of all previous edicts restricting the ordination of priests according to the rites of the Greek church constituted the first official act of the rebel government.[12] This proclamation directly addressed the Venetian government's prohibition of adherents to the Greek church from leaving the island to seek ordination in the Greek church somewhere in the Byzantine Empire. The restriction meant that Greek priests were ordained under the ecclesiastical jurisdiction of the Latin church on the island, and probably according to the Latin rites as well.[13] The second proclamation specified that anyone who wished to become a Greek priest, or *papas*, had the right to go abroad to wherever he wished to be ordained and to return to the island freely without any penalty.[14] The issue at the heart of these first two proclamations was the extension, not the granting, of religious freedom. The Greek liturgy had continued to be celebrated in scores of churches throughout the island after the Venetian occupation. But by restricting the ordination of Greek priests, Venice sought to prevent the filling of vacancies with Greek priests ordained according to the rites of the Greek church and to monitor the principal voice of indigenous dissatisfaction.

De Monacis and historians after him have viewed this provision as little more than a bid for the support of the Greek population of all social ranks. That may be so, but it marks the first time that the colonists attempted to unite with those whom they were meant to control and subjugate, the mass of non-aristocratic Greeks.[15] That the first two proclamations issued by the rebel government should have sought to redress that very situation reflects the extent to which these restrictions had become a sore point with the Greek community.

The proclamations for the rest of the month of August are concerned with security, administration, the regulation of trade in the city of Candia, and the need for a new visual symbol. With regard to the last, it is worth noting that the new regime proclaimed that vessels of all sizes operating under Cretan captains and owners would in future in all parts of the world have to raise the insignia of the Comune of Crete, the figure of St. Tito, special baron and protector of the island, or face the penalty established by the authorities.[16] Despite the apparent smoothness with which the new regime came into power, perhaps the first sign of dissent from the rebel cause appears in a proclamation issued on 20 August, in which some Venetians who had stolen a vessel the previous night were declared outlaws. Unfortunately, shortly after this date no more proclamations of the rebel government were recorded in this register.

News of the revolt reached Venice at the beginning of September. From the start, the Venetian government viewed the revolt taking place on Crete as one of the most formidable challenges to its security, on a par with those posed by Genoa. The matter was of such great concern that responsibility for organizing the campaign against the rebels passed from the Senate to the more powerful College, the council consisting of the doge and his nine councillors. The army that was mobilized by the College to suppress the revolt equalled any that Venice had used at sea or on land against a threat to its interests.[17]

The Venetian reaction to the rebellion can be gauged from the deliberations and letters of the College, which Jegerlehner appended to his study.[18] It decided first to attempt reconciliation with the rebels before resorting to stronger measures. A delegation of patricians representing the Comune went to Crete to negotiate. The delegates were instructed to express the hope of the government that the rebels, as "flesh of our flesh, bone of our bone," would once again become faithful subjects of Venice. The attempt at conciliation between the feudatories and the delegation came to naught; the rebels' response was one of defiance.

Over the course of the next several months the Comune of Venice proceeded to organize an army to crush the revolt. As part of its campaign, it issued appeals for assistance from other states. It solicited aid from the kings of Cyprus and Hungary, Pope Urban V, Giovanna, the queen of Sicily and Jerusalem, the head of the Hospitallers in Rhodes, and the doge in Genoa.[19] The king of Cyprus, the queen of Sicily, and the pope all wrote to the Venetian doge to express their support and issued proclamations forbidding their subjects any commerce or contact with the rebels of Crete.[20] This was also the case with Genoa. Despite the longstanding enmity that existed between Venice and Genoa, the Genoese government prohibited any of its subjects from rendering aid of any kind to the Cretan rebels.

In preparation for their war against the rebels, the Venetian government instituted a search throughout the Italian peninsula for a seasoned commander who would lead the invading army. They finally settled on Luchino dal Verme, a *condottiere*, then living in his native city, Verona, who was formerly in the service of the Visconti family.[21] The army Venice sent out under his command was impressive, consisting of a fleet of galleys, footsoldiers, horsemen, Bohemian mine sappers, Turkish soldiers, and siege engines.

When some of the leaders of the revolt heard of the extent of Venice's military preparations, they deserted the ranks of the rebels. De Monacis turns his narrative to the actions of the remaining rebels. He describes how Leonardo Gradenigo *calogero*, a Latin man from a feudatory family who had abjured the Latin church, was determined to kill all Latins who did not support the rebel cause. Gradenigo joined forces with a Greek monk named Milletos, to whom he promised the most important ecclesiastical position in the Greek church in Candia after their cause had been won. Together with other Greek priests, noblemen, townspeople, and peasants, the two monks set to murdering all Latin feudatories living outside the city of Candia. Indeed the list of people mentioned by De Monacis as having been murdered suggests that the rebels went a long way toward that end.[22]

The Greek population of Crete was much emboldened by these events and sought to profit from them. Ten men whom De Monacis describes as Greek joined the Council of Feudatories. This is in itself interesting, since whatever influence the feudatories had over the regime emanated from the Candiote Senate, not the Council of Feudatories. It is not likely that De Monacis, chancellor of the colony for a number of years, misunderstood the functions of the councils, so we may have arrived at the first relatively obvious distortion of the narrative of events. Why were Greeks inducted into that council and not the others? One explanation might be that the new members were Greek feudatories who had been excluded from membership in the council prior to the revolt. It was noted earlier that they participated in the Great Council and the Senate, but we have no way of knowing whether those families had been on the Council. In addition to the induction of Greeks into the Council of Feudatories, a movement was afoot to convert the liturgy of the cathedral dedicated to St. Tito from the Latin rite to the Greek. Leonardo Gradenigo *calogero* inflamed matters further by inciting an attack on the prisons holding the Venetian officials, but the mob was prevented from doing real harm to the prisoners by those loyal to Venice.

The Greek monk Milletos's murder of Latin families evidently alarmed the Latin rebels to such an extent that they felt compelled to remove him from the scene. Even Leonardo Gradenigo *calogero* distanced himself from his former ally. Having persuaded Milletos to withdraw from the city to a monastery a short distance away, Gradenigo at the head of an armed force attacked the monastery and captured the Greek monk, over whom the Latin rebels had lost control. Gradenigo returned him to Candia, where Milletos was ignominiously thrown down from the top of the ducal palace to the populace below, who slew him.

The vagaries of the crowd are indeed pernicious and frightful, for with scarcely a thought they switch their allegiance when their fortune changes. Many of the Greeks, who had praised the crimes of Milletos and received him avidly as their lord when things looked favorable, consented to and took part in his downfall, now that the outlook was bleak.[23]

The abruptness of this shift in alliances reveals more about De Monacis' desire to craft a particular image of a deed that was heinous in his eyes than it does about the pace of the events themselves. De Monacis is undoubtedly prejudiced in his narration of the revolt, but he is not willing to twist events out of all recognizable shape. He at least strives for coherence. In the above passage, we see that he feels compelled to explain why the Greeks of Candia welcomed and participated in the death of the Greek monk, Milletos. His explanation rests on the inconstancy of the mob rather than on the perfidy of the Greeks. The Greeks of the city, once strong supporters of the insurrection, now drew back from its excesses, a shift which points to a division among the rebels along lines other than ethnic ones.

Milletos's following originated in the countryside. His crime, in addition to the murders he had committed, was that he incited the Greek peasantry to revolt. De Monacis' text reveals not merely a split between Latins and Greeks, but also a split between the urban population, which included the feudatories, and the peasantry. The Latin rebels and the city's residents of all ranks did not fear the violence of Greeks qua Greeks as much as they feared a peasants' revolt, which constituted a far greater danger to the economic life of the colony.

The entire undertaking was unraveling. During the spring of 1364, months after the original rebellion, in the face of the impending arrival of the Venetian army, the feudatories began to fight among themselves about how best to proceed. One faction proposed sending a delegation to Genoa in order to seek assistance and offer the Genoese rule over the island. This proposal progressed to the point of choosing a delegation. However, another faction led by Marco Gradenigo (not the rebel governor) proposed capitulation to Venice. The apostate monk Leonardo Gradenigo accused his kinsman of betrayal and of plotting the extermination of their clan. After arranging the murder of Marco, he had all those suspected of wishing surrender rounded up and imprisoned. Leonardo went on to induct seventy more Greeks into the Council of Feudatories, all amenable to the proposal to approach Genoa.[24] Once the decision had been taken, a delegation including Leonardo *calogero* left for Genoa. In the end, the Genoese disappointed the rebels. The Venetian government had heard rumors about the planned delegation and in time had sent a letter to the Genoese doge, reminding him of his neutrality with regard to the Cretan rebellion. In reply, the Genoese government declared its intention not to meddle in the affairs of Crete. The delegation went away frustrated.

The reconquest of Crete did not wait for the return of the delegation from Genoa. In early April 1364, eight months after the initial overthrow of the island's colonial regime, Luchino dal Verme and his army landed on Crete and approached Candia from the west. As the Venetian army moved in the direction of the city, the rebel forces took flight, allowing Luchino dal Verme and his men to take possession of Candia with very little bloodshed. The rebel governor, Marco Gradenigo, and two of his councillors were captured and executed. The team of provisors sent along with the army to oversee the reinstallation of Venetian dominion immediately set about subduing the other three principal cities of the island. First Chanea, the city furthest away from Candia, surrendered without a fight. Then Rethimno, in the central part of the island, followed by Sithia, at the eastern end, came once again under Venetian rule. The leaders of the revolt who had not been captured fled to the mountains.

Once the colony's capital was again under control, Venice's representatives on Crete began to impose order and eliminate the possibility of another rebellion. All members of the Gradenigo and Venier families who were living in Candia during the rebellion were punished according to the severity of their crimes. The remaining members were banished from residing in any Venetian territory and all their goods were confiscated. The concession granted to the island's first colonists in 1211 was abrogated. The reestablished government set rewards for the capture of fugitive rebels. All those who had demonstrated their fidelity to Venice during the rebellion were invited to reclaim their possessions.

The pacification of the island, however, did not end with the recapture of the principal towns. Once dal Verme's army had established control over Candia, Sithia, Chanea, and Rethimno, it became necessary to turn to the question of the remaining Latin feudatory rebels who had fled to the mountains. Moreover, although the Latin leadership of the revolt had collapsed, the Greek peasantry and sections of the Greek nobility continued to stage violent attacks on the government forces and the feudatories. The provisors in charge of reimposing Venetian authority had to reorient themselves to cope with what they now perceived to be a war between the Greeks and the Venetian government.[25]

This perception was not quite accurate. There were still recalcitrant

Latin feudatories among the remaining rebels. The delegation returning from the fruitless endeavor in Genoa approached Cretan shores only after the capitulation of Candia. Notice of the change in the rebels' fortunes quickly reached the ears of Leonardo Gradenigo, the apostate monk, his kinsman, Leonardo Gradenigo Baiardo, and the other delegates on board the galleys while they were still near the island. A few of the galleys changed course and made for an island lying off the eastern tip of Crete, where the delegates were subsequently captured, brought back to Candia, and executed. As for the other men on the galley returning from Genoa, a considerable number of them landed on Crete and made their way toward the other rebels in hiding, rather than face what awaited them in Candia.

The band of Latin feudatory rebels who remained at large numbered fewer than fifty. According to De Monacis, most fugitives were drawn to a branch of the prominent Greek archontic family, the Calergi, whose land was located in another part of the island. The strongholds of rebellion stretched across the western part of the island. From their base the rebels, under the leadership of Ioannes Calergi, continued their campaign to expel the Venetian authorities. Ioannes Calergi carried before him the insignia of the Byzantine emperor of Constantinople, and, fighting for the faith and for freedom from Latin rule, attacked towns all over the western end of the island.[26]

Eventually the entire western section of the island came once again under the control of the rebels. Venice now authorized the provisors to mount another major campaign against the renegades. Over the next four years, one group of provisors succeeded another as the military campaign continued to move into those areas and bring them under control. The effort required substantial and sustained logistical support, equal to what had been needed in the initial conquest of 1364. The provisors requisitioned horses and troops brought from Turkey. The Venetian doge asked the pope to preach a crusade against the Cretan insurgents. At the request of the Apostolic See, the Latin patriarch of Constantinople, who was the exiled papal legate, preached in Venice on 20 October 1364, promising remission of sins and indulgences to all those who went to fight or contributed resources to that end.

While Venice was organizing the campaign to pacify the entire island, the rebels extended their field of action further east. They entered and won over much of the population in Ierapetra, Mirabello, and Potami. Early in 1365, another group of provisors arrived on the island and took up the campaign to pacify the island where the previous group had left off. In spite of the armed strength of the Venetians, the rebels pushed eastward. The provisors who arrived in 1365 were replaced by another group in April 1366. This group included Niccolò Trevisan, who later wrote a history of Venice in which he devoted one chapter to the rebellion and his campaign to eliminate the remaining rebels.

The value of Trevisan's account of the military campaign lies in its details of the mobilization of the Venetian army. Trevisan participated in the campaign to regain the rebel strongholds in Castro, Stimboli, St. John of Kissamos, and Anapolis. His and his colleagues' purpose was to hunt down and capture "all the Calergi and Tito Venier and a great many other Greek and Latin rebels and traitors and bring the entire island to peace and submission to the Doge's Venetian dominion."[27] The group of rebels grew smaller and smaller. One by one, both Latins and Greeks were captured, conveyed to Candia, and executed. By the end of 1365, Venice had recaptured all the principal towns and fortresses of the island, pushing the outlaws to the interior. It was not until 1368 that the Venetian forces ran the remaining rebels to ground. De Monacis describes in dramatic detail the deaths of Ioannes Calergi and Tito Venier, the two legendary figures, who died cornered in a cave, resisting to the end. With that, so De Monacis tells us, peace descended on the island.

The reestablished Venetian regime immediately turned to cleaning up after the rebels. Residents of Candia pressed suits in court to reclaim land and possessions the rebels had confiscated.[28] Rewards were meted out to those who had remained loyal.[29] The governmental sources and De Monacis would have us believe that the regime exiled families of the principal perpetrators, but the court records and the notarial records seem to suggest that exceptions were made. In one court record from 1374, eleven years after the beginning of the revolt, the court appointed a guardian for the son of a rebel feudatory whom the regime had executed. Manuel Gradenigo, the only surviving son of Leonardo Gradenigo Baiardo, was left without a guardian after the death of his grandmother, Elena Dandolo. The court appointed Mariçoli Venier, his aunt, as his new guardian.[30] Baiardo, as we have seen, figured among the leaders of the revolt. Elena Dandolo and Mariçoli Venier were not, however, peripheral figures. Elena's husband had been Marco Dandolo, who died before the revolt began, but whose sons were among the leaders, and Mariçoli was not only her and Marco's daughter, she was also the widow of the notorious Tito Venier. Either they had never left the island or the regime granted them clemency and allowed them to return. A few months later, the children of Tito's natural brother Marco (the son of a Greek woman from Cerigo and the nobleman Bartholomeo Venier) made a claim to the Venetian Senate for their father's land in the district of Chanea, indicating that they were still in the colony. The Senate referred the matter to the regime in Candia.[31] It is curious that some of the rebel leader families, particularly the relatives of Tito Venier, were allowed to stay.

Then again, perhaps only male kin were expelled. Merely because their names crop up in official records, we ought not to conclude that the sons were resident in the colony at that time. Neither the Venetian Senate nor the Venetian regime in Candia relinquished jurisdiction over the families, once they had exiled them from the island. This is confirmed by a pardon granted in 1391 by the Venetian Senate to the descendants of the 1364 rebels. We learn from the pardon that forty of the rebel kin had originally been sent to Venice at the conclusion of the revolt. Some died in the war with Padua, others in Istria, still others in Zara. Those that survived, among whom figures Manuel son of Leonardo Gradenigo Baiardo, were very young, some infants, when the revolt occurred. The Senate ruled that the descendants could travel and settle anywhere within Venetian territory except Crete. They also now had permission to sit on Venetian councils. The list of the surviving sons confirms the expulsion of not just the Gradenigo family but other rebel feudatory families as well.[32] One of those other rebel families, startlingly enough, was the Calergi. In 1382 the Venetian Senate granted permission to Leo Calergi to reside in Venice or within one hundred miles of Venice on the mainland. Moreover, this rebel, whose brothers only twenty years before were the most feared and hated enemies of the regime, received a pension of twenty-four *lire piccoli*. They could not travel without the permission of the government and they were absolutely forbidden to visit Crete.[33] In Thiriet's French summary Leo is called a "rebelle crétois," not a Greek rebel. Does this signify that Leo had achieved some sort of status in ethnic limbo in the eyes of the Venetian Senate? It certainly cannot be taken as the way Leo would have described himself, since his kinsman, Matteo Calergi, member of the Great Council of Venice, still thought of himself and was thought of by others in Crete as Greek.

Almost thirty years after the rebellion, in 1392, a wealthy feudatory of Rethimno, Giacomo Pascaligo of Venice, made his will in Candia. Among his many bequests figure three whose significance can only be surmised. Giacomo left small pious bequests for the souls of Tito Venier, Matteo Gradenigo, and Giovanni da Vigoncia, three prominent rebels. For whatever reason, the revolt and its main protagonists still occupied a place in the mind of at least one feudatory at the end of the century.

The rebels became protagonists in a much more literal sense four centuries later in a play, presented in Venice at the Teatro Grimani in 1785.[34] The play, *I Coloni di Candia*, by the Venetian playwright Giovanni Pindemonte, has for its theme a revolt in the colony of Crete, the main character of which was a treasonous nobleman of Venetian descent, Tito Venier. The potency of the revolt's example, even reshaped by Pindemonte to suit republican needs, still can be felt in the riot that occurred after the play's opening. The revolt still had a hold on the Venetian imagination centuries later, a testimony to the threat it posed not only to Venetian interests at the time, but perhaps also to the unity that the Venetians imagined they had once enjoyed.

The Rebels

In his account of the suppression of the revolt, Niccolò Trevisan offered his ideas about its causes and the rebels responsible for it:

And in this time, it so happened that God sent a plague over the earth on account of man's sins. Because of the plague, all the old ones who lived on the island died. Gone was love, and faith came to be lacking in the island. Hence, the youth remained, leaving the path of their elders, contenting themselves with the life of youth, which as Solomon said, is like a ship at sea. They broke with good customs and abandoned sane things, giving themselves over to vice, not recognizing their evil, like irrational animals, leaving aside their own nature and that of their ancestors to follow the customs of the Greeks.[35]

In this passage Trevisan places the blame for the revolt on the island's youth, but he implies something more. The choice of the Venetian word *antigi* goes beyond the idea of age. He is also making a point of distinguishing the current inhabitants of the colony from the stock of Venetians who first colonized the island. An illness, he claims, killed the old inhabitants of the island. Thus, in addition to implying that the youth of the island were left without leadership after the Black Death of 1348, he seeks to absolve the original Venetian colonists of any blame for the revolt. As we will see, there is perhaps a little more than a kernel of truth to Trevisan's explanation of how the revolt came about.

Niccolò Trevisan was not the only contemporary commentator to impugn the colonists who led the rebellion. Shortly after news of the insurrection reached Venice, Petrarch, who was residing in the city at the time, expressed in a letter his views about the perpetrators of the rebellion.

> We find the Cretans infamous not only in our own time, but also in antiquity and in apostolic testimony. Their outer aspect deceives us; to look into the hiding-places of their hearts is not for the eye of a mortal: Venetians by name and by custom, they were enemies by design and character. But they, both the living and the dead, will be destroyed by the avenger of deceit and iniquity, CHRIST.[36]

Petrarch certainly knew that the leaders of the revolt were Latin feudatories. Yet he likened them to the Greek Cretans of antiquity. Both Petrarch and Trevisan had reason to distinguish between the rebels and "true" Venetians. Unlike the previous revolts led by Greek archontic families, the participation of Latins in the revolt horrified the patricians of Venice. In Trevisan's and Petrarch's view, repudiating the Venetian origins of the rebels became important not only as a rhetorical flourish, but also as a means of minimizing the dangerous precedent set by the feudatories, the threat of which was not lost on the foreign powers who came to the aid of the Comune of Venice.

Despite Petrarch's wholesale dismissal of the Venetian colonists, De Monacis in his text shows that support for the rebellion among the Latin feudatories was not uniform. While at the beginning of the rebellion the expression of discontent represented the opinion of the majority, thereafter every step toward revolution and usurpation of power narrowed the base of support. In fact, support for the revolt began to dwindle almost immediately. The court records of the colony under the rebel regime confirm that morale among the rebels was sinking as early as November 1363, three months after the initial uprising. The court ruled that certain feudatories be either arrested or sent into exile.[37] The same court records from a period well after the suppression of the uprising show that the rebel regime had confiscated the land of feudatories who refused to support the revolt. For example, although two of his sons-in-law were among the leaders of the revolt, Marino Trevisan, a Venetian-Cretan feudatory, had his land confiscated and his son Pietro had to flee the island.[38]

By the time dal Verme's army had landed on the shores of Crete in the late spring of 1364, a group of feudatories committed to resisting the re-establishment of Venetian dominion had been formed. The Venetian Senate focused its attention on ten rebels, whom it considered the leaders: Marco Gradenigo, Baiardo Gradenigo, Gabriele Abbado, Tito Venier, Bartolomeo Grimaldo, Tito Gradenigo, Marco Fradello, Giorgio Barbo, Theodorello Venier, and Zanachi Rizo.[39] In his chronicle Niccolò Trevisan provides the names of those whom the Venetian government held primarily responsible for the revolt.[40] In the course of his narrative, De Monacis also identifies other key players in the latter stages of the rebellion. Using the membership lists of the Great Council, all of which come from the six-year period immediately preceding the revolt, we can estimate the proportion of the feudatory group that supported the revolt. As we have seen in an earlier chapter, the Great Council consisted of 102 cognomina. The list of forty-five rebels compiled from Trevisan and De Monacis consists of eighteen cognomina.[41] Sixteen of the eighteen rebel cognomina appear in the Great Council lists of 1362–63, accounting for less than 20 percent of the Great Council cognomina.[42] The Gradenigo family contributed the greatest number of rebel participants, at least ten individuals. Undoubtedly, members of other feudatory families took part in the revolt as well, but after the inital enthusiasm of early August 1363, the rebels represented a diminishing proportion of the feudatory group.

In his account, De Monacis emphasizes the solidarity of the families supporting the revolt. Kinship mattered much, for it played a part in the decision whether to join the rebels.[43] He describes how one feudatory, who went on to play a prominent role in the revolt, initially had reservations about joining. Leonardo Gradenigo Baiardo was serving as captain of a galley in the Venetian fleet protecting the Adriatic when he first heard of the revolt, and his first thought, according to De Monacis, was to go directly to Venice and offer his services to the Comune. He changed his mind, however, when he heard that all his family (*prole*) were not only rebels but leaders of the revolt. Leonardo abandoned his post and returned to Crete.[44] At the end of the revolt, according to the records of the Venetian Senate, the surviving members of the Gradenigo family had their property confiscated and were sent into exile.[45] But, oddly, we find a Leonardo Baiardo still in Candia in 1368, involved in a suit concerning his debt of fifty hyperpera to the three sons of Marco Dandolo.[46]

At least three branches of the Gradenigo family participated in the uprising. Leonardo Baiardo and his three brothers, Giovanni, Niccolò, and Pietro, belonged to one branch.[47] Each of these brothers married daughters of other prominent feudatories.[48] Ergina, wife of Pietro Gradenigo, made her will in 1362, which suggests that she had died prior to the revolt. The document provides interesting details about this family.[49] At the beginning of her will, she states, "I had summoned to me the notary Giovanni da

Fermo, whom I asked to write this testament, which I gave to him written in Greek, the tenor of which, word for word, is as follows."[50] The notary translated the will into Latin, which was the version that ultimately came to be entered in his protocol after her death. At the end of her will, a translated statement by the Greek notary appears: "I, Barnabas, monk, *penetentialis* of the monastery of holy Mt. Sinai, resident of the village of Cherissia, wrote this."[51] This information tells us that Ergina very likely first dictated her will in Greek, which accounts for the Greek notary. That he was the confessor at the monastery was incidental and so cannot be taken to mean that Ergina adhered to the rites of the Greek church. But the little more we learn about Ergina's family from her will shows how familiar she and her family were with Greek culture. Her father's brother, Giovanni Grimaldo, married Phylippa, daughter of Marco Muazzo. In Phylippa's will of 1348, she reveals that she had an uncle who was a Calergi and an aunt on her mother's side who was married to a Greek man, Nichitas Naptopulo.[52]

Leonardo Baiardo's family was not the only branch of the Gradenigo clan to have kinship ties with Greek archontes. We have seen that Leonardo Gradenigo *calogero* was a monk in the Greek church. It is impossible to say for now to which branch of the family he belonged, although De Monacis tells us he had a brother named Tito.[53] But, according to De Monacis the monk was the one rebel who very clearly thought in terms of kinship. When the rebels debated whether to capitulate or seek the assistance of Genoa, Leonardo *calogero* accused a kinsman of betrayal. "You seek to betray us! You are advocating the extermination of our *domus*!" he cried in response to the suggestion that the rebels come to terms with the Venetian authorities.[54] The most prominent member of the Gradenigo to participate in the revolt, however, was Marco Gradenigo *maior*, the senior member of the family, who became the leader of the new regime. We have met Marco before, among the most influential feudatories in the colony, who took part in more committees than anyone else, save for Alessio Corner of the Greater House. We know little about his family; we do not even know if he had sons, although he did have one daughter, who married into the Fradello family.[55]

Two other of the most prestigious feudatory families, the Muazzo and Venier, also contributed their share of participants to the rebel cause. The Muazzo were split between those who clung tenaciously to rebellion and those who capitulated early in the revolt. Three of the sons of the late Pietro Muazzo and his Greek wife, Elena, née Ialina, were massacred together with others by Milletos, the Greek monk, after they had abandoned the rebel ranks.[56] Their mother Elena made her will in January of 1360, three years prior to the revolt.[57] In it we learn that Elena continued her devotion to the Greek church after her marriage to a Latin feudatory. She also reveals that her brother was Petros Ialina and her brothers-in-law were Giovanni Ghisi and Andrea Pantaleo, all three of whom subsequently became principal leaders of the revolt.

The name Francesco Muazzo belonged to several members of the feudatory group at that time, making it very difficult to distinguish one from another. Among the rebels figured a Francesco whom it is tempting to identify as the Francesco who had been involved in a controversy with Tito Venier eight years before. In 1355 a matter concerning Francesco Muazzo and Tito Venier had disrupted the political life of the colony. Venice and the colonial regime must have viewed the issue involved as so sensitive that nowhere is there an explanation of what the two feudatories were supposed to have done. All we know is that the Venetian Senate considered their actions dangerous to Venetian authority and consequently confiscated their property.[58] In response, the Council of Feudatories sent a delegation of the most influential feudatories to Venice in order to argue before the doge and his council that the confiscation was unjust.[59] They must have succeeded, for both Francesco and Tito regained their lands and the matter was closed.[60] The incident may not have any connection at all with the revolt, but it is perhaps not entirely coincidental that one of these men, very likely both, led the uprising less than ten years later.

Tito Venier and his family were the rebel Latin feudatory family par excellence. Established in the colony since the first half of the thirteenth century, the Venier were the only other family, along with the Gradenigo, singled out by the Venetian Senate for dispossession and exile. The severity of the penalty, however, may not derive entirely from their role in the St. Tito revolt. Over twenty years previously, members of the Venier family were summoned to Venice to explain their acts of piracy launched from their island of Cerigo against the Catalans.[61] The Venetian Senate had long considered them a nuisance.

The Venier, too, were no strangers to Greek culture. Early in the fourteenth century, Bartolomeo Venier had acquired a share in the island of Cerigo through his marriage to a daughter of one of the island's three Greek lords, who held it in the name of the Byzantine emperor. When his father-in-law became sole lord of the island, he offered it to Bartolomeo. Bartolomeo was apparently not entirely straightforward with his wife and father-in-law, because it turned out that he was already married to a Latin woman, by whom he had several sons, including Tito, the future rebel. As a result, he had to flee from the island. But before this fact became known, Bartolomeo had had a son, Marcos, by his Greek wife. In 1353 Marcos pressed suit in Venice against his half-brothers, who had sought to exclude him from his father's goods and lands and from membership in the council of Chanea. The Venetian Senate sustained Marcos's claim, and thereafter Marcos appears acting in concert with his brothers in legal actions.[62] Tito, we know, became the anti-hero of sorts in the dramatic events of 1363–68. He had married Mariçoli, a daughter of Marco Dandolo, although it is not completely certain that this Marco was the same as the Marco who played such a large role in the Candiote councils in the period immediately before the revolt.[63] In the notarial, governmental, and literary sources, Tito is closely associated with his brother Theodorello.[64]

Other feudatory families figure among those the Venetian authories hunted. Giovanni Ghisi is another figure prominent among the rebels. He belonged to the branch of the family that possessed the island of Amorgos.[65] He married Frangula, daughter of the Greek feudatory, Michael Ialina.[66] Here we have arrived at one particularly vital nexus in the web of kinship among the rebels. We have already encountered Elena, Frangula's sister, married to the rebel Pietro Muazzo. Giovanni Ghisi's daughter, Nicolota, became the wife of a member of the Da Vigoncia family implicated in the rebel cause with Giovanni.[67]

Gabriele and Michele Abbado also appear in De Monacis' list of rebels proscribed by the Venetian Senate.[68] They are mostly likely to be identified with the sons of Giovanni Abbado and Potha, daughter of Maria and Leo Calergi. The will of their grandmother, Maria, revels that she was an adherent of the Latin church, signifying perhaps that she was a Latin woman.[69] The identity of another rebel, Andrea Pantaleo, is the hardest to pin down. Three individuals with that name, but without benefit of a patronymic, appear in the Council lists, although we distinguish three in notarial transactions and the colonial regime's register of *feuda*: Andrea Pantaleo, son of the late Niccolò; another, son of the late Manuel; and another, son of the late Giacomo.[70] One of them was married to Aniça, daughter of Michael Ialina, the Greek feudatory who had married two others of his daughters to future rebels, but this Andrea had died prior to 1360, as his widow's will informs us. Another (or perhaps the same) Andrea married one daughter to a Calergi.[71] Still another Andrea makes an appearance in the will of Helena Pantaleo, widow of Chyrilo. Helena's father, Ioannes Sachlichi, was a Greek feudatory who appears among the members of the Great Council. Her brother Stefano has been identified as the Greek-Cretan poet of the same name.[72] Helena had a son named Andrea, called Chyrilo like his father, who was not yet twelve years old when she made her will in 1348.[73] A notarial transaction recorded in 1340 tells us that Helena's husband,

Chyrilo, was a cousin of Andrea Pantaleo, son of the late Giacomo.[74] We will not get very far trying to pin down the identities any of these various Andreas, but the details are enough to show that there was an extensive network of kinship between those families implicated in the revolt and Greek archontic/feudatory families.

To take this point even further, it is not surprising that the feudatories of Candia were bound by a complex web of kinship as described above, since we have already seen that endogamy was characteristic of that group. Kinship ties are prominent among the rebels, but not exclusionary, because kinship ties between rebels and loyalists also exist. The Corner family of the Greater House, for instance, apparently did not participate in the insurrection, although their close kinsman Marco Gradenigo *maior* did. Nor can it be said that the rebel group had more kinship ties with Greek archontic families than had the loyalists. Both sides in the struggle had intermarried with the Greek noble families of the island. The features distinguishing between the rebel and loyalist factions lie in which Latin feudatory family allied itself in marriage to which Greek archontic family. Some members of the loyalist group display kinship ties with certain branches of the Calergi family, but not all branches of the Calergi family supported the revolt. With all these intersections of rebel and loyal feudatory families and Greek noble families, it is very hard to discern along which lines of calculation families decided whether or not to support the revolt.

A new approach to the matter of the revolt and its adherents is needed. The historical narrative of conflict in the colony of Crete has almost always been framed within the confines of ethnic division and hostility, even though there is ample evidence of conflict between people with little regard to their membership in one ethnic group or another. Specifically, virtually no attention has been paid to tensions within city life, within the feudatory group itself, and between city and countryside. Even if the substance of some of those tensions is undiscoverable, their manifestations in the sources are highly suggestive. Rather than viewing the revolt and other instances of hostility as fundamentally ethnic, we need instead to see the evidence of ethnic hostility within the spheres of urban violence and feudatory factionalism.

Conflict Among the Feudatories

Even a casual perusal of the regime's court records and register of proclamations issued throughout the fourteenth century will convince anyone that Candia was no place to be out and about in after dark. The first noticeable

signs of violence in Candia are the obligatory registrations in the records of
the duke's court of incidents involving loss of blood.[75] Not all the injuries
resulted from malicious violence. Some simply came about as an accident —
a kick from a horse, a fall from a roof.[76] Many others, however, came about
from anger and malicious intent.[77] A typical entry records who was injured,
by whom, on what part of the body the wound was located, and the name
of the attending physician. The regime's proclamations tend to contain
slightly more information. When a ten-year old girl was raped, the government issued a call for the capture of her attacker.[78] The burglary of a building inhabited by Jews prompted a call for relevant information from the
populace.[79] Motives and explanations are not given in either set of sources.
The number of injuries caused by altercations of some sort between individuals is not especially remarkable, since tensions arose from the sort of violence that is typical of cities: robberies, assaults, and so forth.

Violence between individuals motivated by personal animosity was by
no means the only danger in living in Candia. Our awareness of a higher
level of violence, or rather a more endemic problem of violence, that extended beyond a pair or a small group of individuals, comes from the
evident concern of the regime to control behavior that reads suspiciously
like vendetta, or factional fighting. Even as early as 1274 we find the Venetian Senate taking up the problem of what to do with the "Latins, *gasmuli*,
Vlachs and Turks" who rebelled against Venetian domination.[80] The year
before, the Senate outlined the penalties involved if a feudatory, a burger, or
other residents of Candia had any contact with members of the banished
Cortazzi and Skordilakis families.[81]

In specific periods during the fourteenth century, the regime issued
proclamations banning weapons, imposing curfews, and limiting public
and private gatherings. From the beginning of the register, proclamations
appear in which the bearing of swords and other arms is strictly prohibited.[82] It is possible that the bans were issued in periods of heightened
tension in the city, the reasons for which we can only surmise. What is
worth noting is that the violence viewed by the regime as barely manageable is perpetrated by both Latins and Greeks, very likely from the upper
social ranks. The first period of unrest in the city comes from 1319. One of
the first signs is the proclamation that prohibits anyone living in Platea or
the *ruga maistra* from holding arms for anyone else. The ban was repeated
five days later.[83] Spontaneous outbreaks of violence do not seem to be the
fear expressed in these bans. The Platea was the center of the political life of
Candia. It was where the duke's court met in the open air. In it were

situated the public buildings in which the councils met. The *ruga maistra*, the main street of the city running from the port to the Platea, was an extension of it. Apparently, the fear was that tensions might lead to planned violence in the political heart of the colony, whether or not it was directed against the regime. More likely the problem was controlling the violence among the feudatories themselves.

Movement through the city also was a corollary concern of the regime. In this same period of tension, 1319, the city heralds proclaimed that no one was permitted to move about after dark without a torch, nor could anyone loiter near the artisanal shops even with a torch. There was to be no loitering in the streets. Everyone must be on his way to somewhere else. Furthermore, no one was allowed to have more than three guests in his home at one time, nor ride through the city or burg in groups larger than four.[84] Nothing in these proclamations so far gives us any idea of the targets of these bans. They applied, evidently, to the entire population. But the very next proclamation, issued on the same day as the previous, points to their real target: "All feudatories and their sons at least sixteen years of age must appear within three days before the regime to swear an oath of fidelity and obedience."[85] The situation had not apparently cooled off sufficiently for the regime by the following November, for it renewed all the bans on bearing weapons, congregations, and curfews.[86]

The problem lay in the members of the councils, evidently a very volatile group. In fact, this is made explicit. On 13 April 1319, because of an altercation (*briga*) that occurred the night before, the regime had forbidden all feudatories from entering the Platea. Now it revoked that prohibition, except for nine individuals whose names show them to be from the feudatory group.[87] One Greek feudatory, Philippo Caliva, appears among them.[88] The next day, the fourteenth, the regime summoned all feudatories to the Platea, except for the ones named in the proclamation of the day before as well as all their fathers, brothers, uncles, sons, and paternal cousins.[89] A proclamation six days later sheds even more light on whom the regime viewed as responsible for the situation. Whenever the sounds of tumult could be heard in the Platea, the heralds proclaimed, the regime would ring the campanile's bell. All feudatories were to stay in or go to their homes, or be fined the extremely high sum of one thousand hyperpera, and all burgers, merchants, and men resident in the city of whatever condition were to come armed to the ducal palace under penalty of a two-hundred-hyperpera fine.[90] Evidently, the regime was able to do little more than attempt to keep a lid on the feudatories' propensity toward violence. It was even obliged to prohibit the wearing of arms in the Great Council or the Candiote Senate and it strictly forbade anyone from leaving either of those councils without the permission of the regime.[91]

Ten years later, in 1329, tensions had again increased to the point where the regime issued sweeping proclamations circumscribing the social behavior of Candia's residents. The substance of the problems was apparently the same as ten years earlier, since the regime placed restrictions on the movements of some of the feudatories involved in the problems of 1319. In a proclamation issued on 8 March 1329, the regime allowed all feudatories to leave their homes unarmed except for the relatives of Nicoletto Bono, Natale Abramo, and Peracio and Micheletto Gradenigo.[92] From subsequent proclamations we learn that the conflict lay between Bono and Abramo, on one side, and Peracio and Micheletto Gradenigo, on the other. On the same day, sweeping restrictions on the behavior of the feudatories were announced as a means to control potential violence.

The new restrictions show how seriously the regime feared the most well-armed section of Candia's colonists. The first restriction reflects the level of danger. No one was permitted, under strict penalties commensurate to the infraction, either day or night, to carry an iron knife, a sword, or other large weapon, or wear armor. There was to be no drawing of swords in the Platea and the *ruga maistra*, from the Great Gate of the city to the corner where a pharmacist's shop was located. If any feudatory broke these rules, his fine would be doubled. No more than three people could congregate in a private residence at one time. No one was permitted to hold weapons for others. At the sound of the city's bell, all feudatories were to go directly to their homes. All merchants, burgers, and others were to go to the ducal palace. No one was to go about after dark without a torch and no groups larger than six persons were permitted to ride through the city together.[93] In little over a week, the level of tension escalated. Now, no one was allowed to leave home or return home after the third bell. No one was allowed to congregate in groups larger than four persons.[94] The fear underlying these restrictions extends beyond a limited concern to maintain public order in the face of a riot. The regime clearly feared organized violence perpetrated by its most privileged colonists.

The measures were not sufficient to prevent loss of life. Less than ten days later, two of the men prohibited specifically by name, Peracio and Micheletto Gradenigo, broke into the residence of one of the duke's councillors and murdered Nicoletto Bono and Natale Abramo.[95] The regime declared them outlaws, and would confiscate their possessions if they did not appear before the duke within eight days. Two days later a curfew was imposed.[96] At the end of April, the regime found a cache of arms hidden in the loggia and required all those registered as possessing similar arms to appear before the duke. All feudatories and their sons were required to take the oath of fidelity within three days, and those outside the city at that time had three days after their return to do so.[97] The picture that emerges from these proclamations has overtones extending beyond vendetta. There is a whiff of revolt about them.

To the extent that the proclamations and court records are a reliable indicator, life in Candia returned to its normal level of violence between individuals for the next two decades. The traces of yet another vendetta with political overtones in 1351, involving a few feudatories who would play a significant role in the 1363 revolt twelve years later, show up in Venetian sources.

In May 1351, a group of horsemen, consisting of Venetian patrician kinsmen visiting the colony, Giovanni, Giacomo, Donato, and Pietro Dolfin, and two servants, rode out of Candia through the imposing city gate leading to the burg. When they neared the hospital of St. Mary of the Crusaders, they were attacked by a group of Candiotes, among whom figured feudatories: Marco Dandolo, son of the late Donato; Leonardo Gradenigo called Baiardo, son of the late Michael; Philippo Dandolo, son of Donato; Michaletto da Raguseo called Brocalio; Niccolò da Canal called Mauro; Niccolò da Cresenza; Niccolò Corner, son of the late Andrea; and Giovanni Romano. Three additional men accompanying the group headed by Marco Dandolo are set apart in the entry: Giovanni da Raguseo called Brochali, Ugucio da Perosa, and Leo Dandolo, the three who eventually bore the brunt of the guilt. No reason is given for the assault, but as a result Giovanni Dolfin died of wounds to his head and two other Dolfin were wounded. Giovanni, Ugucio, and Leo were taken into custody. A proclamation was issued to summon the Dandolo party to the court to explain their actions. The Dandolo party appeared and apparently defended themselves adequately, because Marco Dandolo and his cohort were absolved, except for Niccoleto da Crescenza, who remained at large, and Niccolò da Canal and Giovanni da Raguseo, who remained in prison. Niccolò da Canal eventually escaped from prison and over the city walls.[98]

Once again, the causes of the violence are obscure. But there are two points worth mentioning. One party to the events of 1351, the Dolfin, were obviously kinsmen. Less obviously, however, the same can be said for some of the other party. Marco Dandolo was one of the most prominent and influential feudatories in the Great Council and the Candiote Senate. Philippo Dandolo son of Donato was probably Marco's grandson, if the Donato who was his father was also the Donato who was Marco's son. Leonardo Gradenigo Baiardo, who was seen playing a role in the events of 1363, was Marco's son-in-law. Nicoletto Corner, son of the late ser Andrea, was Marco's nephew. I have been unable to establish a kinship tie between Marco and the other men who accompanied him. The second point to bear in mind is that one party to the affair were Venetians temporarily residing in Crete, who eventually immigrated to Candia. This point will have greater importance later on.

At the beginning of 1357, we once again find proclamations creating a state of martial law in the colony. A ban on weapons appears in April of that year.[99] Later the regime imposed a curfew again, only this time city residents were prohibited from entering the burg at night with or without weapons.[100] Two years later, again a curfew.[101] Also in 1359, a group of Greeks murdered a Greek feudatory, an act that provoked a meeting of the Council of Feudatories.[102] By 1362, the advent of another epidemic led to food shortages and poverty; to combat this the regime decided to tax all *feuda* to raise money for food.[103] The regime had to take steps again in early 1362 to stop the fighting and the attacks that were occurring at night throughout the city and the burg. The same day, a feudatory was found murdered in his bed.[104] The tension continued up to and throughout the 1363 revolt. In the midst of the suppression of the revolt, the regime proclaimed that no more than six men might gather before or after a wedding and that there was to be no dancing.[105] Thereafter, other notices of feudatory violence aimed at the regime and other feudatories appear in the proclamations.[106]

Again, there is no information at all as to the nature of the disturbances that led to the issuance of these proclamations. All that can be said is that the entire population of Candia was affected and that the feudatories seem to be at the core of the problems. Something was happening, but the cause remains unknown.

Before considering one more indication of tension among the feudatories, this is an opportune moment to think once more about the limitations of the councils' deliberations. The decisions of the councils were not meant to be understood as accurate or objective reflections of what was said in the meetings. The vast majority of the substance of discussion was not recorded, especially when the topic under discussion impinged on matters of great sensitivity, as in the case involving Tito Venier and Francesco Gradenigo in the 1350s. For this reason, the substance of the differences among the feudatories does not emerge from the folios. If any divergence in interests can be pinpointed in the register, it is easiest to come away from a review of the deliberations with the impression that the feudatories stood to one side and the regime and the Venetian Senate stood to the other. This impression is in some respects deliberately created in the way De Monacis deliberately depicted the revolt in a manner that was likely to appeal to his primary intended audience, the patricians in Venice. In other words, both the deliberations and De Monacis' narrative attempt to shape the dissension among the colonists in such a way as to least harm Venetian interests. The best policy, when possible, was simply not to mention the problem. If that could not be avoided, then the tacit policy was to commit as little about the problem as possible to writing. Fortunately for the historian, it was occasionally necessary to allude to a problem, even if the regime succeeded in suppressing the subject matter.

In December 1361, six years after the institution of the *proba* for the Candiote Great Council, twenty-seven electors and three *camerarii* held the *proba* for the following year.[107] The families represented by these men included the most noble of the colony: *Barbadico, Bollani, *Caravello, *Contarini, Corner, *Dandolo, Delfino, Dono, Ghisi, *Gradenigo, Greco, *Grimani, Magno, Marcello, *Molino, *Morosini, *Muazzo, Pasqualigo, Sanudo, *Sagredo, Soranzo, *Trivisano, *Venier, *Zane, Zeno, and one illegible name. Thirteen of these names (those with an asterisk) belonged to families who were present at the beginning of the colony. The others, the Bollani, Corner, Dono, Ghisi, Greco, Magno, Marcello, Pasqualigo, Sanudo, Soranzo, and Zeno families, were all noble families who had immigrated to the island at a subsequent point. Of the other electors, there is no notice of members of the Dolfin family residing permanently in Candia prior to the 1360s. By the time that they had finished their task, they had disqualified twenty-six men, most of whom had held seats on the Great Council since the *proba* was first instituted in December of 1356.

The eighteen families represented by the men who were disqualified from belonging to the Candiote Great Council were the Bicoli, Bicontolo, Bono, Clugia, Flabani, Freganesco, Ghezzo, Gradu, Lago, Lisi, Milovani, Partegon, Paulino, Pino, Rosso, Saclichi, Venetando, and Vido.[108] Most notable among these names are two Greek cognomina, the Flabani and the Saclichi. Domenico Bono, son of the late Stefano, somehow failed to qualify, although other members of the Bono family continued to hold onto their membership. Only two (Ghezzo and Paolino) are noble cognomina in the Trecento, although Bicontolo is a cognomen that appears among the very first tenants of a sergeantry in 1211.[109]

In Chapter One it was explained that in the *proba* for 1362, sixty-two men were added to the Great Council, and for 1363, forty-nine were added. Most of these additions can be explained by young men joining their fathers and brothers on the council. Only a few of these new additions were new families entering the council seemingly for the first time: Baduario, Damiani (1362 only), Dolfin, Duodo, Fraganesco, a new line of the Grimani, Lauredano, Manolesso, Miani, Mocenigo, Nani, and Signolo. Six of these twelve cognomina appear in the *Concessio*, and so more than likely they were not new members of the council. Consequently, although there is a perceptible increase in the members of the Great Council between 1361 and 1362, the number of families there decreased after the *proba* of December, 1361.

The *proba* the electors conducted in December of 1361 for 1362 did not meet with the approval of the regime and the Venetian Senate, for at the start of the following year's *proba*, a letter from the Signoria in Venice prefaced the proceedings. The Venetian Senate and the Quarantia complained that the *proba* of that year had not been carried out in an orderly fashion, because neither were certain procedures followed nor did electors excuse themselves from the voting when their kinsmen's candidacies were under scrutiny. Therefore the Senate required everyone who failed to qualify the previous year to be reviewed once more that year.[110] The regime put together a new group of electors, replacing fourteen of the twenty-seven men from the previous year. For three days in December 1362, the committee of electors oversaw the *proba* for the Great Council membership of 1363, the results of which led to the reinstatement of the seventeen families disqualified in the previous year, except for Stefano Saclichi, who failed once again. The question is, then, which electors made a difference by their absence to the reinstatement of those disqualified? The left column of Table 17 lists the names of the men who were not reelected to the reconstituted committee of electors in 1362; the right column contains the additions to the committee in 1362.

These changes both in the members of the Great Council and in the families represented in the committee of electors are perplexing. The government claimed that one of the problems in the 1361 *proba* was that some electors did not excuse themselves on grounds of kinship from participating in a vote on the membership of a candidate. This leads us to expect the irregular granting of membership to candidates who might otherwise have failed. Instead, kinship led to the disqualification of seventeen families, an action that was reversed when another group of families replaced some of the participants in the earlier committee. The electors were from all noble families, and it is very difficult to see any difference between those on the

TABLE 17.   Electoral Committee Makeup, 1362

Families dropped from 1362 committee	Families added to 1362 committee
Bolani de Venetiis	Balistrario
Ghisi	Barbo
Greco	Dolfin
Magno	Duodo
Marcello	Emo
Morosini	Falier
Pasqualigo	Fradello
Sagredo	Mazamano
Sanudo	Minoto
Soranzo	Muazzo
Zane	Nani
	Quirini

committee of 1361 and those who replaced them in 1362. The disqualified families were largely non-noble by Venetian standards. Despite this, it was the Venetian Senate that took the initiative to call for a more orderly *proba*, resulting in the reinstatement of the non-noble families.

The only speculative conclusion that can be drawn from this puzzle consists of several parts. First, a portion of the electors in 1361 wished to deprive seventeen families of membership on the Candiote Great Council. Kinship appears to have been a factor in their motives. Such a move on the part of these electors supports the notion of factional conflict within the feudatories, but no pattern suggesting a basis for the conflict emerges from the names of electors. The thrust of the move on the 1361 electors' part seems to have been to constrict the feudatory group to a more aristocratic core. Interestingly, the Venetian Senate did not support this move, perhaps having its eye more focused on procedural integrity than on the social composition of the feudatory group. The impetus to cleanse the feudatory group of social inferiors came from the feudatories themselves, rather than from Venice, where the same process had begun with the *Serrata* and would conclude with the legislation we saw enacted in the first half of the fifteenth. The connection between the aristocratization of the feudatory group in Candia and that of the patriciate in Venice deserves more attention, for it may turn out to be the case in this respect as well as in many others that the colony of Crete had influenced Venice, in the same way that Venice had an impact on Crete, if not to the same extent. For the moment, the important point to bear in mind is that all the indications of the unknown nature of strife within the feudatory group can be seen as leading up to and playing a role in the outbreak of the revolt. The scenario of the feudatories against the Venetian state no longer satisfies as a full explanation of the events of the summer of 1363.

The historian Silvano Borsari has extended Jegerlehner's explanation of the revolt's causes by proposing the idea that the feudatories, increasingly excluded from international trade of greatest value in favor of Venetians from the metropolis, felt they were receiving very little in return for all the fiscal and military obligations imposed on them.[111] The virtue of this view is that it takes into account a difference in interests among the Venetians in general, but I believe the situation is far more complex. Most of the families who supported the 1363 revolt had one characteristic in common: they were among the original concessionaire noble families established on the island since 1211. The one open dispute before the revolt that we know of involved, on the one side, the Dolfin, a patrician family that had not yet immigrated to Crete, and on the other, the Dandolo and the Gradenigo, among the noblest and oldest of Candiote feudatory families. I am suggesting that the factionalism in Candia's feudatory group developed over the fourteenth century between the feudatory families who had been in the colony since its inception and the families that had more recently immigrated there. The oldest families, some of whom were later to apply for confirmation of their Venetian noble status, saw themselves seated at the pinnacle of Candiote society. They are also the families with some of the strongest kinship links with Greek archontic families, particularly the Calergi. The Gradenigo, Venier, Muazzo, Dandolo, and others were the ones with the short-lived vision of themselves as a new polity in 1363. We cannot know the specific details of their resentments, but the context is not hard to guess.

The revolt of 1363 has consistently been depicted as an irregular, exceptional, and aberrant occurrence, when for once Venice lost control of the reins. We now see, however, that rebellion on the part of the Latin population, whether feudatory or commoner, did not begin in the 1360s. If, instead, we look for potential variances of interests among the various players in the ever-urgent drama of ruling a distant colony, we may gain some insight into not only what happened in the colony of Crete, but also some fundamental dynamics of the colonial experience, especially one that is charged with ethnic currents.

Where indeed in all the above proclamations and governmental actions is the ethnic strife that interested observers from the fifteenth century down to today have used to explain Candia's history? To be sure, there are indications in the sources throughout the period of that strife on a grand scale, such as the deliberations of Venetian Senate that trace the large archontic-led revolts of the fourteenth century.[112] From the Candiote documents, the significance of traces of more immediate, local tension have not been appreciated to their full extent. For instance, consider the following proclamation from 1314.

> It was publicly proclaimed by Riçardo, herald, that no feudatory supplying a troop may henceforth appear at muster in the presence of the regime wearing a beard, under penalty of ten hyperpera for each time, unless he has the excuse of *mesticie*. And this is to apply to all associates who form part of the *feuda*.[113]

Here is one tangible cause of diverse interests within the feudatory group, but before considering that cause, three points must be elicited from that proclamation. First, the early part of the fourteenth century was still a period marked by open revolt of the archontic families against the Venetian regime. Naturally, the regime wished to be able to distinguish its forces from those of the enemy, one of whose better-known cultural customs was the wearing of beards. Therefore, the regime was instituting one measure to separate Greeks from Latins: but not just any Latins. The second interesting point to be taken from the proclamation is that the regime felt it necessary at all to impose this stricture on its feudatories, the implication being that some Latin feudatories gave the impression of "going native" as early as 1314. Third and mostly important, some Latin feudatories were in fact exempted from the prohibition of beards, on the grounds that they were descended from or the direct products of parents of mixed heritage and so understandably would display that heritage in such a manner. In spite of an apparent insistence on religious conformity, the regime demonstrated a latitude one would not expect it to allow the feudatories. In other words, a mixed heritage was understood to entail the observance of certain cultural customs not traditionally associated with being Latin. No wonder the older and more prestigious feudatory families, with their extensive ties to the noblest Greek families, felt at odds with the more recent patrician *arrivistes*. This insight lends added significance to another change occurring in the early 1360s that is evident in the sources.

An examination of the deliberations of the three Candiote councils from 1360 to 1362 reveals that a change in the feudatories' leadership was taking place immediately prior to the outbreak of the revolt. During the

1350s, five men stand out conspicuously as the leaders of the feudatories: Marco Gradenigo *maior*, Alessio Corner of the Greater House, Pietro Quirini, son of the late Romeo, Marco Dandolo, and Marco Fradello. Let us place each of them briefly in the context of the 1363 revolt.

No other feudatory served on as many committees of the councils as did Marco Gradenigo *maior* and Alessio Corner of the Greater House. Gradenigo's seat on the council dates back to the earliest Senate membership list, in 1349, but he was one of three to be elected to the responsible position of secretary (*camerarius*) to the Candiote Great Council in 1346, and he appears in a notarial transaction from an earlier date.[114] After 1349, his name shows up on fifty different committees, whose purviews involved issues of great concern to both the colony and the feudatories.[115] He frequently served as ambassador to Venice on behalf of the feudatories and was at the center of most discussions concerning defense against Turkish raids. Marco Gradenigo *maior* became the rebel regime's governor. He was from the elder generation of feudatories as well as descended from one of the original settlers, despite what De Monacis has to say about the vagaries of the youthful rebels.

Alessio Corner served nearly as often as Marco Gradenigo on committees and in the capacity of ambassador of the Council of Feudatories to Venice and to the emirates of Asia Minor.[116] Alessio Corner appears for the last time in the councils' deliberations at the end of 1362, a year before the revolt began. His death is substantiated by De Monacis, who describes the murder by Milletos of Alessio's son, "Andrea quondam Alexii."[117]

Pietro Quirini, son of the late Romeo, was the only other feudatory comparable in status and responsibilities, apparently beginning his career at the same as Marco Gradenigo *maior*, when they both were elected *camerarii*. He also died sometime in 1362.

Marco Dandolo, whom we have seen involved in the murder of a visiting Venetian nobleman, died sometime between the autumn of 1360 and the early summer of 1362.[118] Not much is known of the fifth influential feudatory, Marco Fradello, before the revolt, except for the fact that he had two sons, Andrea and Giovanni. Once the revolt began, however, Marco moved immediately into the foreground, joining the revolt and becoming one of the four councillors to the rebel governor, Marco Gradenigo *maior*. Fradello met his end when he, Marco Gradenigo *maior*, and Gabriele dell'Abate were beheaded in Candia after the city fell to Venetian forces in the summer of 1364.

Alessio Corner, Pietro Quirini, and Marco Dandolo died in the years immediately preceding the summer of 1363. The two other feudatories, Marco Gradenigo *maior* and Marco Fradello, emerged at the head of the revolt. The coincidence is purely circumstantial, yet consider those circumstances. We cannot determine on which side Pietro Quirini would have stood in the revolt. Marco Dandolo's kin by and large allied themselves with the rebels. Alessio Corner is a bit of a mystery, but De Monacis offers a revealing moment in the revolt. Alessio's son, Andrea, was killed during the revolt by the monk Milletos.[119] De Monacis describes the murder. On the night that the killings of Latin feudatories in their country estates began, the Greek monk Milletos

in order to avoid arousing suspicion of his plan, stayed with Andrea Corner quondam Alexii, dearest friend to him, in the village of Psonopila. When night fell, Milletos with his companions-in-crime first invaded the aforesaid village. Thoroughly frightened, Andrea Corner said to him: Friend, why have you come? Milletos answered, In order to kill you. And the other: What great misfortune has befallen you that you would wish to kill your intimate friend and benefactor? He responded: So it must be, for friendship gives way to religion and liberty. I took an oath that I would bring us liberty and uproot you schismatics from this island, which is our patrimony. And having said these things, they killed him.[120]

De Monacis makes clear that Milletos was somehow intimately connected to Andrea's household. Obviously Andrea is perceived as one of the enemy. Parenthetically, the Corner of the Greater House were not among the original settlers, although they did become one of the most important families in the colony. The passing of a generation of feudatory leaders brought into being conditions that were all that had been lacking for a major uprising.

To summarize the points I have made thus far pertaining to the feudatories, a close reading of the regime's proclamations and court records, in tandem with the Venetian Senate's deliberations, reveals a fairly continual state of tension throughout most of the fourteenth century within the feudatory group. The feudatories experienced enough problems internal to the group to warrant the attention of the Venetian state to such an extent that it appears the regime averted a revolt in 1329 showing a marked resemblance to the one of 1363. Whatever the source of those tensions, kinship played a central role in their expression. But the evidence suggests that the factions within the feudatory group fell along lines dividing the oldest colonist families from those more recently arrived. The feudatories, however, constituted only one segment of that volatile society.

The colony of Crete resembled a powder-keg in the fourteenth century, but the fault cannot be laid entirely at the doorstep of the feudatory group, to judge from the rapidity with which the revolt spread beyond them. The danger of rebellion, the Venetian state realized, lay not solely in the actions of its most privileged subjects in the colony, but also and perhaps especially in those actions in combination with the mass of indigenous Cretan people, meaning the townspeople and the peasants. De Monacis gives the list of Greeks he says were inducted into the feudatory group after the rebel regime was installed: Carandino, Marmici, Petaço, Ferazo, Raguseo, and Dado. Oddly, these are not Greek cognomina. Neither are they noble. The same is true of the list of rebels brought to Venice for trial in the Venetian sources:

Paladino Premarin
Marco de la Tura
the carpenter Marco Bugato
the jeweler Cavalcante
the refiner Niccolò Rizzo
Francesco da Fermo, brother of the former chancellor of Crete
Vettor Schevagata
Micheletto di Ranieri
Giannino Saymben
Francesco Mudazzo
Giorgio da Molino
Micheletto Falier
Angelo Barozzi
Galeazzo Zancaruolo[121]

   With the exception of the last five, the men listed here are also non-patricians. It cannot be a coincidence that the rebels the Venetian authorities chose to bring back to Venice to make an example of were commoners. The feudatory leaders of the revolt whom they had managed to capture up until that point had been executed in Candia. Thus, the social makeup of the rebels turns out to be far more complex than De Monacis' and Trevisan's descriptions of the revolt as one begun by Latins and usurped by Greeks. Three Cretan groups with three varying interests and responses to the events are discernible in De Monacis' chronicle. The feudatories are obviously the first group, who light the match that sets the fire. The townspeople form the second, who at first support the rebels, but then turn against the excesses of the rebellion out in the countryside. The peasantry under the leadership of some Greek archontes and Latin feudatories constitutes the third, and they are the ones who prolong the revolt literally for years. Emerging slowly and indistinctly from De Monacis' text are the feudatories' and the townspeople's fears of a peasants' revolt, depicted primarily in scenes involving the Greek monk Milletos and his following. The governmental records reveal that the groundswell of popular support for the feudatories' actions within Candia dwindled, once a full-fledged peasants' revolt threatened, led by portions of the Greek nobility.[122] All the above factors must be added to our recognition that the feudatory group was riven by faction to a degree that threatened the stability of the colony's very existence. In other words, what we have here is a colonial situation that very much resembles the colonies of centuries to come. The colonizing power nearly lost possession of its colony to a coalition of a portion of its own elite, permanently settled in the colony, in alliance, however temporary or expedient, with the general population over which those agents were meant to hold sway.

Up to now the history of the Revolt of St. Tito has been categorized as a revolt of the Latin feudatories that got out of hand. According to this view, once the participation of Greeks began to dominate the rebellion, many Latin rebels distanced themselves from the insurrection and thereafter the revolt evolved into an ethnic struggle for independence from Venetian rule. The revolt did not signal a rapprochement between the Latin rebels and the Greek nobility or peasantry, according to one historian, but a temporary convergence of interests between the two groups at the start of the enterprise.[123] To be sure, this perception of the revolt is still valid; but there is much more to be said.

The extent of the kinship ties between the Greek nobility and the feudatories mitigates the notion that any rapprochement between the two groups was one of pure convenience. Ethnic divisions in Candiote society persisted, in spite of kinship, but the Revolt of St. Tito brings into relief other divisions in Cretan life, which had the potential to transform the colony in unprecedented ways. Where else in the Mediterranean of that time can we find a colony on the brink of becoming a postcolonial nation in the modern sense of each of those words, a politically autonomous entity forged on the basis of a coalition between a once-foreign ruling class and popular elements composed of all classes and ethnic groups? Consider the following scene in De Monacis' narrative. In the first days of the rebellion, the rebels convened in the ducal palace to begin the business of governing and establish order once more in the city.

In the palace, the rebels discussed whether they should raise the customary flag of San Marco, or that of San Tito. A crowd ran into the piazza crying, Long live San Tito! And so it was decreed that the figure of San Tito be borne on a standard, on land and sea, and be raised in public everywhere. On the same day, with an excited crowd gathered, the flag of San Tito was raised above the bell-tower, but the figure of the Saint was turned upside down, with the head below the feet. Many of the faithful became frightened.[124]

Putting aside the ill omen, did the hoisting of the banner of St. Tito express a political will that had been biding its time for the right moment to emerge? Or was it rather an instinctive act, emerging out of special conditions, one meant to ignite a sense of political will and by extension the desire and support for political independence, by which the two ethnic communities would be united, if not made all equal? Standards, emblems, and other outward symbols of civic or imperial unity were not new in the Middle Ages. Indeed, the very substitution of the lion of St. Mark by the rebels' own standard attests to the already recognized symbolic power of insignia. Nevertheless, the moment was new. The raising of the standard of St. Tito embodied what was in fact extraordinary about the revolt and the colony itself. The overthrow of the Venetian regime, the establishment of a new one, and the display of public emblems symbolizing the severance of ties with Venice all represent a singular demonstration of political will on the part of colonial agents of a foreign power.

Here today's vocabulary fails most tellingly, for it is difficult to describe the significance of the 1363 revolt without recourse to modern, anachronistic terminology. Modern historiography lacks the vocabulary to define the nature of the bond that once united the Venetian Senate, Venetians of Venice, and the Venetian feudatories long established on Crete. Does the term "national" adequately describe the sentiment shared by Latin Cretans and Venetians of the metropolis, or does it more accurately describe the sentiment that brought Latin Cretans and Greek Cretans together, on equal and unequal terms, in their homes, their families, their marketplaces, the courts of law, and their councils, and ultimately led them to secede from Venice? Short-lived though the revolt may ultimately have been, the raising of the St. Tito standard displayed a flash of imaginative political will that sought to redefine the people of this colony as neither Greek nor Latin, but as Cretan.

Modern colonization arose out of the laboratory in which the Venetian colony of Crete played an important part. The root of the tension in Candia was not merely foreign domination, but a kind of foreign domination unusual for its time: state-sponsored colonization. The overarching political structure imposed on the island of Crete gave rise to social relations among the inhabitants that over time took on unprecedented characteristics. In the conditions prevailing there, at the highest and lowest ends of the social spectrum, are located the harbingers of colonies to come. The elite colonists constituted a class of people who were neither fish nor fowl, neither Greek nor Latin, neither ruler nor completely subject, whose interests were fundamentally divided between those of the colonizing power and those of their cohabitants on the island. At the peak of Candiote society stood the feudatories, whose status before the Venetian state and law placed them on the same side of the governing/governed equation as the indigenous people of the island. Valuing their privileges as Latin feudatories and servants of the Venetian state, they were aware of being at the pinnacle of Candiote society. Their position relative to Venetian society was not as advantageous. They may have been at the peak of Candiote society, but they were pushed below the summit of the Venetian patriciate. The Venetian state recognized the dangers of the feudatories' disaffection and did what it could to keep the feudatories' gaze upward towards the awesome and privilege-granting power of the state. Only trouble could result when the gaze descended. The conflicting pressures led to the tense atmosphere throughout the fourteenth century. The ability of the elite colonists to find common interests with the others in the colony's social pyramid bespeaks the potential for an incipient modern nation, one composed of different classes and categories of privilege, capable of imagining itself for a moment in a way that virtually no other people in the period in that region had the capacity to imitate, not even in Venice itself.

At the same time, the same social relations caused the emergence of a different manner of determining who could and could not benefit from free status on the lowest levels of society. The previous methods, mostly relating to religion, no longer worked in the specific conditions created in Crete, where one Christian population conquered and subjugated another acknowledged Christian population. Although slavery was not a vital component of the Cretan economy, as the Atlantic slave trade would become in the economies of the new American states, slavery was nevertheless an important component of Mediterranean trade, and Crete was one of its important markets, visited by the Venetians, the Genoese, and other Italian merchants, and by the Aragonese. Safeguarding people from enslavement according to religious criteria came to be replaced in Crete by ethnic criteria. From there it is a short step to justifying people's enslavement according to similar and amplified rationales.

5

Conclusion

The Myth of Ethnic Homogeneity

THE TRADITIONAL VIEW OF Venetian Crete, with its heavy emphasis on monolithic, fundamentally antagonistic ethnic groups, is in part the product of the particular way the sources have been manipulated by scholars. The governmental and literary sources, such as the council deliberations and court records, show that ethnic categories in Crete operated on two levels: the official and the popular. In the council records, most symptoms of tension in the colony are described in ethnic terms. The Venetian colonial authorities lent juridical status to the term "Latin" when it passed down rulings in the fourteenth century in its courts that to be Latin was to be free. Furthermore, the official categories "Latin" and "Greek" appear to have been consistent with the sympathies of the island's inhabitants, to judge by the wills made by Latins and Greeks. These are the sources that have received the bulk of scholarly attention.

The notarial registers, in contrast, are filled with the Latins and Greeks of Candia and its district going about their business both jointly and separately. As disadvantageous as Venetian rule was in many ways for Greek Cretans, those who lived in Candia had a better chance of prospering than those in the countryside, not because they were Greek in a different way, but rather because they were not peasants. They made their livings differently, and their material lives were fundamentally different from those of the peasantry. In short, they belonged to a different class of society that, by virtue of the differences in how they made their living and in their material lives, put their interests potentially at variance with those of the Greek peasants. Moreover, the notarial sources show that many Latin and Greek Candiotes came to share cultural attributes. The Latin population, both feudatories and commoners, had absorbed aspects of Greek culture, such as given names, language, customs, and a tolerance of the Greek church, that is sometimes difficult to distinguish from promotion. Marriage between the Latin feudatories and the Greek noble families was not uncommon, as we saw in the case of the Calergi family. Mixed marriages on the lower levels of society were even more common, although at times officially discouraged by the government. Elsewhere I have shown that Greek women, the poorest and least juridically capable section of the population, were engaged in their own right in a variety of economic ventures.[1] Lastly, we have found at least five Greek noble families who held seats in the island's advisory councils.

The problem is how to reconcile the two pictures presented by the different sets of sources, because both are to different degrees valid, and how to explain them in light of the population's continued use of terms like "Latin" and "Greek" when it is obvious that the criteria for what defined "Latin" and "Greek" had evolved considerably over the first two centuries of Venetian rule. After working with these sources closely for a long time, it became clear to me that the defining features of "Latin" and "Greek" were less important, since they changed, than the uses to which the ethnic terms were put and the situations in which they were employed.

Ranging the evidence for unrest in the colony derived from the governmental sources against notarial evidence of economic life brings into relief the antagonistic divisions in Candiote society, which do not appear fundamentally ethnic. Moreover, the traces of major fault lines are clearest as those dividing the town from the countryside and the longest-established colonial families from the newer ones. Scratch beneath the surface of the so-called Greek revolt in the aftermath of the 1363 rebellion, and there will appear something that looks very much like a peasants' revolt. This means that recognizing the concept of ethnicity, however it is defined, and the categories derived from it, to be a tool first and a state of existence second, opens the way to deepening our understanding of how those who have the power to do so manipulate social perceptions and self-perceptions that have an impact on others. Viewing ethnic or national identity as an ideological tool, or at least a factor that comes into play in specific situations and moments, instead of being an all-pervasive, omnivalent state of being, helps to locate and account for behavior that seems to contradict that sense of collectivity.

Two centuries before the settlement of the western hemisphere, Venice, an Old World colonial power, provides the link between colonization and evolving notions of ethnicity. The fourteenth century was a threshold into an age where ethnic distinctions between peoples took on new burdens, many of them linked to the reality of enslavement. The people of the

Mediterranean, in particular, were thrust over that threshold by the exigencies of colonial relations, in which rationales were needed to protect status or, later on, to deprive a person of status, in the aftermath of foreign conquest and the process of consolidating that conquest. The connection between colonization and ethnicity is clearest in colonies; less obvious is the impact of that connection on the mother society.

"Inevitable" is a word that historians correctly shun, but miscegenation does seem to be an almost inevitable result when two or more peoples live side by side. Establishing a colony in an already inhabited land requires not merely the subjugation of those inhabitants, but also the creation of incentives beyond that of economic gain for the colonists to settle there permanently. Sexual partners from among the indigenous population were an important, if unacknowledged, incentive, although in Crete sanctioned sexual alliances in the form of marriages were not encouraged by the regime. Nevertheless, that miscegenation led to children is to state the obvious. In Venetian Crete, where miscegenation was common, sex and ethnicity were inextricably linked. A good portion of Candiote society from top to bottom counted members of both Greek and Latin ancestry among their forebears. But the begetting of illegitimate children in a colony such as Crete had different consequences from those attached to illegitimate children in an independent western European state during the same period. The most important consequence was that miscegenation led to changes in the ethnic composition of the population over time, with the continual growth in numbers of people of mixed backgrounds. This meant that every colonial society had to devise ways to cope with the problem of miscegenation, ranging from including those new members to denying their existence.

The discriminatory process had its limits in this early setting. In Crete the government placed a premium on Latin ancestry, prompting the population to do so as well to varying degrees, depending on their social status. Being "Latin" in Crete came to be little more than a formal category. Not even religious affiliation was sufficient to anchor it to a fixed standard. That a portion of the Candiote population clung to the formal category is a political observation, not a taxonomical one. Since so many Candiotes had mixed ancestry, were bilingual, and displayed mixed cultural attributes in their compendium of customs, a person's "Latin-ness" was not arbitrary so much as it was politically contrived.

The manner in which ethnicity evolved in Crete also had an impact on the patriciate back in the city of Venice. In the appeals for and the reaction to the confirmations of membership in Venice's Great Council there appeared an analogous process of one elite heightening its self-definition by excluding candidates for commensurate status. Colonization's impact on the so-called mother society of Venice is an area of study that deserves more students. The correlation I make between the colonists' applications for noble status in Venice and the legislation of the second *Serrata* suggests that at the same time that feudatories sought increased prestige and economic privilege in Crete through Venice's recognition of their noble status, their kinship with Greek noble families reduced their prestige in the eyes of the mother society's nobility. Specifically, the correlation means that those tainted branches of patrician families were not well received by the Venetian aristocracy, who were at the same time, but perhaps not coincidentally, drawing a circle around themselves even smaller than the one created by the legislation of the first *Serrata*. Although the language of the fifteenth-century legislation is free of the concept of "purity of blood," an uneasiness and a contempt are clearly felt, and the best candidates for the objects of that uneasiness are those Venetian Cretan nobles seeking confirmation of their noble status.

Venetian Cretan nobles immigrated to Venice in increasing numbers over the fourteenth and throughout the fifteenth centuries. Their uneasy reception and integration into Venetian society shows how colonial elites who immigrated to the mother society inadvertently promoted a heightened sense of superiority in the more prestigious nobility, in a way that Venetian commoners and those belonging to non-Venetian ethnic groups already resident in the city never did. It is worth exploring the possibility that the heightened sense of Venetian identity among the patriciate that developed in the fifteenth century emerged in part from the desire to distinguish true Venetian patricians from false ones. The so-called true nobles did not define themselves against non-Venetians or the *popolani* exclusively. Their concern was to exclude those who they felt diminished their corporate purity from within their own ranks. Buried in that concern is the germ of ethnic — and subsequently racial — notions of inclusion and exclusion that are indicative of changes taking place in the same period of time elsewhere in the Mediterranean and most ominously out in the Atlantic Ocean.

The differences between Crete and the Spanish and British colonies of the Caribbean and America can be seen on all social levels. The colonists of New Spain, and other Spanish colonies, developed a creole identity that underlay the foundation of a future national one; the Venetian Cretan feudatories' identity as fourteenth-century "creoles" (if the use of that word may be allowed in that century) led ultimately nowhere, except back to Venice, in the aftermath of the Ottoman conquest of the island in 1669.[2]

Similarly, at work in the later colonial situations of Spanish America and Ireland was the tension between the evident pressures on the colonists to lead lives in close proximity to a population they had conquered and less tangible pressures emanating from the mother society back in Europe or across the sea in England. Acculturation and miscegenation, no matter how limited or extensive, created a confusion of symbols in the colony, particularly among the elite, and the suspicion of colonists' pollution in the eyes of the nobility in the mother country.

Across the Atlantic, a little more than two centuries after the Revolt of San Tito in 1363, another group of colonists expressed a desire for independence from the colonial power that sanctioned their presence in a distant conquered land. Martín Cortés, son of the conqueror of Mexico, and his fellow colonists were unhappy at the news received in 1565 that the Spanish crown planned to do away with the system of land allotment and exploitation known as the *encomienda*. He and his fellow colonists saw an opportunity in this moment. A group of them donned the customary dress of indigenous Mexican chieftains and warriors and marched in procession through Mexico City to Cortés's house, where he received from them a crown of flowers. This political theater reenacted in symbolic fashion the ceding of Mexico's lands by Moctezuma to Cortés's father, Hernán. Although the uprising that followed was more quickly suppressed than the rebellion in Venetian Crete, the assumption of indigenous symbols by a colonial elite as part of a strategy to gain autonomy was very much like the dynamic at work in Candiote society and in the 1363 revolt itself.[3]

No matter how great the privileges they enjoyed, the colonists recognized that they were standing on common ground with the prior inhabitants of the land and were momentarily prepared to recast their self-image from that of loyal Spaniards to that of new men in a new homeland. Anthony Pagden's observation about the Spanish crown's response to this aborted attempt at secession can apply as well to the Venetian state's attitude toward its own colonists: "The revolt was a failure, but a highly significant failure that for the crown marked forever the descendants of the old conquistadores as a social group that could not be trusted."[4] The revolts in the colonies of Crete and New Spain, as Mexico was then called by the Spaniards, were less exceptional historically than they were a logical result of competing spheres of interest in colonial situations. Both events were the results of social relations that can be characterized only as colonial, given the shifting position of colonists, sometimes closer to the distant colonizing power and sometimes closer to the people they were meant to subjugate as part of the process of colonization.

Ireland, too, became the homeland of a nobility whose ancestry was rooted across the Irish Sea in England. Although the authority of the crown weakened in the colony over the fourteenth century and the number of absentee lords grew, the descendants of the Anglo-Irish noble settlers residing in Ireland increasingly took on the cultural attributes of the Gaelic Irish, while nevertheless remaining concerned to maintain their status as English lords.[5] Intermarriage between the Anglo-Irish and the Gaelic-Irish had borne fruit long before.[6] These Anglo-Irish, or the Old English as they would come to be called in the fifteenth and sixteenth centuries, were perceived and apparently perceived themselves to some extent as "the middle nation," looked down upon by the English nobility as literally degenerate, and despised by the Gaelic Irish nobility as foreigners.[7] Tensions very similar to those among the feudatories of Crete emerged in the seventeenth century between the "Old English," the Catholic descendants of the twelfth-century Angevin invaders, and the largely Protestant "New English," who had arrived more recently in the fifteenth and sixteenth centuries. Two revolts by the Old English, in 1579 and 1580, can be seen as early expressions of those tensions.[8] The two groups, however, were able to unite temporarily against the English government in the failed Ulster Rising of 1641, but the Old English ultimately found that they had more interests in common with the Catholic Gaelic Irish, thereby planting the seeds of a conflict that persisted for centuries.[9]

For these reasons, an equally valuable direction of study would be to examine the colonies' impact on the nobilities of Spain and England. The *hildagos* of the Spanish kingdom looked down upon the Spaniards of the colonies, whose status was diminished by their association with a land where there could be little pretense of *limpieza de sangre*.[10] Purity of blood was no more possible in Spain than it was in New Spain, but the advantage was on the Spanish nobility's side in setting the level of the bar leading to high status.[11] The Spaniards of New Spain were irrevocably "tainted." The Anglo-Irish nobility likewise attracted the disdain and contempt of the English nobility for similar reasons. In the sixteenth century, Richard Stanihurst, the son of an Old English family in Ireland, lamented the deterioration of his social group's status and attributed its causes to the abandonment of the English language and customs.[12]

Whether they were Greeks in the fourteenth century, native Americans or Africans in the sixteenth, when a subjugated people initially came into sustained contact with their conquerors, the features the conquerors used to differentiate themselves from their subjects were in one sense reliable, since the populations had not yet had the opportunity to miscegenate. Once miscegenation occurred over time, the need for a more complex system of differentiation in the ongoing process of mastery over humans developed. One historian has noted precisely this process in colonial Mexico.[13] In medieval Crete and Ireland, social relations had not become so complex that anything more than the category of "Latin" or "English" was needed. Spanish and British America, however, developed far more complex colonial societies, in which the evolving economic role of slavery played a major role in shaping relations between the Europeans, the natives, and the Africans brought forcibly to the western hemisphere.

It is not merely an objective perception of Muslims and Jews in fifteenth-century Spain as undesirable, nor the introduction of the concept "race" as a result of increased slave trade with Africa, that presage *limpieza de sangre*. It is rather the increased artificiality of ethnic categories possessing little consistency with those whom they were meant to categorize that set the stage for the complexity of racial categories in the colonies of the Americas. Human beings did not suddenly wake up to the ethnic and racial differences among them, once they all came into contact. The existence of differences is not at issue; whether and how those differences were made significant is.

Behind all this discussion of the relationship between colonization and ethnicity lurks a troubling, and to many, more threatening, insight: the myth of ethnic homogeneity. Over thirty years ago, in his study of the racial categories used by the British in the West Indies and continental colonies, Winthrop Jordan made an observation that underlines the difference between the earlier experiments in colonization and the later ones.

Perhaps he [the American colonist] sensed as well that continued racial intermixture would undermine the logic of the racial slavery upon which his society was based. For the separation of slaves from free men depended on a clear demarcation of the races, and the presence of mulattoes blurred this essential distinction. Accordingly, he made every effort to nullify the effects of racial intermixture: by classifying [the mulatto] as a Negro he was in effect denying that intermixture had occurred at all.[14]

The tendency to ignore miscegenation, or at the very least to underestimate its impact on society in the period prior to the rise of the African slave trade and the development of "race" as an ideological weapon to justify enslavement, has persisted until this day. Jordan's comment about the denial of miscegenation by the American colonist of the past can apply equally to historians of the present. If ethnic homogeneity is a myth, then why do scholars continue to write as if it were not? To take one example from the literature on medieval and early modern colonies, the historian James Lydon argues in his article on nation and race in medieval Ireland that "It can be accepted, then, that just as there were two dominant races in medieval Ireland, so there were two distinct nations."[15] The evidence for his statement is seemingly convincing: the people of that time did indeed use terms to define themselves and others as such. Is his characterization of the population, however, sufficient or even, on further thought, accurate? What do we gain by incorporating such viewpoints from the past into our own? What do we lose by making it a practice? Lydon would be the first to acknowledge that the Anglo-Irish and the Gaelic-Irish had become practically indistinguishable in language and custom by the sixteenth century.[16] Why, then, endorse the myth of homogeneity through the usage of inaccurate terms and concepts associated with outdated notions of homogeneity, if we know it to be false? Analogously, would we adopt into usage one group's derogatory or perjorative terms about another group simply because those are the terms that the first group used? No modern historian is likely to refer to the Anglo-Irish as "degenerate" without qualifying that that was how the English nobility viewed them, not how the historian viewed them. Then why would we do the same with seemingly benign racial and ethnic terms, if we know them to portray the group in question inaccurately?

I am not arguing for the elimination of racial and ethnic terminology in scholarly literature, because, in addition to having their uses, such terms need defending as long as some of the people the terms refer to are threatened with extinction or subordinated under the pretext of being inferior, as Edward Said observed. My argument has instead everything to do with modes of analysis and nothing to do with extinguishing any of the categories that give meaning to people's lives. There ought, however, to be a greater distance between the scholar and his or her subject in matters pertaining to race and ethnicity. We ought not, in fact, to take people at their word when they proclaim, or a government proclaims for them, in categorical terms their identity. The myth of ethnic homogeneity, in other words, is pernicious and still pervasive.

The myth is most obvious in colonial settings, where the interaction between people of very distinct backgrounds can be relatively easily discerned. Even in countries that are traditionally perceived as ethnically homogeneous, such as Greece, Japan, and even France, the myth falls apart rather quickly on close examination. It takes the tacit, and sometimes not-so-tacit, complicity of governments and the societies in which they operate to create a consensus according to which each kind is believed to stick to its own. The illusion of ethnic homogeneity, in the last analysis, shows how politically contrived "ethnicity" is.

The direction the myth took in the western hemisphere had an impulse propelling it different from the earlier forces at work in the Mediterranean. One significant difference between the medieval colonies and the colonies of the later centuries is the economic role of slavery in those societies. Even though the plantation economy of the Americas and the Caribbean did not take off until the seventeenth century, the engine of race was idling.[17] It needed fuel, which in part came from an increasingly emphatic differentiation between those enslaved and those invulnerable to enslavement, the latter of whom had become jurically protected over the course of the thirteenth and fourteenth centuries.

One last story from Venetian Crete. In the late summer of 1367, Tadeo Giustiniani, the Venetian representative in charge of pacifying the island of Crete in the aftermath of the 1363 rebellion, issued a series of proclamations involving insurgents as yet uncaptured. Among the rebels he outlawed figure two Greek Cretans, Sifi Gavala and his mother-in-law Rovithi, both inhabitants of the countryside in the district of Rethimno. Sifi's crime is not specified, but Rovithi's inflammatory words are recorded in the proclamation. She is reported to have said to a fellow Greek Cretan, "Why did you flee from us and from your kin? Why did you go with the Latins? Oh, how I wish I had in my hands the eyes of all those who joined the Latins and the eyes of all Latins!"[18] Throughout all the archival and literary sources surviving from Venetian Crete, there is perhaps no more eloquent and personal expression of Greek-Latin hostility than the words of this village woman, whom the Venetian authorities condemned in absentia to having her own eyes plucked out and placed in her hands, just to drive the lesson home. It would be pointless to argue that Rovithi was evincing anything other than anti-Latin hostility. And it would be hard to argue with all the historians who have subsequently cast the struggles of that island under Venetian rule in ethnic terms. But the thrust of the arguments in this work has been that the resort to ethnic identity as a prima facie explanation for behavior is insufficient. Taking ethnic hostility at face value in Rovithi's case would mean that we would miss the fact that the Greek-Cretan she castigated was a Greek man, a member of the Calergi family branch supporting Venice, but, according to Buondelmonti, also a Greek hero. We can see that the problem for Rovithi, at bottom, was less that she was ruled by Latins than that she was ruled by a rapacious power only marginally kinder to those who lived in the cities than to the servile souls working the land. The townspeople of Candia, the Greek majority and the Latin minority, feared Rovithi as much as the Venetian authorities did. She, however, framed the source of her troubles in ethnic terms, just as the Venetian state and its spokesmen did. Neither our more comprehensive overview nor Rovithi's view is right or wrong, but in the final analysis, neither view is correct without taking account of the other.

Following this reasoning, then, the concept of "ethnic identity" ought to be viewed more as a shibboleth than as a mysterious object of study which we humans imperfectly understand, but one which we still believe we will eventually decipher. To relate it to the broader field of Venetian Crete and Latin Greece, the attempt to describe the construction of Byzantine or Latin identities in the past is tantamount to dissecting the anatomy of a chimera.[19] Perhaps my colleague in the library courtyard was right in one sense about "identity" in the past: we may have created a category, or at least reinforced one, that has taken on a greater life in print than it had in reality. The problem is that the consequences of perpetuating such myths can contribute to a toxic atmosphere, both in the academy and in society at large. The myth of ethnic homogeneity continues to propel scholars into the realm of identity politics of the past, when what we in fact should be engaged in is the dismantling, the deconstruction — literally — of the concept, "ethnic identity," without a worry for its eventual reconstruction.

> That much of what passed as historical fact in academic circles has to be considered as tentative — if not outright fictional — is becoming clear as postgenocidal sobriety compels a growing number of historians to take seriously the political uses to which their writings have been put, and their readers to question the certainty with which many a claim has been advanced.
>
> — Mahmood Mamdani[20]

Appendix 1. Occurrence of Cognomina

Cognomina in the *Concessio insulae cretensis* of 1211

The following seventy-three names of the first colonists to settle in Crete
appear in the Charter of Concession published in G. L. Tafel and G. M.
Thomas, eds., *Urkunden fur älteren Handels- und Staatsgeschichte der Republik Venedig mit besonderer Beziehung auf Byzanz und die Levante*, 3 vols.
(Amsterdam: rpr. 1964), 1: 134–35. Italicized names are found in the Great
Council membership lists of 1356–63. I have retained the spellings as the
names appear in the document; alternate (Latin or Venetian) spellings as
they appear later in the sources are in parentheses.

Alberto	Cavatorta	Marano
Alvovario	Çentiliana	*Marino*
Anno	Circopo	*Mauro*
Auri	*Contareno*	*Mauroceno*
Badoario (Baduario)	*Dandulo*	Minio
Barastro	Dedo (Diedo)	*Molino*
Barbadico	*Dodo* (Duodo)	*Mudacio*
Baroci	*Faletro* (Falier)	*Nani*
Beligno	Fuscari	Natali (Natalis)
Belli	*Fuscolo* (Foscolo)	*Pantaleo* (Pantalio)
Bethani	Girardo	*Paulo*
Bicontolo (Bocontolo)	*Gradonico* (Gradenigo)	Petro
Bocco	*Grimani*	Prando
Bonçi	Indoso	Putheo
Boniolo	*Iulio* (Iuliano)	Rainaldo
Calbo (Calbi)	*Iustiniano*	Rapani (Rampani)
Canale	Iusto	*Rosso*
Çancarolo	Lollini (Lulino?)	Saco
Capello	Longo	*Sagredo* (Secreto)
Caravello	*Macono* (Matono)	*Signolo*
Cauco (Caucho)	Manolesso	*Taliapetra*

Tonisto	Viadro	Vitalis
Valerio	*Vido*	Viviano
Vançago	Vilione	Zane
Venerio (Venier)		

Cognomina of the Sergeants in the
Concessio insulae cretensis of 1211

Of the twenty-four cognomina below, those italicized appear in the Great Council membership lists of 1356–63.

Abramo	Fabro	Semiteculo
Alaistro	Fuscari	*Steno*
Barberio	*Grimani*	Treso
Bicontolo	Ieremia	*Trivixanus*
Bocassus	Marao	Vallero
Cavalairo	Pellaçarius	*Venerio*
Constantinus	Piccolo	*Vido*
Donatus	Rampani	*Vitalis*

Cognomina in the Great Council Membership Lists

Archivio del Ducha di Candia, *Quadernus consiliorum*, Busta 12. Italicized cognomina appear in the *Concessio insulae cretensis* of 1211. I have retained the spellings as the names appear in lists, but have placed their Venetian variant in parentheses.

1358–59

1. Abbate (1)	7. *Barbadico* (4)	12. Beto (2)
(Abbado)	(Barbarigo)	13. Biaqua (1)
2. Acontanto (1)	8. Barbo (3–5)	14. Bocolis (1)
3. Albi (1)	9. *Baroci* (2–3)	15. *Bocontolo* (1)
4. Alvirando (1)	(Barozzi)	(Bicontolo)
5. Avonale (4)	10. Basilio (2)	16. Bolani (1)
6. *Barastro* (1)	11. *Belli* (1)	17. Bono (2–6)

18. Bonsignor (1)
19. Brogodione (1)
    (Brogognone)
20. *Calbo* (1)
21. Caliva (1)
22. *Canale* (1)
23. *Caravello* (2)
24. *Caucho* (1)
    (Cauco)
25. *Contareno* (1–3)
    (Contarini)
26. Cornario (7–10)
    (Corner)
27. Crisencia (1)
    (Criscenza)
28. *Dandulo* (3–5)
    (Dandolo)
29. Dono (1)
30. Dulce (1)
31. *Faletro* (1)
    (Falier)
32. Feriolo (1)
33. Flabani (1)
34. Foscareno (1)
    (Foscarini)
35. Fradello (3)
36. Francho (1)
37. *Fusculo* (1)
    (Foscolo)
38. Geno (3–4)
    (Zen)
39. Gezzo (1)
40. Gisi (2–4)
41. *Gradonico* (12)
    (Gradenigo)

42. Gradu (1)
43. Greco (1)
44. Grimaldo (1)
45. Gritti (1)
46. Habramo (6)
    (Abramo)
47. Ialina (1)
48. *Iuliano* (1)
    (Giuliano)
49. *Iustiniano* (1)
    (Giustiniani)
50. Lago (1)
51. Lando (1)
52. Lisi (1)
53. Magno (2)
54. Marcello (1)
55. *Marino* (1)
56. *Matono* (1)
57. *Mauro* (2)
58. Mazamano (2)
59. Medio (2)
    (Mezzo)
60. Minoto (1)
61. *Molino* (4–5)
62. *Mudacio* (7)
    (Muazzo)
63. *Pantaleo* (3)
    (Pantalio)
64. Paradiso (1)
65. Partegon (1)
66. Pasqualigo (1)
67. Paulino (1)
68. *Paulo* (2)
69. Pino (1)
70. Plachina (1)

71. Plasencia (1)
72. Poltroni (1)
73. Portu (1)
74. Quirino (9)
    (Quirini)
75. Raguseo (1)
76. Rippa (1)
77. Rizzo (1)
78. Rodulfo (1)
    (Rodolfo)
79. *Rosso* (1)
80. Rugerio (1)
81. Ruzini (1)
82. Saclichi (1)
83. Salamono (1)
84. Saxo (1)
    (Sasso)
85. *Secreto* (2)
    (Sagredo)
86. Simeon (1)
87. Stadi (1)
88. Steno (1)
89. *Taliapetra* (2)
90. Truno (1)
91. Truzane (1)
92. Urso (1)
93. Vassallo (2)
94. *Venerio* (4–5)
    (Venier)
95. Venetando (2)
96. *Vido* (2)
97. Vigoncia (2–3)
    (Vigonza)
98. Ystrigo (1)
    (Ystrico)

1360

Clugia (1)

1361

100. *Baduario*(1)   102. *Duodo* (1)   105. *Mauroceno* (1)
     (Badoario)   103. Freganesco (1)   106. *Nani* (2)
101. Damiani (1)   (Fraganesco)   107. Sanuto (1)
     (Damini)   104. Lauredano (1)

1362

108. *Grimani* (2)   110. Miani (1)   112. Trivisano (1)
109. *Manolesso* (1)   111. Mocenigo (1)   (Trevisan)

1363

113. Delfino (1)   114. *Signolo* (1)
     (Dolfin)

Cognomina of Feudatories in 1349

The following list of forty-six names comes from the Deliberations of the Great Council, which in 1349 undertook a minor reform in the distribution of contiguous sergeantries. It is not by any means a complete list of the feudatories of that year. The cognomina below, all explictly called "feudatories," include those who had recently died and those to whom the regime consigned their sergeantries. Those names preceeded by an asterisk appear in the Great Council membership lists of 1356–63. Those italicized appear in the *Concessio insulae cretensis* of 1211.

* Albi	Çaco	Gritolo
Armaki	Caliva	* Ialina
* *Barastro*	* *Contareno*	Iordano
* *Barbadico*	Corario	Kavalario
* Beco	* *Dandulo*	Litini
Bevardo	* Flabani	Litore
* Bono	* Fraganesco	Milano
* Brogodiono	Granella	Modino

*Natalis
* Pantalio
* Pantalio
Pitaruli
Pasqualigo
Pendidari
* Portu
* Quirino

Ragono
* Rosso
* Ruçini
* Saclichi
Sardano
* Sasso
* Steno
Tonisto

Torcello
* Venetando
Venetiano
*Venier
Vidore
* Vigoncia
* Ystrico
Zaco

Appendix 2. *Sale of cavalleria involving Lingiaco Mavristiri, Candiote Jew* [1]

ASV, NDC, NOT. G. GERARDO, BUSTA 101, FOL. 302V, 17 MAY 1341

Die XVII. Manifestum facio ego Alexius Calergi, filius quondam Georgii Calergi, habitator in casali Merona, cum meis heredibus tibi Lingiacho Mauristiri, iudeo, habitatori Candide, et tuis heredibus, quia sum contentus quod merchatum vel emptio cavalarie de lo Castri quod vel quam es facturus vel procuras facere ser Nicolao Venerio sit pro me et meo nomine et teneor solvere et dare pro precio eiusdem cavalarie yperpera in cretensia currentia novem millia et quingenta hoc modo, videlicet yperpera quinque millia dabo in camera comunis in termino quo teneberis et cum conditione qua teneberis et yperpera quingenta dabo ser Nicolao Quirino usque ad unum annum tunc prius venturum ad presam stationis, si dicta cavalaria scripta fuerit cui voluero, sicut secundum Nicolaus Venerio tenebitur tibi, videlicet infra mensem unum proxime venturum. Et reliqua yperpera quatuor millia dabo tibi ex tunc usque ad quinque annos tunc prius venturos et [2] debeo tibi de eis facere cartam ad presam stationis ita tamen quod prode non ascendat ultra yperpera duodecim pro centenario yperperorum in anno, quod prode, siquid fuerit, dabo tibi omni anno sub pena dupla eius quolibet anno cum ista conditione quod suprascripta cavalaria debeat obligari tibi et scribi in catastico dominationis pro tuo signo et pignere yperperorum quatuor millium suprascriptorum quam tenearis facere scribi cui voluero ita quod sit Latinus et feudatus et possit sibi scribi cum conditione suprascripta. Si igitur etc. pena yperpera quinque millia contractu firmo. Testes Nicolaus de Firmo, prestarus, Marcus de Placencia, Andreas Dandulo, filius quondam ser Iohannis et Dominicus de Placencia. Complere et dare. Haec carta remanet anichilata de precepto et ordinamento dominationis.

ASV, NDC, NOT. G. GERARDO, BUSTA 101, FOL. 302V, 17 MAY 1341

Eodem die. Manifestum facio ego suprascriptus Alexius Calergi, cum meis heredibus tibi suprascripto Lingiacho Mauristiri, iudeo, et tuis heredibus,

quia si compleveris tractatum et merchatum cavalarie de lo Castri et feceris
scribi illam cavaleriam cui voluerio secundum quod continetur in carta
suprascripta promitto[3] tibi dare yperpera in Creta currentia sexcenta pro
tua provisione vel tuo labore, que debeam tibi solvere et dare hoc modo,
videlicet, a die quo scripta fuerit illa cavalarie, ut predictum est, in antea
usque ad annos sex proxime venturos videlicet omni anno yperpera centum
salva in terra omni occasione remota. Hec autem que scripta sunt etc. pena
ad rationem yperpera viginti pro centenario yperperorum in ratione anni et
nichilominus solvenda predicta yperpera ut dictum est. Testes suprascripti.
Complere et dare. Haec carta remaneat anichilare de precepto et ordinamento dominationis.

ASV, NDC, NOT. G. GERARDO, BUSTA 101, FOLS. 302V–303R,
17 MAY 1341

Eodem die. Manifestum facio ego suprascriptus Lingiachus, iudeus, cum
meis heredibus, tibi Alexio Calergi suprascripto et tuis heredibus quia si
complevero tractatum vel merchatum quod procuro facere cum ser Nicolao
Venerio de emendo suam cavalariam de lo Castri, promitto tibi quod ipsam
cavalariam tibi conscenciam et debeo cum illis conditionibus et modis atque
pactis que fecero cum ipso te solvente et dante pro eius precio secundum
quod continetur in cartam quam michi fecisti hodiernia die scriptam manu
notarii infrascripti et est sciendum quod si dictus Nicolaus non attendere
vel observare michi pacta que secum fecero tunc debeam tibi concedere
omnia iura que habebo quam illum de penis secundum quod continebun-
tur in carta vel cartis quam vel quas cum ipso exinde fecero vel faciam [Fol.
303r] et dabo opus quantum potero quod excucias ab ipso nomine meo
penam et penas quas vel quam michi incuret vel incurent exinde. Si igitur
etc. pena yperpera quinque millia contractu firma. Testes suprascripti.
Complere et dare. Haec carta remanet anichilata de precepta et ordinamento dominationis.

ASV, NDC, NOT. G. GERARDO, BUSTA 101, FO. 303R, 18 MAY 1341

Die XVIII. Manifestum facimus nos Nicolaus Venerio, filius quondam domini Marci Venerio, habitator Candide, cum meis heredibus, ab una parte,
et Lingiachus Mauristiri, iudeus, habitator Candide, cum meis heredibus,
ex altera parte, una pars nostrum alteri vicisim, quia in Dei nomine ad tales

devenimus concordiam et pactum insimul, videlicet, quod ego suprascriptus Nicolaus do, vendo et transacto tibi Lingiacho meam cavalariam de lo Castri, cum omnibus suis habentiis, pertinentiis, vilanis et omnibus aliis suis iuribus, amodo in antea imperpetuum cum plena virtute et potestate intromittendi, habendi, tenendi, possidendi, dandi, vendendi, transactandi et alienandi atque pro anima iudicandi, cum intrascripta conditione. Precium autem dicte cavalarie iuxta nostre convencionis pactum est yperpera in cretensia currentia sexmillia, quam cavalariam teneor facere scribi ordinate in catastico dominationis, cuicumque volueris dummodo sit persona suficiens et latina ac feudata et data licencia per dominationem quod ipsa cavalaria scribatur in catastico sicut dictum est superius. Tunc teneor ego suprascriptus Lingiachus ex nunc usque ad dies tres proxime venturos vel antea dare et presentare vel presentari facere in camera dominationis de suprascripto precio yperpera quinque millia. Et ego predictus Nicolaus teneor presentare vel concordare /reliqua/ yperpera mille. Verumtamen quod illa yperpera mille ego suprascriptus Lingiachus teneor deducere tibi suprascripto Nicolao de parte capitalis et pene carte quam habeo contra te et Marcum Venerio, in qua est fideiussor Bartholomeus Bono. Item si dominatio nolet ipsam cavaleriam scribi facere sicut superius dictum est, sed velet a capite ponere eam ad incautum, teneor ego dictus Nicolaus Venerio facere illam cavalariam deliberari per dominationem cuicumque volueris dummodo sit persona ydonea ut superius dictum est pro precio yperpera sexmillia, quorum quinque millia ut premissum est presentabis tu Lingiachus in camera comunis ut dictum est et alia yperpera mille presentabo ego Nicolaus ut dictum est superius. Et tunc ego Lingiachus debeo tibi Nicolao deducere yperpera mille sicut superius dictum est de carta quam habeo contra te et Marcum Venerio, nepotem tuum, in qua est pleçius Bartholomeus Bono. Preterea promitens promito ego suprascriptus Lingiachus tibi suprascripto Nicolao quia si feceris deliberari et scribi suprascriptam cavalariam cui voluero et scribi possit sicut superius continetur, tunc teneor tibi donare de parte capitalis et pene cartarum quas habeo contra te, videlicet yperpera duomillia de debitis tui Nicolai, de quibus voluero et alia yperpera mille de quocumque alio debito voluero de debitis que michi /dare/ debet Marcus Venerio, nepos tuus, videlicet infra dies octo postquam requisiveris me /et/ quando factum et completum fuerit illud quod superius dictum est /teneor/ stare ad dandum et solvere pro te Nicolao, ser Nicolao Quirino, yperpera quingenta usque ad unum annum tunc proxime venturum. Item si negocium ut premissum est complebitur, teneor ego suprascriptus Nicolaus Venerio facere quod ser Nicolaus Quirino mutuet cui volueris, te existens pleçio in toto et parte, yperpera in cretensia currentia mille ad presam stationis, solvendo sibi usque ad menses sex tunc proxime venturos, inteligendo quod ipse Nicolaus det tibi dicta yperpera mille, ut dictum est, in tali ora quod possint presentari simul cum aliis dominationi. Item si dominacio velet te Lingiachus compelere quod ponere debeas in camera [Fol. 303v] aliquos alios denarios ultra suprascripta yperpera quinque millia, teneor tunc ego suprascriptus Nicolaus Venerio facere quod non sis astrictus de hoc vel solvere[4] aut presentare dominationi illos denarios pro quibus dominatio ut premissum est te compeletur. Hec autem omnia et singula suprascripta promitimus unus nostrum alteri facere, atendere, complere atque observare amodo usque ad unum mensem proxime venturum vel antea. Si qua igitur predictarum partium contra hanc manifestionis, /venditionis/ promissionis et pacti cartam ire temptaverit et que suprascripta sunt non observaverit, tunc emendare debeat pars non observans cum suis heredibus parti observanti et observare volenti et eius heredibus pro pena et nomine pena inde constituta yperpera in cretensia currentia quinque millia et hec manifestationis, /venditionis/, promissionis et pacti cartam in sua permaneat firmitate. Signum suprascriptorum Nicolai et Lingiachi qui hec rogaverint fieri. Testes presbyter Marcus de Placencia, Albertus Palamonte, Marcus Brino et Petrus de Porto. Complere et dare cuilibet unam. Dedi.

Notes

Sources

1. Silvano Borsari, *Il dominio veneziano a Creta nel XIII secolo* (Naples, 1963).

2. Ernst Gerland, *Das Archiv des Herzogs von Kandia im Königl. Staatsarchiv zu Venedig* (Strassburg, 1899); Maria Francesca Tiepolo, "Note sul riordino degli archivi del Duca e dei notai di Candia nell'Archivio di Stato di Venezia," *Thesaurismata* 10 (1973): 88–100.

3. In 1884, the registers of the Cretan notaries were removed from the Archives of the Duke of Candia and placed in the Notarial Archives of the ASV. Tiepolo, "Riordino degli archivi," p. 88–89.

4. I will present an estimation of the city's population further on in Chapter 2.

5. Beniamino Pagnin, *Il documento privato veneziano* (Padova, 1950), p. 66.

6. Charalambos Gaspares, "He glossa tes Venetikes grafeiokratias: i avtiparathese latinikes kai ellenikes glossas ste mesaionike Krete (130s–os ai)," *Simmeikta* 9, Mneme D. A. Zakithenou (Athens, 1994), 1: 141–56, p. 145.

7. ASV, NDC, not. D. Grimani, Busta 103 and 295, 1356–87.

8. ADC, *Sentenze*, Busta 26, reg. 2, fasc. 1, fol. 11v.

9. "Tabellio" was a term also employed in the early history of the Venetian ducal chancery. See Pagnin, *Documento privato* p. 68.

10. Gasparis, "He glossa," pp. 149–50.

11. ADC, *Sentenze*, Busta 26, reg. 2, fasc. 1, fol. 11v, 14 Feb 1364/65: "Nos Petrus Mauroceno de mandato incliti domini ducis Venetiarum ducha Creta cum nostro consilio notum facimus universis tam latinis quam grecis presentibus et futuris presentem paginam inspecturis quod papas Georgius Spilioti, habitator Chanee, in nostra presentia constitutus nobis humiliter supplicavit ut eum in scriptura greca notarium publicum crearemus. Nos vero habito consilio diligenti de ipsius fama inquiri fecimus diligenter et eum excutiari fecimus iuxta usum et quod inventa est persona legalitatis et bone fame ac sufficiens et ydoneus ad tabellionatus officium exercendum sua petitione admissa auctoritate nostri regiminis eum notarium duximus statuendum volentes et statuentes deinceps quod sit notarius et tabellionatus officio uti debeat fideliter et legaliter secundum quod consuetudo grecorum exigit et requirit ipse vero iuravit fidelitatem domino nostro duci nobis et successoribus nostris erit obediens et fidelis, cartam falsam non faciet et si aliqua carta pervenerit ad manus suas que sibi fraudulenta videatur ipsam presentabit dominationi. Et si ipsam presentare non possit, manifestabit dominio quam citius poterit. Et si vocatus fuerit per dominationem ad videndum aliquam cartam de ipsa diret quod sibi melius approbit utrum sit bona vel mala et si erit insincerus et si requisitus fuerit a curia ut

veniat ad scribendum in servicio comunis universa scripta faciet que sibi iniuncta fuerint fideliter et legaliter credentias celabit que dicte fuerint sibi donec per dominationem fuerint absolute scriptum aliquod non faciet quod sit contra honorem domini nostri ducis Venetiarum nostrum et successoriorum nostrorum nec contra latinos Crete insule commorantes. Item teneatur observare formam consilii cuius tenor per omnia tale est: quod nullus notarius grecus decetero audeat facere cartam alicuius condictionis vel tenoris nisi testes inde rogentur ab aliis qui fieri faciunt cartam in presentia ipsius notarii modo aliquo vel ingenio quod si fecerit nullius valentie vel vigoris erit et nichilominus solvere teneatur hyperpera decem pro pena et si privatus ab officio tabellionatus et hec addit debeat in capitulariis notariorum grecorum. Unde ad futuram rei memoriam et sepedicti papatis Georgii cautellam presentem scriptam sibi fieri fecimus et ipsum nostro sigillo cereo pendenti iussimus comuniri in eo propriis manibus subscribentes. Ego Petrus Mauroceno ducha Creta mm ss. Ego Nicolaus Ciurano, consiliarius Crete, mm ss. Ego Lodovicus de Molino, consiliarius Crete, mm. ss. Actum Candidam, anno Domini millesimo trecentesimosexagesimoquarto, mense februarii, die quartodecimo, indicione tercia, manu mei Marci Vassallo, scribe palatii Candide." A similar entry appears in the same busta, fasc 2.2, fol. 154r–v, 14 Aug 1370. A very brief summary of both entries appears in French in *Régestes des arrêts civils et des mémoriaux (1363–1399) des archives du Duc de Crète*, ed. Elisabeth Santschi (Venice, 1976), nos. 28, 210.

12. Pagnin, *Documento privato*, pp. 64, 66.

13. Priest-notaries of Candia: Iohannes Belli, capellanus duche Crete; Petrus Dandulo; Marcus Donçorçi; Victor Grafaro, plebanus ecclesie S. Marie Matris Domini; Iohannes Granella; David Lamoniti, papas; Niccolò Piacenza; Iohannes Traversario; Dominicus de Valdagno; Iohannes Zuffo de Venetiis, notarius canonicus; Michael Zusto.

14. Notaries of Candia: Fregona, 36 years; L. Quirino, 22 years; A. Bellamore, 24 years; G. Gerardo, 31 years; Z. de Fredo, 33 years; G. de Milano, 24 years; M. Zusto, 25 years; G. Morgano, 21 years; D. Grimani, 38 years.

15. Notaries of Candia: L. Marcello, 12 years; B. de Milano, 17 years; A. Maza, 19 years; A. Negri, 14 years; A. Rodolfo, 10 years; N. Gradenigo, 12 years; M. Piacenza, 13 years; A. Bocontolo, 15 years; P. Longo, 12 years; F. Malpes, 15 years; N. de Milano, 10 years; M. Donzorzi, 14 years; G. Emo, 18 years; L. Cavisino, 11 years; H. Focha, 10 years.

16. Sally McKee, "Households in Fourteenth-Century Venetian Crete," *Speculum* 70 (1995): 27–67.

Introduction

1. Dimitris Tsougarakis, *Byzantine Crete from the 5th Century to the Venetian Conquest*, Historical Monographs 5 (Athens, 1988), p. 89.

2. Edward Said, "Between Worlds," *London Review of Books* 20/9, 7 May 1998: 3–7, p. 7.

3. Malcolm Chapman, Maryon McDonald, and Elizabeth Tonkin, "Introduc-

tion—History and Social Anthropology," in *History and Ethnicity*, ed. Malcolm Chapman, Maryon McDonald, and Elizabeth Tonkin (New York, 1989), pp. 1–21, p. 11.

4. This is particularly evident in *Concepts of National Identity in the Middle Ages*, ed. Simon Forde, Lesley Johnson, and Alan V. Murray, Leeds Texts and Monographs n.s. 14 (Leeds, 1995).

5. David Nirnberg, *Communities of Violence: Persecution of Minorities in the Middle Ages* (Princeton, N.J., 1996); *Medieval Frontier Societies*, ed. Robert Bartlett and Bernard Hamilton (Cambridge, 1989); Forde et al., *Concepts of National Identity in the Middle Ages*.

6. For additional overviews of the colony, see the following works: Freddy Thiriet, *La Romanie vénitienne au moyen âge: le développement et l'exploitation du domaine colonial vénitien (XII–XV siècles)* (Paris, 1959); David Jacoby, "Social Evolution in Latin Greece," in *A History of the Crusades*, ed. K. M. Setton (Madison, Wisc., 1989), 6: 175–221; Chryssa Maltezou, "The Historical and Social Context," in *Literature and Society in Renaissance Crete*, ed. David Holton (Cambridge, 1991), pp. 17–47; Mario Gallina, *Una società coloniale del Trecento: Creta fra Venezia e Bisanzio* (Venice, 1989).

7. Felipe Fernández-Armesto makes brief mention of Crete only twice in his *Before Columbus: Exploration and Colonization from the Mediterranean to the Atlantic, 1229–1492* (Philadelphia, 1987). Freddy Thiriet, a notable scholar of Venetian Crete and Latin Greece, also saw little distinction between the Venetian merchant quarters in cities around the Mediterranean and the colony established in Crete: "Une colonie vénitienne, c'est d'abord un groupe assez nombreus de Vénitiens. . . . Mais quel que soit le nom donné à l'établissement vénitien, l'organisation administrative est partout à peu près identique" (*La Romanie vénitienne*, pp. 182–83).

8. The best introductions to the Cretan Jews are Joshua Starr, "Jewish Life in Crete Under the Rule of Venice," *Proceedings of the American Academy for Jewish Research* 12 (1942): 59–114; David Jacoby, "Venice and Venetian Jews in the Eastern Mediterranean," in *Gli Ebrei e Venezia: Secoli XIV–XVIII, Atti del convegno internazionale organizzato dall'Istituto di storia della società e dello stato veneziano della Fondazione Giorgio Cini*, ed. Gaetano Cozzi and R. Bonfil (Milan, 1987), pp. 29–58; Steven Bowman, *The Jews of Byzantium (1204–1453)* (Birmingham, Ala., 1985).

9. Regarding the immigration of Armenians to Crete, see *Régestes des délibérations du Sénat de Venise concernant la Romanie*, ed. Freddy Thiriet (Paris, 1959), p. 105, n. 407, 8 June 1363.

10. R. R. Davies, "Lordship or Colony?" in *The English in Medieval Ireland: Proceedings of the First Joint Meeting of the Royal Irish Academy and the British Academy, Dublin, 1982*, ed. James Lydon (Dublin, 1984), pp. 142–60, p. 151.

11. Thiriet, *La Romanie vénitienne*, p. 182: "Mais entre les comptoirs en terre étrangère et les possessions directes, les différences de statut sont, dans l'ensemble, négligeables."

12. Joshua Prawer, *Crusader Institutions* (Oxford, 1980), pp. 219, 226.

13. For example, Robert Bartlett, *The Making of Europe: Conquest, Colonization and Cultural Change 950–1350* (Princeton, N.J., 1993), p. 307: "The expansion

through replication had, as its characteristic agents, not the powerful monarchies—
we might be tempted to say, not the state—but consortia, entrepreneurial associations of Frankish knights."

14. The bibliography on merchant compounds in the Mediterranean is vast.
The following are merely a starting point and the most germane to this discus-
sion. Elyahu Ashtor, *Levant Trade in the Later Middle Ages* (Princeton, N.J., 1983);
Michel Balard, "Communes italiennes, pouvoir et habitants des états francs de
Syrie-Palestine au XIIe siècle," in *Crusaders and Muslims in Twelfth-Century Syria*, ed.
Maya Shatzmiller (Leiden and New York, 1993), pp. 43–64; idem, ed., *Etat et
colonisation au Moyen Age et à la Renaissance* (Lyon, 1989); Laura Balletto, *Genova,
Mediterraneo, Mar Nero (secc. XIII–XV)* (Genoa, 1976); Maurice H. Chéhab, *Tyr à
l'époque des Croisades*, vol. 2, *Histoire sociale, économique et réligieuse* (Paris, 1979);
David Jacoby, *Recherches sur la Méditerranée orientale du XIIe au Xve siècle: peuples,
sociétés, économies* (London, 1979); idem, "Byzantine Crete in the Navigation and
Trade Networks of Venice and Genoa," in *Oriente e Occidente tra medioevo ed età
moderna: studi in onore di Geo. Pistarino*, ed. Laura Balletto (Genoa, 1997), pp. 517–
40; Joshua Prawer, *The Latin Kingdom of Jerusalem: European Colonialism in the
Middle Ages* (London, 1972).

15. Michel Balard, "La lotta contro Genova," in *Storia di Venezia dalle origini
alla caduta della Serenissima*, vol. 3, *La formazione dello stato patrizio* (Rome, 1997),
pp. 87–126.

16. For the most recent survey, see Donald Queller and Thomas Madden, *The
Fourth Crusade: The Conquest of Constantinople*, 2nd ed. (Philadelphia, 1997).

17. Gabriella Airaldi, *Studi e documenti su Genova e l'oltremare* (Genoa, 1974);
Michel Balard and Alain Ducellier, eds., *Coloniser au moyen âge* (Paris, 1995); Michel
Balard, Angeliki E. Laiou, and Catherine Otten-Froux, *Les italiens à Byzance: édition
et présentation de documents* (Paris, 1987).

18. A select bibliography on this subject would include David Abulafia, *Com-
merce and Conquest in the Mediterranean, 1100–1500* (London, 1993); Fernández-
Armesto, *Before Columbus*, pp. 96–120; Michel Balard, "Communes italiennes," pp.
43–64; Maurice H. Chéhab, *Tyr à l'époque des Croisades*; Dennis Deletant, "Genoese,
Tatars and Rumanians at the Mouth of the Danube in the Fourteenth Century,"
Slavonic and East European Review 62 (1984): 511–30; Elisaveta Todorova, "The
Greeks in the Black Sea Trade During the Late Medieval Period," *Etudes balkaniques*
28, 3–4 (1992): 45–47.

19. Jacques Heers, "Origines et structures des compagnies coloniales génoises
(XIIIe–XVe siècle)," in *Etat et colonisation au Moyen Age et à la Renaissance*, pp. 17–
33, p. 17.

20. Heers, "Origines et structures," p. 21; Fernández-Armesto, *Before Columbus*, p. 99.

21. Philip Argenti, *The Occupation of Chios by the Genoese and Their Administration of the Island, 1346–1566: Described in Contemporary Documents and Official Dispatches*, 3 vols. (Cambridge, 1958), 1: 106–7, 116–17. See the interesting note on
page 117 citing Lopez, who wrote "the delegation on paper of the functions of the
State to an association of shipowners and a private commercial company and other

public elements amounts to giving the Mahona of Chios the right to be considered as the remote precursor of the famous East India Company."

22. Argenti, *Occupation of Chios*, 1: 438–39; Michel Balard, "Les grecs de Chio sous la domination genoise," *Byzantinische Forschungen* 5 (1977): 5–16.

23. As part of a larger argument about the connection between Genoese and Iberian expansion, Fernández-Armesto likens the Genoese colony of Chios to Crete, but he ignores fundamental differences in the ways the colonies were governed. Fernández-Armesto, *Before Columbus*, pp. 102–3.

24. Fernández-Armesto, *Before Columbus*, pp. 154–55.

25. Charles Verlinden, *The Beginnings of Modern Colonization* (Ithaca, N.Y., 1970), p. 6.

26. Eduardo Aznar Vallejo, "The Conquest of the Canary Islands," in *Implicit Understandings: Observing, Reporting, and Reflecting on the Encounters Between Europeans and Other Peoples in the Early Modern Era*, ed. Stuart B. Schwartz (Cambridge, 1994), pp. 134–56, p. 137.

27. J. H. Elliott, "The Spanish Conquest," in *Colonial Spanish America*, ed. Leslie Bethell (Cambridge, 1987), pp. 1–58, p. 11.

28. Elliott, "The Spanish Conquest," p. 15.

29. Antony M. Stevens-Arroyo, "The Inter-Atlantic Paradigm: The Failure of Spanish Medieval Colonization of the Canary and Caribbean Islands," *Comparative Studies in Society and History* 35/3 (1993): 515–43, p. 520.

30. Fernández-Armesto, *Before Columbus*, pp. 116–20; Verlinden, *Beginnings of Modern Colonization*, pp. 6–7, 12–13, 130–31. See also Verlinden's pamphlet, "Précédents médiévaux de la colonie en Amérique" (Mexico City, 1954) and his "Italian Influences in Iberian Colonization," *Hispanic American Historical Review* 33 (1953): 199–211.

31. Robert Burns, *Medieval Colonialism: Postcrusade Exploitation of Islamic Valencia* (Princeton, N.J., 1975), p. 15.

32. Burns, *Medieval Colonialism*, p. 215.

33. Fernández-Armesto, *Before Columbus*, pp. 13, 18–19.

34. Fernández-Armesto, *Before Columbus*, p. 28; Antoni Riera Melis, *La Corona de Aragón y el reino de Mallorca en el primer cuarto del siglo XIV*, vol. 1, *Las repercusiones arancelarias de la autonomía Balear (1298–1311)* (Madrid and Barcelona, 1986), p. 55.

35. J. N. Hillgarth, *The Spanish Kingdoms, 1250–1516*, 2 vols. (Oxford, 1976), 1: 251.

36. Riera Melis, *Corona de Aragón*, p. 54: "La situación cambió notablemente a la muerte del Conquistador, cuando la confederación . . . se escinde en dos Estados soberanos e independientes: la Corona de Aragón, integrada por los reinos de Aragón y Valencia y el principado de Cataluña, y el reino de Mallorca, constituido por el archipíelago balear, los condados del Rosellón y la Cerdaña, el señorío de Montpellier y el vizcondado de Carlades."

37. T. N. Bisson, *The Medieval Crown of Aragon: A Short History* (Oxford, 1986), pp. 95–97, 104, 110.

38. Bartlett, *The Making of Europe*, p. 313.

39. R. R. Davies, *Dominion and Conquest: The Experience of Ireland, Scotland, and Wales* (Cambridge, 1990), pp. 30–31.

40. Davies, *Dominion and Conquest*, p. 58.

41. W. L. Warren, *Henry II* (Berkeley and Los Angeles, 1973), pp. 192–93, 197–99.

42. Warren, *Henry II*, p. 194; A. J. Otway-Ruthven, *A History of Medieval Ireland* (New York, 1980), pp. 47–48.

43. Otway-Ruthven, *Medieval Ireland*, p. 102.

44. Bartlett, *The Making of Europe*, p. 32. For an argument against the characterization of de Courcy's raid as rash, see Seán Duffy, "The First Ulster Plantation: John de Courcy and the Men of Cumbria," in *Colony and Frontier in Medieval Ireland: Essays Presented to J. F. Lydon*, ed. T. B. Barry, Robin Frame, and Katharine Simms (London and Rio Grande, 1995), pp. 1–27.

45. Otway-Ruthven, *Medieval Ireland*, p. 107.

46. Otway-Ruthven, *Medieval Ireland*, p. 108.

47. Bartlett, *The Making of Europe*, pp. 170–71.

48. Otway-Ruthven, *Medieval Ireland*, Chapter V, "The Government of the Norman-Irish State," pp. 144–90, supplied much of this information.

49. Davies, "Lordship or Colony," p. 151.

50. Robert Bartlett, *The Making of Europe*, pp. 214–15.

51. For background to these points, see Bartlett, *The Making of Europe*; Manlio Bellomo, *The Common Legal Past of Europe, 1000–1800*, trans. Lydia G. Cochrane (Washington, D.C., 1995); Julius Kirshner, "Between Nature and Culture: An Opinion of Baldus of Perugia on Venetian Citizenship as Second Nature," *Journal of Medieval and Renaissance Studies* 9, 2 (1979): 179–208.

52. Bartlett, *The Making of Europe*, p. 238.

53. G. Mac Niocaill, "The Interaction of Laws," in *The English in Medieval Ireland* (Dublin, 1985), pp. 105–17, p. 109; Robin Frame, *The Political Development of the British Isles, 1100–1400* (Oxford, 1990), p. 86; Nicolas Canny, "Identity Formation in Ireland: The Emergence of the Anglo-Irish," in *Colonial Identity in the Atlantic World, 1500–1800*, ed. Nicholas Canny and Anthony Pagden (Princeton, N.J., 1987), pp. 159–212, p. 161.

54. Davies, *Dominion and Conquest*, pp. 66–67.

55. James Lydon, "The Middle Nation," in *The English in Medieval Ireland* (Dublin, 1985), pp. 1–26, p. 1.

56. Lydon, "The Middle Nation," p. 18.

57. Lydon, "The Middle Nation," pp. 2, 18.

58. For the former view, see Otway-Ruthven, *Medieval Ireland*, Chapter IV, p. 126; for the latter, J. A. Watt, *The Church and the Two Nations in Medieval Ireland* (Cambridge, 1970), p. 40.

59. Watt, *The Church and the Two Nations*, p. 40.

60. Otway-Ruthven, *Medieval Ireland*, p. 129; Watt, *The Church and the Two Nations*, p. 116.

61. John Watt, "*Ecclesia inter Anglicos et inter Hibernicos*: Confrontation and Coexistence in the Medieval Diocese and Province of Armagh," in *The English in Medieval Ireland* (Dublin, 1984), pp. 46–64, p. 47.

Chapter 1

1. *Acta Urbani V* (Rome, 1965), p. 253, n. 153, 28 Jul 1368: "sicut gratanter audivimus, in insula Cretensis . . . dilecti filii dux et Commune Venetiarum super Latinos et Graecos plenius solito dominentur." Gill translated "plenius solito" as "more complete," but I do not believe we are in contradiction to each other: Joseph Gill, "Pope Urban V (1362–1370) and the Greeks of Crete," *Orientalia Christiana Periodica* 39 (1973): 461–68, p. 461.

2. Frederic C. Lane, *Venice: A Maritime Republic* (Baltimore, 1973), pp. 225–28.

3. Prior to the founding of the Cretan colony, Venice's other colonial endeavors all were merchant colonies. Their *modus operandi* was one characterized more by economic infiltration of distant land than by conquest of territory, very similar to Genoa's experience: Julian Chrysostomides, "Venetian Commercial Privileges Under the Palaeologi," *Studi veneziani* 12 (1971): 267–356; Bernard Doumerc, "Les Vénitiens à la Tana au XVe siècle," *Moyen-âge* 94 (1988): 363–80; Mario Gallina, "L'affermarsi di un modello coloniale: Venezia e il Levante tra Due e Trecento," *Thesaurismata* 23 (1993): 14–39; David Jacoby, "Vénitiens naturalisés dans l'empire byzantin: un aspect de l'expansion de Vénise en Romanie du XIIIe au milieu du XVe siècle," *Travaux et mémoires du Centre de Recherche d'Histoire et Civilisation de Byzance* 8 (1981): 217–35, rpt. in *Studies on the Crusader States and on Venetian Expansion* (London, 1989); "L'expansion occidentale dans le Levant: les Vénitiens à Acre dans la seconde moitié du 13e siècle," *Journal of Medieval History* 3 (1977): 225–65.

4. Silvano Borsari, "I Veneziani delle colonie," in *Storia di Venezia dalle origini alla caduta della Serenissima*, vol. 3, *La formazione dello stato patrizio* (Rome, 1997), pp. 127–58, p. 147.

5. Julian Chrysostomides, "Venetian Commercial Privileges Under the Palaeologi."

6. R. Cessi, *Venezia nel duecento, tra oriente e occidente* (Venice, 1985), pp. 28–37.

7. *Urkunden für älteren Handels- und Staatsgeschichte der Republik Venedig mit besonderer Beziehung auf Byzanz und die Levante*, ed. G. L. Tafel and G. M. Thomas, Fontes rerum austriacarum, Diplomataria et acta, XII–XIV, 3 vols. (Vienna, 1856–1857; rpt. Amsterdam, 1964), 1: 512, "Refutatio Crete," 12 Aug 1204; G. B. Cervellini, "Come i veneziani acquistarono Creta," *Nuovo archivio veneto* n.s. 16 (1908): 262–78, esp. 269–71.

8. Freddy Thiriet, *La Romanie vénitienne*, pp. 105–6.

9. Borsari, *Dominio veneziano*, pp. 21–25; Georges Jehel, "The Struggle for Hegemony in the Eastern Mediterranean: An Episode in the Relations Between Venice and Genoa According to the Chronicles of Ogerio Pane (1197–1219)," *Mediterranean Historical Review* 11, 2 (1996): 196–207.

10. Gerola found only three edifices dating to the Venetian period: Giuseppe Gerola, *Monumenti veneti nell'isola di Creta: Ricerche e descrizioni fatte per incarico del R. Istituto*, 4 vols. (Venice, 1905–32), 3: 202–8.

11. *Itinerarium Symonis Semeonis ab Hybernia ad Terram Sanctam*, ed. and trans.

Mario Esposito (Dublin, 1960), p. 43. For an discussion of one Cretan export, cheese, see David Jacoby, "Cretan Cheese: A Neglected Aspect of Venetian Medieval Trade," *Medieval and Renaissance Venice*, ed. Ellen E. Kittell and Thomas F. Madden (Urbana and Chicago, 1998), pp. 49–68.

12. Ruthi Gertwagen, "The Venetian Port of Candia, Crete (1299–1363): Construction and Maintenance," in *Mediterranean Cities: Historical Perspectives*, ed. Ira Malkin and Robert L. Hohlfelder (London, 1988), pp. 141–58, p. 141.

13. Gertwagen, "Venetian port of Candia," pp. 146–48.

14. For examples of the kinds of activities occurring in the port of Candia, see Silvano Borsari, "I Movimenti del Porto di Candia AA. 1369–1372," *Annali della facoltà di lettere e filosofia, Università di Macerata* 30–31 (1997–1998): 323–46.

15. Freddy Thiriet, "Candie, grande place marchande dans la première moitié du XVe siècle," in *Pepragmena tou A' Diethnou Kretologikou Sinedriou* [Proceedings of the 1st International Cretan Studies Center], vol. 2 (Irakleio, 1961–62), pp. 338–52; rpt. in *Etudes sur la Romanie Greco-vénitienne (Xe–XVe siècle)* (London, 1977), 9: 338–52.

16. A few examples: ADC, Proclami e Banni, Busta 14bis, fol. 20v, n. 50; fol. 24r, nn. 65–68.

17. Thiriet, *La Romanie vénitienne*, p. 268.

18. Thiriet, *La Romanie vénitienne*, p. 268: the *ruga maistra* ran 600 meters from port to *platea*. See now Maria Georgopoulou, "The Meaning of the Architecture and the Urban Layout of Venetian Candia: Cultural Conflict and Interaction in the Late Middle Ages" (Ph.D. diss., University of California Los Angeles, 1992), pp. 7, 115.

19. Thiriet, "Candie, grande place," p. 344.

20. Gallina, *Società coloniale*, p. 25.

21. Jacoby, "Venice and Venetian Jews," p. 37.

22. Gallina, *Società coloniale*, p. 25; city ordinance that all buildings facing on the *ruga maistra* be constructed of stone and "calcina": *Deliberazioni del Maggior Consiglio di Venezia*, ed. Roberto Cessi, Accademia dei Lincei. Commissione per gli atti delle assemblee costituzionali italiane (Bologna, 1931–50), 2: 345.

23. Georgopoulou, "The Meaning of the Architecture," p. 277.

24. Gerola, *Monumenti*, 3: 200.

25. M. Margaret Newett, *Canon Pietro Casola's Pilgrimage to Jerusalem in the Year 1494* (Manchester, 1907), pp. 201–2.

26. Georgopoulou, "The Meaning of the Architecture," p. 123.

27. Roberto Cessi, *Gli statuti veneziani di Jacopo Tiepolo del 1242 e le loro glosse* (Venice, 1938).

28. Thiriet, *La Romanie vénitienne*, pp. 191–93.

29. Thiriet, *Déliberations du Sénat*, p. 40, n. 90, 2 Apr 1339: "le Sénat décide que 3 Juges de Proprio e de Petizion seront élus à Venise et envoyés à Candie, ou ils exerceront leur office avec les 3 autres Juges locaux. De même, les 4 Domini di notte de Candie seront choisis par le Grand Conseil de Venise." (*Misti*, 18, ff. 18r–v); *Apophasis Meizonos Symbouliou Venetias, 1255–1669*, ed. S. M. Theotokes (Athens, 1933), 1: 178–79.

30. Theotokes, *Apophasis*, 1: n. 9, 1261: rectors (inc. duke and his councillors) may not engage in commerce; Thiriet, *La Romanie vénitienne*, p. 196.

31. Thiriet, *La Romanie vénitienne*, p. 199; Gallina, *Società coloniale*, pp. 4–5.

32. Thiriet, *La Romanie vénitienne*, p. 201.

33. E. Gerland edited the *capitularium* in *Das Archiv des Herzogs*, p. 93: "4. Item omnes sententias, quas ego et socii mei proferemus, illas iuxta formam statutorum Uenetiarum dabo. Et si aliqua questio apparuerit, de qua statuta non faciant aliquam mentionem, et in ipsis inueniretur aliquod simile, procedere et iudicare debeo de simili ad simile in questione, et si aliquod simile non reperiretur in eisdem, iudicare et proferre debeo sententiam iuxta bonam consuetudinem approbatum. Et si consuetudo non haberetur, iudicabo et procedam secundum meam bonam conscientiam."

34. For fifteenth-century Venetian colonial rule and law, see James S. Grubb, *Firstborn of Venice: Vicenza in the Early Renaissance State* (Baltimore and London, 1988), p. 29.

35. Gerland, *Das Archiv*, p. 98.

36. Gerland, *Das Archiv*, p. 98: "Excepto de ratione repromissearum [sic], de quibus procedere et iudicare debeo iuxta usum Grecorum." Gaetano Cozzi noted the same exception in his discussion of Venetian law in Crete: Gaetano Cozzi, "La politica del diritto," in *Stato, società e giustizia nella repubblica veneta (sec. XV–XVIII)*, ed. Gaetano Cozzi (Rome, 1981), pp. 17–152, p. 33: "Non è chiaro cosa fossero le 'repromissae' per cui si faceva eccezione: è importante comunque che in un caso si tenesse conto esplicitamente di un 'usus' dei Greci."

37. Chryssa Maltezou, "Byzantine 'consuetudines' in Venetian Crete," *Dumbarton Oaks Papers* 49 (1995): 269–80, pp. 270, 273, 275.

38. ASV, NDC, not. A. Bellamore, Busta 9, fol. 175v, 5 Dec 1328: "Eodem die. Manifestum facimus nos presbyter Antonius Rizardi, archidiaconus Crete ecclesie, yconomus, procurator, gubernator, actor, factor et amminstrator episcopatus et ecclesie Chironensis, ut de yconomatu et procuracione atque mandato huiusmodi patet publico instrumento manu Bartholomei de Hengelardi, imperiale auctoritate notarii, publice scripto, facto anno a Nativitate Domini nostri Yhesu Christi et canonici ecclesie Chironensis."

39. *Statuta Judaeorum Candiae eorumque memorabilia (Takkanot Candia)*, ed. E. S. Artom and H. M. D. Cassuto (Jerusalem, 1943). In Hebrew.

40. Patrick Geary, "Ethnic Identity as a Situational Construct in the Early Middle Ages," *Mitteilungen der Anthropologischen Gesellschaft in Wien* 113 (1983): 15–26.

41. Maltezou, "The Historical and Social Context," p. 20.

42. Marco Pozzo, "La cancelleria," in *Storia di Venezia*, vol. 2, *L'età del Comune* (Rome, 1995), pp. 349–69, p. 362.

43. Tafel-Thomas, *Urkunden*, 2: 131.

44. Stanley Chojnacki, "In Search of the Venetian Patriciate: Families and Factions in the Fourteenth Century," in *Renaissance Venice*, ed. J. R. Hale (London, 1973), pp. 47–90; Stanley Chojnacki, "Social Identity in Renaissance Venice: The Second Serrata," *Renaissance Studies* 8, 4 (1994): 341–58.

45. Tafel-Thomas, *Urkunden*, 2: 129–36. See Borsari, *Dominio veneziano*, p. 29, n. 7 for correction of the edited *Concessio*.

46. Later in the fourteenth century, these divisions were replaced by the older Byzantine system of dividing the island into four *turme*: Candia, Chanea, Rethimno and Sitia. Gallina, *Società coloniale*, pp. 4–5; Thiriet, *La Romanie vénitienne*, pp. 125–26.

47. Tafel-Thomas, *Urkunden*, 2: 130: "Reliquum uero tocius insule sit uestri iuris; ita tamen, quod unusquisque miles ex uobis sex partes possideat, et quilibet peditum habeat unam partem tantum."

48. Among the best-known historians of Venetian Crete, two make clear that they consider both *cavallerie* and sergeantries to have been kinds of *feuda*, or fiefs, while two others state unequivocally that only a *cavalleria* constituted a *feudum* and its tenant a feudatory. The proponents of *cavallerie* and sergeantries equaling *feuda* are Borsari, *Dominio veneziano*, p. 28: "Naturalmente gli obblighi militari dei titolari dei due tipi di feudo erano diversi."; Maltezou, "The Historical and Social Context," p. 20: "The colonists were divided into two categories: the *milites*, who received as their fiefs the *cavallerie*, . . . and the *pedites*, who were allocated less extensive fiefs, the *serventarie*." Freddy Thiriet makes the association between the first *milites* and the status of feudatory: *La Romanie vénitienne*, pp. 126–27; while David Jacoby, "Social Evolution," p. 192, does not view both units of property as *feuda*: "The settlers who belonged to the old Venetian families were called in Crete *milites* or *feudati*, knights or feudatories; they were provided with military tenements called *militiae, cavallerie*, or *feuda*. . . . The *popolani* or members of non-noble families were given smaller tenures called *serventarie* or sergeantries."

49. For one explanation of the economic structure of the colony, with particular attention to *feuda*, see Elisabeth Santschi, *La notion du "feudum" en Crète vénitienne (XIIIe–XVe siècles)* (Montreux, 1976). For a more general background on the agrarian organization, see the very welcome and informative study of Charalmabos Gaspares, *He ge kai oi agrotes ste mesaionike Krete, 13os–14os ai* [*Land and Peasants in Medieval Crete, 13th–14th c.*] (Athens, 1997) (In Greek, with English summary).

50. David Jacoby, *La féodalité en Grèce médiévale: Les "Assises de Romanie": sources, applications et diffusion* (Paris, 1971).

51. Jacoby has made this point in several places, but recently in "Social Evolution," pp. 192–93, esp. n. 30.

52. Borsari, *Dominio veneziano*, p. 77; Gasparis, *He ge*, pp. 49–53.

53. Gallina, *Società colonial*, p. 6; Brunehilde Imhaus, "Les maisons de la Commune dans le district de Candie au XIVe siècle," *Thesaurismata* 10 (1973): 124–37.

54. Gallina, *Società colonial*, pp. 37–38. For concise definitions of the predominant forms of allocating and renting land, see the glossary in Gasparis, *He ge*, pp. 41–45.

55. Borsari, *Dominio veneziano*, p. 73.

56. Gallina, *Società coloniale*, pp. 33–36; Gasparis, *He ge*, pp. 55–60.

57. Maltezou, "The Historical and Social Context," p. 26; Jacoby, "Social Evolution," pp. 209–211; Gasparis, *He ge*, p. 41.

58. Borsari, *Dominio veneziano*, pp. 77–78.

59. See Appendix A for list of cognomina.

60. Tafel-Thomas, *Urkunden*, 2: 129–36.

61. Borsari, *Dominio veneziano*, pp. 75–78. Men from north central Italy, very likely serving as men-at-arms, appear among the tenants of *serventarie* in the thirteenth century, and more rarely among the tenants of *cavallerie*.

62. Jacoby, "Social Evolution," p. 197.

63. David Jacoby, "Les états latins en Romanie: phénomènes sociaux et économiques (1204–1305 environ)," in *XVe Congrès International d'Études Byzantines*, vol. 1, *Histoire: Rapports* (Athens, 1976), pp. 3–15; rpt. in *Recherches sur la Méditerranée orientale du XIIe au Xve siècle* (London, 1979), p. 20.

64. Thiriet, *Délibérations du Sénat*, p. 64, n. 214, 12 Aug 1348; pp. 116–17, n. 455, 18 Mar 1368; p. 145, n. 580, 8 Jul 1376. *Documents inédits pour servir à l'histoire de la domination vénitienne en Crète de 1380 à 1485*, ed. Hippolyte Noiret (Paris, 1892), p. 54, 11 Mar 1393, and p. 92, 28 Apr 1398; Gallina, *Società coloniale*, p. 30.

65. Tafel-Thomas, *Urkunden*, 2: 234–49, n. 263; Borsari, *Dominio veneziano*, pp. 30–40.

66. ADC, *Proclami e Banni*, p. 16, n. 29, 2 Apr 1314.

67. Maltezou, "The Historical and Social Context," p. 20.

68. Tafel-Thomas, *Urkunden*, 2: n. 263, pp. 246–47: "cum autem, Domino concedente, ad Cretam junxeritis, transactis duobus annis, quibus, ut supradictum, debetis ibi continue comorari, licitum vobis esse debet mutare milites servitores ipsos, quos hinc illuc tuleritis, vel per tempora ibidem habueritis pro Venetis vel forinsecis, sed non Grecis: videlicet militem pro militie, peditem pro pedite cambiare, tamen cum voluntate Ducis, qui in eadem insula est vel erit per nos nostrumque consilium."

69. Tafel-Thomas, *Urkunden*, 2: 470–80; Thiriet, *La Romanie vénitienne*, p. 131.

70. ASV, NDC, not. A. Brixiano, Busta 11, fol. 213v, 1370.

71. Gerland, *Das Archiv*, p. 58, doc. 7: "Primo super puncto loquente, quod consilium maius Candide vadit in desolationem occasione personarum indigenarum, que fiunt de ipso consilio."

72. The names of the electors began to be recorded in 1359. Only two of those names belong to men who were not among the most influential feudatories: Franciscus Caravello and Andreas Pantaleo quondam Iacobi.

73. ADC, *Proclami e Banni*, Busta 15, fol. 2r, 5 Dec 1356: "Die quinto decembris, indicione X. Clamatum fuit publice per Iohannem Marino, gastalidionem, quod cum dominatio scridari fecerit quod illi qui sunt de maiori consilio se faciant scribi ut approbentur secundum formam litterarum ducalium et forsam aliqui qui non sunt de dicto maiori consilio se fecerent scribi ad hoc quod sint provisi dominus ducha et eius consilium mandant quod quicumque se faciet scribi pro dicta proba qui non est vel deberet esse racionabiliter de predicto maiori consilio incurrerent penam advocatoribus comunis que est yperpera L."

74. An interesting and probably unanswerable question is whether this supposed legal dependence implies a joint household as well. The field of Venetian studies lacks a study of emancipation, such as Thomas Kuehn's *Emancipation in Late Medieval Florence* (New Brunswick, N.J., 1982).

75. The Corner family had between seven and ten family groupings; the Gradenigo twelve; the Muazzo seven; the Quirini nine. I am relying on Chojnacki's list

of families who were unquestionably members of the Venetian patriciate in the Trecento: Chojnacki, "In Search of the Venetian Patriciate," pp. 72–75.

76. For an interesting challenge to the notion that family numbers on councils are commensurate to their political power, see David B. Rheubottom, "Genealogical Skewing and Political Support: Patrician Politics in Fifteenth-Century Ragusa (Dubrovnik)," *Change and Continuity* 9 (1994): 369–90, p. 375.

77. The estimation of 4.5 members per family group may very likely be a low one for the feudatory group. I have entered the members of both the Great Council and the Senate into a genealogical database. Culling data from the notarial sources and court records, when I found reliable information about additional members of the feudatory family groups spanning the fourteenth century I have entered their names into the family group to which they belonged. The results are as follows: feudatories with four or more known children: 55; feudatories with two or three known children: 113. The significance of these numbers is limited to showing that possibly a quarter to a third of the feudatories had two or more children, suggesting further that the estimate of 4.5 is a conservative one.

78. The cognomina are Alberto, Baduario, Balbi, Baldu, Bragadino, Busenago, Cavatorta, Delfino, Fuero, Georgii, Gezo, Grimani, Grioni, Lauredano, Malipetro, Manolesso, Mauroceno, Mazamano, Michael, Minio, Mocenigo, Nani, Paradiso, Pisani, Pizamano, Romano, Ruzini, Sanuto, Trivisano, Vituri.

79. Thiriet, *Deliberations du Sénat*, n. 547, 22 Jun 1348, p. 214. Concerned to restore population levels to their former levels as fast as possible, the Great Council of Venice offered economic incentives to potential immigrants.

80. For this and what follows, see Appendix A.

81. *Quaternus consiliorum*, n. 219, pp. 119–22, 29 Mar 1349.

82. *Imbreviature di Pietro Scardon (1271)*, ed. Antonino Lombardi (Turin, 1942), n. 4, 1271, quoted in Peter Topping, "Viticulture in Venetian Crete (XIIIth c.)," *Pepragmena tou D' Diethnous Kretologikou Sinedriou* [Proceedings of the 4th International Cretan Studies Congress] (1981), 2: 509–20, p. 510.

83. *Duca di Candia: Quaternus Consilarum (1340–1350)*, ed. Paola Ratti Vidulich, Fonti per la storia di Venezia. Sez. I: Archivi pubblici (Venice, 1976), pp. 210–11, 25 Nov 1348.

84. *Duca di Candia: Quarternus consiliorum*, p. 11, 24 Nov 1344.

85. For background to the Serrata, see Stanley Chojnacki, "In search of the Venetian patriciate"; Guido Ruggiero, "Modernization and the Mythic State in Early Renaissance Venice: the Serrata Revisited," *Viator* 10 (1979): 245–56; Reinhold Mueller, "Espressioni di status sociale a Venezia dopo la 'Serrata' del Maggior Consiglio," in *Studi veneti offerti a Gaetano Cozzi* (Venice, 1992), pp. 53–61.

86. ADC, *Quaternus consiliorum*, Busta 12, fol. 124r, 22 Mar 1359.

87. Those names, found in volume 3, the index, of *Wills from Late Medieval Venetian Crete, 1312–1420*, ed. Sally McKee, 3 vols. (Washington, D.C., 1998), are Marcus Cornario, ducha Crete, Gilbertus Dandulo, consiliarius, Nicolaus Delphyno, consiliarius, Iohannes Gradonico, duca Crete, Federico Iustiniano, consiliarius, Iustinianus Iustiniani, ducha Crete, Iohannes Mauroceno, ducha Crete, Marinus Mauroceno, ducha Crete, Petrus Mozenigo, ducha Crete, Baldus Quirino, consiliarius, Bernardus Victuri, consiliarius.

88. *Wills*, 3: index, s.v. "dominus": Frater Marcus Catelan, Frater Marcus Griffo, prior of S. Petrus.

89. *Wills*, 3: index, s.v. "dominus": Civrano de confinio S. Pantaleonis; Nicolaus Coppo, civis Veneciarum; Marcus Iustiniano de contrata S. Marie Formose, Nicolaus Vituri de Venetiis. In 1328, "nobilis vir Iohannes Gradonico," "moved by natural and primitive love and desire of the *patria*," that is, Venice, moved to Venice from Crete and now receives permission to sell off his possessions in Candia: ASV, *Maggior Consiglio*, Avog. di Comune, reg. 22/5, Brutus, fol. 85r, 2 Aug 1328.

90. Chojnacki, "In Search of the Venetian Patriciate," pp. 72–73.

91. Borsari, "Veneziani delle colonie," p. 128.

92. John Knight Fotheringham, *Marco Sanudo* (Oxford, 1915).

93. Peter Lock in *The Franks in the Aegean, 1204–1500* (London and New York, 1995), p. 148, presents the lords of the Archipelago as separate from the feudatories of Candia, when in fact the principal residence of some was in Candia. The most accessible evidence of this is found in *Wills*: Will 183, Nicolaus Venerio *maior*, 1351, resident of Candia: "Preterea dimitto Tito Venerio et Marco Venerio, fratribus, nepotibus meis, totam meam quartam partem insule Cederici"; Will 239, Marcus Cornario *de domo maiori*, 1326: "Residuum vero omnium bonorum meorum insule Crete, Scarpanti et Venetiis dimitto filio meo, Andree . . ."; Will 329, Angeloti, daughter of the late Iohannes Gisi, wife of Thomas Fradello, 1346/47: "Item quicquid michi tengerit de insula de Murgo in parte mea dimitto filio meo, Iohanni suprascripto"; Will 345, Auroplase, widow of *dominus* Iacobus of Venice, 1329: "meos fidei commissarios Andreas Barozi, filium meum, dominatorem insule Sancte Herini et Thirassie atque admiratum Imperii Romanie, Agnetem et Marchesinam, filias meas, omnes habitatores Candide."

94. ADC, *Quaternus consiliorum*, Busta 12, fol. 57r, 13 Apr 1351.

95. ASV, NDC, not. N. da Milano, Busta 144, fol. 58r, 7 Dec 1362: "Florencia, filia quondam bone memorie egregii domini Iohannis Sanuto, Egey Pallagi ducis, dominatrix insularum Egey Pallagi suprascripti, relicta nobilis viri domini de le Carcere, habitatrix Candide."

96. Charles and Kathleen Frazee, *The Island Princes of Greece: The Duke of the Archipelago* (Amsterdam, 1988), pp. 41–42.

97. ASV, NDC, not. N. Tonisto, B273, fasc. 2, fol. 59v, 6 Oct 1387: "Eodem die. Manifestum facio ego Nicoletus Dondi, habitator Candide, patronus unius barche presentialiter existentis in portu Candide, cum meis heredibus, tibi done Gradenige Pisani, relicte domini Nicolai Pisani de Venetiis, habitatrici Candide et successoribus tuis, quia in Christi nomine nauliço tibi dictam barcham meam armatam cum hominibus septem a remo super qua vero debeo levare ser Iohannem Pisani, filium tuum, et ser Dominicum Suriano, socium eius, cum arnisis, familiis et panaticha eorum et teneor recedere hinc ad sequendum viagium insularum S. Santurini, Naxie et Serfii per totam diem crastina, salvus tamen impedimentum Dei et Domini. Et in Serfio debeo cum barcha mea comorare per dies V faciendo expensas marinariorum meorum oris. Si vero infra dies V predictos (*sic*) homines ipsius insule noluissent aliquo modo recipere pro domino suo ser Iohannem filium tuum predictum, tunc ipsum ser Iohannem et socium et familiam eorum hinc Candide transducere debeo. Et tunc teneris mihi dare pro nabulo barche et marinariorum

meorum yperpera XXXV, de quibus ad presens confiteor habuisse yperpera XXV, et residuum in reditu meo de presenti viagio. Si vero homines insule Serfii voluerint accipere pro domino suo dictum ser Iohannem Pisani infra predictos V dies, tunc debeo cum barcha mea ipsum ser Iohannem et socium expectare a die quo aplicuerimus cum barcha mea in dicta insula Serfii donec percompleverint dies XV. Et si dictus ser Iohannes et socius cum familia sua voluerint hic rediere teneor ipsos in barcha mea levare et hic deduare. Si autem ipse ser Iohannes et socius voluerint ire ad insulas infrascriptas, scilicet, Nigroponte, Micono et Tine, tunc tibi nec eorum tenear in aliquo nisi tenear dictis nauliçare barcham meam armata itero precio racionabiliter et nauliçamenta iterum facto inter me et dictum ser Iohannem et ser Dominicum mihi teneris hic Candide tu rendere et solvere de denariis tuis. Verum est quod a diebus V postquam in Serfio applicuimus in antea usque ad dies X, dictus filius tuus teneatur facere expensas oris dictis meis marinariis et mihi, ut tu mecum concors fuisti. Ad hec autem ego Gradonica Pisani predicta sum contenta de omnibus suprascriptis et teneor atendere et observare omnia et singula suprascripta. Si qua igitur etc. Pena yperpera L. Contractu firmo. Testes Na. de Montello et Da. Rodino. Complere et dare."

98. *Wills*, Will 683, Constancius Avonale, 1376.

99. The numbers of the members may be admittedly off by one or two names, given the damaged quality of the folios on which they were recorded. Even if a name is no longer legible, it is possible to see where it once was.

100. Chojnacki, "In Search of the Venetian Patriciate," pp. 72–73.

101. ADC, *Quaternus consiliorum*, Busta 12, fol. 58r, 4 Aug 1351.

102. ADC, *Quaternus consiliorum*, Busta 12, fols. 99r, 101v, 106r, 107r, 110v, 115v, 116r, 125r, 126v, 127r, 129v, 130r, 131v, 132r, 148v, 150r, 151r, 152v, 162v, 163r, 166v, 168v.

103. ADC, *Quaternus consiliorum*, Busta 12, policing: fols. 106r, 110r, 116r, 120r, 137v, 161v; internal defense: fols. 111r and 112r.

104. ADC, *Quaternus consiliorum*, Busta 12, fol. 4r, 2 Apr 1345; fol. 10v, 28 Sep 1345; fol. 14r, 23–27 May 1346; fol. 14v–15r, 21 Apr–3 May 1346; fol. 16v, 9 May 1346; fol. 17r, 11 May 1346; fol. 71v, 21 Oct 1352.

105. ADC, *Quaternus consiliorum*, Busta 12, fols. 8v–9v; fols. 34v–35r, 31 Jan 1348/49; fol. 77v, 2 Jan 1353/54; fol. 90v, 20 May 1356; fol. 91r, 29 May 1356.

106. Gerland, *Das Archiv*, n. 4, 1325, p. 49: "Nono quod mandatum siue preceptum [fuit] eis per ducam et consiliarios, quod ipsi non possent ponere partes pro suis agendis; supplicant, quod seruare valeant, prout semper fecerunt antecessores sui, cum ipsi non possint uti iuribus suis coram nostra dominatione nec coram duca Crete, si consilium inter eos non fiat et [partes] inter eos non ponantur."

107. Gerland, *Das Archiv*, p. 49.

108. Thiriet, *La Romanie vénitienne*, p. 261. The plague reached Crete in the fall of 1347 and returned several more times in the following fifteen years.

109. ADC, Quaternus consiliorum, Busta 12, fol. 26r, 31 May 1347; fol. 29v, 26 Feb 1347/48; fol. 79v, 23 Apr 1356; fol. 124r, 15 Apr 1359; fol. 138v, 12 Jul 1360; fol. 143v, 21 Sep 1360; fol. 146v, 22 Nov 1360; fol. 152r, 23 Apr 1361; fol. 159r, 9 Jan 1361/62; fol. 163r, 18 Jun 1362; fol. 165r, 27 Sep 1362.

110. This is suggested by the fact that the list of senators are divided into three columns, each consisting of approximately thirty names. At the head of the first column is written "Ad vocem domini duche," which translates roughly as "at the summons of the duke." The summoners in the other two lists were the duke's two councillors.

111. The number of *rogati* without family representation on the Great Council may be greater than the table shows. A few of the *rogati* whose family had more than one branch residing in Crete attached the sobriquet "de Venetiis" to their name, indicating that they were recent immigrants to the colony, or at least the most recent of that particular clan.

112. *Duca di Candia, Quaternus Consiliorum (1340–1350)*, pp. ix–x.

113. Elizabeth A. Zachariadou, *Trade and Crusade: Venetian Crete and the Emirates of Menteshe and Aydin (1300–1415)* (Venice, 1983), p. 5.

114. ADC, *Quaternus consiliorum*, Busta 12, fols. 54v–55r, 10 May 1351; fols. 145r–146r, 8 Nov 1360.

115. ADC, *Quaternus consiliorum*, Busta 12, fol. 73r, 2 Dec 1352.

116. ADC, *Proclami e Banni*, Busta 14bis, fols. 1v–2r, 2r, 17v, 41v, 48r, 65r, 81r.

117. The feudatories convinced the doge to reverse the rule prohibiting the joining of several sergeantries. This reversal is mentioned in the deliberations, because the duke of Crete was not allowing sergeantries to be combined. Hence the Council of Feudatories prepared a delegation to the doge. ADC, *Quaternus consiliorum*, Busta 12, fol. 37v, 5 May 1349 (p. 127 in *Duca di Candia: Quaternus consiliorum*).

Chapter 2

1. Chojnacki, "In Search of the Venetian Patriciate," pp. 48–49.

2. Adrian J. Boas, "The Frankish Period: A Unique Medieval Society Emerges," *Near Eastern Archaeology* 61, 3 (1998): 138–73, p. 143.

3. Tafel-Thomas, *Urkunden*, 2: 131. Similar requirements can be found in other Venetian dependencies. See Susan Mosher Stuard, *A State of Deference: Ragusa/Dubrovnik in the Medieval Centuries* (Philadelphia, 1992), p. 42.

4. Thiriet, *Déliberations du Sénat*, p. 48, n. 95, 28 Aug 1339.

5. ADC, *Proclami e Banni*, Busta 14bis, fols. 1v–2r, 2r, 17v, 41v, 48r, 65r, 81r.

6. ADC, *Libri feudorum*, Catastico SS. Apostolorum, fol. 81: "Propter presentem guerram miliciam suam secure non poterat habitare, set si habet peccuniam unde posset turrim unam hedifficare in terra dicte milicie, tunc ibi securius habitaret." Cited in Borsari, *Dominio veneziano*, p. 81, n. 78.

7. *Pietro Pizolo: Notaio in Candia*, Tom. I (1300), ed. Salvatore Carbone, Fonti per la storia di Venezia. Sez. III: Archivi notarili (Venice, 1978), n. 499, 1347, Petrus Dono.

8. ADV, NDC, not. N. da Milano, Busta 144, fol. 44r, 29 Nov 1361.

9. Laurentius De Monacis, *Chronicon de Rebus Venetis* (Venice, 1758), p. 179. *Wills*, Will 612, Ergina, daughter of ser Bartholomeus de Grimaldo, wife of ser

Petrus Gradonico, 1362. ASV, NDC, not. L. Marcello, n. 297, 21 Oct 1280: Vidota, widow of Albertino Taliapetra, resident in *Castrum Themali*. *Pietro Pizolo: Notaio in Candia*, Tom. I (1300), ed. Salvatore Carbone, Fonti per la storia di Venezia. Sez. III: Archivi notarili, 2 vols. (Venice, 1978), 1: n. 162, 6 Mar 1300: Iohannes Lumbino, son of the late Constantino Lumbino, resident in the village of Rustica, and his brother Niccolò Lumbino, resident of Candia, possessor of three sergeantries in the villages of Lanopoli et Rustica; v. 1 n. 368, 6 April 1300: Marinus de Molino, resident of the village of Ambrusia.

10. Ennio Concina, *A History of Venetian Architecture* (Cambridge, 1998), p. 95.

11. Georgopoulou, "The Meaning of the Architecture," p. 283.

12. Juergen Schulz, "The Houses of the Dandolo: A Family Compound in Medieval Venice," *Journal of the Society of Architectural Historians* 52 (1993): 391–415, p. 391.

13. Schulz, "Houses of the Dandolo," pp. 405–7.

14. Thiriet, *Délibérations du Sénat*, p. 42, n. 99, 22 Feb 1340.

15. *Wills*, Will 271, Petrus Taliapetra Buali, 1 December 1362: "Item volo quod commissarius meus debeat affictare prout sibi bonum videbitur domus meas in quibus ad presens habito et eciam illas que fuerunt de ca' Ialina. Et afficcitur earum det annuatim Fratribus Minoribus de Candida . . . Item dimitto dicte uxori mee domus meas, in quibus habito ad presens, per annos undecim ad omnem suam utilitatem, ipsa viduante et ipsa solvente onus dictarum domorum de quanto ipsam tetigerit de iure dicto tempore."

16. ASV, NDC, not. N. Tonisto, Busta 73, fol. 32v, 24 Jun 1386: Stamatio Chaviari and Filipo Anelli agree "facere lobis de arte nostra murarie." No mention of the family's main house appears in the 1328 post mortem division of the estate belonging to Marco Corner *de domo maiori* among his sons and two of his brothers, Giovanni and Alessio, the uncles of the men contracting to build a loggia. Text of division of Marco's estate: Gasparis, *Hege*, pp. 324–30. In Marco's will, however, he stipulates that if his daughter married a Corner, he is to receive his share of the island Scarpanthos and his share of the *"domus magna"*: *Wills*, Will 239, Marcus Cornario, 1326.

17. Concina attributes such an arrangement to an increased interest in light: Concina, *Venetian Architecture*, p. 95.

18. ASV, NDC, not. N. de Milano, Busta 144, fol. 44v, 12 Dec 1361: "Die XII. Manifestum facio ego Iohannes Bono filium quondam ser Petri Bono, habitator Candide, cum meis heredibus, de licencia et auctoritate nobilium virorum dominorum Mathei Mudacio et Iohannis Dandulo, iudium proprii. . . . Candide tibi ser Nicolao Bono filio quondam ser Antonii, habitatori Candide, et tuis heredibus quod cum per dominium Crete deliberata fuerit tibi dimidia serventaria pro indiviso de tribus meis serventariis de Stirona, et convenerimus insimul quod pro suprascripta dimidia serventaria tibi do domum meam magnam sitam in civitatem Candide que est porticus unus et due camere, cum hac conditione, quod non possim impedire sive accipere lumen balchionis existentis de supra puteum nec alteri superiori balchionis existentis de supra dictum balchionem. Et insuper non possim laborare a conducto respiniente de versus partem ponentis muri qui extendat vel transendat ultra solerium magne porte porticus suprascripti. Tu vero teneris murare

magnam portam porticus antedicti. Amodo in antea imperpetuum cum plena virtute et potestate."

19. My method for determining whether a testator was a feudatory or a member of his family consists of weighing the name against the evidence of wealth and property along with kinship to other known members of the feudatory group.

20. The nineteen marriage contracts between Venetian Cretan feudatory families are Biaqua and Corario, not. A. de Bellamore, Busta 9, fol. 23r, 1 Feb 1319/20; Sclavo and Trivixano, not. G. Similante, Busta 244, fol. 31r, 5 Jul 1326; Signolo and da Molin, not. A. de Bellamore, Busta 9, fol. 228r, 4 Dec 1329; Dono and Barbarigo, not. M. da Piacenza, Busta 186, fasc. 2, fol. 46r, 27 Jul 1342; Quirini/da Giordano and Venerio, not. G. Gerardo, Busta 100, fol. 321r, 20 Nov 1348; da Canal and Zeno, not. G. Gerardo, Busta 100, fol. 238r, 29 Aug 1348; Corner and Caravello, not. G. Gerardo, Busta 100, fol. 313r, 12 Nov 1348; Caravello and Corner/Contareno, not. G. Gerardo, Busta 100, fol. 320v, 28 Nov 1348; Avonal and Corner, not. G. Gerardo, Busta 100, fol. 343v, 11 Jan 1348/49; Venerio and Venerio, not. G. Gerardo, Busta 100, fol. 337r, 17 Jan 1348/49; Urso and Franco, not. G. da Milano, Busta 143, fol.22v, 23 Sept 1349; Polo and Natale, not. G. Gerardo, Busta 101, fol. 4v, 23 Jan 1350/51; Gradenigo and Quirini, not. D. Grimani, Busta 103, fols. 53v–54r, 24 Oct 1356; Gradenigo/Natale and Abramo, not. D. Grimani, Busta 103, fol. 56r, 5 Dec 1356; Coco and Polo, not. A. Brixiano, Busta 11, fasc. 1, fol. 185r, 11 Nov 1369; Bolani and Polo, not. E. Valoso, Busta 13, fasc. 1, fol. 86r, 17 Feb 1370/71; Avonal and Vassallo, not. G. Aymo, Busta 1, fol. 88v, 20 Apr 1371; Quirini and Dandolo, not. A. Brixiano, Busta 11, fasc. 2, fol. 560r, 7 Jul 1390; Corner and Dandolo, not. A. Brixiano, Busta 11, fasc. 2, fol. 591r, 31 Oct 1390.

21. Christiane Klapisch-Zuber, "The 'Cruel Mother': Maternity, Widowhood, and Dowry in Florence in the Fourteenth and Fifteenth Centuries," in *Women, Family, and Ritual in Renaissance Italy*, trans. Lydia G. Cochrane (Chicago, 1985), pp. 117–31, esp. p 118: "Women, then, were not permanent elements in the lineage. Memory of them was short."; Mark Phillips, *The Memoir of Marco Parenti: A Life in Medici Florence* (Princeton, N.J., 1987), p. 48: "But for Gostanza [daughter of the family] herself, marriage effectively removed her from the family, placing her beyond Marco's protection, unless by misfortune she should become widowed and so return to her family."

22. Chojnacki takes a similar, broadly sketched approach: Stanley Chojnacki, "Gender and the Early Renaissance State," in *Gender and Society in Renaissance Italy*, ed. Judith C. Brown and Robert C. Davis (London and New York, 1998), pp. 63–86, esp. 67–68.

23. *Wills*, Wills: 20, 23, 159, 219, 222, 238, 263, 271, 275, 276, 296, 324, 328, 358, 451, 490, 498, 521, 771.

24. *Wills*, Wills 201 and 222.

25. *Wills*, Wills 66, 71, 123, 201, 218, 261, 278, 297, 301, 382, 418, 517, 636, 644, 695, 781, and 784.

26. *Wills*, Will 239, Marcus Cornario *de domo maiori*, 30 Aug 1326.

27. *Wills*, Will 659, Maria, widow of *dominus* Iohannes Cornario son of the late *dominus* Andreas *de domo maiori*, 11 Nov 1415; Will 275, Andreas Cornario, son of *dominus* Alexius Cornario *de domo maiori*, 19 Jun 1360.

28. ASV, NDC, not. G. Gerardo, Busta 100, fol. 337r, 17 Jan 1348/49.

29. *Wills*, Will 239, Marcus Cornario *de domo maiori*, 30 Aug 1326.

30. *Wills*, Will 275, Andreas Cornario, son of *dominus* Alexius Cornario *de domo maiori*, 19 Jun 1360. For a description of Andrea's death, see De Monacis, *Chronicon*, p. 179.

31. *Wills*, Will 256, Marçoli, wife of ser Andreas Cornario, son of *dominus* Alexius Cornario *de domo maiori*, 31 Aug 1351.

32. ADC, NDC, not. G. Gerardo, Busta 100, fol. 320v, 1348; not. N. da Milano, Busta 144, fol. 89v, 1369.

33. ADC, NDC, not. N. da Milano, Busta 144, fol. 80r, 1368.

34. De Monacis, *Chronicon*, p. 179.

35. *Wills*, Will 536, Elena, widow of ser Marcus Dandulo, 26 Jul 1369. ASV, NDC, not. A. de Bellamore, Busta 9, fol. 283r, 10 Nov 1331.

36. ASV, NDC, not. N. da Milano, Busta 144, fol. 50r, 30 Jul 1362. This notarial transaction reveals also that Margarita's will was first taken down in Greek by a Greek notary.

37. *Wills*, Will 544, Iohannes Dandulo, son of the late *dominus* Marcus, 18 Mar 1376.

38. Dowry quittance, ASV, NDC, not. N. da Milano, Busta 144, fol. 17v, 12 Mar 1360; Will 271, Petrus Taliapetra Buali, 1 Dec 1362. The second wife, Phylippa, daughter of Alexios II Calergi, married Niccoló in 1368: ASV, NDC, not. N. da Milano, Busta 144, fol. 80r, 12 Jan 1367/68.

39. *Wills*, Will 536, Elena, widow of ser Marcus Dandulo, 26 Jul 1369.

40. One example of a marriage alliance between families of two Cretan towns: ASV, NDC, not. G. Gerardo, Busta 101, fol. 79r, 14 Nov 1356: Marchesina de Molino, wife of Antonius, *habitatrix Chanee*, was the daughter of the lord Marco Corner, resident of Candia.

41. ADC, *Proclami e Banni*, Busta 14bis, n. 79, fol. 73v, 19 Apr 1361.

42. Gallina, *Società coloniale*, pp. 123–26; Zachariadou, *Trade and Crusade*.

43. ASV, NDC, not. G. Gerardo, Busta 101, fol. 126v, 20 Dec 1357: "Die vigesimo. Manifestum facio ego Hemanuel Beto, habitator Candide, quia recepi cum meis heredibus a te ser Marco Beto, habitatore dicte Candide, et tuis heredibus yperpera cretensia centum et septem et grossos venetos octo, que debeo portare mecum super navigium quod nunc dominatio Crete mittit in Palatia et ibi et alio ubicumque mihi videbitur in partibus Turchie licitis et non vitatis per dominium Crete debeo negociare et merceri sicut mihi videbitur pro meliori emendo et vendendo portando vel mittendo Candide cum uno vel pluribus navigiis ad omne tuum periculum et fortunam di maris et gentium [*sic*]."

44. ADC, *Memoriali*, Busta 19, fasc. 15, fols. 8v–9r, 17 Sep 1366; fols. 9v–10r, 21 Sep 1366.

45. ASV, NDC, not. G. Catacolo, Busta 24, fol. 2r, 22 May 1389: "Die XXII. Manifestum facimus nos Marcus Dandulo quondam domini Thome, habitator Candide, ex una parte, et Anastassius Laudopulo de Nigroponte, ad presens existens Candide, patronus unius galeote bancorum XVI existentis in portu Candide ex altera parte, una pars alteri vicissim, cum nostris heredibus, quia concordes sumus hoc modo, videlicet, quod ego Anastassius suprascriptus nauliço tibi suprascripto

ser Marco Dandulo totam dictam meam galeotam, videlicet, cum hominibus pro remo XXIIII, nauclerio uno, patrono uno et balisteriis III meis pro viagio Nigropontis, in qua galeota teneor caricari facere mille libras thimiama grece vocatum et libras II^C lini et caretellum unum vini, que omnia mihi presentare debes in rippa portus Candide. Teneor eciam levare cum dicta mea galeota de Candida omnes illa personas quas volueris de quibus omnibus teneris dedisse mihi expeditionem usque ad dies XXVI, mense maii instantis, ad quem terminum teneor recedere de dicto portu Candide cum dicta galeota, salvo impedimento Dei et Signorie, et ire Chaneam et de Chanea levare omnes illas personas quas volueris cum eorum rebus et arniseis expectando te ibidem per duos dies quibus elapsis inde recedere debeo et ire retto tramitte Nigropontem et non possimus nec audeam levare nec ponere aliquid aliud in dicta mea galeota. Tu vero pro meo nabulo, videlicet, medietatem eorum hic Candide antequam recedam de Candida et reliquam medietatem in Nigroponte infra dies V postquam illuc applicuero cum dicta galeota. Ego vero suprascriptus Marcus Dandulo versa vice sum contentus de omnibus et singulis suprascriptis promittens inviolabiliter observare omnia que ad me spectant pro mea parte. Si qua igitur nemo partium etc. pena ducatorum auri L. Contractu firmo. Testes Andronicus Rampani et Georgius Rodino. Complere et dare unam cartam cuilibet parti. Dedi."

46. ASV, NDC, Busta 244, fasc. 1, fol. 111r, 4 Jul 1331: "Die IIII. Manifestum facimus nos Marcus Cumaniti, habitator in burgo Candide, ex parte una, et Petrus Vidro, habitator Candide, ex altera, cum nostris heredibus quia ad tale concordium devenimus in simul, videlicet, quod ego suprascriptus Marcus nauliço tibi dicto Petro meum lusterium quod ad presens est in portu Candide cum quo recedere debeo die crastina et ire in Nixiam et Parium cum litteris quas mihi das ad presens quas presentare debeo domino Nicolao Sanuto et ab eo recepere litteras recipusales et inde recedere et ire ad Thebas et ibi presentare tuas litteras factori tuo et expectare ad recipiendum sclavos XIII diebus X post presentacionem dictarum litterarum, quod Candidam debeo portare tibi. Tamen licitum est mihi stare in insula Policandi pro meis agendis diebus II. Ego autem predictus Petrus tibi dare debeo pro nabulo dicti lusterii pro dictis viaticis yperpera XXII de quibus ad presens tibi dedi yperpera XII et reliqua yperpera X debet tibi ad tuum redditum dare et si in Thebis steteris ultra dictis X diebus deffectum mei faceris debeo tibi dare tuas et tuorum marinariorum expensas illis diebus quibus steteris. Hec autem etc. pars non obervans parti observanti pena yperperorum XXV. Contractu firmo. Testes Iohannes Mussele, presbyter Michael Felicis, Marcus Mauro et Iohannes de Bononia. Complere et dare."

47. Gallina, *Società coloniale*, pp. 99–106.

48. Thiriet, *Délibérations des assemblées*, p.107, n. 100, 21 Jun 1304.

49. Examples: ASV, NDC, not. F. della Croce, Busta 22, fol. 5r, 13 Jan 1338/39; not. G. Gerardo, Busta 101, fol. 166v, 3 Sep 1358; not. G. Gerardo, Busta 101, fol. 160v, 13 Oct 1358; not. A. Cocco, Busta 23, fol. 37v, 1 May 1400.

50 *Wills*, Wills: n. 46, Catarina de Molino, wife of ser Facinus de Molino of Venice, 1348; n. 55, Agnes Paradiso, wife of ser Simonetus Paradiso of Venice, 1348; n. 56, Marçoli, wife of ser Andreas Iustiniano of Venice, 1348; n. 64, Marinus Quirino, son of the late *dominus* Nicolaus Quirino called Turin of Venice, 1348; n.

260, ser Marinus Venerio, son of the late Blasius, 1362; n 272, Michaletus Mauroceno, son of the late *dominus* Franciscus of Venice, 1363; n. 274, Ser Belellus Nani of Venice, 1362; n. 521, Michaletus Bragadino, *de confinio Sancti Ieminiani de Venetiis*, 1348.

51. ASV, NDC, not. G. Gerardo, Busta 101, fol. 136r, 10 Mar 1358.

52. ASV, NDC, not. G. Gerardo, Busta 101, fol. 166r, 1 Sep 1358. Other examples may be found in the same notarial register, fol. 63r, 2 Jul 1356; fol. 94r, 24 Mar 1357 and in not. A. Brixiano, Busta 11, fol. 221r, 30 Aug 1370.

53. ASV, NDC: not. G. Similante, Busta 244, fol. 3v, 8 Mar 1326; not. G. Similante, Busta 244, fol. 49r, 14 Dec 1327; not. G. da Milano, Busta 143, fol. 8r, 15 Dec 1345; not. G. da Milano, Busta 143, fol. 11r, 19 Jul 1346; not. A. Bocontolo, Busta 10, fol. 33v, 23 Oct 1346; not. G. Gerardo, Busta 101, fol. 94r–v, 29 Mar 1357; not. A. Brixiano, Busta 11, fol. 72r, 13 Dec 1366.

54. ASV, NDC, not. G. Gerardo, Busta 100, fol. 221v, 6 Feb 1347/48.

55. Sally McKee, "Households in Fourteenth-Century Venetian Crete," p. 41; Stanley Chojnacki, "Dowries and Kinsmen in Early Renaissance Venice," *Journal of Interdisciplinary History* 4 (1975): 571–600, p. 571.

56. ASV, NDC, not. G. Similante, Busta 244, fol. 49r, 14 Dec 1327: marriage contract between Nicolaus Dandulo Bellino and Francesca, daughter of the late Angelus Teocari.

57. Tsougarakis, *Byzantine Crete*, p. 81.

58. Theotokes, *Apophasis*, 1: n. 6, 1255.

59. Thiriet, *Délibérations des assemblées*, p. 193, n. 472, 4 Jul 1339.

60. Borsari, *Dominio veneziano*, pp. 76–77.

61. Thiriet, *Délibérations des assemblées*, 1: 114, n. 134, 1 Jul 1307.

62. Thiriet, *Délibérations des assemblées*, 1: 124, n. 171, 11 Mar 1309.

63. ADC, *Memoriali*, Busta 29, fasc. 15.3, fol. 3v, 2 Mar 1368.

64. *Le deliberazione del Consiglio dei Rogati (Senato), serie "Mixtorum"*, ed. Roberto Cessi and P. Sambin (Venice, 1960), 1: 201, n. 284; *Apophasis*, 1: 144–45, n. 40; David Jacoby, "Les états latins," p. 31.

65. Thiriet, *Déliberations du Sénat*, p. 207, n. 880, 27 Jul 1395; Noiret, *Document inédits*, p. 70, 27 Jul 1395.

66. See Appendix D for full texts of the documents.

67. Gerland, *Das Archiv*, p. 62: "Feudati non possint obligare feuda sua Iudeis in catasticis uel aliis actis curie."

68. Full text in Gerland, *Das Archiv*, p. 52.

69. *Apophasis*, vol. 1, *Liber Cerberus*, n. 2, 1283: Consilia ad ducham [...] 13. Any Latin with a *feudum* or *burgesia* cannot be related by marriage to Greeks without loss of that property: David Jacoby, "From Byzantium to Latin Romania," *Latins and Greeks in the Eastern Mediterranean After 1204*, ed. Benjamin Arbel, Bernard Hamilton, and David Jacoby (London, 1989), pp. 1–44, here 9–10. For the prohibitions against intermarriage, see R. Cessi, *Deliberazioni del Maggior Consiglio di Venezia*, 3: 337–38. See also Jacoby, "Les états latins en Romanie," pp. 29–30.

70. As one example among many, many of which can be found in *Wills*, a notarial transaction from 1339 involves Marino Quirini, son of the late lord Pietro,

resident of Candia, and his *cognatus*, Costancio Cutaioti. ASV, NDC, not. F. da Croce, Busta 22, fol. 4v, 4 Jan 1338/39.

71. Cessi, *Deliberazioni* , 2: 155, n. 72; Theotokes, *Apophasis*, 1: 4, 1272: the daughters of Manuel Dragondopulis are permitted to be married to Latin men. K.D. Mertzios, "He syntheke Veneton-Kallergi kai hoi synodeuontes auten katalogoi," *Kretika Chronika* (1949): 262–92, p. 269: "Item quo (sic) tu et omnes qui fuerunt rebelles possitis facere parentelas cum latinis."

72. *Apophasis*, 1: 31, n. 13. I have not seen this reference, but have taken it from Peter Topping, "Co-existence of Greeks and Latins in Frankish Morea and Venetian Crete," in *Studies on Latin Greece* (London, 1977), 11: 3–23, p. 21, n. 59.

73. *Wills*, Will 82, Cali, wife of Constantinus Vlasto, 22 Apr 1349 (kin with Cornario); Will 160, Fradela, widow of Albertinus Cornario, 11 Jan 1341/42 (kin with Calergi); Will 224, Helena, widow of Chyrilus Pantaleo, 6 May 134; Will 482, Agnes, widow of ser Iohannes Vaxalo, daughter of the late ser Iohannes Caliva, 7 Oct 1341; Will 558, Margarita Calergi, 2 Jul 1377 (kin with Mudacio and Secreto); Will 566, Herchiolda Quirini, 8 October 1375 (kin of Quirino, Marcello); Will 766, Mariçoli, wife of ser Iohannes Ialina, 18 Mar 1376 (kin with Habramo).

74. *Wills*, Will 43, Paulus Quirino, son of the late *nobilis vir* Hemanuel Quirino, 23 Jan 1347/48.

75. *Wills*, Will 20, Iacobus Cordeferro, 15 Nov 1330.

76. Angeliki Laiou, "Venetians and Byzantines: Investigations of Forms of Contact in the Fourteenth Century," *Thesaurismata* 22 (1992): 29–43.

77. *Wills*, Will 418, Stephanus Bono, *notarius*, 27 Sep 1331.

78. *Wills*, Will 224, Helena, widow of Chyrilus Pantaleo, 6 May 1348.

79. A. F. Van Gemert, "O Stefanos Saxlikis kai i epoxi tou," *Thesaurismata* 17 (1980): 36–130.

80. ASV, *Avogaria di Comun*, 1334/35; ASV, NDC, not. A. Bocontolo, 1345. Topping, "Co-existence," pp. 18–19.

81. *Délibérations du Sénat*, p. 32, n. 44, 28 Feb 1334/35.

82. *Wills*, Will 123, Iohannes de Rugerio, son of the late Hemanuel, 26 Jul 1336.

83. For background on Buondelmonti, see J. P. A. Van Der Vin, *Travellers to Greece and Constantinople*, 2 vols. (Louvain, 1980), 1: 133–651.

84. Cristoforo Buondelmonti, *Description des Îles de l'Archipel Grec*, ed. Emile Legrand (Amsterdam, 1974). From *Descriptio insule Candie*, pp. 101–37: "Capimus post gravem iter ab alia parte montis Yde rus Meronam, quod in monte erat hedificatum: ubi sic prospiciebam infinitas nucum arbores domesticaque arbusta sub altis videbam montibus, caloerus quidam talia dixit: 'Dum noster sanctissimusque totius mundi atque Polis imperator divisam atque maculatam vestram ecclesiam in suis dimisit erroribus et in sanctam hortodocxamque fidem, mediante nostro summo patriarcha, nos confirmavit, capitaneum Calerghi, ut ab insidiis vestrorum hominum defenderet, ad nos misit, qui in tanto amore atque fidelitate nos gubernavit, quod in hodiernum diem sui descendentes non tanquam homines sed tanquam divinos in terra ista tenentur. Insula tota sub spe ipsorum substentatur et quidquid minimus illorum precipit, presto in anima cum corpore sumus. Et, ut a vestris

Franchis mei domini non decipiantur, nunquam in eodem loco insimul habitant, sed supra iuga montis Dicteique Leuci, cum maiore ipsorum qui hic resedit, concorditer convalescunt. Videsne planum cum magnis ruribus ornatum? In eum cum asperisque periculosis vallibus intratur: exules, cuiuscumque condictionis sint, huc convolant et coram domino Matheo Calerghi ducuntur et bene tractantur. . . . Caloerus, postquam versus orientem omnia dixit, ad domum eius domini me conduxit, qui propter nostram civitatem in sui gratiam me reponit; et dum in latinoque greco multa dicemus, in montem ipse cum suis satrapis lentis gradimur passis, cuius in radicibus centum fontes recentem fluunt aquam, in quibus rura amplissima Romanorum habitant. Ubi talia audivi, avidissimus ut protopapa narraret exoravi, qui libratis verbis sic est orsus: 'Postquam chir Foca ex parte nostri imperatoris insulam totam subiugaverat, filius dicti imperatoris cum nobilibus duodecim principalioribus Romanorum Polis diuque civibus in hanc insulam venit, qui omnibus istis nobilibus dominium et loca concessit; deinde, magno tempore peratto, ex continuis preliis iam fessi in istis montibus conduxere, qui hodie arma et nomen portantes in tanta devenerunt quantitate, quod, si essent concordes, leve eis foret insulam possidere. Et primo sunt Ghortazi, id est Saturi, quingenti in numero; Mellissini, id est Vespasiani, qui sunt trecenti: Lighni, id est Suctiles, qui sunt mille sexcenti; Ulasti, id est Papiniali, qui sunt ducenti; Cladi, id est Ramuli, qui sunt centum octuaginta; Scordili, id est Agliati, qui sunt octingenti. Venerunt denique post longum tempus due alie generationes, qui ab istis nobilibus gratiose recetti fuerunt, scilicet Arculeades, id est Ursini, qui sunt centum, et Colonni, id est Colonnenses, qui fere treginta remanserunt et versus Settiam non cum aliis concordes locum eligere.'

85. I am immensely grateful to Robert Rogers for pointing this out to me.

86. For the serious problems in Van Spitael's edition, see Dimitris Tsougarakis, "Some Remarks on the ⟨⟨Cretica⟩⟩ of Cristoforo Buondelmonti," *Ariadne* 3 (1985): 88–108. For the interpretations placed on such a problematic text, see Francesca Luzzatti Laganá, "La funzione politica della memoria di Bisanzio nella Descriptio Cretae (1417–1422) di Cristoforo Buondelmonti," *Bulletino dell'Istituto Storico Italiano per il Medio Evo e Archivio Muratoriano* 94 (1988): 395–420, p. 420: "And so, it is evident that the resentments of archontic as well as ecclesiastic power against the Franks' usurpations are grafted onto the jealously-preserved memory of Byzantium. In conclusion, it is possible to affirm that Buondelmonti served the sentiments of a nobility that had known how to shape the Cretan collective memory for their own political needs, making it an instrument of self-interested defense in the face of the colonial power, but also evidently an instrument of ideological pressure and hegemony over the population in the name of a common 'national' sentiment" (my translation); Chryssa Maltezou, "Byzantine 'consuetudines,'" 279: "the Byzantine idea, which the *archon* class promoted and disseminated in order to further its own political claims, appealed to the popular imagination and strengthened the client relationship of the masses with the *archontes*."

87. Mertzios, " Syntheke," pp. 262–92.

88. Mertzios, " Syntheke," p. 269.

89. Ernest Gerland, "L'Histoire de la noblesse crétoise au moyen-âge," Part I, *Revue de l'Orient latin* 10 (1903–4): 172–247; Part II, 11 (1905–8): 7–144.

90. Venice, Museo Correr, Mss. Provenienze Diverse 676 c/II.

91. Gerland, "L'histoire," pp. 224–26.

92. ASV, NDC, not. N. Brixiano, Busta 10, fol. 46v, 2 Mar 1347.

93. Gerland, "L'histoire," p. 222; Borsari, *Dominio veneziano*, pp. 49, 51.

94. Venice, Museo Correr, Mss. P.D. 676 c/II, fasc. 1; Gerland, "L'histoire," pp. 236–38.

95. ASV, NDC, not. Stephano Bono, Busta 8, fol. 59r, 19 Dec 1317. One of the documents in the Museo Correr suggests that Alexios I made his will in 1321, but this is obviously an error: Venice, Museo Correr, Mss. P.D. 676 c/II, fasc. 4.

96. For example, Jacoby, "Social Evolution," p. 203.

97. *Pietro Pizolo*, 1: 44, nn. 782, 783, 18 Jun 1304 and n. 934, 22 Oct 1304.

98. The examples will be documented further on. Some of the female Calergi descendants were themselves products of mixed marriages.

99. For future reference, I invite the reader to compare the families into which the Calergi married with the cognomina listed in the *Concessio* of 1211 (Appendix A).

100. Venice, Museo Correr, Mss. P.D. 676 C/II, fasc. 4.

101. ASV, NDC, not. L. Quirini, Busta 233, fol. 39r, 2 Nov 1316: Antonius Bono son of the late lord Nicolaus Bono and Georgius Calergi son of the nobleman Alexios Calergi, his *cognatus*.

102. ASV, NDC, not. G. Gerardo, Busta 101, fol. 6r, 30 Jan 1351/52. In an earlier transaction from 1346, the sergeantries of the late Georgios Calergi in the *turma* of Millopotamo were sold. The location of the land connects this Georgios with the Georgios son of Alexios I: ADC, *Liber incantorum*, Busta 25, fol. 19v, 9 Mar 1347.

103. *Pace* Thiriet (*La Romanie vénitienne*, p. 178, n. 2), I believe the brothers inducted into the Great Council of Venice to be the sons of Alexios II.

104. ASV, NDC, not. G. Gerardo, Busta 100, fol. 221v, 6 Feb 1347: "Die sexto. Manifestum facimus nos Alexius Calergi, habitator in casali Castri, filius quondam nobilis viri Georgii Calergi, ex una parte, et Marcus Gradonico de Venetiis, filius divisus domini Iohannis Gradonico, habitator Candide, ex altera, cum nostris heredibus vicissim quia in Christi Dei nomine ad tales concordiam et pactum devenimus, videlicet quod ego Marcus teneor facere hinc per totum mensem septembris proxime venturos vel antea quando tu Alexius volueris, quod Cecilia Gradonico, filia mea, accipiat Matheum Calgeri, filium tuum in suum virum legittimum, secundum canonicas sanctiones pro eius quidem Cecilie repromissa teneor dare ipsi Matheo quandocumque volueris libras mille ad grossos hic in Candida omni occasione remota sub pena grossi unius pro quolibet yperpero nichilominus solvendo capitale, teneor eciam dare ei donna honorabilia secundum usum nobilium mulierum quando dictus Matheus debebit transducere Ceciliam predictam et pro repromissa suprascripta bona tui Alexii mobilia et immobilia debeant esse obligata. Ad hec autem ego Alexius suprascriptus sum contentus et teneor facere quod suprascriptus Matheus filius meus accipiat suprascriptam Ceciliam in suam uxorem legittimam cum repromissa et donnis suprascriptis modo et ordine predictis. Si qua igitur partium etc. pena yperperorum mille. Contractu firmo. Testes ser Andreas Dandulo, ser Nicolaus Quirino quondam domini Marini, Al. Palamonte, Lau. de Bello Amore, Titus [. . .] Complere et dare."

105. Venice, Museo Correr, Mss. P.D. 677 C/III, fol. 6.

106. ASV, NDC, not. A. Brixiano, Busta 11, fol. 50r, 19 Apr 1366.

107. ASV, NDC, not. A. Brixiano, Busta 11, fol. 76r, 18 Jan 1366/67.

108. A notarial transaction of 1358 involves Ioannes, son of the late Alexios, and his father-in-law Benedetto Quirini. Benedetto was the brother of Bampanino, father of Georgios' first wife. ASV, NDC, not. G. Gerardo, Busta 101, fol. 166r, 1 Sep 1358.

109. ASV, NDC, not. G. Emo, Busta 1, fol. 55r–v, 22 Jun 1370; marriage contract, not. N. da Milan, Busta 144, fol. 80r, 12 Jan 1367.

110. These families' links come from the family trees located in Venice, Museo Correr, Mss. P.D. 676, C/II, fragment.

111. Venice, Museo Correr, Mss. P.D. 676, C/II, fasc. 4. The document reads under Georgios's name for 1332: "catastico in nome de Andrea Gradenigo genero." ASV, NDC, not. A. Bellamore, Busta 9, fol. 193r, 6 Feb 1328/29: "Eodem die. Plenam et irrevocabilem securitatem facio ego Andreas Gradonico filius quondam domini Leonardi Gradonico, habitator Candide, cum meis heredibus, tibi Mariçoli filie nobilis viri domini Georgii Calergi, dilecte uxori mee, habitatrici eiusdem Candide, et tuis successoribus, de tota illa repromissa magna vel parva quam suprascriptus dominus Georgius, pater tuus, michi dare promisit pro te tempore nostre disponsationis, que vero repromissa fuit desuper toto in denariis et aliis rebus extimatis yperpera in cretensia currentia duomille, nunc autem quia de predictis dictus pater tuus me tuo nomine bene et perfecte appacavit etc. Si igitur etc. secundum usum obligans tibi pro ipsa repromissa omnia et singulis bona mea mobilia et immobilia habita et habenda in Crete insule tantum et non alia. Testes Nicolaus Marcel, Iohannes Barbadico, Iohannes de Bello Amore. Complere et dare. Eodem die. Plenam et irrevocabilem securitatem facio ego suprascriptus Andreas Gradonico, cum meis heredibus, tibi nobili viro domino Georgio Calergi, dilecto socero, habitatori in casali Verona et tuis heredibus de quantocumque habui ad dicendum, petendum vel requirendum aut habeo seu tu michi dare debuisti vel debes vel meum dare faciendum habuisti vel habes quocumque modo et quantacumque ratione vel causa cum carta et sine carta in curiam et extra curiam ab initio usque modo nunc autem etc. secundum usum salvum quantum potestatem etc. Testes suprascripti. Complere et dare."

112. ASV, NDC, not. A. Bellamore, Busta 9, fol. 302v, 10 May 1341.

113. ASV, NDC, not. A. Brixiano, Busta 11, fol. 19r, 10 May 1350: "Richiolda, relicta quondam ser Georgii Calergi" and "Agnes, filia sua"; not. A. Brixiano, Busta 11, fol. 52r, 31 May 1366.

114. ASV, NDC, not. Andreas de Bello Amore, Busta 9, fol. 274v, 12 Sep 1331: "Eodem die. Post suprascriptam securitatis cartam per virtutatem et potestatem unius testamenti carte testate et roborate manu notarii infrascripti facte sub anno dominice incarnatione millesimo trecentesimo vigesimonono, mense novembris, die decimooctavo, intrante indictione XIII, Candida, per quam cartam Andreas Calergi, filius quondam domini Alexii Calergi, habitator in loco qui dicitur Castri, insula Crete, instituit suos fideicommissarios Iacobum Cornario Cornarachi, cognatum eius, Iohannes et Alexius Cornario fratres de domo maiore, nepotes eius, Michaelem, Iacobum et Nicolinum Cornario fratres cognatos eius, omnes habi-

tatores Candide, dante sibi virtutem inter cetera post mortem suam faciendi cartas securitatis et commissionis, manifestationis, obligationis et quamcumque vel quascumque aliam vel alias cartas cuiuscumque modi et forma opportunas etc., / ut in ea legitur /, manifestum facimus nos suprascripti Iacobus, Alexius, Michael, Iacobus et Nicolaus nomine quo supra / cum suprascriptis Iohanne Cornario renunciavit commissariam cum meis successoribus/vobis suprascriptis Iacobo et Marco Matono fratribus filii quondam Pascalis Matono, habitatores Candide et tuis heredibus quia pro residuo solvere yperpera quingentorum que dominus Alexius Calergi pater quondam dicti Andree Calergi commissariam dimisit suprascripto Pascale quondam patruo vestrum per suum testamentum sumus contenti vobis dare yperpera in Creta currentia ducenta amodo usque ad unum annum proxime venturum vel ante hic in Candida, salvum in terra, omni occasione remota. Hec autem etc. et pro pena grossi unius. tt. suprascripti. complere et dare."

115. ASV, NDC, not. G. Gerardo, Busta 101, fol. 79r, 14 Nov 1356.

116. *Délibérations du Sénat*, p. 66, n. 227, 17 Jul 1349.

117. The decision is in *Délibérations du Sénat*, p. 80, n. 289, 5 Apr 1356. The relevant clause in the treaty between Alexios Calergi and Venice is in Mertzios, "Syntheke," pp. 267–68: "Item volumus quod possis emere quolibet anno tu cum tuis heredibus equos quindecim ab armis vel rocinos ad tuam voluntatem. Et si non posses eos habere ad emendum quod signoria teneatur dari facere tibi et tuis heredibus quolibet anno pro justo precio equos decem ab armis si tibi tot deficerent a numero dictorum quindecim de allis qui sunt extra guarnicionem."

118. ASV, NDC, not. G. Gerardo, Busta 101, fol. 208v, 21 Oct 1361.

119. Venice, Museo Correr, Mss. P.D., 676 C/II, fasc. 4.

120. Venice, Museo Correr, Mss. P.D., 676 C/II, fasc. 4.

121. In the deliberations of the Venetian Senate there is mention of Leo, grandson of Alexios I, who rebelled against Venice in 1344. Very likely this is Leo, son of Georgios, grandson of Marcos, great-grandson of Alexios I, since as far as I know no other Leo appears among Alexios I's grandsons or great-grandsons. *Délibérations du Sénat*, p. 57, n. 176, 21 Feb 1345.

122. Venice, Museo Correr, Mss. P.D., 676 C/II, fasc. 4.

123. ASV, NDC, not. N. da Milano, Busta 144, fol. 39r, 9 Sep 1361.

124. The nickname Trulidi, or occasionally Turlidi, appears primarily among Leo's descendants, but it crops up now and then among the descendants of his brothers.

125. ADC, *Atti Antichi*, Busta 10, fol. 35v, Jun 1334; Venice, Museo Correr, Mss. P.D. 676 C/II, fasc. 4.

126. ASV, NDC, not. S. Bon, fol. 59r, 19 Dec 1317. The parties involved are Georgius *quondam domini Alexii*, his brother Marcus, and their nephew, Alexius *quondam Trulidhi*.

127. Alexios is alive in Jul of 1331: ASV, NDC, not. Andreas de Bello Amore, Busta 9, fol. 264v, 1 Jul 1331: Alexius Calergi *quondam Leonis Calergi dicti Trulidhi, habitator in casali Sivudhanites* and Iohannes Gradonico *quondam Francisci* Gradonico, *eius avunculus*; listed as in October of the same year: ASV, NDC, not. Andreas de Bello Amore, Busta 9, fol. 277v, 20 Oct 1331: Georgius Calergi son of

the late lord Alexius Calergi and the late Alexius Calergi dictus Trulidhi. See also ADC, *Atti antichi*, Busta 10, fol. 35v, 1334; ASV, NDC, not. F. Croce, Busta 22, fol. 17r, 15 Apr 1339.

128. ASV, NDC, not. G. Gerardo, Busta 101, fol. 94r, 24 Mar 1357; fol. 105v, 10 Jul 1357.

129. Venice, Museo Correr, Mss. P.D. 676 C/II, fasc. 4, fragment.

130. *Wills*, Will 417, Agnes, daughter of the late *nobilis vir dominus* Alexius Calergi, wife of Cornarachus Cornario, 9 Feb 1330/31. See also Renas I. Vlachaki, "H diatheke tes Agnes kores tou Alexiou Kallergi (1331) kai o orthodoxos episkopos Makarios." *Pepragmena tou E' Diethnous Kretologikou Suvedpriou* (Hagios Nikolaos, Crete, 1981), 2: 56–63.

131. *Wills*, Will 209, Iacobus Cornario, son of the late ser Iacobus Cornario, 25 Feb 1348/49. "Cornaraki" is a Greek-Cretan diminutive, which suggests that Giacomo's environment was Greek.

132. This is not the fulfillment of an unfulfilled testamentary bequest of his first wife, since there is no mention of Andrea or his children in Agnes's will.

133. Venice, Museo Correr, Mss. P.D. 676, C/II, fasc. 4.

134. ASV, NDC, not. G. Gerardo, Busta 101, fol. 196v, 6 May 1359.

135. The notarial entry also provides the information that Beata's aunt was Marchesina, widow of Marinus Baroci. The Calergi family archive shows Ioannes to have had a daughter married to Marcus Baroci, son of the late Marinus. Somewhere in the midst of all these genealogical details about the existence of a fifth son is an error, but it would not detract from my main point, the existence of a fifth son.

136. ADC, *Memoriali*, Busta 29, 16.1, fol. 51r–v, 26 May 1369. *Régestes des arrêts civils*, *Sentenze*, p. 36, n. 157; *Memoriali*, p. 151, n. 430.

137. ADC, NDC, not. L. Quirino, Busta 233, fol. 149v, 14 Nov 1318.

138. ADC, *Sentenze*, Busta 29, fasc. 2, fol. 41r, 5 Jul 1324.

139. *Wills*, Will 23, Petrus Mudacio called Parlatus, 1325; Will 43, Paulus Quirino, son of the late nobleman Hemanuel Quirino, 1347/48; Will 54, Iohannes Iallina, son of the late ser Michael, 1348; Will 228, Nicolaus Habramo, son of the late ser Marinus Habramo, 1353; Will 271, Petrus Taliapetra Buali, 1362; Will 650, Bertucius Gradonico, son of the late ser Petrus Gradonico, 1362.

140. *Wills*, Will 218, Daniel Greco, 1348; Will 219, Marcus de Canale, 1348; Will 275, Andreas Cornario, son of the *dominus* Alexius Cornario *de domo maiori*, 1360; Will 557, Petrus de Grimaldo, son of the late ser Iohannes, 1375; Will 567, Thomas Bollani, son of the late ser Thomas, 1375.

141. ADC, *Memoriali*, Busta 29, 15.3, fol. 4r, 2 Mar 1368. *Régestes des arrêts*, *Sentenze*, p. 13, n. 50; *Memoriali*, p. 128, n.194.

142. ADC, *Memoriali*, Busta 29, 16.1, fol. 51, 11 Jun 1369. *Régestes des arrêts*, *Memoriali*, p. 151, n. 432.

143. ASV, *Maggior Consiglio*, *Avogari di Comune*, reg. 22/5, Brutus, fol. 49v, 12 Mar 1327.

144. *Wills*, Will 239, Marcus Cornario *de domo maiori*, 1326.

145. *Wills*, Will 498, Petrus Dono, son of the late *dominus* Paulus, 1346/47.

146. *Wills*, Will 280, Franciscus Caravello, son of the late *dominus* Marcus, 1371.

147. Borsari, *Dominio veneziano*, p. 78; Charles Verlinden, "Traite des esclaves au XIV et XV siècles," in *Studi in onore di Amintore Fanfani*, 3 vols. (Milan, 1962), 3: 593–669; Elisabeth Santschi, "Quelques aspects du statut des non-libres en Crète au XIVe s.," *Thesaurismata* 9 (1972): 104–36.

148. The wills in which the former slaves appear are, in numerical order: *Wills*, Wills 78, 81, 214, 219, 247, 259, 290, 297, 335, 371, 439, 482, 529, 547, 581, 610, 653, 658, 666, 670, 678, 685, 686, 701, 730, 733, 739, 775, 777, 782.

149. *Wills*, Will 411, Chali, former slave of Nicolaus Vasmulo, 1329; Will 422, Herini, former slave of Petrus Lio, now free, wife of Stephanus Nigro, 1332; Will 450, Xenus Doto, former slave of Matheus Doto, now free, 1330; Will 483, Lio Taliapetra, former slave of Matheus Taliapetra, now free, 1342; Will 613, Iohannes Segredho, former slave of ser Iohannes Segredho, 1362.

150. *Wills*, Will 483, Lio Taliapetra, former slave of Matheus Taliapetra, now free, 1342.

151. For instance, Michele Orso, *marinarius* and resident of Venice, arranges for his brother, Nichitas (a Greek name), to apprentice. ASV, NDC, not. G. Gerardo, fol. 53r, 1355.

152. Johannes Jegerlehner, "Beiträge zur Verwaltungsgeschichte Kandias im XIV. Jahrhundert," *Byzantinische Zeitschrift* 13 (1904): 435–79, pp. 464–66.

153. Maria Georgopoulou, "Mapping Religious and Ethnic Identities in the Venetian Colonial Empire," *Journal of Medieval and Early Modern Studies* 26 (1996): 467–96.

154. Since giving the residences of both parties to notarial transactions does not appear to have been obligatory, the numbers in the tables will not correspond to the number of documents.

155. The figure of one hundred and forty-four Greek names among the wills' executors is without question a conservative accounting. For one thing, not all executors' names, many of them Greek, are accompanied by their places of residence. Second, I counted only those names which were indisputably Greek, leaving aside those to which too much ambiguity adheres. See *Wills*, passim.

156. Those professions are: bowmaker (*arcerius*); goldsmith (*aurifex*); crossbowman (*balistrarius*); barber (*barbitonsor*); butcher (*beccarius, macellator*); goatherder (*bordonarius*); bottlemaker (*buticlarius*); caldronmaker (*calderarius*); caulker (*calefatus*); cobbler (*caligarius, sutor, cerdo*); cabinetmaker (*capsellarius*); leatherworker (*cimator*); locksmith (*claverius*); armorer (*clibanarius*); cook (*cochus*); (*corrigarius?*); knifesmith (*cultellarius*); (*curtinarius?*); guard (*custos*); customs agent (*daçarius*); ironsmith (*faber*); baker (*fornarius*); harness maker (*frenarius*); herald (*gastaldus, preco*); (*manegoldus?*); carpenter (*maragnonus*); farrier (*marescalcus*); sailor (*marinarius*); physician (*medicus*); measurer (*mensurator*); merchant (*mercator*); miller (*molendinarius*); muledriver (*mulinarius*); mason (*murarius*); shepherd (*peccorarius*); furrier (*peliparius, varotarius*); painter (*pictor*); potter (*pignatarius*); fisherman (*piscator*); porter (*portarius*); bell-ringer (*pulsator*); arrowsmith (*sagittarius*), meatseller (*salumerus*); tailor (*sartor, iuparius*); bag or purse maker (*scarselarius*); notary (*notarius, scriba*) stonecutter (*speçapetra*); grocer/pharmacist (*speciarius*); tavernkeeper (*tabernarius*); weaver (*textor*); dyer (*tintrix*); banker (*tratarius*); secondhand dealer (*venderigolus*).

157. Sally McKee, "Women Under Venetian Colonial Rule in the Early Renaissance: Observations on Their Economic Activities," *Renaissance Quarterly* 51 (1998): 34–67; Chryssa Maltezou, "Métiers et salaires en Crète vénitienne (XVe siècle)," *Byzantinische Forschungen* 12 (1987): 323–41.

158. Elisabeth Santschi, "Contrats de travail et d'apprentissage en Crète vénitienne au XIVe siècle d'après quelques notaires," *Revue Suisse d'histoire* 19 (1969): 34–74.

159. Santschi, "Contrats de travail," p. 59.

160. ASV, NDC, not. N. Tonisto, Busta 273, fol. 52r, 16 Jul 1387.

161. According to Achille Vitali, *La moda a Venezia attraverso i secoli: lessico ragionato* (Venezia, 1992), Santschi is incorrect in defining "cerdo" as tanner: cf. Santschi, "Contrats de travail," 62.

162. Vitali, *Moda a Venezia*, s.v. "calzatura," see esp. pp. 84–85.

163. ASV, NDC, not. A. Bocontolo, Busta 10, fol. 31v, 15 Oct 1346.

164. ASV, NDC, not. N. Tonisto, Busta 273, fol. 57r, 26 Sep 1387: "[Marcus Vergici, cerdo,] teneor servire dictis masculis filiis vestris in calciatu sicut mihi dixerint et ordinaverint, videlicet, insolare solatas suas, facere eis subtelare cum punctu vel sine punctu et aptare, scilicet, scapinare stivalia eorum, tenendo ipsos et ipsas semper bene caligatas. Dictis vestris filiabus teneor aptare stivalia earum et facere eis subtelare cum pontu vel sine ut mihi ordinaverint et omnes subtelare laceratos omnium predictorum filiorum et filiarum vestrorum apud me retinere debeo."

165. Cf. Charalmabos Gasparis, "Oi epaggelmaties tou Chandaka kata ton 14° aiona skeseis me ton katanalote kai to kratos," *Simmeikta* 8 (1989): 83–133, p. 102.

166. *Wills*, Will 14, Cali, wife of Hemanuel Habramo, *aurifex*, 1324: 110 pp; Will 187, Georgius Rosso, *aurifex*, 1352: 200 pp; Will 230, Maria, wife of Georgius Selopulo, *aurifex*, 1345: 200 pp; Will 248, Marchesina, widow of Nicolaus de Plasencia, *aurifex*, 1329: 180 pp; Will 400, Caterina, daughter of Nicolaus de Plansença, wife of Iohannes Rapani, 1324: 250 pp; Will 478, Petrus Çangisiti, *aurifex*, 1339: 200 pp; Will 637, Aniça, daughter of Dionnisius Gramaticopulo, *aurifex*, wife of Petrus Çane da Mantoa, *spatarius*, 1362: 225 pp. Marriage contract, n. 6: 230 pp; n. 69: 300 pp: n. 101: 200 pp.

167. ADC, *Proclami e Banni*, Busta 15, fol. 13r, 10 Sep 1357, fol. 81v, 3 Oct 1361, fol. 114r, 18 Oct 1364. Gaspares, "Oi epaggelmaties," p. 103.

168. ASV, NDC, not. E. Valoso, Busta 13, fol. 27r, 25 May 1370: "Eodem die. Manifestum facio ego Andreas Malandrin, marangonus, habitator Candide, cum meis heredibus tibi Georgio Cavoso, aurifici, et tuis heredibus quoniam promitto tibi et sum contentus debere tibi facere banchum unum novum cum meo lignamine, cum bonis tabulis et omnibus meis expenssis, cum tribus anixi et cum bancheta de subter et unum armarium apano, talem qualem tibi ostendi amodo usque ad dies XV proxime venturos. Que banchum et armarolum debeant esse bene laborata sic quo per omnes magistros marangonos quibus mihi placuerit dicatur quod fuit dictum banchum et armarium bene et sufficienter laboratum. Et si dicti magistri dicant non esse bene laborata, non tenearis ad accipiendum dictum banchum et armarium nec pro eis solvere mihi. Et si ipsi magistri dicant esse bene et sufficienter facta et laborata tenearis ea accipere et pro meo laborerio sive solutione tenearis mihi

dare yperpera novem, completo dicto servicio. Si quis etc. et pro pena inde constituta yperpera quinque. Contractu firmo. Testes presbyter Iohannes Sclença, Leonardus Qurino et Iohannes Ploreo, spatarius. Complere et dare."

169. ADC, *Proclami e Banni*, Busta 15, 9 Nov 1365. Gaspares, "Oi epaggelmaties," p. 104.

170. ASV, NDC, not. G. Similante, fasc. 1, fol. 11r, 22 Jul 1326: "in tua stacione . . . eciam ire extra per casalia secundum consuetudinem aurificorum quando mihi preciperis."

171. ASV, NDC, not. G. Similante, fasc. 1, fol. 21r, 14 Feb 1326/27.

172. ASV, NDC, not. G. Gerardo, Busta 101, fol. 30rbis, 14 Jan 1354/55: "servire in dicta arte tua in statione tua et extra in burgo et in casalibus ubicumque illum in tua societate acceperis pro dicta arte tua exercenda."

173. The two goldsmiths who moved from the burg into the city are Nicolaus Vaceta, resident of the burg in 1381 (ASV, NDC, not. Antonio Brixiano, Busta 12, fol. 82r, 16 May 1381) and of the city in 1385 (ASV, NDC, not. N. Tonisto, Busta 273, fasc. 2, 14v, 18 Nov 1385) and Georgius Xathomali, resident of the burg in 1386 and of the city in 1387 (ASV, NDC, not. N. Tonisto, Busta 273, fol. 38r, 22 Nov 1386).

174. ASV, NDC, not. N. Tonisto, Busta 273, fol. 28v, 12 Apr 1386: "Die suprascripto. Manifestum facio ego Dimitrius Salonicheo, speciarius, habitator Candide, cum meis heredibus tibi ser Petro Brocardi de Florentia, speciario, habitatori Candide, et heredibus tuis quia afirmo me tecum amodo in antea usque ad annos duos proxime venturos, hoc modo, videlicet, quod in dicto tempore tibi servire debeam bene et legaliter tam in stacione tua speciarie, faciendo candellas, confectiones et alia servicia dicte stationis et vendendo ipsa iuxta posse et scire meum die noctuque quam eciam in aliis tuis serviciis prout mihi preceperis."

175. ADC, *Proclami e Banni*, Busta 14, fol. 91v, 12 Sep 1333: "Clamatum fuit publice per Petrum Vido, gastaldionem, quod amodo in antea nullus spatarius, faber, arcerius, et sagitarius qui habitat in burgo Candide audeant laborare aliquid de arte sua nisi inter in civitatem et laborare quod ipsi fecissent usque modo debeant ponere in civitatem cras per diem. Et si fabri habitantes in burgo haberent ferrum laboratum debeant illud scribi iuxta ordinem factum per dominium sub pena medietatis valoris rei. Et haec conmittatur advocatoribus comunis qui inquirant et exigant penas a contrafacientibus de quibus accusatores habeant terciam partem et terciam partem ipsi advocatori et reliquam terciam partem comuni."

176. *Wills*, Will 445, Helena, wife of Petrus Paulo, *faber*, daughter of the late Nicolaus Naptopuli of Caronissi, 1339.

177. ASV, NDC, not. B. Francisci, Busta 97, fol. 59v, 29 May 1339.

178. *Wills*, Will 35, Nicolota, widow of Nicolaus Naptopulo, 1347/48; Will 53, Hemanuel Paulo, son of the late Petrus Paulo, *faber*, 1347/48. It was customary for women, especially Greek ones, to revert to their natal names in widowhood.

179. *Wills*, Will 635, Petrus Çane of Mantoa, *spatarius*, 1362; Will 637, Aniça, widow of Petrus Çane, *spatarius*, 1362.

180. *Wills*, Will 231, Antonius Chandachyti, *filius indivisus* of Michael Chandachyti, *arcerius*, 1361.

181. The Jewish physicians are Açargias, 1323; Bonus, 1301; Magister Elyas,

1374; Magister Iacob, theotonicus; 1370–78; Magister Ioste, 1389; Moyses, 1355; Rebi Michael, 1319; Samuel, sacerdos, 1368; Solomon, son of the late Bonus, 1355–63; Laçarus de Serre, 1353.

182. The obviously Greek physicians are Theodorus Gemisto of Constantinople, 1350; Magister Marcus Granella, 1333; Magister Cosmas Rosso, 1389; Yacintho, monacus, 1353.

183. Magister Iacobus de Alexandria, 1345; Antonius, 1352; Antonius Apussicius, 1316; Egidio de Assissio, 1458; Magister Iohannes de Bonaldis, 1345; Magister Iacobus de Bonivento, 1376–87; Magister Michaletus Bonaviturdo, 1360; Magister Bonazunta, 1345; Magister Leonardus de Caneto, 1387; Magister Bernardus de Crispis de Mutina, 1358; Magister Thomas de Fano, 1370; Magister Fredericus, 1333; Magister Georgius de Maiorica, 1301; Magister Marcus, 1301; Magister Marinus, 1341; Marcus Pagano, 1349; Magister Iohannes de Monte Galdella de Padua, 1356; Iohannes de Parma, 1355; Marcus Piloso, 1326; Pucius de Sicilia, 1367; Petrus de Rena, *ianuens, habitator Veneciarum*, 1367; Magister Franciscus de Senis, 1351; Magister Gregorius de Spinis de Laude, 1348; Benet Surianus de Tauresio, 1355; Victor, *magister*, 1340.

184. ASV, NDC, not. G. Gerardo, Busta 10, fol. 53v, 13 Jun 1355 (canceled): "Eodem die. Manifestum facimus nos Benet medicus surianus de Tauresio, nunc morans Candide, ex una parte, et Petrus Cornario, filius ut dico divisus ser Alexii Cornario de domu maiori, habitator Candide, ex altera cum nostris heredibus vicissim quod ad tales concordiam et pactum devenimus quod ego Benet teneor incipere ad medicandum et curandum te Petrum de infirmitate raucedinis quam pateris ita quod mediante auxilio Dei venias in statu vere sanitatis et libereris a dicto malo et vox tua sit solida et stagna. Tu vero pro mea provisione dicte curationis teneris mihi dare ducatos venetos auri quinquaginta infra dies decem postquam de dicta infirmitate sanatus fueris. Tamen pro expenssis medicinarum quas me opportet tibi facere recepi nunc a te ducatos auri decem. Et si amodo usque ad menses duos proximos de dicta infirmitate non eris sanatus hac carta remaneat vacua, nec tenearis mihi dare aliquid nec ego tenear tibi reddere aliquid de predictis decem ducatis expenssarum. Nota quod partes fuerunt in discordia antequam preces darent et ideo hec scriptura nichil vallet." Fol. 53v, 18 Jun 1355, same text as above with this difference: "recepi nunc a te ducatos auri decem ultra scriptascriptos . . . nec tenearis mihi dare aliquid de decem ducatis expenssarum. Ad hec autem ego suprascriptus Petrus sum contentus et illa tenear observare. Sciendum est quod cum suprascriptus Benet non intelligat linguam latinam vel grecam, turçumanus eius fuit Costas de Romania, famulus eius. Si qua igitur partium etc. pena ducatorum auri decem. Contractu firmo. Testes Iohannes Sclavo quondam Georgii, Nicolaus Stando, Georgius Garguli. Complere et dare." I am very grateful to Leslie MacCoull for drawing my attention to Benet having very probably been Christian.

185. ADC, *Quaternus Consiliorum*, Busta 12, fol. 3r, 30 Jan 1344/45; fol. 3v, 5 Feb 1344/45; fol. 5r, 3 May 1345; fol. 8v, 21 Sep 1345; fol. 12v, 23 Nov 1345; fol. 13v, 14 Jan 1345/46; fol. 15v, 3 May 1346; fol. 19r, 30 Oct 1346; fol. 21v, Feb 1346/47; fol. 16 Feb 1346/47; fol. 25r, 31 May 1347; fol. 26r, 31 May 1347; fol. 29r, 23 Dec 1347; fol. 31v, 18–22 Mar 1348; fol. 32r, 28 May 1348; fol. 32v, 18 Jun 1348; fol. 33r, 30 Jul 1348; fol. 36v, 2 Apr 1349; fol. 37r, 23 Apr 1349; fol. 39v, 26 Sep 1349;

fol. 42r, 14 Feb 1349/50; fol. 44v, 1 May 1350; fol. 49v, 14 Aug 1350; fol. 52v, 30 Dec 1350; fol. 57v, 2 Aug 1351; fol. 57v, 2 Aug 1351; fol. 58r, 4 Aug 1351; fol. 63r, 15 Mar 1352; fol. 71r–v, 18–22 Oct 1352; fol. 76v, 19–24 Aug 1353; fol. 80v, 27 Aug 1354 and 1 Oct 1354; fol. 81v, Mar 1355; fol. 84v, 13 Jul 1355; fol. 89r, 12 Mar 1356; fol. 92r, 3 Jul 1356; fol. 92v, 18 Sep 1356; fol. 94v, 11 Nov 1356; fol. 100v, 20 Jul 1357; fol. 101v, 14 Sep 1357; fol. 110r, 3 Apr 1358; fol. 113v, 6 Aug 1358; fol. 114v, 14 Sep 1358; fol. 120r, Dec 1358; fol. 123r, 2 Mar 1359; fol. 124r, 15 Apr 1359; fol. 124v, 25 Apr 1359; fol. 126r, 26 Jul 1359; fol. 128v, 5 Sep 1359; fol. 132r, 20 Nov 1359; fol. 136r, 25 Feb 1359/60; fol. 136v, 15 Mar 1360; fol. 138v, 12 Jul 1360; fol. 143v, 21 Sep 1360; fol. 144r, 28 Sep 1360; fol. 146v, 22 Nov 1360; fol. 152r, 23 Apr 1361; fol. 153r, 13 Jun 1361; fol. 156r, 19 Sep 1361; fol. 159r, 9 Jan 1361/62; fol. 159v, 18 Jan 1361/62; fol. 163r, 18 Jun 1362; fol. 165r, 27 Sep 1362.

186. The town of Chanea had no physician to attend the colonists there in 1353: ADC, *Quaternus Consiliorum*, Busta 12, fol. 77r, 5 Sep 1353. By 1354, the Candiote feudatories employed only one physician: ADC, *Quaternus Consiliorum*, Busta 12, fol. 79v, 23 Apr 1354.

187. *Délibérations du Sénat*, p. 214, n. 547, 22 Jun 1348.

188. ASV, NDC, not. S. Bon, Busta 8, fol. 16r, 4 Sep 1303 (*caligarius/murarius*); not. A. Bellamore, Busta 9, fol. 268r, 23 Sep 1331; not. G. Gerardo, Busta 100, fol. 40v, 27 Oct 1331; not. M. de Piacenza, Busta 186, fasc. 2, fol. 30r, 28 May 1341; not. G. Paço, Busta 189, fol. 15v, 9 Mar 1384; *cerdo/texatrix*, not. G. Siligardo, Busta 244, fol. 169r, 27 Jan 1339/40. Marriage contracts: *faber/aurifex*, not. B. Francisci, Busta 97, fol. 59v, 29 May 1333?; *preco/sutor*, not. M. de Piacenza, Busta 186, fasc. 2, fol. 48r, 9 Nov 1342; *mercatrix/specialis*, not. G. de Milano, Busta 143, fol. 45v–46r, 5 Mar 1347; *peliparius/sutor*, not. G. de Milano, Busta 143, fol. 17v, 6 Aug 1348; *furnarius/furnarius*, not. G. Gerardo, Busta 101, fol. 46v, 29 Apr 1355; *sutor/calefatus*, not. D. Grimani, Busta 103, fol. 55v, 1356; *speçapetra/cerdo*, not. A. Brixiano, Busta 11, fol. 78v, 27 Jan 1366/67; *marinarius/buticlarius*, not. A. Brixiano, Busta 11, fol. 105r, 3 Oct 1367; *botarius/aurifex*, not. A. Brixiano, Busta 11, fol. 149v, 1 Nov 1368; *calderanus/iuparius*, not. G. Emo, Busta 1, fols. 26v–27r, 29 Jan 1369/70; *preco/sutor*, not. A. Brixiano, Busta 12, fol. 154v, 14 Dec 1382; *venderigolus/murarius*, not. G. Catacalo, Busta 24, fol. 16r, 21 Jul 1389; *curtinarius/barbitonsor*, not. G. Catacalo, Busta 24, fol. 22r, 25 Aug 1389; *preco/marinarius*, not. G. Catacalo, Busta 24, fol. 26v, 8 Sep 1389.

189. *Pietro Pizzolo*, 1: n. 390, 13 April 1300. The other contracts showing interartisanal marriages leading to improved social standing are all in ASV, NDC: *barbitonsor/aurifex*, not. G. Gerardo, Busta 100, fol. 16v, 20 Feb 1329/30; *ex-slave/cimator*, not. G. Gerardo, Busta 100, fol. 28r, 13 Jul 1331; [?] not. G. Siligardo, Busta 244, fol. 157r, 5 Jul 1339; *villanus/faber*, not. F. de Croce, Busta 22, fol. 24v, 30 Nov 1339; *marinarius/marangonus-calefatus*, not G. Gerardo, Busta 101, fol. 53r, 12 Jun 1355; *arcerius/iuparius*, not. N. de Milano, Busta 144, fol. 15v, 8 Oct 1355; *spatarius/marangonus*, not. N. de Milano, Busta 144, fol. 8v, 17 Oct 1355; *iuparius/aurifex*, not. G. Gerardo, Busta 101, fol. 70r, 5 Sep 1356; *caligarius/iuparius*, not. G. Gerardo, Busta 101, fol. 184r, 25 Mar 1359; *fusarius/aurifex*, not. N. de Milano, Busta 144, fol. 28v, 14 May 1360; *preco/peliparius*, not. A. Brixiano, Busta 12, fol. 108r, 9 Dec 1381; *cerdo/peliparius*, not. G. Paço, Busta 189, fol. 32r, 12 Sep 1384; *clibanarius/*

peliparius, not. G. Paço, Busta 189, fol. 43v, 7 Nov 1384; *villanus/iuparius*, not. N. Tonisto, Busta 273, fol. 13v, 29 Oct 1385; *cerdo/iuparius*, not. G. Catacalo, Busta 24, fol. 34v, 27 Sep 1389; *soldatus/cerdo*, not. G. Catacalo, Busta 24, fol. 35v, 28 Sep 1389.

Chapter 3

1. William Shakespeare, *Troilus and Cressida*, Act IV, scene V, lines 135–51.

2. A selective bibliography on these matters begins with Patrick Amory, "The Meaning and Purpose of Ethnic Terminology in the Burgundian Laws," *Early Medieval Europe* 2, 1 (1993): 1–28; Benedict Anderson, *Imagined Communities: Reflections on the Origin and Growth of Nationalism* (London, 1983); Geary, "Ethnic Identity"; Eric Hobsbawm, *Nations and Nationalism Since 1780* (Cambridge, 1990); Anthony Smith, "National Identities: Modern and Medieval?" in *Concepts of National Identity in the Middle Ages*, ed. Simon Forde, Lesley Johnson and Alan V. Murray (Leeds, 1995), pp. 21–45.

3. Bartlett, *The Making of Europe*.

4. Gina Fasoli, "Nascita di un mito," in *Studi storici in onore di Gioacchino Volpe* (Florence, 1958), 1: 445–79; Grubb, "When Myths Lose Power: Four Decades of Venetian Historiography," *Journal of Modern History* 58 (1986)), 43–94; Gregory Jusdanis, *Belated Modernity and Aesthetic Culture: Inventing National Literature* (Minneapolis, 1991).

5. Basing my view on the proposition that what the nobility believes is not necessarily representative of what lower ranks of society believe, I have sought substantiation of the often-cited "Greekness," resentment against Latins qua Latins, and so forth of the peasantry, but I find only assertions without substantiation. In my view, such a priori assumptions are the very first thing to be jettisoned in any investigations of collective sentiment in the past.

6. For noble feudatories' desire for their daughters to marry as noble women, see *Wills*, Will 159, Nicolaus Dandulo Bellinus, 1351; Will 197, Phylippus Çane, son of the late *dominus* Nicolaus Çane, 1348; Will 301, Dominicus Quirino, son of the late ser Andreas Quirino, 1365; Will 590, Iacobus Baroci, son of the late ser Marinus, 1376.

7. Fredrick Barth, ed., *Ethnic Groups and Boundaries: The Social Organization of Culture Difference* (Boston, 1969); Hans Vermeulen and Cora Govers, eds., *The Anthropology of Ethnicity: Beyond "Ethnic Groups and Boundaries"* (The Hague, 1994).

8. *Diplomatarium veneto-levantinum, sive acta et diplomata res venetas, Graecas atque Levantis illustrantia*, ed. G. M. Thomas and Riccardo Predelli, 2 vols. (Venice, 1880–99; rpt. 1966), 1: 3–4, n. 3: "Item narrabitis, quod, cum in concessione Candide et Chanee contineatur, quod aliquis bastardus non possit habere feudum, nec esse de consilio, nec habere castellanariam, nec iudicatum, quod de cetero hoc non sit quia iam tota Chanea est corupta, quia cotidie fiunt bastardi castellani et iudices; et quia plura feuda in eorum manibus sunt peruenta: unde omni modo tractetis, quod hoc non fiat, et etiam dicere quod aliquis Grecus non possit habere feudum, nec esse de consilio."

9. Thiriet, *Délibérations des assemblées*, 1: 96–97, n. 66, 23 Aug 1302.

10. Relying on Thiriet's registers, David Jacoby identifies two other feudatory families as Greek, an attribution that I do not share: Franguli Greco (a cognomen attested to in Venice prior to the occupation of Crete) and Zanachi Partegon called Milonensis, who is more likely to have come from the Dalmatian coast: Jacoby, "Les états latins," 31, n. 163; *Délibérations du Sénat*, 1: 315–31, pp. 319–22.

11. *Délibérations du Senat*, 1: 102, n. 391, 5 Jul 1362.

12. David Jacoby sees in this resistance to the offspring of Latin feudatories and humble Greek women a resentment of the preferential treatment these young men received. Jacoby, "Les états latins," pp. 30–31.

13. A succinct explanation of the doctrinal issues dividing the Greek and Latin churches may be found in John Meyendorff, *Byzantine Theology: Historical Trends and Doctrinal Themes* (New York, 1974), Chap. 7, "Schism Between East and West," pp. 91–102.

14. Peter Lock, *Franks in the Aegean*, p. 196.

15. For an overview of the two churches in Latin Greece and the Aegean, see Lock, *Franks in the Aegean*, pp. 193–221; Giorgio Fedalto, *La chiesa latina in Oriente*, 3 vols. (Verona, 1973–78); R. L. Wolff, "The Organization of the Latin Patriarchate of Constantinople, 1204–1261: Social and Administrative Consequences of the Latin Conquest," *Traditio* 6 (1948): 44–60.

16. Fedalto, "La chiesa latina a Creta (1204–1261)," *Kretika Chronika* 24 (1972): 145–76, pp. 149–50.

17. Borsari, *Dominio veneziano*, p. 107. There were two Greek bishops in the Latin hierarchy in the first half of the thirteenth century and at least one in the fourteenth century. See Vlachaki, "He diatheke tes Agnes."

18. Thomas, *Diplomatarium*, 2: 132.

19. Thomas, *Diplomatarium*, 2: 132–33.

20. ADC, *Proclami e Banni*, Busta 14bis, fol. 54r, 1360.

21. Fedalto, "La chiesa latina a Creta," pp. 153–56.

22. For instance, *Déliberations du Senat*, 2: 201, n. 848, 13 Apr 1394.

23. For an example of two Greek priests excusing themselves from participating in a case before the court, see *Régestes des arrêts, Memoriali*, p. 108, n. 71, 3 Jul 1366. Regarding marriages, see ASV, NDC, not. E. Valoso, Busta 13, fol. 37v, 1 Aug 1370: "Eodem die. Manifestum facio ego Nicolaus Trivixano, cerdo, habitator Candide, cum meis heredibus tibi Caliçe Nasimbene dicte Cortacopulena, habitatrici Candide, et tuis successoribus quoniam promitto tibi et sum contentus debere comparere tuo nomine in curia archiepiscopatus Candide, coram dominis vicariis in . . . dicte archiepiscopate, vacante sede tociens quociens opus fuerit, pro procurando et exercendo quod Nicoletus Foscolo quem dicis esse virum tuum cogatur per dictos dominos vicarios sentenciam diffinitam debet te accipere in suam uxorem legittimam secundum normam Sancte Matris ecclesie. Tu vero pro meo labore et salario teneris per te vel tuum missum dare et solvere mihi vel meo misso si devicero dictam questionem infra tres dies postquam fuerat pronunciata sentencia in tuo favore contra dictum Nicoletum Foscolo yperpera cretensia decem et par unum persutorum. Et similiter tenearis mihi dare et solvere dicta yperpera et persutuos, si concors forte fueris cum eo ante fine litis. Si vero non obtinuero sentenciam in tuo favore sec pronuncietur in favore dicti Nicoleti, tenearis tunc mihi dare et solvere

grossis XII. Ad hec autem ego Thimia Contareno, calogrea, mater dicte Caliçe, constituo me pleçiam tibi suprascripto Nicolao Trivixano pro dicta Caliça filia ita quod de dicta solutione possis te tenere in tota et parte tam ad me quam ad predictam Caliçam. Si igitur etc. et pro pena inde constituta yperpera X. Contractu firmo. Testes Filareto Muscolo et Iohannes Sclavo filius Hemanuelis. Complete et dare."

24. For a more detailed account from the archbishop's point of view, see Tsirpanles's article on an unedited codex containing material pertaining to the archbishop's complaints: Z. Tsirpanles, "Anekdote pege gia ten ekklesiastike istoria tes Kretes." *Kretika Chronika* 22 (1970): 79–98.

25. Freddy Thiriet, "La situation religieuse en Crète au début du XVe siècle," *Byzantion* 36 (1966): 201–12, pp. 204–5. Too many Greek priests from Candia, the burg, and villages of the district appear in notarial documents with full legal capacity for Thiriet's statement to be strictly speaking true.

26. *Wills*, Will 517, Michael Chanioti, 1348: "fratalia Sancte Marie grecorum."

27. Gill, "Pope Urban V," p. 465.

28. *Délibérations du Sénat*, 2: 147–48, n. 599, 4 Jul 1379; Maltezou, "The Historical and Social Context," p. 27; Gill, "Pope Urban V," p. 464.

29. Jacoby, "Social Evolution," p. 218.

30. Georgopoulou, "The Meaning of the Architecture," p. 24.

31. ADC, *Quaternus consiliorum*, Busta 12, fol. 144r–v, 19–23 Oct 1360; *Proclami e Banni*, Busta 14bis, fols. 58v–59r, n. 24, 25 Oct 1360.

32. ADC, *Memoriali*, Busta 29, fasc. 22.4, fol. 6v, 14 Mar 1391: "Magnificus dominus Dominicus Bono, honorabilis ducha Crete, et eius consilium in concordio dixerunt quod Hemanuel Psatopulo de Sancto Vassilio de Crovata quocienscumque habuerit etatem legittimam possit promoveri ad sacerdocium secundum ritum grecorum et quod postquam pervenerit ad etatem ad omnes eius requisicionem fieri debeant sibi litere ad dominos castellanos Coroni et Mothoni in quibus contineatur licencia sibi data per hoc regiminem quod per aliquem episcopum grecorum promoveri possit ad sacerdocium et predicta concessio et gratia sibi faca est quia suprascriptus Hemanuel operatus fuit personam suam pro quodam arduo negocio dominicionis unde domini consiliarii promiserant sibi in Apano Viano ubi tunc erant facere ei gratiam suprascriptam." ADC, Memoriali, Busta 29, fasc. 22.4, fol. 33v, 18 Mar 1391: "Data fuit licencia Georgio Murisco, habitatori burgi in Neamoni, eundum extra insulam pro faciendo se ordinari clericum grecum ab episcopo greco. Et hoc ad petitionem magistri Masiliani, sutoris. Die V aprilis 1391. Similis licencia dada fuit Iohanni Lalacho, habitatori casalis Calivia, ad petitionem ser Donati Dandulo. Die XVIII maii 1391. Similis licencia data fuit Hemanueli da Credo, habitatori casalis Acrea predicto casali ad petitionem ser Georgii Secreto. Datus die suprascripto, die XVIII maii 1391, similis licencia data fuit calogero Ianichi Scodili habitatori Sancti Iohannis Sisi ad petitionem ser Andree Venerio quondam ser Marci de Neacasi. Die suprascripto. Similis licencia data fuit Ionne Pangalo, calogero, habitatori casalis Apano Archanes, per supplicationem quam ipse fecit dominio. Die VIIII iunii 1391. Similis licencia data fuit Iohanni da Gredo, habitatori casalis Cato Acrea ad petitionem ser Marci Diedo. Die X mensis iulii 1391. Similis licencia data fuit calogero Iorassimo Vlagho, habitatori [S . . .] ad petitionem [incomplete]."

33. The existence of hostilities did not prevent some exceptional instances,

such as the participation of a Greek monk, Hemanuel Capsodassi, and his son Leo who fought on the Venetian side in their war with Padua: Noiret, *Document inédits*, p. 88, 1397.

34. Maria Vassilakis-Mavrakakis, "Western Influences on the Fourteenth Century Art of Crete," *Jahrbuch des Osterreich* 32, 5 (1982): 301–11, p. 301, n. 2.

35. The total number of wills in the edition amounts to 790, but the edition includes two wills by the same testator and other non-Cretans.

36. I do not make a comparison of these figures to the total number of Latin and Greek testators, because I believe them to be meaningless, given the randomness of the sample.

37. *Wills*, Will 178, Iohannes Ialina, 1353; Will 591, Petrus Cutaioti, son of the late ser Constantius, 1376; Will 686, Iohannes Garguli, son of the late ser Andreas, 1376.

38. *Wills*, Will 673, Marula, wife of ser Dominicus Castrofilacha, 1415.

39. All found in *Wills*: Will 49, Georgius de Filaretis, *notarius*, 1348; Will 54, Iohannes Iallina, son of the late ser Michael, 1348; Will 149, Maria, widow of Leo Calergi, 1346; Will 222, Petrus Çampani, son of the late ser Iohannes Çampani, 1348; Will 224, Helena, widow of Chyrilus Pantaleo, 1348; Will 240, Agnes, wife of Hemanuel Gavala, 1322; Will 290, Sofia Gulyaçena, 1363; Will 356, Stamatini, wife of Iohannes Iustiniano, 1325/26; Will 500, Kali, widow of Theodorus Rapani, 1347; Will 566, Herchiolda Calergi, 1375.

40. *Wills*, Will 222, Petrus Çampani, son of the late ser Iohannes Çampani, 1348; Will 54, Iohannes Iallina, son of the late ser Michael, 1348. Although both men lived too early in the century to show up in the Great Council membership lists, the "ser" attached to their fathers' names is indicative of their feudatory status.

41. *Wills*, Will 178, Iohannes Iallina, 1353. His daughter's large dowry of fifteen hundred hyperpera places her father firmly among the noble branch of the Ialina.

42. *Wills*, Will 231, Antonius Chandachyti, *filius indivisus* of Michael Chandachyti, *arcerius*, 1361: "Item volo quod suprascripti mei commissarii expendant in opere necessario ecclesie Dei Genitricis de Chera Ialini, in qua meam elligo sepulturam, yperpera decem. Item dimitto presbytero Nicolao qui officiat eam ut scribat me in suo condice, yperpera tria."

43. *Wills*, Will 45, Nicolaus Plachina, 1348. "Converso" here would have signaled a convert from Judaism.

44. *Wills*, Will 23, Petrus Mudacio Parlatus, 1325; Will 123, Iohannes de Rugerio, 1336; Will 135, Marinus Gisi, 1383/84; Will 205, [first name unknown] Cornario, son of the late Andreas of Venice, 134?; Will 209, Iacobus Cornario, 1349; Will 221, Antonius Secreto, 1348; Will 265, Nicolaus Ragusio, 1362; Will 304, Petrus Gulielmo, 1338; Will 469, Iulianus Natale, 1334; Will 498, Petrus Dono, son of the late lord Paulus, 1347; Will 529, Donatus Truno, 1348; Will 596, Marinus Gisi, 1383; Will 627, Georgius Geno, 1360; Will 650, Bertucius Gradonico, 1362; Will 687, Michaletus Manfredo, 1376; Will 772, Nicolaus Cornario, son of the late ser Iohannes, 1376.

45. *Wills*, Will 125, Iacobina, wife of Nicolaus Habramo, 1336; Will 144, Marchesina, widow of Nicolaus Habramo, 1339/40; Will 198, Mariçoli, wife of

Nicolaus Pantaleo, 1348; Will 326, Francisca, daughter of Stephanus Bono, wife of Matheus Gradonico, 1348; Will 536, Elena, widow of Marcus Dandulo, 1369; Will 595, Aniça, wife of ser Nicolaus Cavalaro, 1378; Will 630, Agnes, widow of ser Signoretus Betto, 1362; Will 693, Aniça Ruçino, 1376; Will 737, Marula, wife of Matheus Mudacio, 1366.

46. *Wills*, Will 469, Iulianus Natale, 9 Mar 1334.

47. *Wills*, Will 687, Michaletus Maufredo, 1376.

48. ASV, NDC, not. G. Similiante, Busta 244, fasc. 1, fol. 61v, 30 Apr 1328: "Die ultimo mensis aprilis. Manifestum facio nos presbyter Marinus Valerio, principale, et Petrus Cornario, plexius eius, ambo habitatores Candide, cum nostris heredibus et successoribus tibi Nicoletus Dandulo dicto Belino de Venetiis, nunc habitatoris Candide, et tuis heredibus quia ex pacto et conventione habitis inter me presbyterum Marinum et te debeo et teneor venire et celebrare in ecclesia tua Sancte Marie, que est prope Sanctum Titum, cotidie a kallendis mensis aprilis presentis in antea usque ad annos tres proxime venturos completos. Cuius ecclesie redditus, introytus et proventus ac dimissorias dimissas in dicta ecclesia havere debeo. Et pro predicta celebratione facienda contentus et confessus sum me a te recepisse calicem unum argentis deauratum, amittum unum, camisum unum, cingulum I de lino, stolam I deauratam, calusulam unam viridem, messale unum et altraiole unum. Tu autem pro meo labore et soldo pro celebracione dicte ecclesie mihi dare debes annuatim yperpera XII, videlicet in principio quorumlibet mensium VI medietatem ipsorum sub pena unius paris caponum et nichilominus valoris peramentorum suprascriptorum. Testes Georgius de Molino, Antonius Piloso et Marcus Avonale. Complere et dare."

49. ASV, NDC, not. G. Gerardo, Busta 101, fol. 40r, 10 Mar 1355: "Die decimo. Manifestum facimus nos Iohannes et Vitalis Dandulo, filii quondam ser Nicolai Dandulo dicti Belini, habitatores cum nostris heredibus tibi Nemfo, ieromonacho, habitatori burgi Candide, et tuis successoribus quod cum ecclesia Dei Genitricis de Fraschea sita super locum quem dictus quondam pater noster accepit ad afficctum a comuni Crete esset ruinata et iam modico tempore relevaretur sed adhuc non fuerit completa et tu intendas et vellis eam complere et reducere in culmine ad tuas expenssas quod maximum pietatis opus est, damus et concedimus tibi eamdem ecclesiam cum terra mensuratarum trium vel circa amodo in antea usque ad illud tempus pro quo dictus pater noster accepit suprascriptum locum a comuni Crete, renovando tibi cartam sicut nobis et Thome Dandulo, fratri nostro, renovabitur ab ipso comuni cum plena virtute et potestate dictam ecclesiam cum terra pro anima eiusdem patris nostri intromittendi, habendi, tendendi, possidendi et omnes tuas utilitates in ea et ex ea et dicta terra faciendi, nemine tibi contradicente tamen cum onere suo. Preterea teneris ipsam ecclesiam studiose et cum omni temore Dei officiare die noctuque iuxta regulam ecclesiasticam et habitare aput eam et conservare eam in culmine, faciendo quamcitius poteris fornatam unam calcis ad complendum illam ecclesiam, de eo quod ipsa indiget et liceat tibi laborare domos super terram predictam et recipere monacos ad habitandum in eis et serviendum dicte ecclesie et in ipsa terra liceat tibi seminare et plantare et facere omnes utilitatem tuam et havere aquam sitam aput ipsam terram ad omnes tuam utilitatem, non contradicendo aliis personis que voluerint accipere de ea. Et quicquid havere poteris de usufructu seminaciarum et plantacionis quas facies super eam debeat esse tuum

amore Dei et pro anima suprascripti patris nostri. Nec tenearis solvere nobis aliquid, inde hac tamen conditione addita et expressa quod si ante finem suprascripti termini obieris dicta ecclesia et hedificia et plantatio que fecisses in ipsa terra remaneant in nostra potestate ad concedendum ea aliis monacis qui volverint habitare in dicto loco et servire ipsi ecclesie et tu non possis te de eis ordinare. Si igitur etc. pena yperperorum centum. Contractu firmo. Testes Papas Georgius Marmara, Th. Domestico, He. de Iordano, Marcus de Portu quondam Pauli, Iohannes de Gradu. Complere et dare. Die XI mensis maii, indicione octava, contenti fuerunt suprascripte partes quod hec carta cancellarentur."

50. The text of the Dandolo brothers' division of their father's goods appears in Gasparis, *Hege*, pp. 338–41.

51. ASV, NDC, not. G. Similante, Busta 244, fol. 49r, 14 Dec 1327.

52. ASV, NDC, not. N. Tonisto, Busta 273, fol. 34v, 9 Aug 1386: "Die nono. Manifestum facio ego papas Iohannes Mussuro, habitator Candide, cum meis heredibus, tibi ser Georgio de Porta quondam ser Stamati, habitatori in eadem Candide, et heredibus tuis quoniam promitto tibi et sum contentus venire et habitare cum familia mea in tuo casali Gurnes amodo in antea usque ad annos tres proxime venturos, dando michi ecclesiam dicti casalis nomine Sancti [blank] quam officiare debeam toto dicto tempore bene iuxta usum et ritum grecorum. Tu autem teneris dare michi quolibet anno salmam unam frumenti et salmam unam vini, que esse debeant pro anima tua. Et teneris facere quod quilibet homo dicti casalis, videlicet, illi qui habent par unum bovum teneatur dare michi quolibet anno mensuras dua furmenti (*sic*) et illi qui non habent par I bovum teneatur dare michi mensuram unam frumenti quolibet anno donec percompleverit anni III predicti. Et tenearis concedere michi illam vineam tuam Atiri positam apud dictam ecclesiam apoxilu in antea usque ad dictum tempus, aptando et gubernando ipsam bene iuxta usum vinearum suis temporibus congruis et consuetis et tempore vindemiarum tenear super [patitorium] dare tibi totam et integram partem tocius vini et usufructur exinde proventuros, reliquis duabus partibus in me retentis, sub pena dupli pro quolibet termino non observato. Quam vineam tenear in complemento dictorum annorum trium tibi inculmine refutare et ullo modo tu cum tuis heredibus infra dictum tempus non possis me de dicta ecclesia vel casali depeli nec ego ullo modo possem recedere con familia mea /inde/. Teneris quoque dare michi pro habitacione mea et familie mee in dicto casali domos duas. Ad haec autem manifestum facio ego predictus Georgius de Portu cum meis heredibus promittassem tibi predicto papati Iohanni et heredibus tuis et sum contentus omnia et singula suprascripta atendere et observare. Si qua igitur etc. pena yperperorum XXV. Contractu firmo."

53. *Wills*, Will 417, Agnes, daughter of the late *nobilis vir dominus* Alexios Calergi, wife of Chornarachus Cornario, 1330/31.

54. *Wills*, Will 175, Elena, widow of ser Petrus Mudacio, 23 Jan 1359/60.

55. *Wills*, Will 415, Marina, widow of Nicolaus Çancaruolo, 27 Aug 1331.

56. Dorothy Abrahamse, "Rituals of Death in the Middle Byzantine Period," *Greek Orthodox Theological Review* 29 (1984): 125–34, pp. 131–32.

57. *Wills*, Will 482, Agnes, widow of ser Iohannes Vaxalo, son of the late ser Iulianus, daughter of the late ser Iohannes Caliva, 1341.

58. The Calergi family is an exception owing to the terms of the treaty between

themselves and Venice and to the fact that they preferred to reside in their ancestral lands ouside Rethimno.

59. *Wills*, Will 186, Cherana, wife of Nicolaus Corfioti, *habitatrix in casali Bassia*, 1351/52.

60. *Wills*, Will 445, Marcus Franchus, *barbitonsor*, 1340: bequest of wine to "calogero seu presbytero qui tenet et officiat ecclesiam de lo Christo de lo Vicuta"; Will 611, Benedicta, wife of Iohannes de Vlero, 1361: one legatee is called both a *monaca* and a *calogera*; Will 618, Cali Pronicadhena, 1362/63: her mother is a *monaca* and her brother is a *papas*; Will 629, Maria, widow of Iohannes Modhino, *monacha*, 1361: despite being a *monacha*, all her bequests are to the Greek church; Will 749, Anica, wife of Franculus Cauco Clida, 1383: instructs a *presbyter* to enroll in her the traditional Greek commemorative codex.

61. *Wills*, Will 627, Georgius Geno, son of the late Iohannes Geno, 1360.

62. *Wills*, Will 627: "Item volo et ordino quod dicti mei commissarii dare debeant alicui presbytero greco qui sit bona persona ecclesiam meam Sancte Anne positam in civitate Candide ad officiandum eam usque ad annos quinque proximos, hoc modo quod medietas introitus et proventus ipsius ecclesie sit et esse debeat dicti presbyteri. Et reliqua medietas devenire debeat in dictos meos commissarios pro substentatione suprascripti Çanachi, filii mei. Et quod transactis quinque annis suprascriptis dicti comissarii mei quam cicius fieri poterint emere debeant de partibus Turchie vel de aliis seu hiis partibus unum sclavum qui sit presbyter grecus et ipsum debeant deputare ad officiandum suprascriptam ecclesiam Sancte Anne pro animabus et remissione pecatorum Anchone quondam uxoris mee, mea et omnium mortuorum meorum. Et quod ipse presbyter remaneat liber quia dicta uxor mea quondam sicut me ordinavit in obitu eius ad faciendum."

63. *Wills*, Will 480, Stephanus Capelario, *habitator. in castro Themensis*, 1339: "Item volo et ordino quod presbyter Theodhorus, papas Georgius et papas Andreas sint in mea sepultura, quibus dimitto cuilibet ipsorum yperperum unum."

64. *Wills*, Will 6, Marcus Capaci, *caligarius*, 1321; Will 10, Potha, wife of Nicolaus Cauco, 1323; Will 16, Anastassu, widow of Nicolaus Caravello, 1328; Will 73, Mabilia, daughter of Thomas Moço, 1348; Will 114, Cali de Mothono, 1335; Will 310, Iacobina, daughter of Georgius Languvardo, wife of Albertus de Savimonis, *ianuens*, 1342; Will 354, Maria, widow of Michael Barbo, 1312; Will 366, Iacobina, wife of Marinus Longo, 1316; Will 440, Iohannes de Rugerio, natural son of Paulus de Rugerio, 1340; Will 444, Marcus Franchus, *barbitonsor*, 1340; Will 461, Maria, daughter of Thomas Avonale, *hab. in casali Colena*, 1333/34; Will 462, Thomasina, daughter of Thomas Avonale, *habitatrix in casali Colena*, 1333/34; Will 501, Nicolaus Filaretis, 1348; Will 592, Nicolaus Romeopulo, 1376.

65. These issues are covered in Maria Georgopoulou, "Late Medieval Crete and Venice: An Appropriation of Byzantine Heritage," *Art Bulletin* 77 (1995): 479–96. I am not persuaded by Georgopoulou's citation of an entry in the court records to support her statement that the *protopapas* of Candia carried the icon of the Virgin *Mesopanditissa* in procession as early as 1368, since the entry makes no mention of the *protopapas*, nor of that specific icon, and applied only to the residents of the burg and not of the city, where the icon was housed in the cathedral. Art historians are better positioned than I am to decide if the most revered icon in the city would be

transported to the burg every Tuesday for procession. For a summary in French, see Santschi, *Régestes des arrêts*, p. 138, n. 298. However, the complete, corrected text of the court record, ADC, Busta 29bis, *Memoriali*, fasc. 15/3, fols. 38v–39r, 10 Jun 1368, is as follows: "Eodem die. Per dominum ducham et eius consilium dictum et ordinatum est quod pro reverencia gloriose virginis Marie illi qui deputati sunt ad levandum eius ymaginem que quolibet [not 'quobus'] die martis levatur ad honorem Dei Genitricis et ad laudem dominacionis et comunis veneciarum non cogantur amodo in antea per capitaneum burgi vel per alios officiales ad faciendum vaitam que fieri solet per habitatores dicti burgi, sed sint ipsi exempti de ipsa vaita, qui sunt numero persone VIII. Nomina eorum sunt hec: Dimitrius Seriga, Iohannes Brati, Georgius Quirino, Stamati Gisi, Elias Simbrago, Stamati Cumnino, Michael Longovardo, Nichiforus Paleologo (Santschi and Georgopoulou read "Michael Paleologo")."

66. For requests to be buried or have commemorative masses according to Greek custom, see *Wills*, Will 10, Potha, wife of Nicolaus Cauco, 1323; Will 35, Nicolota, widow of Nicolaus Naptopulo, 1347/48; Will 37, Maria, wife of Nicolaus Brexiano, *notarius*, 1347/48; Will 88, Nicoleta Marcello, wife of Georgius Marcello, 1372; Will 414, Nicola, son of the late *papas* Hemanuel Agapito, 1331; Will 424, Herini Charadina, wife of Georgius Sichini *da ca' Çeno*, 1331/32; Will 430, Nichita Adhamo, 1337; Will 436, Michael Stadhiati called Mauro, 1338; Will 656, Chalinichi Misinena, *chalogrea*, 1408; Will 670, Hergina, widow of Georgius Sclavo, 1343. An example of a Greek dowry: ASV, NDC, not. N. da Milano, Busta 144, fol. 82v, 20 Sept 1368, "de yperperis septuagintaduo pro libra una solita pro repromissa more grecorum."

67. Maltezou, "The Historical and Social Context," pp. 33–34; Nicolaos Panagiotakes, "The Italian Background of Early Cretan Literature," *Dumbarton Oaks Papers* 49 (1995): 282–323, pp. 296–98.

68. Panagiotakes, "Italian Background," pp. 291, 293–94.

69. Twenty-five testators state either that they had written some document such as a will in their own hand (but none of the female testators listed) or that some other non-notary had written one. *Will* 49, Georgius de Filaretis, notarius, 1348; Will 64, Marinus Quirino, son of the late *dominus* Nicolaus Quirino called Turin of Venice, 1348; Will 75, Antonius Belli, 1348; Will 197, Phylipus Çane, son of the late *dominus* Nicolaus Çane, called Pançono, of Venice, 1348; Will 209, Iacobus Cornario, son of the late ser Iacobus Cornario, 1348/49; Will 214, Magdalena, *monacha*, widow of Iohannes Afrato, 1349/50; Will 257, Andreas Quirino of Venice, 1364; Will 260, ser Marinus Venerio, son of the late Blasius, *de contrata S. Thodorie* of Venice, 1361; Will 261, Iohanninus Cornario, son of *dominus* Marcus, 1362; Will 272, Michaletus Mauroceno, son of the late *dominus* Franciscus of Venice, 1363; Will 276, Laurentius Quirino, son of the late *dominus* Nicolaus, 1362; Will 296, Iohannes Dandullo, son of the late ser Belinus Dandulo, 1362; Will 297, Grafeus Saxo, 1364; Will 544, Iohannes Dandulo, son of the late *dominus* Marcus, 1376, Will 533, Thomasinus Sancti, 1366; Will 560, Honesta Taliapetra, wife of ser Nicolaus Taliapetra, 1373; Will 594, Matheus Tarono of Venice, 1377; Will 635, Petrus Çane da Mantoa, *spatarius*, 1362; Will 636, Antonius Greco, 1362; Will 683, Constancius Avonale, 1376; *nobilis vir* Bernardus Vituri of Venice, 1381; Will 717,

Lodovicus de Medio, son of the late *dominus* Iacobus de Medio of Venice, 1382; Will 725, Marinus Trivisano, son of the late *dominus* Victor Trivisano of Venice, 1380; Will 769, Phylippus Cornario, son of ser Marcus Cornario, 1376; Will 774, Nicolaus Dandulo, son of the late *dominus* Marcus Dandulo, 1376.

70. ADC, *Memoriali*, Busta 29, fasc. 21, fols. 11v–13v, 10 Dec 1387: "MCCCLXXXVII, die XXVI octubris, indicione Xa. Nobilis vir ser Iohannes Mauro, habitator Candide, testis, iuravit et dixit quod cognoscit literam hic notatam quam dixit fuisse factam manu Ursi Ramella quondam habitatoris Candide, cuius quidem Ursi literam benenovit. Ser Nicolaus Dado habitator Candide testis iuravit et dixit quod cognoscit literam hic notatam et dixit eam fuisse factam [fol. 13v] manu Ursi Ramella quondam habitatoris Candide sicut sibi videtur quoniam iste bene novit formam literarum dicti quondam Ursi Ramella."

71. Agostino Pertusi's article, "Lorenzio Pilato" contains the best documentary summary of what we know about education in Venetian Crete. Geanakoplos offers another brief summary (in need of some revision): Deno John Geanakoplos, *Byzantine East and Latin West: Two Worlds of Christendom in the Middle Ages and the Renaissance* (Oxford, 1966), Chapter 5, "The Cretan Role in the Transmission of Greco-Byzantine Culture to Western Europe via Venice," pp. 139–64, esp. pp. 140–42.

72. ASV, NDC, not. G. Gerardo, Busta 100, fol. 49v, 10 Mar 1332. For a helpful guide to sorting out the different titles pertaining to teachers, see Ronald Witt, "What did Giovannino Read and Write? Literacy in Early Renaissance Florence," *I Tatti Studies: Essays in the Renaissance* 6 (1995): 83–114, esp. 89–94. Witt has observed in Florence and elsewhere in northern and central Italy a link between grammar teaching and schools for notaries, which may be relevant for Venetian Crete as well.

73. ASV, NDC, not. G. Similiante, Busta 244, fasc. 1, fol. 48r, 6 Dec 1327. For the location of Pietro's school, not. G. Similiante, Busta 244, fasc. 1, fol. 88r–v, 27 Feb 1328/29 and fol. 98v, 27 Jun 1329. Text in Pertusi, "Lorenzio Pilato," 376.

74. *Wills*, Will 311, Bartholomeus de Hengelardis, 1342: "Item debeo dare domino Petro Liberi pro tempore anni secundi quo tenui magaçenum eius, in quo regebam scolas, yperpera duo et grossos octo usque ad medium mensem septembris presentis." The text of his will, minus the one typographical error in the wills edition, may be found in Pertusi, "Lorenzio Pilato," 378–79.

75. ASV, NDC, not. G. Similiante, Busta 244, fasc. 1, fol. 24r, 23 Mar 1327. Text in Pertusi, "Lorenzio Pilato," 372–73.

76. ASV, NDC, not. G. Similiante, Busta 244, fasc. 1, fol. 48r, 6 Dec 1327 and fol. 9r–v, 16 Apr 1329. Cited also in Pertusi, "Lorenzio Pilato," 374–75.

77. ASV, NDC, not. G. Similiante, Busta 244, fasc. 1, fol. 17v, 22 Dec 1326; fol. 55v, 22 Feb 1327/28 (canceled); fol. 56r, 28 Feb 1327/28. Cited in Pertusi, "Lorenzio Pilato," pp. 372–77.

78. ASV, NDC, not. G. Similiante, Busta 244, fasc. 1, fol. 56v, 6 Mar 1328 and fol. 76v, 22 Oct 1328 (canceled).

79. *Wills*, Will 311, Bartholomeus de Hengelardis, 1342. Text also in Pertusi, "Lorenzio Pilato," pp. 378–79.

80. ASV, NDC, not. A. Bellamore, Busta 9, fol. 175v, 5 Dec 1328: "Eodem die. Manifestum facimus nos presbyter Antonius Rizardi, archidiaconus Crete ecclesie, yconomus, procurator, gubernator, actor, factor et amministrator episcopatus et

ecclesie Chironensis, ut de yconomatu et procuracione atque mandato huiusmodi patet publico instrumento manu Bartholomei de Hengelardi, imperiale auctoritate notarii, publice scripto, facto anno a Nativitate Domini nostri Yhesu Christi et canonici ecclesie Chironensis."

81. *Wills*, Will 311, Bartholomeus de Hengelardis, cited above: "Ex quibus dictus dominus Marcus, divino ductus amore, recuperavit et emit per incantum certam quantitatem librorum in una cassa cipressi pro yperperis quinquaginta et yperperis sexaginta, quibus ipse dominus Marcus redemit a domino Iohannino Aymo apparatum decretalium Bernardi, Codicem et Decretum. De quibus denariis ante ruptam stationem mei generi ego solveram ser Iohanni Secreto de quadam sentencia yperperorum sexaginta fidei commissario nomine dicti Leonis, mei generi, necnon de yperperis vigintiquinque Andreas de Iordano pigneratos tenebat plures libros meos, occasione cuiusdam sentencie ante rupturam ipsius stationis. Summatim debeo et recognosco yperpera in cretensia currentia octuaginta. Item debeo dare discreto viro presbytero Petro Dandulo, notario, yperpera quindecim pro quibus tenet a me quandam Decretalem cum apparatu Bernardi, quam tenebam ab Albertino Maça, notario, et quandam sentenciam ordinis iudiciarii secundum Egidium de Fuscarariis et quondam annulum de auro cum bula mea." Worth noting is that Albertino Maza was not an imperial notary, but a Venetian-licenced one who worked in Candia and many of whose redacted wills have survived.

82. *Duca di Candia, Quaternus consiliorum*, n. 46, p. 24, 19 Jun 1345.

83. ASV, NDC, not. N. da Milano, Busta 144, fol. 22v, 10 Apr 1360.

84. ASV, NDC, not. A. Brixiano, Busta 12, fol. 28v, 4 Jan 1360/61.

85. ASV, NDC, not. G. Paço, Busta 189, fol. 29v, 4 Aug 1384.

86. ASV, NDC, not. G. Paço, Busta 189, fol. 55r, 20 Jan 1384/85.

87. ASV, NDC, not. G. Paço, Busta 189, fol. 32r, 14 Sept 1384.

88. ASV, NDC, not. G. Paço, Busta 189, fol. 12v, 8 Feb 1383/84.

89. ASV, NDC, not. N. Tonisto, Busta 273, fasc. 2, fol. 54r, 16 Sept 1387.

90. ASV, NDC, not. L. Quirino, Busta 233, fol. 36r, 22 Oct 1317. Text in Pertusi, "Lorenzio Pilato," p. 371.

91. ASV, NDC, not. G. Paço, Busta 189, fols. 59v–60r, 22 Feb 1384/85.

92. ASV, NDC, not. N. Tonisto, Busta 273, fasc. 2, fol. 54r, 16 Sept 1387.

93. ASV, NDC, not. N. Tonisto, Busta 273, fol. 70v, 1 Dec 1387. One other contract between a Greek priest and a father arranging for his son to learn Greek: not. N. Tonisto, Busta 273, fol. 66v, 6 Nov 1387.

94. *Wills*, Will 418, Stephanus Bono, *notarius*, 27 Sept 1331. See also Laiou, "Venetians and Byzantines," pp. 37–38; Robin Cormack, *Painting the Soul: Icons, Death Masks, and Shrouds* (London, 1997), pp. 205–6.

95. ASV, NDC, not. G. Catacalo, Busta 24, fol. 24r, 31 Aug 1389.

96. ASV, NDC, not. A. Brixiano, Busta 12, fol. 59v, 8 Nov 1380.

97. ASV, NDC, not. N. Tonisto, Busta 273, fol. 65r, 30 Oct 1387.

98. Van Gemert, "O Stefanos Saxlikis," pp. 36–130.

99. M. I. Manoussacas, *Leonardou Ntellaporta Poiemata (1403/1411)* (Athens, 1995).

100. G. Hofmann, "La biblioteca scientifica del monastero di San Francesco a Candia nel medio evo," *Orientalia Christiana Periodica* 8 (1942): 317–60.

101. ASV, NDC, not. E. Valoso, Busta 13, fol. 23v, 11 May 1370: "Eodem die.

Plenam et irrevocabilem securitatem facio ego frater Georgius Faletro, prior conventus fratrum Heremitarum Candide, cum meis successoribus, tibi yconomo Synaitorum, habitatori Candide, et tuis successoribus, de libro uno nominato Vulgari et uno alio libro psaltereo scriptis in lingua grecorum, que mihi dedisti et restituisti. Qui libri fuerunt tibi pignorati pro grossis decemnovem quod quidam tibi dederit dictos libros ad vendendum et dictos grossos XVIIII tibi dedi et persolvi. Nunc autem quia dictos libros mihi dedisti et deliberasti amodo in antea te securum reddo pariter et quietum et promitto cum meis successoribus te extrahere ab omni dampno expenssis et interesse que possent tibi occurere dictorum librorum occasione. Quia etc. Testes presbyter Marchus Durcios et Franciscus Coppe. Complere et dare."

102. ASV, NDC, not. G. Gerardo, Busta 101, fol. 145r, 26 Apr 1358: "Die vigesimosexto. Manifestum facio ego Lodovicus de Costula de Parma, clericus, quia cum meis successoribus do, vendo et in perpetuum transacto tibi magistro Bernardo de Crispis de Mutina, physico, habitatori Candide, et tuis heredibus octo volumina meorum librorum de medicina et phylosofia quia magister Iohannes de Costula, physicus, frater meus quondam, per cartam sui testamenti dimisit mihi ut venderem et emerem libros in iure canonico. Que quidem volumina sunt hec: scilicet, unum Galieni magnum et aliud parvum unum Petri de Abano vocatum conciliator, unum Guillelmi de Placencia et unum Iohannis da Messeni, unum naturialium Avicene, unum Serapionis in simplicibus et aliud diverssarum questionum, videlicet, amodo in antea ipsa volumina librorum cum plena virtute et potestate intromittendi, habendi, tenendi, possidendi, dandi, donandi, vendendi, alienandi, pro anima iudicandi et omnes tuos utilitates in eis et ex eis faciendi, nemine tibi contradicente. Tu vero pro ipsorum precio et solutione integra iuxta nostre conventionis pactum dedisti et persolvisti mihi ducatos venetos auri sexagintaduos, de quibus et dictis voluminibus te reddo securum et quietum quia nichil inde remansit unde te amplius requirere sed [compare?] valleam per ullum ingenium sive modum. Si igitur etc. pena auri librarum quinque. Contractu firmo. Testes Michael de Ceca, ser Blasius de Rippa et Hemanuel de Iordano. Complere et dare. Dedi." Pietro d'Abono (1250–1315), philosopher, physician, astrologer and composer; Giovanni Serapion, physician, mentioned in 1553. *Dizionario biografico*.

103. *Wills*, Will 209, Marcus Cavalcante, 15 Apr 1349. The works collected in one volume, Prospero, or *Ex sententiis Augustini*, Aesop, and Cato were commonly associated with one another in medieval school curricula: Paul F. Grendler, *Schooling in Renaissance Italy: Literacy and Learning, 1300–1600* (Baltimore and London, 1989), pp. 113, 115.

104. *Wills*, Will 104, Marcarius, *monacus de Troia*, 1332. A copy of this will with the same date was entered into another notary's protocol. In the wills edition, it is Will 453. According to Du Cange, σματολόγιον is the liturgical book containing the ordo for monastic ordination. Du Cange, *Glossarium ad scriptores mediæ et infimæ Graecitatis in qvo graeca vocabula novatae significationis, aut usus rarioris, barbara, exotica, ecclesiastica, liturgica, tactica, nomica, jatrica, botanica, chymica explicantur, eorum notiones & originationes reteguntur . . . Et libris editis, ineditis veteribusque monumentis* (Lyon, 1688), s.v. "σματολόγιον."

105. Giuseppe De Gregorio, "Per uno studio della cultura scritta a Crete sotto il dominio veneziano: I codici greco-latini del secolo XIV," *Scrittura e civiltà* 17 (1993): 104–201.

106. De Gregorio, "Codici greco-latini," pp. 116–30.

107. In a postscript to his article on the Italian background of Cretan literature, Panagiotakes objected to De Gregorio's harmonious vision of "la civiltà veneto-cretese soprotutto nei secoli XV–XVII" as one that did not take sufficient account of historical realities: Panagiotakes, "Italian Background," pp. 321–22. At the risk of appearing unwilling to take sides, I believe that the viewpoints of both scholars have merit. To my mind, Panagiotakes places too much unnuanced stress on Latin-Greek hostilities and De Gregorio places too great an evidentiary burden on six manuscripts.

108. Geanakoplos, *Byzantine East and Latin West*, p. 140.

109. I am much obliged to Arthur Lesley for his help in interpreting this contract.

110. ASV, NDC, not. G. Similiante, Busta 244, fasc. 1, fol. 7r, 7 May 1326.

111. ASV, NDC, not. G. Similiante, Busta 244, fasc. 1, fol. 91v, 30 Mar 1329.

112. ASV, NDC, not. A. de Bellamore, Busta 9, fol. 46v, 23 Feb 1320/21: Iohannes and Nicolaus, *tubatores*, sons of the late Vaxilius, *tubator*, residents of the village Helea; not. G. Gerardo, Busta 101, fol. 71r, 3 Oct 1356: Georgius, *tubator*; not. G. Paço, Busta 189, fol. 15r, 5 Mar 1384: ser Marcus Boni, *sonator*, resident of Candia's burg.

113. ASV, NDC, not. G. Granela, Busta 244, fol. 148r, 14 Nov 1333.

114. ASV, NDC, not. G. Gerardo, Busta 101, fol. 63r, 29 Jun 1356. The text of this notarial entry can be found in Nikolaos Panagiotakes, "Martiries gia te mousike sten Krete kata te Venetokratia." *Thesaurismata* 20 (1990): 9–169, pp. 34–36.

115. The dean of Cretan art history remains M. Chatzidakes, whose bibliography is too extensive to list here. More recently, see the works of Maria Konstantoudaki, Sharon Gerstel, Maria Georgopoulou, and Maria Vassilakis-Mavrakakis. For the presence and influence of Italian painters, see Mario Cattapan, "Nuovi elenchi e documenti dei pittori in Creta dal 1300 al 1500," *Thesaurismata* 9 (1972): 202–35; Maria Vassilakis-Mavrakakis, "Western Influences on the Fourteenth Century Art of Crete."

116. Chryssa Maltezou, "Venetike moda stin Krete (Ta foremata mias Kallergopouloas)," in *Vizantion Afieroma ston Andrea N. Strato*, 3 vols. (Athens, 1986), 1: 139–47; the text of the document begins on p. 145.

117. In spite of a 1323 ban on claims to free status by villeins, cases continued to be brought before the court. ADC, *Proclami e Banni*, Busta 14, fol. 30v, 13 Sep 1323. *Duca di Candia, Quaternus consiliorum*, pp. 131–32, n. 345.

118. ADC, *Proclami e Banni*, Busta 14bis, n. 28, fol. 60r, 27 Oct 1360; n. 81, fol. 125r-v, 12 Oct 1365: "1365, die XII octubris, inditione quarta. Clamatum fuit publice per Nicoletum de Molino, gastaldus, in lobio et extra portas civitatis Candide quod cum alias infrascriptum bannum fuerit proclamatum dominacio nunc facit illud renovari, cuius tenor est talis. Quod quilibet grecus qui amodo quando sibi preceptum fiet per precones ad respondendum alicui fecerit sibi precipi pro latino cada pro qualibet vice qua sibi sic precepi premisserit et fecerit pro latino in pena yperperorum quinque. Et is ob illud tale preceptum factum illi greco pro latino sentencia aliqua [fol. 125v] fiet illa sentencia sit nullius valoris et nichilominus ille talis grecus cui preceptum factum fuerit pro latino solvat omnes expensas dicte sentencie. Et quilibet preco qui fecerit preceptum aliquod alicui greco dicenti se esse

greco et rediderit illud curie proprii pro latino cadat similiter pro qualibet vice in penam yperperorum duorum cuius pene medietas sit comunis et alia medietas avocatoribus comunis. Et si accusator inde fuerit dividatur per tercium, tercium comuni, tercium accusatori, et tercium avocatoribus comunis quibus hoc comittatur declarando quod ordines notati infra curia proprii reserventur."

119. Verlinden, "Traite des esclaves."

120. Verlinden, "Traite des esclaves," p. 622.

121. Gerland, *Das archiv*, pp. 98–100.

122. ADC, *Sentenze*, Busta 29, fasc. 1, fol. 1v, 7 Sep 1319.

123. ADC, *Sentenze*, Busta 29, fasc. 1, fol. 4v, 27 Sep 1319: "Vaxilus Mileo intendit probare per infrascriptos testes contra Franciscum Gisi quod pater suus fuerat Latinus et francus et erat oriendus in hac insula et prima ivit ad insulam Melli et ibi eciam transiebat pro latino"; fasc. 1, fol. 7r, 10 Oct 1319: "Per infrascriptos testes intendunt probare Georgius et Michael, fratres, Cortesi contra Franciscum Gisi ad probandum quod ipsi sunt Latini et filii Latini veneti."

124. ADC, *Sentenze*, Busta 29, fasc. 1, fol. 19r, 19 Jan 1319/20 (two cases); fasc. 2, fol. 3v, 17 Nov 1323; fasc. 2, fol. 7r, 1 Dec 1323; fasc. 2, fol. 8v, 8 Dec 1323; fasc. 2, fol. 10r, 15 Dec 1323; fasc. 2, fols. 14v–15r, 24 Jan 1323/24; fasc. 2, fol. 155v–16r, 26 Jan 1323/24 (two cases); fasc. 2, fol. 17r, 26 Jan 1323/24; fasc. 2, fol. 22r, 1 Mar 1324 (two cases); fasc. 2, fol. 28r, 29 Mar 1324; fasc. 2, fol. 32r, 10 May 1324; fasc. 2, fol. 35v, 31 May 1324; fasc. 2, fol. 41r, 5 Jul 1324; fasc. 2, fol. 41v, 5 Jul 1324; fasc. 3, fol. 10v, 25 Feb 1331/32; fasc. 4, fol. 26v, 23 Sep 1336; fasc. 5, fol. 60r–v, 18 Nov 1340; fasc. 6, fol. 14r, 29 Feb 1339/40; fasc. 7, fol. 33v, 16 Mar 1345; fasc. 8, fol. 24r, 6 Jul 1346 (two cases); fasc. 9, fol. 4r, 21 Aug 1347; fasc. 13, fol. 10v, 24 Nov 1360; fasc. 13, fol. 12v, 10 Dec 1360.

125. ADC, *Sentenze*, Busta 29, fasc. 2, fol. 10r, 15 Dec 1323: "Die XV decembris. Absolutum est per dominum ducham et eius consilium concorditer et sententialiter Nicolaus de Calabria, filius quondam [blank] de Calabria, quem camerarii comunis volebant facere pignorari pro villano comunis, cum ipse probaverit se fuisse filium dicti quondam [blank] de Calabria, qui fuit filius quondam Nicolai de Calabria, qui Nicolaus venit ad habitandum in Cretam iamdudum et nesciebat linguam grecam, qui et dictus et iste Nicola quem petebant modo dicti camerarii pro villano semper transiverunt pro latinis."

126. ADC, *Sentenze*, Busta 29, fol. 17r, 26 Jan 1323/24: "Absolutus per dominum ducham et eius consilium concorditer et sententialiter quod Michael qui se dicit filium naturalem quondam Pauli Done et petitionem quam sibi faciebant camerarii comunis qui eum petebant pro villano comunis, videlicet pro filio naturali Iohannis Condo, vilani comunis, cum ipsi camerarii comunis intentionem suam non probaverint, videlicet dictum Michaelem esse filium naturalem dicti Iohannis Condo et cum ista conditione, quod si dictus Michael portabit umquam barbam secundum morem gregorum vel ibit ad officium grecorum et non vivere tamquam latinus quod ipse esse debeat villanus comunis." In one other case the court imposed similar conditions: fasc. 2, fol. 32r, 10 May 1324.

127. ADC, *Proclami e Banni*, Busta 14, fol. 4r, n. 53, 15 Jul 1314. *Régestes des arrêts*, p. 20. For the ethnic significance of hair, see Robert Bartlett, "Symbolic Meanings of Hair in the Middle Ages," *Transactions of the Royal Historical Society* 6th ser. 4 (1994): 43–60.

128. Thiriet, *Délibérations du Senat*, p. 125, n. 492, 10 Feb 1371.

129. ADC, *Sentenze*, Busta 29, fasc. 2, fol. 8v, 8 Dec 1323, "quem genuit cum uxore villani"; fasc. 2, fol. 22r, 1 Mar 1324: "natus ex Kerana, quondam uxore ipsius Leondari [villein]"; fasc. 2, fol. 32r, 10 May 1324: "quem genuit cum uxore dicti Georgii [villani], ipso Georgio existente extra terra magno tempore"; fasc. 2, fol. 35v, 31 May 1324: "quem genuit cum Erini, uxore sua, [a villein of the comune]"; fasc. 4, fol. 26v, 23 Sep 1336: "quem ipse habuit cum Maria, eius femina"; fasc. 7, fol. 33v, 16 Mar 1345: "qui tentabat vendere et alienare Demitrium et Andronicum, filios Theodore, sclave sue, tamquam suos sclavos et servos eo quod nati fuerant ex ipsa sua sclava"; fasc. 9, fol. 4r, 21 Aug 1347: "ex qua eum habuit Nicolaus Vassalo, pictor"; fasc. 13, fol. 10v, 24 Nov 1360.

130. ADC, *Sentenze*, Busta 29, fasc. 2, fol. 22v, 1 Mar 1324.

131. ADC, *Sentenze*, Busta 29, fasc. 5, fol. 60r–v, 18 Nov 1340: "Cum esset questio inter providum virum magistrum Victorem, physicum, procuratorem ser Iohannis Marchesini, et Iacobelli de Marchisino, eius filii, canonici Crete, de cuius procuratorio constat publico instrumento scripto manu presbiteri Petri Dandulo, notarii, sub anno Domini MCCCXXXVIIII, mense maii, die IIII, indicione VII, ex parte una petentem et Iohannem Strongillo, ex altera, deffendentem. Petebat quos dictus magister Victor, nomine procuratorii predicti, predictum Iohannem Strongillo pro villano prebende dicti Iacobelli, canonici Crete, et propterea requirebat . . . sententiare et mandare dictum Iohannem esse villanum dicte prebende et eis servire et respondere more aliorum villanorum. Et respondebat autem dictus Iohannes Strongillo peticioni predicte predicti magistri Victoris quod non erat villanus dicte prebende nec debebat servire nec respondere in aliquo dicto magistro Victori, nomine villanatus dicte prebende. Nam dicebat se fuisse filium naturalem Hemanuelis Cavalla quondam, qui fuit feudatus et archondopolus grecus et propterea petebat absolui a dicta petitione sibi facta per dictum magistrum Victorem. [fol. 60v] Per magnificum dominum Nicolaum de Priolis, honorabilem ducam Crete et dominum Franciscum Dandulo, consiliarum, absente domino Marco Eruzo, altero consiliario, propter sui corporis infirmitatis, concorditer et sententialiter auditis utriusque partis, rationibus et examinatis diligenter testibus introductis per utramque partem ac omnibus facientibus ad causam hanc sufficienter discussis habitique matura deliberatione consilioque superinde et dictum et illatum est quod dictus Iohannes Strongillo est et sit et esse debeat villanus dicte prebende dicti Iacobelli Marchisini, cuius dictus magister Victor est procurator ut superius patet et debeat servire sibi et respondere tamquam villanus ipsius prebende quemadmodum faciunt certi villani et tamquam filius dicti Iohannis Strongillo villani quondam dicte prebende cum dictus magister Victor physicus procurator dictorum ser Iohannis Marchisini, qui nomine procuratorio predicto obtulit se probare quod dictus Iohannes Strongillo fuit filium Iohannis Strongillo quondam qui fuit villanus dicte prebende plene probaverit suam intentionem predictam et eciam patuerit dominacionem relatione domini archiepiscopi et fratris Pasini super hoc interogatorum quod dictus Iohannes Strongillo fuit confessus in eorum presencia se fuisse [fol. 61r] filium dicti Iohannes Strongillo quondam et quod ipsi Iohanni qui absens fuerat de insula per aliquod tempus dederat vineas et domos quas olim dictus Iohannes pater dicti Iohannis in loco dicte prebende possederat dedit et assignavit tamquam filio dicti Iohanni quondam et villano dicte prebende et quod ipso beneficio huiusque nomine

villanatus predicti usus fuerat et cum ipse Iohannes qui obtulit se probare quod fuit filius Hemanuelis Cavala, arcondopuli, non probaverit suam intentionem."

132. ADC, *Sentenze*, Busta 29, fasc. 12/3, fol. 9r, 17 Oct 1360: "Die XVII predicti mensis octubris. Dictum est per dominum ducham et eius consilium concorditer et sententialiter quod Nicolaus Monovassioti, habitator casalis Dimillie, debeat solvere dacium comunis tamquam villanus forensis et sicut solvunt alii villani dicti comunis forenses, salvo tamen iure comunis et Nicolaus predicti si quo tempore probaret ipse Nicolaus se fuisse archondopulum in suis partibus unde venit ad insulam Crete."

133. ASV, NDC, not. G. Gerardo, Busta 101, fol. 247r, 29 Oct 1353.

134. It cannot be a coincidence that, just as there are no cases of women seeking recognition of their Latin paternity, there are no instances of a woman designating herself *filia divisa* to signal her legal independence from her *patria potestas*. Emancipation and its connection to the transfer of the dowry deserves the attention of Venetian scholars, as scholars of Florence have benefited from Thomas Kuehn's attention to those topics: Thomas Kuehn, "Women, Marriage and *Patria Potestas* in Late Medieval Florence," in *Law, Family and Women: Toward a Legal Anthropology of Renaissance Italy* (Chicago and London, 1991), pp. 197–211, esp. pp. 201–4.

135. Stanley Chojnacki, "Social Identity in Renaissance Venice: The Second *Serrata*," *Renaissance Studies* 8, 4 (1994): 341–58.

136. Chojnacki is paraphrasing an enactment of 1414: "Social identity in Renaissance Venice: the second *Serrata*," p. 344.

137. Chojnacki, "Social identity," pp. 343–44.

138. Chojnacki, p. 344.

139. ASV, Avogari di Comune, *Raspe*, reg. 3643/3 (1361–78), fol. 8v, 10 Jun 1361, "Parlatus Mudacio de Candida"; fol. 95v, 22 Jun 1367, "Barbus Barbo de Candida"; fol. 95v, 22 Jun 1367, "Frangulius de Molino filius quondam ser Manueli de Candida"; fol. 96v, 2 Jul 1367, "Nicolaus Dandulo quondam ser Marci de Candida"; fol. 165r–v, 13 Apr 1372, "Francischinus Quirino dictus Franghya de la Canea"; fol. 239r, 4 Jan 1376/77, "Andreas Barbadico quondam ser Michaleti de Candida"; fol. 253v, 8 Dec 1377, "Georgius de Molino filius quondam ser Rigaçii de Molino de Candida"; reg. 3644/4 (1378–1393): fol. 41r, 20 Mar 1382, "Iana Trun filius quondam nobilis viri ser Nicolai Truno de Candida"; fol. 50r–v, 28 Jan 1382/83, "Marinus Ghysi quondam ser Nicolai de Candida"; fol. 51r, 20 Feb 1382/83, "Iana Bono filius quondam ser Bartholomei Bono de Candida"; fol. 105r–v, 13 Jul 1387, "pro parte nobilis pueri Antonii Gradonico filii nobilis viri ser Petri Gradonicho quondam ser Athonii de Candida"; fol. 111r, 12 Dec 1387, "Nicolaus Geno quondam ser Iohannis de Candida dictus Collucius Geno"; fol. 117r, 17 Jul 1388, "Çanachi Quirino quondam ser Angeli de Candida"; fol. 131v, 3 Jul 1389, "Georgius Gradonico quondam ser Iohannis de Candida"; fol. 138v, 14 Oct 1389, "Righus de Molino quondam ser Antonii quondam ser Marci, habitator Canee"; fol. 139r–v, 1 Dec 1389, "Iohannes Mudacio quondam ser Laurentii de Rethimo filii quondam ser Luce fratris quondam ser Petri"; fol. 139v, 11 Dec 1389, "Petrus Mudacio quondam ser Luce de Canea quondam ser Petri"; fol. 139v, 12 Dec 1389, "Georgius Cornario quondam ser Petri quondam ser Iacobi Cornario dicti Mazaro"; fol. 155v,

3 Feb 1390/91, "Mapheus Signolo filius ser Mari Signolo, habitator Canee"; fol. 161r, 5 Jun 1391, "Nicoletus Barbadico quondam ser Laurencii de Candida," "Manoli Gradonico quondam ser Leonardi Baiardo de Candida"; fol. 163r, 24 Jul 1391, "Francischinus Mudazo quondam ser Parlati de Candida"; fol. 177r, 23 Feb 1391/92, "Georgius de Molino quondam ser Zanachii quondam ser Marci de Candida"; fol. 182r, 20 May 1392, "Georgius Panthalio quondam ser Andree filii quondam ser Iacobi quondam ser Nicolai de Candida"; fol. 183v, 1 Aug 1392, "Frangias Venerio quondam ser Petri olim filii ser Marci quondam ser Petri de Candida"; fol. 185v, 6 Sep 1392, "Çanachius Sagredo quondam filius nobilis viri ser Laurencii Sagredo quondam filii nobilis viri ser Iohannis Sagredo quondam ser Laurencii Sagredo de Candida"; fol. 60r, 4 Nov 1396, "Marcus Cornario quondam ser Petri quondam ser Iacobi dicti Mazaron de Candida"; fol. 60r, 4 Nov 1396, "ser Petrus Çancarolo de Canea quondam ser Iohannis quondam ser Petri de Canea"; fol. 63v, 6 Feb 1396/97, "Angelo Barbadicho quondam ser Andree quondam ser Marci de Candida"; fol. 67r–v, 15 May 1397, "Michaletus Truno de Candida quondam ser Pasqualis quondam ser Nicolai quondam ser Michaelis"; fol. 123r, 20 Aug 1400, "Petrus Venerio de Candida quondam ser Iohannis quondam ser Francisci quondam ser Marci"; fol. 131r, 9 Apr 1401, "Iohannes Mudacio de Candida quondam ser Iacobi quondam ser Francisci de Candida"; fol. 131v, 18 Apr 1401, "Andreas Corario quondam ser Ieronimi quondam ser Andree de Candida" and "Marinus de Molino ser Iohannis quondam ser Marini de Candida"; fol. 135v, 16 Jun 1401, "Nicolaus Abramo quondam ser Iohannis quondam ser Marci quondam ser Leonardi de Candida"; fol. 162r–v, 14 Dec 1402, "Donatus Truno quondam ser Bartholomei quondam ser Nicolai"; reg. 3646/6 (1406–1417): fol. 68v, 20 Aug 1409, "ser Nicolaus Quirino de Candida quondam ser Stamati quondam ser Pauli quondam ser Nicolai dicti Turin"; fols. 93v–94r, 14 Nov 1410, "Laurencius Pasqualigo quondam Marini quondam Laurencii de Candida"; fol. 107r–v, 16 Jul 1411, "Leonardo Maçamano quondam ser Iohannis quondam Leonardi de Candida"; fols. 112v–113r, 26 Oct 1412, "Marino Bono de Candida quondam Antonii quondam ser Marini"; fols. 155v–156r, 13 Mar 1413, "Nicoleto Quirino quondam Georgii quondam Petri de Candida"; fol. 156r, 11 Mar 1413, "Marino Dandulo ser Marci de Candida quondam ser Iohannis"; fol. 156v, 13 Mar 1413, "Chirlo Quirino sive Karolus, ser Andree quondam Marini de Candida"; fols. 156v–157r, 13 Mar 1413, "Nicolaus Cornario quondam Thome quondam Marci de Candida"; fol. 159r, 15 May 1413, "Angelo Simitecullo quondam Iohannis quondam Georgii quondam Blasii de Rethimo"; fol. 163v, 28 Jun 1413, "Andreas Quirino ser Iacobi quondam ser Angeli de Candida"; fol. 179v, 24 Nov 1413, "Andreas Geno quondam ser Bartholomei quondam ser Zanachii de Creta"; fol. 205r, 20 Dec 1414, "Michael Cornario quondam Nicolai quondam Andree de Candida"; fol. 210v, 20 Feb 1414/15, "Domenico Venerio ser Petri quondam Angeli de Candida"; fol. 234r, 21 Jan 1415/16, "Leonardus Gradenigo de Candida ser Maphey"; fol. 244r–v, 18 Jul 1416, "Anthonio Çancarolo de Canea"; fol. 244r, 18 Jul 1416, "Çanachio Dandulo quondam ser Andree quondam Zanachii quondam Marci de Candida"; reg. 3647/7 (1417–1428): fol. 248v, 8 Jan 1426/27, "Tito Gradonico de Candida ser Franguli quondam ser Francisci quondam ser Nicolai de Candida."

140. ASV, Avogari di Comune, *Raspe*, reg. 3644/4 (1378–1393), fol. 95v, 5 Sep

1386, "Iohannes Simitecholo quondam ser Georgii de Rethymo"; reg. 3646/6 (1406–1417), fol. 32r–v, 17 Aug 1407, "Nicolaus Matono Andree de Candida"; fol. 35r, 23 Aug 1407, "Marinus Bono de Candida quondam ser Anthonii"; fol. 215r–v, 26 Apr 1415, "Nicolaus Avonal de Rethimo quondam ser Iacobi quondam Dominici"; fols. 221r–222r, 12 Jul 1415, "Petrus Simitecullo de Rethimo quondam Zanachii quondam Petri de Rethimo."

141. ASV, Maggior Consiglio, Avogari di Comune, reg. 22/5, *Brutus*, fol. 85r, 2 Aug 1328: "nobilis vir Iohannes Gradonico, motus amore et desiderio naturalis primitive patrie, scilicet, civitatis Veneciarum."

142. Stanley Chojnacki, "Political Adulthood in Fifteenth-Century Venice," *American Historical Review* 19 (1986): 791–810, p. 797.

143. For example, ASV, Avogari di Comune, *Raspe*, reg. 3644/4 (1378–1393), fol. 161r, 5 Jun 1391, cited above: "Cum nobilis vir ser Nicoletus Barbadico quondam ser Laurencii de Candida propter partem captam in consilio rogatorum de faciendo gratiam illis nobilibus qui privati fuerant de maiori consilio ob delicta suorum progenitorum, videlicet, propter rebelionem Crete, se scribi fecerit in libris quarantie." The others are cited above: fol. 161r, 5 Jun 1391; fol. 163r, 24 Jul 1391; fol. 177r, 23 Feb 1391/92. One other entry, immediately following the last, may also involve the son of a rebel: fol. 182, 20 May 1392.

144. Crete was not the only source of petitioners of noble rank. ASV, Avogari di Comune, *Raspe*, reg. 3644/4 (1378–1393), fol. 62r, 18 Sep 1383, "Bartholomeus Ghisi quondam ser Georgii dominius unius terçerii Nigropontis."

145. Francesco Petrarca, *Epistole de rebus senilibus*, ed. U. Dotti (Torino, 1978), Lib. III, IX.

146. Stanley Chojnacki, "Nobility, Women and the State: Marriage Regulation in Venice, 1420–1535," in *Marriage in Italy, 1300–1650*, ed. Trevor Dean and K. J. P. Lowe (Cambridge, 1998), pp. 128–51, p. 132.

147. There are numerous *prove di nobilità* involving Cretan feudatories from the fifteenth century listed in Indice 86bis of the *Avogari di Comun*.

148. *Benvenuto de Brixano, Notaio in Candia, 1301–1302*, ed. Raimondo Morozzo della Rocca (Venice, 1950), p. 180, n. 503, 16 Dec 1301: "quia facio te liberum et heredes tuos tam qui nati sunt quam qui de cetero nascituri erunt, tali modo quod libero de cetero sis et tracteris, in omnibus eficiaris Romanus et totum quod habes et acquisiveris de cetero sit in tua potestate et ex eis facias tuum velle nec ex eo in aliquo molesteris ab aliquo modo aliquo."

Chapter 4

An earlier version of portions of this chapter appeared in Sally McKee, "The Revolt of St. Tito in Fourteenth-Century Venetian Crete: A Reassessment," *Mediterranean Historical Review* 9 (1995): 173–204.

1. For the thirteenth-century revolts, see Borsari, *Dominio veneziano*, pp. 27–66 ("Guerre e rivolte").

2. Borsari, *Dominio veneziano*, p. 33.

3. Thiriet, *Délibérations du Sénat*, 1: 50, n. 146, 25 Aug 1342; 51, n. 150, 12 Mar 1343.

4. In the eighteenth century, Flamino Corner, a Venetian scholar, edited for the first and last time De Monacis' *Chronicon*.

5. Eric Cochrane, *Historians and Historiography in the Italian Renaissance* (Chicago, 1981), pp. 77–78.

6. Agostino Pertusi, "Le fonti greche del '*De gestis, moribus et nobilitate ciuitatis Venetiarum*' di Lorenzo de Monacis," *Italia medioevale e umanistica* 8 (1965): 161–211.

7. M. Poppi, "Ricerche sulla vita e cultura del notaio e cronista veneziano Lorenzo de Monacis, cancelliere (ca. 1351–1428)," *Studi veneziani* 9 (1967): 153–86.

8. J. Jegerlehner, "Der Aufstand der kandiotischen Ritterschaft gegen das Mutterland Venedig, 1363–65," *Byzantinische Zeitschrift* 12 (1903): 78–125.

9. S. M. Theotokes, "He dethen aforme e prokalesa ten apostasian tes Kretes tou 1363," *Epeteris Htaireias Byzantinon Spoudon* 8 (1931): 206–13; idem, "O Petrarxes kai i Kretike apostasia tou 1363," in *Istorike Kretike Melete, Imeroloion tes Megales Ellados* (Athens, 1929): 295–306; Thiriet, *La Romanie vénitienne*, p. 174; M. I. Manoussacas, "Ta diplomatika diavemata tes Venetias pros tes Europaïkes divameis gia to nautiko apokleimo tes Kretes kata ten apostasia tou 1363/64," *Panegerike Sinedria tes 28 Dekemvriou 1995, Akademia Athenon* 70 (1995): 721–40.

10. The rebel proclamations are in ADC, *Proclami e banni*, Busta 14bis, fols. 107r–109v. Jegerlehner edited these particular proclamations and appended them to his study, "Der Aufstand," 101–7.

11. ADC, *Proclami e Banni*, Busta 14bis, fol. 106v: "Tempore regiminis magnifici Marci Gradonico gubernatoris et rectoris Crete suique consilii."

12. Jegerlehner, "Der Aufstand," 101: "Clamatum fuit publice [. . .] quod ordo et bannum facti tempore regiminis domini Marini Grimani quondam duche Crete et sui consilii de promotione illorum Grecorum volentium effici papates, sit et esse debeat totaliter revocatus et annulatus."

13. Georgio Fedalto, "Le Sénat vénitien et les églises chrétiennes de Crète au XIVe siècle," in *Pepragmena tou G' Diethnous Kretologikou Synedriou* (Athens, 1976), 2: 94–101, pp. 100–101.

14. Jegerlehner, "Der Aufstand," 94–101: "Et decetero sit licitum cuilibet uolenti effici papatem ire quocunque ad ⟨quencunque⟩ uoluerit, ad faciendum se fieri papatem et redire ad insulam libere et absque aliqua pena."

15. De Monacis, *Chronicon*, p. 174: 'pro captanda eorum beneuolentia.'

16. Jegerlehner, "Der Aufstand," p. 103: "Clamatum fuit [. . .] quod omnia et singula nauigia magna et parua cuiuscunque conditionis, solita portare insignia, que patroniçabuntur decetero per homines Cretenses et habitatores in insula Crete, debeant portare pro insigni comunis Crete per omnes partes mundi, ubicunque nauigabunt, figuram sancti Titi huius insule specialis baronis et protectoris, sub pena ad uoluntatem dominii pro quolibet contrafaciente et qualibet uice."

17. The extent of Venice's preparations can be gauged from the calendar of the deliberations of the Collegium: *Délibérations des assemblées*, 1: 258–66; 2: 15–29. For a recent review of the call for an embargo, see Manoussacas, "Ta diplomatika diavemata tes Venetias."

18. Jegerlehner, "Der Aufstand," pp. 107–25.

19. Jegerlehner included the letters sent by the Senate to these rulers in the apprendix of his article, "Der Aufstand," pp. 111–25.

20. The rulers' responses appear as an appendix to *Diplomatarium*, vol. 1: letters of Ludovicus, king of Hungary, p. 391; the doge of Genoa, p. 392; the queen of Sicily and Jerusalem, p. 392.

21. For Petrarch's letters to dal Verme on the occasion of his employment by Venice, see Francesco Petrarca, *Francesco Petrarca e Luchino dal Verme, condottiere dei Veneziani nella Guerra di Candia*, ed. Marco Tabarrini (Rome, 1892).

22. De Monacis, *Chronicon*, p. 179.

23. De Monacis, *Chronicon*, p. 180: "quippe perniciosa, & tremenda est instabilitas vulgi, nam levissimis animis fidem cum fortuna permutant; multi enim ex Graecis, qui in secundis rebus laudaverant scelus Milleti, ipsumque in Dominum cupide accepissent, nunc in adversis consenserunt, & interfuerunt suae ruinae."

24. Taking into account the presence of a number of Greeks among the feudatories at this time, it is interesting that the rebels at this point did not think to turn to the Byzantine emperor, a proposal that De Monacis would have been sure to mention. Cf. below, n. 27.

25. References in the sources to the revolt from this point on refer to the rebellion of the Greeks; for example, ADC, *Proclami e Banni*, Busta 14bis, fol. 113r, n. 18, 4 Oct 1364: "Cum occasione rebellionis Grecorum conmorancium."

26. De Monacis, *Chronicon*, p. 186: "ipse Johannes cum multitudine rebellium publice se hostiliter detegens decimo Augusti ferens ante se vexillum, & insignia Imperatoris Constantinopolis, ac divulgari faciens pugnare pro fide, & libertate contra Latinos, invadit casale Agiomiri."

27. Venice, Biblioteca nazionale, Cl. VII, Cod. 519 (coll. 8438), fol. 118r, col. A: "tutti li Calergi, e Titto Venier et moltissimi altri rebeli e traditori Greci e Latini e metesemo tutta lisola in pase et all obedientia del Dogal dominio veneto."

28. The Venetian Senate noted the numerous complaints of dispossession: Thiriet, *Délibérations du Sénat*, 2: 113, n. 438, 15 Nov 1366. One example of a specific case brought to the duke's court can be found in ADC, *Memoriali*, Busta 29bis, fasc. 21, fols. 26v–29v, 11 May 1368.

29. Thiriet, *Délibérations du Sénat*, 2: 115, n. 447, 3 Oct 1367.

30. ADC, *Sentenze*, Busta 26, 2.4, fol. 239v, 14 Mar 1374.

31. Thiriet, *Délibérations du Sénat*, 2: 134, n. 539, 3 Jun 1374.

32. Noiret, *Documents inédits*, pp. 43–45, 30 May 1391. The list consists of Iacobellus Quirino *quondam ser Pauli*, Marcus Gradonico *quondam Titi* and his brother Andreas, Petrus Gradonico *quondam Antonii*, Manoli Gradonico *quondam Leonardi Bajardo*, Nicolaus Barbadico *quondam Laurencii*, Georgius de Molino *quondam Zanachii* and his brother Francischinus, Marcus de Firmo and his brother Paulus, *populares*, and Petrus Bono.

33. Thiriet, *Délibérations du Sénat*, 2: 155, n. 635, 21 Nov 1382.

34. The original work was entitled *I Coloni di Candia: Tragedia di Giovanni Pindemonte* (Filadelfia, 1801). See *Poesia e lettere di Giovanni Pindemonte*, ed. Giuseppe Biadego (Bologna, 1883): xviii–xxv. A critical review of the play is found in MS Biblioteca Marciana, Venice, 8°, 1785, Misc. 498.1; Drama, 1442.4. For references to the play and the review, see Emanuele Antonio Cicogna, *Saggio di bibliografia veneziana* (Bologna, 1847). For a more recent treatment of Pindemonte, see Franca Barricelli, "Civic Representations: Theatre, Politics, and Public Life in Venice, 1770–1806" (Ph.D. dissertation, University of Wisconsin-Madison, 1995).

35. Venice, Biblioteca Marciana Mss Cl. VII, Cod. 519 (coll. 8438), fol. 115, fol. A: "et in questo tempo cussi fatto, Dio volse, per li pecati deli homeni, mandar una mortalitade sopra la terra, per la quas quasi tutti li antigi che abitana in la ditta isola mori: Vade lamor ella fede vena a manchar, in la preditta isola: Unde li zoveni romase lassando la via deli antigi, contentando la via deli zoventude, laqual segondo come dise Salamono si come la nave in mar: corompano li boni costumi, et lassano le sanie cosse e danosi alli vicii, assi insteli non cognosendo el mal suo simile alli anemali inrationali, lassando la sua propria natura di suoi antecessori, seguitando li costumi de Greci." Freddy Thiriet also transcribed this passage for his study of the B.M. manuscripts relating to Venetian Crete, but gave two variations in his reading that differ from mine. Where I read "corompano," he read "ci rompano"; where I read "sanie," he read "savie." Freddy Thiriet, "Les chroniques vénitiennes de la Marcienne et leur importance pour l'histoire de la Romanie gréco-vénitienne," *Mélanges d'archéologie et d'histoire publiées par l'Ecole française de Rome* 66 (Paris, 1954), rpt. in Thiriet, *Etudes sur la Romanie gréco-vénitienne (Xe–XVe siècles)* (London, 1977), no. III: 241–92.

36. Francesco Petrarca, *Senilium Rerum Libri*, IV, 3, in *Epistole di Francesco Petrarca*, ed. Ugo Dotti (Torino, 1978), Lib. III, IX: "Cretenses tamen invenimus non praesenti tantum nostro, sed antiquo tam poetico, quam apostolico testimonio infames. Fefellit nos adspectus exterior; pectorum latebras introspicere non est mortalis obtuitus: habitus ac nominibus Veneti, proposito atque animis hostes erant, quos vivos ac mortuos male perdet mendaciorum et nequitiae ultor CHRISTUS."

37. ADC, *Memoriali*, Busta 26, fol. 14r–v, 2 Nov 1363.

38. ADC, *Sentenze*, Busta 26.2, fols. 1r–2v, 20 Jan 1368.

39. Noiret, *Documents inédits*, p. 44, 30 May 1390.

40. Venice, B.M. Mss. Cl. VII, Cod. 519 (coll. 8438), fol. 116r, cols. A–B.

41. This list does not include any Calergi family members, since they resided in the district of Rethimno, far from Candia.

42. The two rebel cognomina that do not appear in the Great Council lists are Lulino and Siurino. Angelo Lulino, who became rebel rector of Sithia, probably was a Greek Candiote and possibly a feudatory. Iohannes Siurino quondam Pauli has not turned up in any document examined thus far.

43. The Comune of Venice also recognized the importance of family solidarity. In 1342 a Greek boy six years of age, Paulos Scordilis, belonging to one of the island's archontic families, was brought to Venice after the suppression of a revolt in which his family had participated. Fourteen years later the Venetian Senate granted Paulos permission to travel anywhere except to Crete: Thiriet, *Délibérations du Sénat*, 1: 81, n. 295; 22, 3 May 1356.

44. De Monacis, *Chronicon*, p. 176: "Leonardus Gradonico aberat a Capitanea, cum habuit de rebellione notitiam. Huic primo fuit impetus ire Venetias, & destestando scelus rebellium, praesentare, & offerre se Ducali potentiae; sed ut innotuit, omnes de prole sua fuisse nedum rebelles, sed auctores rebellionis."

45. *Délibérations des assemblées*, 2: 24–25, n. 753, 12 Jun 1364.

46. ADC, *Sentenze*, Busta 26, fol. 5v, 12 Feb 1367/68. Santschi, *Régestes des arrêts*, p. 12, n. 45.

47. The three brothers appear in the Great Council membership lists. They are also mentioned in the will of their mother, Maria, widow of Michael Gradonico, 20 Jun 1348, *Wills*, Will 70. In De Monacis, *Chronicon*, see pp. 175, 177.

48. Giovanni, called El Grasso, married Aurumplasa, sister of Agnes, wife of Niccolo Venier: ASV, NDC, not. A. Brixiano, Busta 11, fol. 31v, 25 Oct 1359. Leonardo Baiardo married a daughter of Marino Trevisan, who did not support the revolt: ASV, NDC, not. A. Brixiano, Busta 11, fol. 42v, 26 Feb 1364/65. Pietro Gradenigo married Ergina, daughter of Bartolomeo de Grimaldo, one of the principal rebels.

49. *Wills*, Will 612, Ergina, daughter of ser Bartholomeus de Grimaldo, wife of ser Petrus Gradonico, 22 Jun 1362.

50. *Wills*, Will 612: "vocari feci ad me Iohannem de Firmo, notarium, ipsumque rogavi ut hoc meum scriberet testamentum que sibi dedi in littera greca, cuius tenor de verbo ad verbum."

51. *Wills*, Will 612: "Ego geromonacus Varnavas, Sancti Montis Sinay penetencialis, habitator casalis Cherissia, hoc scripsi."

52. *Wills*, Will 259, Phylippa, daughter of the late Marcus Mudacio, wife of Iohannes de Grimaldo, 30 May 1348.

53. De Monacis, *Chronicon*, p. 177.

54. De Monacis, *Chronicon*, p. 181: "Ergo, proditor tu vis, & consulis exterminium totius domus nostrae."

55. ADC, *Sentenze*, Busta 26.2, fol. 88r, n. 246, 11 Dec 1370.

56. De Monacis, *Chronicon*, p. 179.

57. *Wills*, Will 175, Elena, widow of ser Petrus Mudacio, 23 January 1359/60.

58. Thiriet, *Délibérations du Sénat*, 1: 78, n. 277, 25 Aug 1355.

59. ADC, *Quaternus consiliorum*, Busta 12, fol. 86r, 6 Oct 1355.

60. *Istorika kretike eggrafa. Ekdidomena tou Archeiou tes Benetias. Thespismata tes Benetikes Gerousias, 1281–1385*, ed. S. M. Theotokes, 2 vols. (Athens, 1936–37), 2: 18–20 (25 Aug 1355); 22 (19 Jan 1356). Thiriet, *Délibérations du Sénat*, 1: 79, n. 283, 19 Jan 1356.

61. Thiriet, *Délibérations du Sénat*, 1: 43, n. 103, 28 Mar 1340.

62. Thiriet, *Délibérations du Sénat*, 1: 75–76, n. 264, 17 Dec 1353; n. 268, 29 Jul 1354; p. 134, n. 539, 3 Jun 1374.

63. *Wills*, Will 536, Elena, widow of ser Marcus Dandulo, 26 Jul 1369.

64. In addition to appearing near each other in the Great Council lists, Tito and Theodorello appear in notarial transactions, a few of which follow. ASV, NDC: not. N. Brixiano, Busta 10, fol. 133v, 14 Feb 1339/40; not. F. Croce, Busta 22, fol. 25v, 8 Dec 1339; not. G. Gerardo, Busta 101, fol. 68r, 19 Aug 1356 and fol. 69v, 2 Sep 1356.

65. The genealogy of the Ghisi family is at this point very difficult to sort out. The evidence in the wills conflicts not only with portions of Raymond-Joseph Loenertz's reconstruction of the Ghisi family tree, which is contradictory in itself, but also with the documents on which he based his conclusions: R.-J. Loenertz, *Les Ghisi: dynastes vénitiens dans l'Archipel, 1207–1390* (Florence, 1975), pp. 43, 72–72, 371–72. Giovanni's father, however, was Marino, a well-known member of the Great Council. Giovanni also appears to have been related to several other rebel families. ADC, *Sentenze*, Busta 26.2, fols. 29r–30r, n. 116, 17 Oct 1368.

66. *Wills*, Will 175, Elena, widow of Petrus Mudacio, 23 Jan 1359/60.

67. Though the relationship between Nicolota's husband and the rest of the da

Vigoncia family is not clear, Filipo da Vigoncia, a rebel feudatory whose name shows up in notarial transaction as early as 1339, was married to Marchesina, niece of Alexios Calergi. ADC, *Sentenze*, Busta 26, 1368. *Régestes des arrêts*, n. 116. It is equally difficult to ascertain which Alexios Calergi is meant. ASV, NDC, not. N. Brixiano, Busta 10, fol. 112r, 18 Nov 1339; not. A. Brixiano, Busta 11, fol. 24v, 3 Oct 1358; *Apophasis*, Lib. XXVIII, fols. 51–52, 21 May 1358. Moreover, Filipo da Vigoncia had a sister married to a Marco Gradenigo, but there is no patronymic or nickname to indicate which one he was: *Wills*, Will 266, Marchesina de Canale, widow of ser Marinus de Canale, 25 Aug 1362.

68. Michele Abbado fled to Rhodes when the Venetian forces advanced towards the city of Candia from the point of disembarcation, and Gabriele was captured and beheaded: De Monacis, *Chronicon*, pp. 177, 184.

69. *Wills*, Will 149, Maria, widow of Leo Calergi, 1346.

70. ADC, *Libri pheudatorum*, Busta 23, fols. 42v–43v.

71. *Wills*, Will 558, Margarita Calergi, 1377.

72. Van Gemert, "O Stefanos Saxlikes," p. 37.

73. *Wills*, Will 224, Helena, widow of Chyrilus Pantaleo, 1348.

74. ASV, NDC, not. N. Brixiano, Busta 10, fol. 167r, 26 Jun 1340.

75. The first time that the regime proclaimed the obligation to report injuries comes from 1359: ADC, *Proclami e Banni*, Busta 14bis, fol. 42r, n. 67, 1359. The reports in the court records, however, much predate that date.

76. One example of this kind of entry can be found in ADC, Proclami e Banni, *Memoriali*, Busta 15, fasc. 1, fol. 11v, 21 Oct 1366: "Die XXI octubris, inditione quinta. Anatolli, filius Calo de Rodo, puer annorum septem, habitator Candide, die predicto, per magistros Heliam, iudeum, fisicum, Pucium de Scicilia et Melchielem, theotonicum iudeum, cirurgicos, coram dominatione datus est extra periculum mortis de fractura ossis quam habebat in brachio dextro quam sibi nullus fecit, sed cecidit." For a summary in French, see Santschi, *Regéstes des arrêts*, p. 111, no. 86.

77. For examples, see Santschi, *Regéstes des arrêts*, passim.

78. ADC, *Proclami e Banni*, Busta 14bis, fol. 12v, n. 6.

79. ADC, *Proclami e Banni*, Busta 14bis, fol. 22r, n. 57.

80. *Déliberations des assemblées*, p. 37, 7 Jun 1274.

81. *Déliberations des assemblées*, p. 36, 15 Nov 1273.

82. ADC, *Proclami e Banni*, Busta 14bis, n. 42, 28 Jul 1314: "Nullus audeat decetero portare spatam vel alia arma maiore mensura cultelli." Renewed: n. 180, 17 Jan 1318. See Santschi, *Regestes*: n. 224, 20 Apr 1319; nn. 249–57, 2 Nov 1319; nn. 340, 341, 6 May 1323; n. 471, 8 Mar 1329; fol. 4v, n. 91, 19 Apr 1357.

83. *Duca di Candia. Bandi*, p. 78, n. 214, 13 Apr 1319; p. 79, n 217, 18 Apr 1319.

84. *Duca di Candia. Bandi*, p. 81, nn. 222, 223, 225, 20 Apr 1319.

85. *Duca di Candia. Bandi*, p. 82, n. 226, 20 Apr 1319.

86. *Duca di Candia. Bandi*, pp. 92–94, nn. 249–257, 2 Nov 1319.

87. *Duca di Candia, Bandi*, p. 78, n 215, 13 Apr 1319. The names are Peracio Gradonico, Marino Maçamano, Marco Gretolo, Anatale Habramo, Petro Donno quondam Pauli, Nicoleto Marcello, Hemanueliçio and Georgius Quirino, Philippo Caliva, and Angelo Ponte.

88. *Duca di Candia, Bandi*, p. 85, n. 230, 5 Jun 1319. One from the list, Angelo de Ponte, appears two months later in another altercation, this time with an individual, possibly a Greek, Zanachi Vitale Zagara, who drew his sword against him.

89. *Duca di Candia, Bandi*, pp. 78–79, n. 216, 14 Apr 1319.

90. *Duca di Candia. Bandi*, pp. 80–81, nn. 219, 220, 221, 20 Apr 1319.

91. *Duca di Candia. Bandi*, pp. 113–14, n. 303, 15 Jul 1321. Here we have another indication of the distinctions between the councils. The regime did not appear concerned about the Council of Feudatories.

92. *Duca di Candia. Bandi*, p. 192, n. 470, 8 Mar 1329.

93. *Duca di Candia. Bandi*, pp. 192–94, n. 471, 8 Mar 1329.

94. *Duca di Candia. Bandi*, p. 196, n. 475, 19 May 1329.

95. *Duca di Candia. Bandi*, pp. 195–96, n. 474, 17 Mar 1329.

96. *Duca di Candia. Bandi*, p. 196, n. 475, 19 Mar 1329.

97. *Duca di Candia, Bandi*, pp. 196–97, nn. 476, 477, 28 Apr 1329.

98. ASV, Avogaria di Comun, *Raspe* 3641/2, 1341–1361, fols. 211r–212r, 21 Nov 1353.

99. ADC, *Proclami e Banni*, Busta 14bis, fol. 4v, n. 91, 19 Apr 1357.

100. ADC, *Proclami e Banni*, Busta 14bis, fol. 26r–v, n. 9 and n. 11, 1357.

101. ADC, *Proclami e Banni*, Busta 14bis, fol. 33r, n. 39, 1359.

102. ADC, *Proclami e Banni*, Busta 14bis, fols. 34v–35v, 1 Aug 1359.

103. ADC, *Quaternus consiliorum*, Busta 12, fol. 163v, 27 Jun 1362.

104. ADC, *Proclami e Banni*, Busta 14bis, fol. 101v, n. 16, 1362; fol. 102r, n. 17, 7 Feb 1361/62.

105. ADC, *Proclami e Banni*, Busta 14bis, fol. 118r, n. 51, 3 Feb 1364/65.

106. ADC, *Proclami e Banni*, Busta 14bis, fols. 111v–112r, n. 11, 8 Sep 1364; fol. 122r, n. 67, 2 Jun 1365.

107. ADC, *Quaternus consiliorum*, Busta 12, fol. 156v, 11 Dec 1361.

108. ADC, *Quaternus consiliorum*, Busta 12, fol. 158r, 11 Dec 1361.

109. Stanley Chojnacki, "La formazione della nobiltà dopo la Serrata," in *Storia di Venezia dalle origini alla caduta della Serenissima*, vol. 3, *La formazione dello stato patrizio* (Rome, 1997), pp. 641–725, pp. 655, 657.

110. ADC, *Quaternus consiliorum*, Busta 12, fol. 168r, 10 Dec 1362: "Infrascripti ceciderunt ad probam magni consilii anno nuper ellapso. Sed virtute ducalium litterarum missarum dominio Crete . . . fuerunt positi ad probam et remanserunt illi quorum nomines inferius notabuntur. Tenor autem dictarum litterarum ducalium in quantum tanget probe negocium est tale. Cum proba nobilium de Crete de maiori consilio non fuerit facta cum ordine anno preterito quia ad ipsam probam . . . citra XXVIII, sicut habetur expositione predictorum, non expulsis presentibus nec servatis solemnitatibus que servantur apud nos et iusta sit quod quilibet in . . . iure conservetur mandamus vobis cum nostris consiliis maioris, rogatorum et XLta, quod si est veritas quod parentes non exierint vel non fuerit servata alia solemnitas que servare debuisset per formam ordinum nostrorum faciatis iterum fieri dictam probam a capite tam de illis qui cecidissent quam qui remanssissent, observantes formam partis alias capte in rogatis de dicta proba sicut iacet et cetera, prout in ipsis ducalibus litteris plenius continetur. Cum magnificus

dominus Leonardus Dandulo, miles clare memorie etc., honorificus ducha Crete, et dominus Iacobus Dado, consiliarius, non existente in eorum oppinione domino Stephano Gradonico, altero consiliario, habuerint concorditer per testes productos et per sacramentum examinatos quod proba nobilium de Crete de maiori consilio anno nuper preterito non fuit facta cum ordine quia parentales non exiverunt neque fuit servata solemnitas que servari debuit iuxta ordines dominii, ideoque determinaverunt concorditer quod fiat iterum proba a capite esse de illis qui ceciderant quam de illis qui remanserant etc. iuxta formam mandati ducalis predicti. [names of those reinstated] Stephanus Saclichi quondam Iohannis qui fuit de numero predictorum qui ceciderunt anno nuper ellapso cecidit ad [folio torn at this point]."

111. Borsari, "Veneziani delle colonie," p. 142.

112. For two examples of the Senate's preparations to confront a revolt taking place in Crete, see *Déliberation du Sénat*, 1: 30, n. 35, 14 Oct 1333; 50, n. 146, 25 Aug 1342.

113. *Duca di Candia. Bandi*, p. 20, n. 53, 15 Jul 1314.

114. *Régestes des délibérations des assemblées vénitiennes concernant la Romanie, 1160–1399*, ed. Freddy Thiriet, 2 vols. (Paris, 1966), p. 21, n. 531, 4 Dec 1346; ASV, NDC, not. N. Brixiano, Busta 10, fol. 21v, Mar 1338.

115. ADC, *Quaternus consiliorum*, Busta 12, fols. 34r, 39v, 42r, 43v, 44v, 45r (twice), 46v, 47r, 56v, 57r, 64r, 64v, 57v, 60r, 64r, fol. 69r (twice), 69v, 72r, 77v, 81r–v, 84r (twice), 85r–v, 87r, 89v, 90v, 92v, 92v (twice), 94r–v, 98r, 100r, 106r, 109v, 110r, 112r–v, 115r, 121r, 123v, 124v, 125r, 149v, 152v, 158r.

116. ADC, *Quaternus consiliorum*, Busta 12, fols. 35r, 38r, 43v, 53r, 56v, 57r, 64v, 69v, 72r, 73r, 75r, 76v, 78r, 80v, 81r, 83v, 84r (two committees), 85v, 86r (two committees), 92v (two committees), 98r, 100r, 103r, 108r, 110, 112v, 115r, 124r, 125v, 127r, 142v, 144r, 158r, 166v.

117. De Monacis, *Chronicon*, p. 179.

118. Marco Dandolo is referred to as "quondam" in ASV, NDC, not. N. da Milano, Busta 144, fol. 50r, 30 Jul 1362.

119. Andrea's will has survived: *Wills*, Will 275, Andreas Cornario, son of *dominus* Alexius Cornario *de domo maiori*, 1360.

120. De Monacis, *Chronicon*, p. 179: "Milletus ad auertendam omnem suspicionem hujus tractatus mansit cum Andrea Cornario quondam Alexii sibi amicissimo in casali Psonopila; ut nox superuenit, dictus Milletus cum sociis scelerum primo inuadit casale praedictum, ad quem Andreas Cornario territus dixit: amice ad quid uenisti? Milletus respondit, ut te interficiam; & ille: potest ne in te cadere tantum scelus, ut amicum familiarem, & benefactorem tuum occidas? Respondit: sic oportet fieri, nam amicitia cedit religioni, & libertati: Haec conjuratio facta est, ut uendicam nos in libertatem, & eradicem uos scismaticos de hac insula, quae est nostrum patrimonium; hisque dictis eum interficiunt."

121. *Déliberations des assemblées*, 2: 26, n. 757, 27 Jul 1365.

122. A proclamation of 1367 lists the names of the "archondopouloi" living in the villages whom the regime sought to capture for their role in carrying on the revolt: Constantinus [illegible], of the village Papianopulo; Costas Vlasto quondam Fimi; Iani Curtazi; Georgius Lubino; Dimitrius Vlasto; Nicolaus Vlasto; Georgius Capadoca; Theodorus Vanigha.

123. Jacoby, "Social Evolution," p. 204.

124. De Monacis, *Chronicon*, p. 175.

Chapter 5

1. Sally McKee, "Women Under Venetian Colonial Rule: Some Observations on Their Economic Activities," *Renaissance Quarterly* 51 (1998): 34–67.

2. As a rich source of parallels and contrasts, the studies pertaining to the definitions of "creole" and the differences between creole societies of the Caribbean ought to be required reading for all scholars of Mediterranean colonization and cultural encounters in the fourteenth and fifteenth centuries. I have found the following articles most helpful in acquainting myself with the terms and issues of Creole studies: Carolyn Allen, "Creole Then and Now: The Problem of Definition," *Caribbean Quarterly* 44 (1998): 33–49; Ira Berlin, "From Creole to African: Atlantic Creoles and the Origins of African-American Society in Mainland North America," *William and Mary Quarterly* 53 (1996): 251–88; Nigel O. Bolland, "Creolisation and Creole Societies: A Cultural Nationalist View of Caribbean Social History," *Caribbean Quarterly* 44 (1998): 1–32.

3. D. A. Brading, *The First America: The Spanish Monarchy, Creole Patriots, and the Liberal State, 1492–1867* (Cambridge, 1993), p. 290.

4. Anthony Pagden, "Identity Formation in Spanish America," in *Colonial Identity in the Atlantic World, 1500–1800*, ed. Nicholas Canny and Anthony Pagden (Princeton, N.J., 1987), pp. 51–93, pp. 54–56.

5. Robin Frame, *English Lordship in Ireland, 1318–1361* (Oxford, 1982), pp. 75, 77.

6. Lydon, "The Middle Nation," p. 11.

7. Lydon, "The Middle Nation," p. 18.

8. Nicholas Canny, "Identity Formation," pp. 164–65.

9. Andrew Hadfield, "English Colonialism and National Identity in Early Modern Ireland," *Eire-Ireland* 28 (1993): 60–86, pp. 70–73.

10. Patricia Seed, *To Love, Honor, and Obey in Colonial Mexico: Conflicts over Marriage Choice, 1574–1821* (Stanford, Calif., 1988), p. 21.

11. Brading, *The First America*, p. 21.

12. Hadfield, "English Colonialism," pp. 74–75.

13. Seed, *To Love, Honor and Obey in Colonial Mexico*, p. 220: "One consequence of using race as the sole means of expressing substantial social inequality was to exaggerate the extent of equality within racial groups; another was to exaggerate the extent to which racial differences were the critical markers of social distinctions between groups."

14. Winthrop D. Jordan, "American Chiaroscuro: The Status and Definition of Mulattoes in the British Colonies," *William and Mary Quarterly* 3rd ser. 19 (1962): 183–200, p. 200.

15. James F. Lydon, "Nation and Race in Medieval Ireland," in *Concepts of National Identity in the Middle Ages*, pp. 103–24, p. 117.

16. Lydon, "The Middle Nation," p. 15.

17. Robin Blackburn, *The Making of New World Slavery: From the Baroque to the Modern, 1492–1800* (London and New York, 1997), p. 8.

18. ADC, *Proclami e Banni*, Busta 14bis, fol. 138v, 5 Sep 1367: "Item cum Papadia Rovithu, socrus Sifi Gavala, habitatrix casalis Orthea, districtus Rethemi, insule cretensis, tempore rebellionis et guerre proxime preterite, pessima femina extiterit contra honorem ducalis dominii et status insule cretensis cumque habita triumphali victoria per nostros predecessores de grecis rebellibus et proditoribus facta fuerit gratia remissio dicte Papadie Rovithu et ceteris ad gratiam et obedienciam prefate dominationis reddire volentibus suis demerits non inspectis, cumque dicta Papadia Rovithu, inmemor et ingrata talis et tante gratie, maligno spiritu, instigata in suo malo proposito . . . usa fuerit verbis turpibus et enormibus in obprobrium danum preiudicium et detrimentum prefate dominationi et status insule cretensis animo et intentione volendi subvertere mentes et animos aliorum et eos promovere in rebellione prefate dominacioni et inter cetera habuerit dicere Leoni Calergi, filio quondam ser Georgii dicti Sileo, habitatori casali Orthea, qui fuit et est fidelis et obediens dominacioni haec verba, videlicet, Et quare fugiebas nobis et a domo tua et quare ibas tu cum latinis. Quod utinam haberem ego in meis manibus occullos erutos omnium illorum qui a nobis recesserunt et eciam latinis iverint et eciam occulos omnium latinorum."

19. For the most recent examples of these efforts: Maria Georgopoulou, "Mapping Religious and Ethnic Identities in the Venetian Colonial Empire," *Journal of Medieval and Early Modern Studies* 26 (1996): 467–96; Chryssa Maltezou, "Byzantine 'consuetudines' in Venetian Crete"; Leonidas Maurommates, "Romaïke Tautoteta, Ellenike Tautoteta," *Simmeikta* 7 (1987): 183–91.

20. Quoted in Philip Gourevitch, *We wish to inform you that tomorrow we will be killed with our families. Stories from Rwanda* (New York, 1998), p. 48.

Appendix 2

1. See Chapter 2, note 66.
2. *ad presens* deleted.
3. *debea tibi* deleted.
4. *facere* deleted.

Bibliography

Unpublished Primary Sources

Archivio di Duca di Candia, Archivio di Stato di Venezia

Atti Antichi, Busta 10
Liber incantorum, Busta 25
Liber pheudatorum, Busta 30
Memoriali, Busta 29

Proclami e Banni, Busta 14 and 14bis
Quaternus consiliorum, Busta 12
Sentenze, Busta 26

Notai di Candia, Archivio notarile, Archivio di Stato

Andreas de Bello Amore, Busta 9
Giovanni de Hugolinis, Busta 295
Giovanni Belli, Busta 295
Michele Iusto, Busta 295
Angelo Bocontolo, Busta 10 and 295
Pietro Longo, Busta 295
Antonio Brixiano, Busta 11–12
Albertinus Maça, Busta 295
Niccolo Brixiano, Busta 10
Filippo Malpes, Busta 143
Leonardus Cavisino, Busta 295
Niccolo Manduga, Busta 295
Michele de Ceca, Busta 295
Antonius Marci, Busta 295
Giorgio Chandachyti, Busta 25
Benedetto da Milano, Busta 142
Francesco della Cruce, Busta 22
Georgio da Milano, Busta 143
Giovanni Dario, Busta 295
Giovanni Morgano, Busta 295
Marco Donçorçi, Busta 295
Albertus Palamonte, Busta 295

Giorgio Emo, Busta 1
Tito de Pena, Busta 295
Petrus Facio, Busta 295
Avanço de Pesellis, Busta 295
Giovanni de Firmo, Busta 295
Marco da Piacenza, Busta 186
Hemanuel Focha, Busta 295
Bartholomeus Quirino, Busta 10
Donato Fontanela, Busta 97
Leonardus Quirino, Busta 233
Bartholomeus Francisci, Busta 97
Antonius Rodolfo, Busta 295
Bonacursius de Fregona, Busta 295
Georgius Siligardo, Busta 244
Giovanni Gerardo, Busta 100–101
Giovanni Similiante, Busta 244
Francesco Gezzo, Busta 103
Giovanni de Torcello, Busta 925
Niccolo Gradenigo, Busta 295
Egidio Valoso, Busta 13
Domenico Grimani, Busta 103
Andreas de Veduaciis, Busta 295

Archivio di Stato di Venezia

Avogaria di Comune, Raspe

Venice, Museo Correr, Mss. P.D. 676 c/II, Alberi genealogici vari anche a stampa, frammento di un libro delle nozze di Ca' Calergi (sec. XVII).
Venice, Biblioteca Marciana, Mss. Cl. VII, Cod. 519 (coll. 8438).
Biblioteca Marciana, Venice, 8, 1785, Misc. 498.1; Drama, 1442.4.

PRINTED PRIMARY SOURCES

Archivio di Duca di Candia, Archivio di Stato di Venezia

Duca di Candia: Quaternus Consiliorum (1340–1350), ed. Paola Ratti Vidulich. Fonti per la storia di Venezia. Sez. I: Archivi pubblici. Venice, 1976.
Duca di Candia: Banni (1313–1329), ed. Paola Ratti Vidulich. Fonti per la storia di Venezia. Sez. I: Archivi pubblici, Venice, 1965.
Régestes des arrêts civils et des mèmoriaux (1363–1399) des archives du Duc de Crète, ed. Elisabeth Santschi. Venice, 1976.

Notai di Candia, Archivio notarile, A.S.V.

Imbreviature di Pietro Scardon (1271), ed. Antonino Lombardi. Turin, 1942.
Benvenuto de Brixano, Notaio in Candia, 1301–1302, ed. Raimondo Morozzo della Rocca. Venice, 1950.
Pietro Pizolo: Notaio in Candia. Tom. I (1300), ed. Salvatore Carbone. Fonti per la storia di Venezia. Sez. III: Archivi notarili. Venice, 1978.
Zaccaria de Fredo: Notaio in Candia. (1352–1360), ed. Freddy Thiriet. Fonti per la storia di Venezia. Sez. I: Archivi pubblici. Venice, 1978.

Acta Urbani V. Rome, 1965.
Apophasis Meizonos Symbouliou Venetias, 1255–1669, ed. S. M. Theotokes. Athens, 1933.
Buondelmonti, Cristoforo. *Description des Îles de l'Archipel Grec*, ed. Émile Legrand. Amsterdam, 1974.
Buondelmonti, Cristoforo. *Descriptio Insule Crete et Liber insularum*, Cap. XI: *Creta*, ed. Marie-Anne van Spitael. Irakleio, 1981.
Cessi, Roberto. *Gli statuti veneziani di Jacopo Tiepolo del 1242 e le loro glosse*. Venice, 1938.
Deliberazioni del Maggior Consiglio di Venezia, ed. Roberto Cessi. Accademia dei Lincei: Commissione per gli atti delle assemblee costituzionali italiane. Bologna, 1931–50.
Le deliberazione del Consiglio dei Rogati (Senato), serie "Mixtorum", ed. Roberto Cessi and P. Sambin. Venice, 1960.
De Monacis, Laurentius. *Chronicon de Rebus Venetis*. Venice, 1758.
Diplomatarium veneto-levantinum, sive acta et diplomata res venetas, Graecas atque

Levantis illustrantia, ed. G. M. Thomas and Riccardo Predelli. 2 vols. Venice, 1880–99. Rpt. 1966.

Documents inédits pour servir à l'histoire de la domination vénitienne en Crète de 1380 à 1485, ed. Hippolyte Noiret. Paris, 1892.

Istorika kretike eggrafa: Ekdidomena tou Archeiou tes Benetias. Thespismata tes Benetikes Gerousias, 1281–1385, ed. S. M. Theotokes. 2 vols. Athens, 1936–37.

Itinerarium Symonis Semeonis ab Hybernia ad Terram Sanctam, ed. and trans. Mario Esposito. Dublin, 1960.

Petrarca, Francesco. *Senilium Rerum Libri*, IV, 3, in *Epistole di Francesco Petrarca*, ed. Ugo Dotti. Torino, 1978.

———. *Francesco Petrarca e Luchino dal Verme, condottiero dei Veneziani nella Guerra di Candia*, ed. Marco Tabarrini. Rome, 1892.

Pindemonte, Giovanni. *I Coloni di Candia: tragedia di Giovanni Pindemonte*. Filadelfia, 1801.

Poesia e lettere di Giovanni Pindemonte, ed. Giuseppe Biadego. Bologna, 1883.

Régestes des délibérations des assemblées vénitiennes concernant la Romanie, 1160–1399, ed. Freddy Thiriet. 2 vols. Paris, 1966.

Régestes des délibérations du Sénât de Venise concernant la Romanie, ed. Freddy Thiriet. Paris, 1959.

Statuta Judaeorum Candiae eorumque memorabilia (Takkanot Candia), ed. E. S. Artom and H. M. D. Cassuto. Jerusalem, 1943. In Hebrew.

Thespismate tis Benetikis Gerousias, 1281–1385, ed. S. M. Theotokes. 2 vols. Athens, 1936.

Urkunden für älteren Handels- und Staatsgeschichte der Republik Venedig mit besonderer Beziehung auf Byzanz und die Levante, ed. G. L. Tafel and G. M. Thomas. Fontes rerum austriacarum, Diplomataria et acta, XII–XIV, 3 vols. Vienna, 1856–57. Rpt. Amsterdam, 1964.

Volumen statutorum, legum ac iurium D. Venetorum. Venice, 1586.

Wills from Late Medieval Venetian Crete, 1312–1420, ed. Sally McKee. 3 vols. Washington, D.C., 1998.

SECONDARY LITERATURE

Abrahamse, Dorothy. "Rituals of Death in the Middle Byzantine Period." *Greek Orthodox Theological Review* 29 (1984): 125–34.

Abulafia, David. *The Western Mediterranean Kingdoms, 1200–1500: The Struggle for Dominion*. London and New York, 1997.

———. *Commerce and Conquest in the Mediterranean, 1100–1500*. London, 1993.

Airaldi, Gabriella. *Studi e documenti su Genova e l'oltremare*. Genoa, 1974.

Allen, Carolyn. "Creole Then and Now: The Problem of Definition." *Caribbean Quarterly* 44 (1998): 33–49.

Amory, Patrick. "The Meaning and Purpose of Ethnic Terminology in the Burgundian Laws." *Early Medieval Europe* 2, 1 (1993): 1–28.

Anderson, Benedict. *Imagined Communities: Reflections on the Origin and Growth of Nationalism*. London, 1983.

Argenti, Philip. *The Occupation of Chios by the Genoese and Their Administration of the*

Island, 1346–1566. Described in Contemporary Documents and Offical Dispatches. 3 vols. Cambridge, 1958.

Ashtor, Elyahu. *Levant Trade in the Later Middle Ages.* Princeton, N.J., 1983.

Aznar Vallejo, Eduardo. "The Conquest of the Canary Islands." In *Implicit Understandings: Observing, Reporting, and Reflecting on the Encounters Between Europeans and Other Peoples in the Early Modern Era*, ed. Stuart B. Schwartz. Cambridge, 1994. 134–56.

Bagnall, Roger S. *Reading Papyri, Writing Ancient History.* London and New York, 1995.

Balard, Michel. "La lotta contro Genova." In *Storia di Venezia dalle origini alla caduta della Serenissima*, vol. 3: *La formazione dello stato patrizio.* Rome, 1997. 87–126.

———. "Communes italiennes, pouvoir et habitants des états francs de Syrie-Palestine au XIIe siècle." In *Crusaders and Muslims in Twelfth-Century Syria*, ed. Maya Shatzmiller. Leiden and New York, 1993. 43–64.

———, ed. *Etat et colonisation au Moyen Age et à la Renaissance.* Lyon, 1989.

———. "Les grecs de Chio sous la domination genoise." *Byzantinische Forschungen* 5 (1977): 5–16.

Balard, Michel and Alain Ducellier, eds. *Coloniser au moyen âge.* Paris, 1995.

Balard, Michel, Angeliki E. Laiou, and Catherine Otten-Froux. *Les italiens à Byzance: édition et présentation de documents.* Paris, 1987.

Balletto, Laura. *Genova, Mediterraneo, Mar Nero (secc. XIII–XV).* Genoa, 1976.

Barricelli, Franca. "Civic Representations: Theatre, Politics, and Public Life in Venice, 1770–1806." Ph.D. dissertation, University of Wisconsin-Madison, 1995.

Barth, Fredrik, ed. *Ethnic Groups and Boundaries: The Social Organization of Culture Differences.* Boston, 1969.

Bartlett, Robert. "Symbolic Meanings of Hair in the Middle Ages." *Transactions of the Royal Historical Society* 6th ser. 4 (1994): 43–60.

———. *The Making of Europe: Conquest, Colonization and Cultural Change 950–1350.* Princeton, N.J., 1993.

Bartlett, Robert and Bernard Hamilton, eds. *Medieval Frontier Societies.* Cambridge, 1989.

Bellomo, Manlio. *The Common Legal Past of Europe, 1000–1800*, trans. Lydia G. Cochrane. Washington, D.C., 1995.

Berlin, Ira. "From Creole to African: Atlantic Creoles and the Origins of African-American Society in Mainland North America." *William and Mary Quarterly* 53 (1996): 251–88.

Bisson, T. N. *The Medieval Crown of Aragon: A Short History.* Oxford, 1986.

Blackburn, Robin. *The Making of New World Slavery: From the Baroque to the Modern, 1492–1800.* London and New York, 1997.

Renas I. Vlachaki, "H diatheke tes Agnes kores tou Alexiou Kallergi (1331) kai o orthodoxos episkopos Makarios." *Pepragmena tou E' Diethnous Kretologikou Suvedpriou.* Hagios Nikolaos, Crete, 1981. 2: 56–63.

Boas, Adrian J. "The Frankish Period: A Unique Medieval Society Emerges." *Near Eastern Archaeology* 61, 3 (1998): 138–73.

Bolland, Nigel O. "Creolisation and Creole Societies: A Cultural Nationalist View of Caribbean Social History." *Caribbean Quarterly* 44 (1998): 1–32.

Borsari, Silvano. "I Movimenti del Porto di Candia AA. 1369–1372." *Annali della facoltà di lettere e filosofia, Università di Macerata* 30–31 (1997–1998): 323–46.

——. "I Veneziani delle colonie." In *Storia di Venezia dalle origini alla caduta della Serenissima*, vol. 3: *La formazione dello stato patrizio*. Rome, 1997. 127–58.

——. *Studi sulle colonie veneziane in Romania nel XIII secolo*. Naples, 1966.

——. *Il dominio veneziano a Creta nel XIII secolo*. Naples, 1963.

Bowman, Steven. *The Jews of Byzantium (1204–1453)*. Birmingham, Ala., 1985.

Brading, D. A. *The First America: The Spanish Monarchy, Creole Patriots, and the Liberal State 1492–1867*. Cambridge, 1993.

Burns, Robert. *Medieval Colonialism: Postcrusade Exploitation of Islamic Valencia*. Princeton, N.J., 1975.

Canny, Nicholas. "Identity Formation in Ireland: The Emergence of the Anglo-Irish." In *Colonial Identity in the Atlantic World, 1500–1800*, ed. Nicholas Canny and Anthony Pagden. Princeton, N.J., 1987. 159–212.

Canny, Nicholas and Anthony Pagden, eds. *Colonial Identity in the Atlantic World, 1500–1800*. Princeton, N.J., 1987.

Cattapan, Mario. "Nuovi elenchi e documenti dei pittori in Creta dal 1300 al 1500." *Thesaurismata* 9 (1972): 202–35.

Cervellini, G. B. "Come i veneziani acquistarono Creta." *Nuovo archivio veneto* n.s. 16 (1908): 262–78.

Cessi, Roberto. *Venezia nel duecento, tra oriente e occidente*. Venice, 1985.

——. *Gli statuti veneziani di Jacopo Tiepolo del 1242 e le loro glosse*. Venice, 1938.

Chaireti, M. "Nea stoixeia peri tes xeipotonia orthodoxov Kretes epi Venetokratias." In *Pepragmena tou G' Diethnous Kretologikou*, Athens, 1974. 2: 333–41.

Chapman, Malcolm, Maryon McDonald, and Elizabeth Tonkin. "Introduction — History and Social Anthropology." In *History and Ethnicity*, ed. Malcolm Chapman, Maryon McDonald, and Elizabeth Tonkin. New York, 1989. 1–21.

Chéhab, Maurice H. *Tyr à l'époque des Croisades*, 2 vols. Vol. 2, *Histoire sociale, économique et réligieuse*. Paris, 1979.

Chojnacki, Stanley. "Gender and the Early Renaissance State." In *Gender and Society in Renaissance Italy*, ed. Judith C. Brown and Robert C. Davis. London and New York, 1998. 63–86.

——. "Nobility, Women and the State: Marriage Regulation in Venice, 1420–1535." In *Marriage in Italy, 1300–1650*, ed. Trevor Dean and K. J. P. Lowe. Cambridge, 1998. 128–51.

——. "La formazione della nobiltà dopo la Serrata." In *Storia di Venezia dalle origini alla caduta della Serenissima*, vol. 3, *La formazione dello stato patrizio*. Rome, 1997. 641–725.

——. "Social Identity in Renaissance Venice: The Second Serrata." *Renaissance Studies* 8, 4 (1994): 341–58.

——. "Political Adulthood in Fifteenth-Century Venice." *American Historical Review* 19 (1986): 791–810.

——. "Dowries and Kinsmen in Early Renaissance Venice." *Journal of Interdisciplinary History* 4 (1975): 571–600.

——. "In Search of the Venetian Patriciate: Families and Factions in the Fourteenth Century." In *Renaissance Venice*, ed. J. R. Hale. London, 1973. 47–90.

Chrysostomides, Julian. "Venetian Commercial Privileges Under the Palaeologi." *Studi veneziani* 12 (1971): 267–356.

Cicogna, Emanuel Antonio. *Saggio di bibliografia veneziana*. Bologna, 1847.

Cochrane, Eric. *Historians and Historiography in the Italian Renaissance*. Chicago, 1981.

Concina, Ennio. *A History of Venetian Architecture*. Cambridge, 1998.

Cormack, Robin. *Painting the Soul: Icons, Death Masks and Shrouds*. London, 1997.

Cozzi, Gaetano, ed. *Stato, società e giustizia nella repubblica veneta (sec. XV–XVIII)*. Rome, 1981.

Cozzi, Gaetano and Michael Knapton, *La Repubblica di Venezia nell'età moderna: dalla guerra di Chioggia al 1517*. Turin, 1986.

Spiridione, Alessandro, Curuni and Lucilla Donati. *Creta veneziana: l'istituto Veneto e la Missione Cretese di Giuseppe Gerola. Collezione fotografica, 1900–1902*. Venice, 1988.

Davies, R. R. "Lordship or Colony?" In *The English in Medieval Ireland: Proceedings of the First Joint Meeting of the Royal Irish Academy and the British Academy, Dublin, 1982*, ed. James Lydon. Dublin, 1984: 142–60.

Davies, R. R. *Dominion and Conquest: The Experience of Ireland, Scotland and Wales*. Cambridge, 1990.

De Gregorio, Giuseppe. "Per uno studio della cultura scritta a Creta sotto il dominio veneziano: I codici greco-latini del secolo XIV." *Scrittura e civiltà* 17 (1993): 104–201.

Deletant, Dennis. "Genoese, Tatars and Rumanians at the Mouth of the Danube in the Fourteenth Century." *Slavonic and East European Review* 62 (1984): 511–30.

Dizionario biografico degli Italiani. Istituto della enciclopedia italiana. Rome, 1960–.

Doumerc, Bernard. "Les Vénitiens à La Tana au XVe siècle." *Moyen-âge* 94 (1988): 363–80.

Du Cange. *Glossarium ad scriptores mediæ et infimæ Graecitatis in qvo graeca vocabula novatae significationis, aut usus rariorus, barbara, exotica, ecclesiastica, liturgica, tactica, nomica, jatrica, botanica, chymica explicantur; eorum notiones & originationes reteguntur . . . Et libris editis, ineditis veteribusque monumentis*. Lyon, 1688.

Duffy, Seán. "The First Ulster Plantation: John de Courcy and the Men of Cumbria." In *Colony and Frontier in Medieval Ireland: Essays Presented to J. F. Lydon*, ed. T. B. Barry, Robin Frame, and Katharine Simms. London and Rio Grande, 1995. 1–27.

Elliott, J. H. "The Spanish Conquest." In *Colonial Spanish America*, ed. Leslie Bethell. Cambridge, 1987. 1–58.

Fasoli, Gina. "Nascita di un mito." In *Studi storici in onore di Gioacchino Volpe*. Florence, 1958. 1: 445–79.

Fedalto, Giorgio. *Stranieri a Venezia e a Padova, Storia della cultura veneta. III/1: Dal primo Quattrocento ad Concilio di Trento*, 3 vols. Vicenza, 1976.

———. "Le sénat vénitien et les églises chretiennes de Crète au XIVe siècle." *Pepragmena tou G' Diethnous Kretologikou Sinedriou*. Athens, 1974. 2: 94–101.

———. *La chiesa latina in Oriente (1204–1261)*, 3 vols. Verona, 1973–78.

———. "La chiesa latina a Creta." *Kretika Chronika* 24 (1972): 145–76.

Ferluga, Jadran. "Veneziani fuori Venezia." In *Storia di Venezia*, vol. 1, *Origini–età ducale*. Rome, 1992. 693–722.

Fernández-Armesto, Felipe. *Before Columbus: Exploration and Colonization from the Mediterranean to the Atlantic, 1229–1492*. Philadelphia, 1987.

Forde, Simon, Lesley Johnson, and Alan V. Murray. *Concepts of National Identity in the Middle Ages*. Leeds Texts and Monographs, n.s. 14. Leeds, 1995.

Fotheringham, John Knight. *Marco Sanudo*. Oxford, 1915.

Frame, Robin. *The Political Development of the British Isles, 1100–1400*. Oxford, 1990.

———. *English Lordship in Ireland, 1318–1361*. Oxford, 1982.

Frazee, Charles and Kathleen Frazee. *The Island Princes of Greece: The Duke of the Archipelago*. Amsterdam, 1988.

Gallina, Mario. "L'affermarsi di un modello coloniale: Venezia e il Levante tra Due e Trecento." *Thesaurismata* 23 (1993): 14–39.

———. *Una società coloniale del Trecento: Creta fra Venezia e Bisanzio*. Venice, 1989.

Charalambos Gaspares. *H ge kai oi agrotes ste mesaionike Krete, 13os–14os ai*. Athens, 1997. [In Greek, with English summary.]

———. "E glossa tes Venetikes grafeiokratias: i avtiparathese latinikes kai ellenikes glossas ste mesaionike Krete (130s–150s ai)." *Simmeikta 9, Mneme D. A. Zakithenou*. Athens, 1994. 1: 141–56.

———. "Oi epaggelmaties tou Chandaka kata ton 14° aiona skeseis me ton katanalote kai to kratos." *Simmeikta* 8 (1989): 83–133.

Geanakoplos, Deno John. *Byzantine East and Latin West: Two Worlds of Christendom in the Middle Ages and the Renaissance*. Oxford, 1966.

———. *Greek Scholars in Venice: Studies in the Dissemination of Greek Learning from Byzantium to Western Europe*. Cambridge, Mass., 1962.

Geary, Patrick. "Ethnic Identity as a Situational Construct in the Early Middle Ages." *Mitteilungen der Anthropologischen Gesellschaft in Wien* 113 (1983): 15–26.

Georgopoulou, Maria. "Mapping Religious and Ethnic Identities in the Venetian Colonial Empire." *Journal of Medieval and Early Modern Studies* 26 (1996): 467–96.

———. "Late Medieval Crete and Venice: An Appropriation of Byzantine Heritage." *Art Bulletin* 77 (1995): 479–96.

———. "The Meaning of the Architecture and the Urban Layout of Venetian Candia: Cultural Conflict and Interaction in the Late Middle Ages." Ph.D. dissertation, University of California Los Angeles, 1992.

Gerland, Ernst. "Histoire de la noblesse crétoise au moyen-âge." *Revue de l'Orient latin*, Part 1, 10 (1903–4): 172–247; Part 2, 11 (1905–8): 7–144.

———. *Das Archiv des Herzogs von Kandia im Königl. Staatsarchiv zu Venedig*. Strassburg, 1899.

Gerola, Giuseppe. *Monumenti veneti nell'isola di Creta: Richerche e descrizioni fatte per incarico del R. Istituto*. 4 vols. Venice, 1905–32.

Gertwagen, Ruthi. "The Venetian Port of Candia, Crete (1299–1363): Construction and Maintenance." In *Mediterranean Cities: Historical Perspectives*, ed. Ira Malkin and Robert L. Hohlfelder. London, 1988. 141–58.

Gill, Joseph. "Pope Urban V (1362–1370) and the Greeks of Crete." *Orientalia Christiana Periodica* 39 (1973): 461–68.

Gourevitch, Philip. *We wish to inform you that tomorrow we will be killed with our families: Stories from Rwanda*. New York, 1998.

Grendler, Paul F. *Schooling in Renaissance Italy: Literacy and Learning, 1300–1600*. Baltimore and London, 1989.

Grubb, James S. *Firstborn of Venice: Vicenza in the Early Renaissance State*. Baltimore and London, 1988.

———. "When Myths Lose Power: Four Decades of Venetian Historiography." *Journal of Modern History* 58 (1986): 43–94.

Hadfield, Andrew. "English Colonialism and National Identity in Early Modern Ireland." *Eire-Ireland* 28 (1993): 60–86.

Heers, Jacques. "Origines et structures des compagnies coloniales génoises (XIIIe–XVe siècle)." In *Etat et colonisation au Moyen Age at à la Renaissance*, ed. Michel Balard. Lyon, 1989. 17–33.

Hillgarth, J. N. *The Spanish Kingdoms, 1250–1516*. 2 vols. Oxford, 1976.

Hobsbawm, Eric. *Nations and Nationalism Since 1780*. Cambridge, 1990.

Hofmann, G. "Il pensiero religioso nelle donazioni e nei testamenti dei Veneziani di Creta." *Civiltà Cattolica* 10 (1944): 220–26.

———. "La biblioteca scientifica del monastero di San Francesco a Candia nel medio evo." *Orientalia Christiana Periodica* 8 (1942): 317–60.

Imhaus, Brunehilde. *Le minoranze orientali a Venezia, 1300–1510*. Rome, 1997.

———. "Enchères des fiefs et vignobles de la République vénitienne en Crète au XIVe siècle." *Epeteris Hetaireias Byzantinon Spoudon* 51 (1974): 195–210.

———. "Les maisons de la Commune dans le district de Candie au XIVe siècle." *Thesaurismata* 10 (1973): 124–37.

Jacoby, David. "Cretan Cheese: A Neglected Aspect of Venetian Medieval Trade. In *Medieval and Renaissance Venice*, ed. Ellen E. Kittell and Thomas F. Madden. Urbana and Chicago, 1998. 49–68.

———. "Byzantine Crete in the Navigation and Trade Networks of Venice and Genoa." In *Oriente e Occidente tra Medioevo ed Età Moderna: studi in onore di Geo Pistarino*, ed. Laura Balletto. Genoa, 1997. 517–40.

———. "Social Evolution in Latin Greece." In *A History of the Crusades*, ed. K. M. Setton. Madison, Wisc., 1989. 6: 175–221.

———. "From Byzantium to Latin Romania." In *Latins and Greeks in the Eastern Mediterranean After 1204*, ed. Benjamin Arbel, Bernard Hamilton, and David Jacoby. London, 1989. 1–44.

———. "Vénitiens naturalisés dans l'empire byzantin: un aspect de l'expansion de Vénise en Romanie du XIIIe au milieu du XVe siècle." *Travaux et mémoires du Centre de Recherche d'Histoire et Civilisation de Byzance* 8 (1981): 217–35. Reprinted in *Studies on the Crusader States and on Venetian Expansion*. London, 1989.

———. "Venice and Venetian Jews in the Eastern Mediterranean." In *Gli Ebrei e Venezia, secoli XIV–XVIII: atti del convegno internazionale organizzato dall'Istituto di storia della società e dello stato veneziano della Fondazione Giorgio Cini*, ed. Gaetano Cozzi and R. Bonfil. Milan, 1987. 29–58.

———. *Recherches sur la Méditerranée orientale du XIIe au XVe siècle: peuples, sociétés, économies*. London, 1979.

———. "Les états latins en Romanie: phénomènes sociaux et économiques (1204–1305 environ)." In *XVe Congrès International d'Etudes Byzantines*, vol. 1, *Histoire, Rapports*. Athens, 1976. 3–15. Reprinted in *Recherches sur la Méditerranée orientale du XIIe au Xve siècle*. London, 1979.

———. "L'expansion occidentale dans le Levant: les Vénitiens à Acre dans la seconde moitié du 13e siècle." *Journal of Medieval History* 3 (1977): 225–65.

———. "The Encounter of Two Societies: Western Conquerors and Byzantines in the Peleponnese after the Fourth Crusade." *American Historical Review* 78 (1973): 873–906.

———. *La féodalité en Grèce médiévale: les "Assises de Romanie": sources, applications et diffusion*. Paris, 1971.

Jegerlehner, Johannes. "Beiträge zur Verwaltungsgeschichte Kandias im XIV. Jahrhundert." *Byzantinische Zeitschrift* 13 (1904): 435–79.

———. "Der Aufstand der kandiotischen Ritterschaft gegen das Mutterland Venedig (1363–1365)." *Byzantinische Zeitschrift* 12 (1903): 78–125.

Jehel, Georges. "The Struggle for Hegemony in the Eastern Mediterranean: An Episode in the Relations Between Venice and Genoa According to the Chronicles of Ogerio Pane (1197–1219)." *Mediterranean Historical Review* 11, 2 (1996): 196–207.

Jordan, Winthrop D. "American Chiaroscuro: The Status and Definition of Mulattoes in the British Colonies." *William and Mary Quarterly* 3rd ser. 19 (1962): 183–200.

Jusdanis, Gregory. *Belated Modernity and Aesthetic Culture: Inventing National Literature*. Minneapolis, 1991.

Kirshner, Julius. "Between Nature and Culture: An Opinion of Baldus of Perugia on Venetian Citizenship as Second Nature." *Journal of Medieval and Renaissance Studies* 9, 2 (1979): 179–208.

Klapish-Zuber, Christiane. "The 'Cruel Mother': Maternity, Widowhood, and Dowry in Florence in the Fourteenth and Fifteenth Centuries." In *Women, Family, and Ritual in Renaissance Italy*, trans. Lydia G. Cochrane. Chicago, 1985. 117–31.

Kuehn, Thomas. "Women, Marriage, and *Patria Potestas* in Late Medieval Florence." In *Law, Family, and Women: Toward a Legal Anthropology of Renaissance Italy*. Chicago and London, 1991. 197–211.

———. *Emancipation in Late Medieval Florence*. New Brunswick, N.J., 1982.

Luzzati Laganà, Francesca. "La funzione politica della memoria di Bisanzio nella Descriptio Cretae (1417–1422) di Cristoforo Buondelmonti." *Bulletino dell'Istituto Storico Italiano per il Medio Evo e Archivio Muratoriano* 94 (1988): 395–420.

Laiou, Angeliki. "Venetians and Byzantines: Investigations of Forms of Contact in the Fourteenth Century." *Thesaurismata* 22 (1992): 29–43.

———. "Quelques observations sur l'économie et la société de Crète vénitienne (ca. 1270–ca. 1305)." In *Bisanzio e l'Italia: raccolta di studi in memoria di Agostino Pertusi*. Milan, 1982. 177–198.

Lane, Frederic C. *Venice: A Maritime Republic*. Baltimore, 1973.

Lock, Peter. *The Franks in the Aegean, 1204–1500*. London and New York, 1995.

Loenertz, R.-J. *Les Ghisi: dynastes vénitiens dans l'Archipel, 1207–1390*. Florence, 1975.

Lydon, James. "The Middle Nation." In *The English in Medieval Ireland*, ed. James Lydon. Dublin, 1984. 1–26.

———. "Nation and Race in Medieval Ireland." In *Concepts of National Identity in the Middle Ages*, ed. Simon Forde, Lesley Johnson, and Alan V. Murray. Leeds Texts and Monographs n.s. 14. Leeds, 1995. 103–24.

Mac Niocaill, G. "The Interaction of Laws." In *The English in Medieval Ireland*, ed. James Lydon. Dublin, 1984. 105–17.

Maltezou, Chryssa. "Byzantine 'Consuetudines' in Venetian Crete." *Dumbarton Oaks Papers* 49 (1995): 269–80.

———. "The Historical and Social Context." In *Literature and society in Renaissance Crete*, ed. David Holton. Cambridge, 1991. 17–47.

———. "Métiers et salaires en Crète vénitienne (XVe siècle)." *Byzantinische Forschungen* 12 (1987): 323–341.

———. "Venetike moda stin Krete (Ta foremata mias Kallergopouloas)." In *Byzantion Afieroma ston Andrea N. Strato*. Athens, 1986. 1: 139–47.

Manousakas, M. I. *Leonardou Ntellaporta Poiemata (1403/1411)*. Athens, 1995.

———. "Ta diplomatika diavemata tes Venetias pros tes Europaïkes divameis gia to nautiko apokleimo tes Kretes kata ten apostasia tou 1363/64." *Panegerike Sinedria tes 28 Dekemvriou 1995, Akademia Athenon* 70 (1995): 721–40.

Margetić, Lujo. "Il diritto." In *Storia di Venezia*, vol. 1, *Origini–età ducale*. Rome, 1992. 677–92.

Maurommates, Leonidas. "Romaïke Tautoteta, Ellenike Tautoteta." *Simmeikta* 7 (1987): 183–91.

McKee, Sally. "Women Under Venetian Colonial Rule in the Early Renaissance: Observations on Their Economic Activities." *Renaissance Quarterly* 51 (1998): 34–67.

———. "Households in Fourteenth-Century Venetian Crete." *Speculum* 70 (1995): 27–67.

———. "The Revolt of St. Tito in Fourteenth-Century Venetian Crete. A Reassessment." *Mediterranean Historical Review* 9 (1995): 173–204.

———. "Greek Women in Latin Households of Fourteenth-Century Venetian Crete." *Journal of Medieval History* 19 (1993): 229–49.

Mertzios, K. D. "Sintheke Eveton-Kallerge kai oi sinodeuontes auten katalogoi." *Kretika Chronika* 3 (1949): 262–92.

Meyendorff, John. "Schism Between East and West" Chapter 7. In *Byzantine Theology: Historical Trends and Doctrinal Themes*. New York, 1974. 91–102.

Mueller, Reinhold C. "Espressioni di status sociale a Venezia dopo la 'Serrata' del Maggior Consiglio." In *Studi veneti offerti a Gaetano Cozzi*. Venice, 1992. 53–61.

———. "The Procurators of San Marco in the 13th and 14th Century: A Study of the Office as a Financial and Trust Institution." *Studi veneziani* 13 (1971): 105–220.

Newett, Margaret M. *Canon Pietro Casola's Pilgrimage to Jerusalem in the Year 1494*. Manchester, 1907.

Nirnberg, David. *Communities of Violence: Persecution of Minorities in the Middle Ages*. Princeton, N.J., 1996.

Otway-Ruthven, A. J. *A History of Medieval Ireland*. New York, 1980.

Pagden, Anthony. *Spanish Imperialism and the Political Imagination*. New Haven, Conn., 1990.

———. "Identity Formation in Spanish America." In *Colonial Identity in the Atlantic World, 1500–1800*, ed. Nicholas Canny and Anthony Pagden. Princeton, N.J., 1987. 51–93.

Pagnin, Beniamino. *Il documento privato veneziano*. Padova, 1950.

Panagiotakes, Nikolaos M. "The Italian Background of Early Cretan Literature." *Dumbarton Oaks Papers* 49 (1995): 281–323.

———. "Martiries gia te mousike sten Krete kata te Venetokratia." *Thesaurismata* 20 (1990): 9–169.

Papadia-Lala, Anastasia, *Euage kai Nosokomeiaka Idrimata ste Venetokratoumene Krete*. Venice, 1996.

Pertusi, Agostino. "Lorenzio Pilato a Creta prima del 1358–1359: scuola e cultura a Creta durante il XIV secolo." *Kretika Chronika* 15–16 (1969): 363–80.

———. "Le fonti greche del *De Gestis, moribus et nobilitate civitatis venetiarum* di Lorenzo de Monacis, cancelliere di Creta (1388–1428)." *Italia medioevale e umanistica* 8 (1965): 161–211.

Phillips, Mark. *The Memoir of Marco Parenti: A Life in Medici Florence*. Princeton, N.J., 1987.

Poppi, M. "Ricerche sulla vita e cultura del notaio e cronista veneziano Lorenzo de Monacis, cancelliere (ca. 1351–1428)." *Studi veneziani* 9 (1967): 153–86.

Pozzo, Marco. "La cancelleria." In *Storia di Venezia*, vol. 2, *L'età del Comune*. Rome, 1995. 349–69.

Prawer, Joshua. *The Latin Kingdom of Jerusalem: European Colonialism in the Middle Ages*. London, 1972.

———. *Crusader Institutions*. Oxford, 1980.

Queller, Donald and Thomas Madden. *The Fourth Crusade: The Conquest of Constantinople*. Philadelphia, 1997.

Rheubottom, David B. "Genealogical Skewing and Political Support: Patrician Politics in Fifteenth-Century Ragusa (Dubrovnik)." *Change and Continuity* 9 (1994): 369–90.

Riera Melis, Antonio. *La Corona de Aragón y el reino de Mallorca en el primer cuarto del siglo XIV*, vol. 1, *Las repercussiones arancelarias de la autonomía Balear (1298–1311)*. Madrid and Barcelona, 1986.

Ruggiero, Guido. "Modernization and the Mythic State in Early Renaissance Venice: The *Serrata* Revisited." *Viator* 10 (1979): 245–56.

Said, Edward. "Between Worlds." *London Review of Books* 20, 9, 7 May 1998: 3–7.

Santschi, Elisabeth. *La notion du "feudum" en Crète vénitienne (XIIIe–XVe siècles)*. Montreux, 1976.

———. "Contrats de travail et d'apprentissage en Crète vénitienne au XIVe siècle d'après quelques notaires." *Revue Suisse d'histoire* 19 (1969): 34–74.

———. "Quelques aspects du statut des non-libres en Crète au XIVe s." *Thesaurismata* 9 (1972): 104–36.

Sarnataro, Maria Maddalena. "La rivolta di Candia del 1363–65 nelle fonti veneziane." *Studi veneziani* 31 (1996): 127–53.

Svoronos, Nikos. "To noema kai e tipologia ton Kretikon epanastaseon tou 13ou ai." *Simmeikta* 8 (1989): 1–14.

Schulz, Juergen. "The Houses of the Dandolo: A Family Compound in Medieval Venice." *Journal of the Society of Architectural Historians* 52 (1993): 391–415.

Seed, Patricia. *To Love, Honor, and Obey in Colonial Mexico: Conflicts over Marriage Choice, 1574–1821.* Stanford, Calif., 1988.

Smith, Anthony. "National Identities: Modern and Medieval?" In *Concepts of National Identity in the Middle Ages*, ed. Simon Forde, Lesley Johnson and Alan V. Murray. Leeds Texts and Monographs n.s. 14. Leeds, 1995. 21–45.

Spanakes, S. "He threskeutiko-ekklesiastike katastase sten Krete ton XVI aiona." *Kretika Chronika* 21 (1969): 134–52.

Starr, Joshua. "Jewish Life in Crete Under the Rule of Venice." *Proceedings of the American Academy for Jewish Research* 12 (1942): 59–114.

Stevens-Arroyo, Anthony M. "The Inter-Atlantic Paradigm: The Failure of Spanish Medieval Colonization of the Canary and Caribbean Islands." *Comparative Studies in Society and History* 35, 3 (1993): 515–43.

Stuard, Susan Mosher. *A State of Deference: Ragusa/Dubrovnik in the Medieval Centuries.* Philadephia, 1992.

Theotokes, S. M. "He dethen aphorme e prokalesa ten apostasian tes Kretes tou 1363." *Epeteris Etaireias Byzantinon Spoudon* 8 (1931): 206–13.

———. "O Petrarxes kai I kretike apostasia tou 1363." In *Istorike Kretike Melete: Imeroloion tes Megales Ellados.* Athens, 1929. 295–306.

Thiriet, Freddy. "La situation religieuse en Crète au début du XVe siècle." *Byzantion* 36 (1966): 201–12. Rpt. in *Etudes sur la Romanie Greco-vénitienne (Xe–XVe siècle).* London, 1977.

———. "Candie, grande place marchande dans la première moitié du XVe siècle." In *Pepragmena tou A' Diethnou Kretologikou Sinedriou* 2. Irakleio, 1961–62. 338–52. Rpt. in *Etudes sur la Romanie Greco-vénitienne (Xe–XVe siècle).* London, 1977.

———. *La Romanie vénitienne au moyen âge. Le développement et l'exploitation du domaine colonial vénitien (XII–XV siècles).* Paris, 1959.

———. "Sui dissidi sorti tra il Comune di Venezia e i suoi feudatori di Creta nel Trecento." *Archivio storico italiano* 114 (1956): 699–712.

———. "Les chroniques vénitiennes de la Marcienne et leur importance pour l'histoire de la Romanie greco-vénitienne." *Mélanges d'archéologie et d'histoire publiées par l'Ecole française de Rome* 66 (1954): 241–92. Rpt. *Études sur la Romanie Greco-vénitienne (Xe–XVe siècle).* London, 1977.

Tiepolo, Maria Francesca. "Note sul riordino degli archivi del Duca e dei notai di Candia nell'Archivio di Stato di Venezia." *Thesaurismata* 10 (1973): 88–100.

Todorova, Elisaveta. "The Greeks in the Black Sea Trade During the Late Medieval Period." *Études balkaniques* 28, 3–4 (1992): 45–47.

Tomadakis, N. "La politica religiosa di Venezia verso I cretesi ortodossi dal XIII al XV secolo." In *Venezia e il Levante fino al secolo XV*, vol. 1, pt. 2. Florence, 1973. 783–800.

Topping, Peter. "Viticulture in Venetian Crete (XIIIth c.)." *Pepragmena tou D' Diethnous Kretologikou Sinedriou* 2 (1981): 509–20.

————. "Co-existence of Greeks and Latins in Frankish Morea and Venetian Crete." In *Studies on Latin Greece*. London, 1977. 11: 3–23.

Tsirpanles, Z. "Anekdote pege gia ten ekklesiastike istoria tes Kretes." *Kretika Chronika* 22 (1970): 79–98.

Tsougarakis, Dimitris. *Byzantine Crete from the 5th century to the Venetian Conquest*. Historical Monographs 5. Athens, 1988.

————. "Some Remarks on the of Cristoforo Buondelmonti." *Ariadne* 3 (1985): 88–108.

Van Der Vin, J. P. A. *Travellers to Greece and Constantinople*. 2 vols. Louvain, 1980.

Van Gemert, A. F. "O Stefanos Saxlikis kai i epoxi tou." *Thesaurismata* 17 (1980): 36–130.

Vassilakis-Mavrakakis, Maria. "Western Influences on the Fourteenth Century Art of Crete." *Jahrbuch des Osterreich* 32, 5 (1982): 301–11.

Verlinden, Charles. *The Beginnings of Modern Colonization*. Ithaca, N.Y., 1970.

————. "Traite des esclaves au XIV et XV siècles." In *Studi in onore di Amintore Fanfani*. 3 vols. Milan, 1962. 3: 593–669.

————. *Précédents mediévaux de la colonie en Amérique*. Mexico City, 1954.

————. "Italian Influences in Iberian Colonization." *Hispanic American Historical Review* 33 (1953): 199–211.

Vermeulen, Hans and Cora Govers, eds. *The Anthropology of Ethnicity: Beyond "Ethnic Groups and Boundaries." The Hague, 1994*.

Vitali, Achille. La moda a Venezia attraverso i secoli: lessico ragionato. Venezia, 1992.

Warren, W. L. *Henry II*. Berkeley and Los Angeles, 1973.

Watt, J. A. *The Church and the Two Nations in Medieval Ireland*. Cambridge, 1970.

————. "*Ecclesia inter Anglicos et inter Hibernicos*: Confrontation and Coexistence in the Medieval Diocese and Province of Armagh." In *The English in Medieval Ireland*. Dublin, 1984. 46–64.

Witt, Ronald. "What Did Giovannino Read and Write? Literacy in Early Renaissance Florence." *I Tatti Studies: Essays in the Renaissance* 6 (1995): 83–114.

Wolff, R. L. "The Organization of the Latin Patriarchate of Constantinople, 1204–1261: Social and Administrative Consequences of the Latin Conquest." *Traditio* 6 (1948): 44–60.

Zachariadou, Elizabeth A. *Trade and Crusade: Venetian Crete and the Emirates of Menteshe and Aydin (1300–1415)*. Venice, 1983.

Index

This index uses two abbreviations: m. for "marriage of," and *q.* for "quondam," or "the late." The index was prepared by students in the Scholarly Publishing Program at Arizona State University.

Corfioti, Cherana, 112–13
Corfioti, Nicolaos, 112–13
Cornario. See Corner
Corneraki, Giacomo Corner, 80
Corner (Cornario) family: marriage patterns, 64, 80; status, 40, 44, 157, 181; Agnes, 111, m. 80; Albertino, 81; Alessio, 61, 65, 85, 98, 148, career, 55–56, m. 65; q. 61; Alessio, q. 162–163; Alexios, 80; Andrea, 38, 59, 61, 77, 163; descendants, 64–65, 85; m. 65; q. 155, 162; Constantino (illegitimate), 85; Dimitri, 119; Elena, m. 65; Francesco (illegitimate), 85; Georgio (goldsmith), 96; Giacomo, 80; Giacomo Cornaraki, m. 82; Giovanni, 61, 80; m. 65, 81; q. 38, 61; Leo, 213n.121; Lucia, 65; Marchesina, m. 80; Marco, 64, 85; q. 77, 80; Maria, m. 81; ser Micaliço, q. 59; Michele, 80; Niccolò, 65, 80, 155; Pietro, 81, 98; m. 65; q. 61
Corner family, of the Greater House, 45, 60–61, 64–65, 151, 163
Coron, 22
Corsica, 10
Cortazzi family, 152
Cortez, Martin, 172
Costula, Lodovico di, 121
councillors, of duke of Venice, 27, 55
Council of Chalcedon, 104
Council of Feudatories, 156, 162; composition, 50, 133; duties, 51; and Great Council of Candia, 49; meetings, 51, 55; records, 30–31, 168; and Revolt, 139; rights, 50–51
Council of the Rogati. See Senate (Candia)
countryside: and city, viii, 140, 169; feudatory holdings, 58–59; pacification, 142–43
courts; ecclesiastical, 105; records, 168
creoles, 171–72
Cresenza, Niccolò da, 155–56
Cretans, identity, 166–67
Crete: administration, 20–21; conquests, 1–2; economic value, 22, 23–24; Greek character, 1; settlements, 22; unique characteristics, 19–20. See also Candia
Crisencia, 181
crowding, 61
Cruscholo, Ianni, 131–32
culture, shared, 168–69. See also acculturation
Cumaniti, Marcos, 66

curfews, 152, 155, 156
Cyprus, king of, 138

D'Acri, Niccolo (cobbler), 95
Dado family, 164
Damiani family, 47, 158, 182
Dandolo (Dandulo) family, 44, 65–66, 79–80, 157, 160, 179, 181, 182; Andrea, 135; Beatrice, m. 79; Donato, 155; q. 155; Elena, 143; Enrico, 22; Francesca, m. 110; Giovanni, 110; m. 65; Leo, 155–56; Lorenzo, q. 79; Marchesina, 65; Marco, 66, 73, 79, 130, 143, 150; assault by, 155–56; death, 66, 102–3, 162–163; m. 65; sons, 147; Mariçoli, m. 150; Niccolò, 130; m. 65, 79; Niccolò Bellino, 110; Nicolota, 73; Philippo, 155–56; Rigo, m. 79; Thomas, q. 66; Vidal, 110
Dandulo. See Dandolo
Davies, R. R., 7, 8, 14, 15
debt, of feudatories, 71
de Clare, Richard fitz Gilbert, 14
de Courcy, John, 14
Dedo, 179
defense, occupations related to, 92, 96–98
de Lacy, Hugh, 14
Delfino. See Dolfin
De Monacis, Lorenzo, 82, 135–40, 137, 138, 142, 143, 146, 147, 157, 162–66
depopulation, 98
Dermata, 26, 94
Desde, Gerardo (ex-slave), 125
Dhamavolus, 59
Di Monaci, Lorenzo. See De Monacis, Lorenzo
Dodo, 179, 182
Doge of Venice, 26–27. See also Venice
Dolfin (Delfino, Dolfino) family, 47, 53, 157, 158, 160, 182; Donato, 155–56; Giacomo, 155–56; Giovanni, 155–56; Pietro, 155–56
domestic service, 92
Dominicans, bequests to, 72, 108, 109
"dominus," defined, 44
"domus," meanings of, 59
Donato family, 44, 155, 180
Dondi, Niccoletto, 46
Dono family, 157, 181; Frangula (illegitimate), 85; Michael (illegitimate), 126; Paoletto (illegitimate), 85; Paolo, 126; Pietro, 59, 85

Iocuda, Solomon de (teacher), 120
Iohannes despoliti, Brother, 109
Iordano. *See* Giordano
Irakleion. *See* Candia
Ireland, 13–18, 173, 175
ironworkers, 92
Isaac, son of Mordochai, 122
Istria, 144
Italian language, 115, 119
iudex di prosopo, 28
Iuliano, 181
Iulio, 179
ius commune, 16, 29
Iustiniani. *See* Giustiniani
Iustinian. *See* Giustiniani
Iusto. *See* Zusto

Jaume I, 12–13
Jaume II, 13
Jegerlehner, J., 136, 138, 160
Jews, 6–7; laws applied to, 28; occupations, 96, 98, 120, 122; perception, 174; residence, 25, 94–95; restrictions, 71
John (king of England), 15
John XXII (pope), 106
judges *di petizion*, 27–28
judges *di proprio*, 27, 61

Kaffa, 10
Kavalario family, 41, 182
kinship: and feudatory tensions, 163; and qualification for Great Council, 159; in Revolt, 147–51, 165. *See also* families
knifemakers, 97
knights, 33, 36, 38
Kyprioti, Frangulio, 38

Lagniti, Michael, 119
Lagniti, Nichitas, 119
Lago family, 157, 181
Lambardo family, 82
land: allotment, 21, 33–38; of archontes, 69; disputes over, 54; laws applied to, 29; *See also feuda*
Lando, 181
language: and choice of notaries, x; and culture, 115, 123, 124; as ethnic marker, 126; teaching, 119–20
Latin, teaching of, 119
"Latin," use of, 168, 169, 170

Latins; murder of, 139; as Venetian subjects, 21. *See also* feudatories
Laudopulo, Anastassios (galley captain), 66
Lauredano family, 47, 158, 182
law: Byzantine, 28–29; canon, 125; and ethnicity, 15–16, 28; martial, 156; situational nature, 29–30; sources, 28
legal system, described, 27–30
Leinster, 14
Levant, crusader states, 8
Liberi family, 44
libraries, 120–23
linen, export of, 66
Lisi family, 157, 181
literacy, 115–16
literature, 120–23
Litini family, 41, 182
Litore family, 41, 182
loitering, bans on, 153
Lollini, 179
Lombardo, Baldovino, 59
Longo family, 179; Marino, 97; Pietro, 67
Lulino, Angelo, 239n.42

Macarios (monk), library of, 121
MacMurrough, Dermot, 14
Macono. *See* Matono family
Magno family, 52, 157, 181; Madio, 52; Sclavo, 52
Mahona, 11
Majorca, 12–13
Maladrin, Andrea (carpenter), 95
Manolesso family, 47, 158, 179, 182
manumission, of slaves, 87–88, 113, 121, 127, 131–32
manuscripts, 120–23
Marano, 179
Marao, 180
Marcello family, 79–80, 157, 181; Elena, 79; Phylippo, *q.* 79; Pietro, m. 79
Marino, 179, 181
Marmici family, 164
marriage: of artisans, 98; contracts for, xiii; outside Candia, 66–67; patterns, 61–69; within feudatory group, 61–66. *See also* intermarriage; miscegenation
martial law, 156
masons, 92
Matono family, 82, 179, 181; Andrea, 84; Giacobina (illegitimate), 84; Giacomo, *q.* 84; Pasquale, 84

Acknowledgments

Several institutions have supported my work in the State Archives of Venice over the past number of years. As a scholar whose subject is Venice and Latin Greece, I have benefited from the best of both funding worlds. In addition to supporting the publication of this volume, the Gladys Krieble Delmas Foundation has provided me on more than one occasion with the means to spend the necessary weeks and months in Venice. The Hellenic Institute of Byzantine and Post-Byzantine Studies in Venice became one of my homes away from home. Dumbarton Oaks and the Trustees of Harvard University offered me shelter in the initial stages of writing. Arizona State University provided me with the funds to return to Venice to bring the project to a conclusion. The Arizona Center for Medieval and Renaissance Studies at ASU provided a warm and welcoming base from which to work.

The individuals who generously gave me time, wisdom, hints, suggestions, moral support and companionship are legion. Each deserves a paragraph of thanks, but I hope that Irene Alm, Benjamin Arbel, Michel Balard, Andrew Barnes, Franca Barricelli, Robert Bjork, Patrizia Bortolozzo, Sandro Bosato, Stanley Chojnacki, Allison Coudert, Michela Dal Borgo, Robert C. Davis, T. J. Davis, William Eamon, Sharon Gerstel, Brian Gratton, Molly Greene, James Grubb, Linda Guzzetti, Vassos Hadzilacos, the Hadzilacos family in Athens and Larissa, Diane Owen Hughes, David Jacoby, Kevin Johnson, Angeliki Laiou, Asunción Lavrin, Beth Luey, Leslie MacCoull, Chryssa Maltezou, Francesco Martusciello, Ann Matchette, Cathy McKee, Ian McKee, Marcy McKee, Reinhold Mueller, Patrice O'Neill, the late Nicolaos Panagiotakes, Sergio Perini, Diamante Rigacou (not forgotten this time!), Robert Rogers, Dennis Romano, Alessandra Sambo, Philip Soergel, Alan Stahl, Susan Stuard, Alfred Vincent, Gordon Weiner, Ronald Witt, and Julia and Tao Zervas all accept this token expression of my deep gratitude for their help, friendship and support.